COUNT ON EMC. 1911 2011

Author   Various
Creative Direction   Duane Wood
Design/Art Direction   Eric C. Johnson
Editor   Sherry Sackfield
EMC Publications Committee   Lisa L. Hamilton
   Robert L. Link
   James M. Moore
Editorial Assistance   Lori P. Drafahl

During the writing of this manuscript, care was taken to ensure the accuracy, completeness, and reliability of the content. The information is based on available historical records and personal recollections; therefore, the accuracy of the information cannot be guaranteed.

The titles and terminology that correlate with each time period were used in this narrative. For example, the company is referred to as "Employers Mutual Casualty Association" (EMCA) prior to 1924 and as "Employers Mutual Casualty Company" (EMCC) until 1980, when "EMC Insurance Companies" became the company's commonplace name. "Workmen's compensation" becomes "workers' compensation" after 1975, when the name was changed by law. The photo captions throughout the book use the trade name EMC Insurance Companies.

EMC Insurance Companies, EMC, the flag design, Count on EMC, EMC Choice, Employers National Life Company, Employers Modern Life Company, and EML are registered trademarks of Employers Mutual Casualty Company.

First published in the United States of America by
WDG Communications Inc.
1615 32nd Street NE
Suite 2
Cedar Rapids, Iowa 52402-4072
Telephone: (319) 396-1401
Facsimile: (319) 396-1647
E-mail: mail@wdgpublishing.com
Web: www.wdgcom.com

Library of Congress Cataloging-in-Publication Data

100 year & counting : EMC Insurance Companies / editor, Sherry Sackfield.
    p. cm.
Includes bibliographical references and index.
ISBN 978-0-9826138-2-5 (alk. paper)
1. EMC Insurance Companies. 2. Insurance companies–United States–History.
3. Insurance companies–Iowa–History. I. Sackfield, Sherry. II. Title: One hundred and counting.
HG8540.E47A14 2011
   368.00973–dc23
                            2011045249

Printed in the United States of America
10 9 8 7 6 5 4 3 2 1

TABLE *of* CONTENTS

DEDICATION

Dedicated to Richard E. Haskins

This book is dedicated in memory of Richard E. Haskins, who was associated with EMC Insurance Companies from 1946, when he began working part time while attending Drake University Law School, until his retirement in 1992. He served as a claims adjuster and supervisor, manager and vice president of the Surety and Assumed Reinsurance Departments, and president and chief operating officer of EMC Reinsurance Company. During his career, he held offices in a number of industry organizations and taught insurance courses at Drake University. Following retirement, he spearheaded the acquisition and compilation of information that appears in this book and guided the production of the narrative until his death on January 14, 2011. Without his interest, enthusiasm, and dedication, what follows would have been vastly less detailed and informative. ▪

...

Left: Attendees at the Fifth Annual Sales Conference in Des Moines, February 4 and 5, 1946.

INTRODUCTION

Starting in 1911, a group of Iowans launched what has become EMC Insurance Companies, and they made critical decisions that allowed our company to survive and thrive. In this book, we attempt to answer the questions of why our enterprise has lasted and how it has prospered.

100 Years and Counting was written primarily, but not exclusively, for the people of EMC. Some will read this book from beginning to end. Many will browse and choose to follow the story of a particular branch or department, specific people or events, examine the facts and figures, or focus on the photos. Whatever your approach, you will meet the people and learn more about how our company became what is it today.

This book includes discussions of business practices and processes to give you a better understanding of the property and casualty industry. Other parts of the book share unique features of EMC, its people, and the traditions that guided us throughout our history. It is our hope that employees and retirees reading this book will enjoy this historical account, and those who are unfamiliar with EMC will find the book an enlightening guide to the growth of an enduring insurance company.

100 Years and Counting tells the story of EMC through historical narrative, photos, and captions, taking the reader on EMC's journey to success over the past 100 years. In celebration of the centennial of EMC Insurance Companies, this book is presented as a tribute to those who have made EMC the strong and stable company it is today.

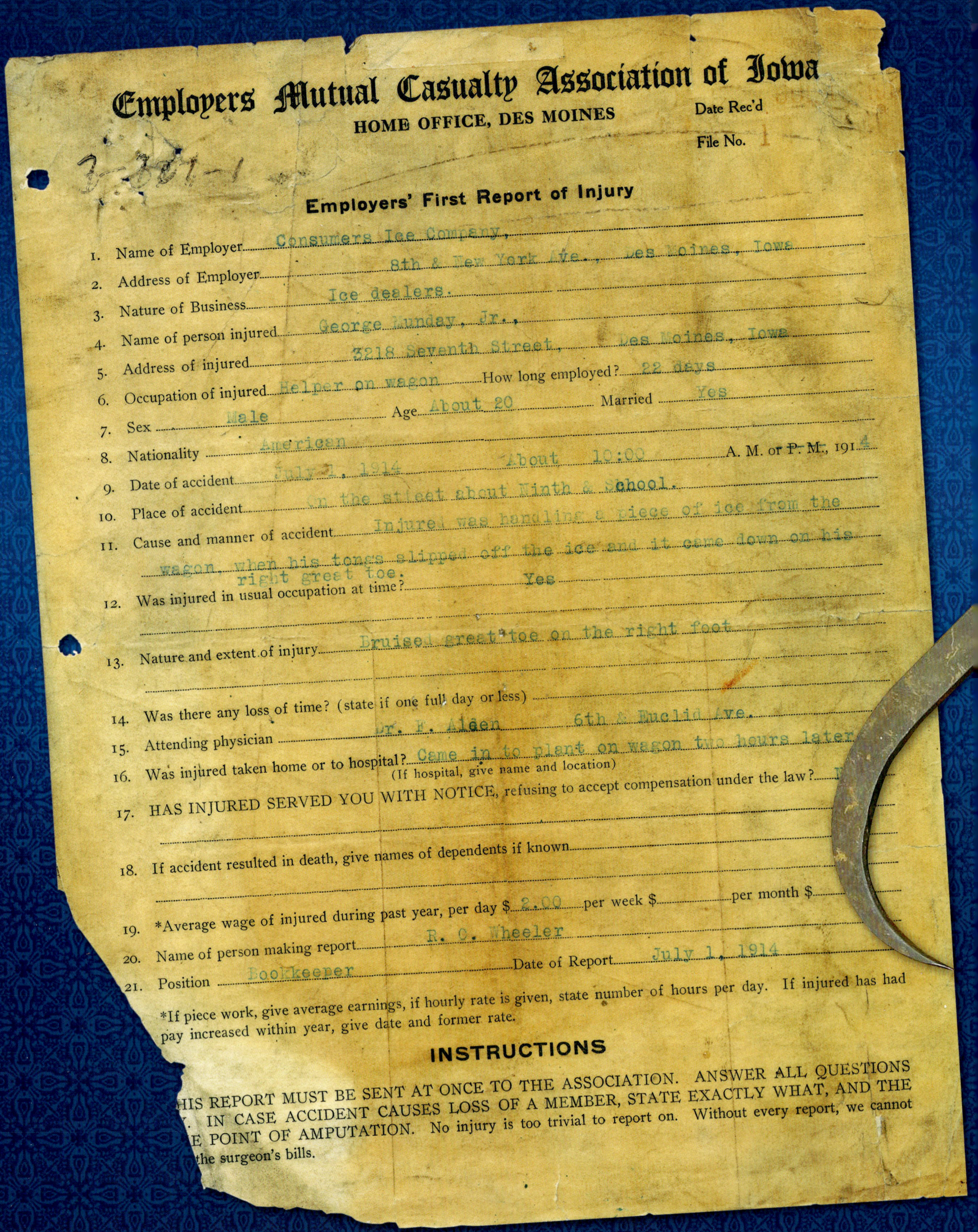

Employers Mutual Casualty Association of Iowa

HOME OFFICE, DES MOINES

Date Rec'd

File No.

3-301-1

Employers' First Report of Injury

1. Name of Employer ... Consumers Ice Company,
2. Address of Employer ... 8th & New York Ave., Des Moines, Iowa
3. Nature of Business ... Ice dealers.
4. Name of person injured ... George Munday, Jr.
5. Address of injured ... 3218 Seventh Street, Des Moines, Iowa
6. Occupation of injured ... Helper on wagon ... How long employed? 22 days
7. Sex ... Male ... Age About 20 ... Married Yes
8. Nationality ... American
9. Date of accident ... July 2, 1914 ... About 10:00 ... A. M. or P. M., 1914
10. Place of accident ... on the street about Ninth & School.
11. Cause and manner of accident ... Injured was handling a piece of ice from the wagon when his tongs slipped off the ice and it came down on his right great toe? Yes
12. Was injured in usual occupation at time? ... Yes

13. Nature and extent of injury ... Bruised great toe on the right foot

14. Was there any loss of time? (state if one full day or less)
15. Attending physician ... Dr. F. Aldeen ... 6th & Euclid Ave.
16. Was injured taken home or to hospital? Came in to plant on wagon two hours later
    (If hospital, give name and location)
17. HAS INJURED SERVED YOU WITH NOTICE, refusing to accept compensation under the law?

18. If accident resulted in death, give names of dependents if known

19. *Average wage of injured during past year, per day $ 2.00 ... per week $ ... per month $
20. Name of person making report ... R. O. Wheeler
21. Position ... Bookkeeper ... Date of Report July 1, 1914

*If piece work, give average earnings, if hourly rate is given, state number of hours per day. If injured has had pay increased within year, give date and former rate.

INSTRUCTIONS

THIS REPORT MUST BE SENT AT ONCE TO THE ASSOCIATION. ANSWER ALL QUESTIONS
IN CASE ACCIDENT CAUSES LOSS OF A MEMBER, STATE EXACTLY WHAT, AND THE
POINT OF AMPUTATION. No injury is too trivial to report on. Without every report, we cannot
the surgeon's bills.

CHAPTER ONE

Left: EMC's first workers' compensation claim, filed July 1, 1914.

Above: Two young men with ice tongs slung over their shoulders pose beside a mule-drawn ice delivery wagon, circa 1910.

Photo/Wichita-Sedgwick County Historical Museum.

The Birth of Employers Mutual Casualty Association: Roots – 1914

Twenty-year-old George Mundy Jr. was making his rounds on a horse-drawn ice wagon for Consumers Ice Company in Des Moines, Iowa, on July 1, 1914. Mundy was new to the job — supplying customers' iceboxes — this was only his twenty-second day. Suddenly, at Ninth and School Streets, a block of ice slipped from his tongs and crashed onto his great right toe. Two hours later, when he returned the wagon to the plant, the pain sent him to Dr. Fred Alden, who bound up his bruise. The fledgling Employers Mutual Casualty Association of Iowa picked up the tab.

That was the first workmen's compensation claim — called "medical only" — of Employers Mutual Casualty Association of Iowa (EMCA). It was filed the first day the workmen's compensation section of the Iowa Employers Liability and Workmen's Compensation statute became effective, the first day EMCA could legally do business as a workmen's compensation insurer.

■ ■ ■

Turn-of-the-century factories posed dangerous risks for American workers.

At the turn of the century, the United States led the world in the number of industrial accidents. Serious injuries had become so prevalent that many states, Iowa included, began investigating working conditions in factories. An Iowa commission documented about 140 accidents weekly in 1905.

Besides the trauma of injuries and deaths, workers and their families suffered the economic hardships of unaffordable medical expenses and serious loss of income. Accidents increased costs for employers as well. Time was lost when injured workers were absent or lost ability to function. Replacement of disabled and deceased workers resulted in down time and training expenses. Efficiency was reduced when other workers became distraught over an accident. All served to decrease production and endanger profits. In addition, employers were faced with unpredictable legal costs from injured employees' suits, and their liability insurance

Public Debate

At the turn of the century, the only relief available to injured workers was to prove fault or negligence on the part of their employers. Done in court, under employers' liability laws based on English common law, this was a difficult task at best. The laws stated that employers were not liable if negligence by injured parties or fellow workers contributed to accidents in any way. Employees, on the other hand, were assumed to have accepted that their compensation covered all customary risks when they took their jobs. Often, as a prerequisite for getting a job, employees were required to sign contracts releasing employers from all liability.

Public debate turned the tide toward advocacy for some form of workmen's compensation that would replace fault litigation with schedules of fixed compensation rates according to class of injury, disability, time lost, and death.

The question of employers' liability and workmen's compensation became a hot topic nationally. The dominant opinion emerged that the state was the most neutral actor and that industrial society could best be humanized through law. Employers began to study ways to improve working conditions by increasing safety and efficiency. ▪

rates were high due to the uncertain costs. Something had to be done.

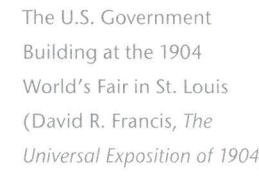

...

The U.S. Government
Building at the 1904
World's Fair in St. Louis
(David R. Francis, *The
Universal Exposition of 1904*).

An Iowa Response: Iowa Manufacturers Association

A broad-based group of Iowa manufacturers, eager to promote their state's role in industrial development, gathered in Des Moines to plan an exhibit for another world exposition, the "World's Greatest Fair" to be held in 1904 at St. Louis. As they put together their exhibit, the Iowa manufacturers sensed a more enduring purpose and incorporated the Iowa State Manufacturers Association to further promote their interests. Soon renamed the Iowa Manufacturers Association, or IMA, and eventually the Iowa Association of Business and Industry (ABI, January 1, 1984), the young organization's interests quickly expanded to

include industry working conditions that resulted in costly accidents in the workplace.

IMA's minutes and its own publication, *Iowa Factories*, reflect the wide variety of opinions held by its members. But by about 1906, the organization as a whole finally concluded that consensus had crystallized and that radical change was inevitable. The two major causative factors were industry's failure to heed calls to improve safety standards and negative public sentiment about the way injury claims were addressed. Business would have to adjust.

In anticipation of the Iowa statute, IMA had organized Employers Mutual Casualty Association (EMCA) in 1911, two years before the bill was enacted. Sensing a forthcoming bonanza from "compulsory" insurance,

•••
1914 letterheads from original policyholders,
along with a letter soliciting business from
Iowa employers.

existing stock casualty companies were raising their employers' liability rates. IMA thought it could lessen costs to its members by forming its own mutual company to insure its members' compensation risk.

The Legislative Solution: Workmen's Compensation

The Iowa Manufacturers Association lobbied Iowa's biennial legislature — not merely to promote the enactment of a workmen's compensation law, which was inevitable, but, more important, to influence the content of the law. George A. Wrightman, Secretary of IMA and a founder of Employers Mutual Casualty Association, spoke at the first meeting of a commission created by the 34th General Assembly in 1911 to investigate "all phases of the question" and to provide material for framing a workmen's compensation bill. This commission surely became well acquainted with IMA.

In 1913, the 35th Iowa General Assembly approved the Employers Liability and Workmen's Compensation Act on April 18. Parts II and III, which became effective on July 4, 1913, created the Iowa Industrial Commission and required all employers to insure their liability through self-insurance or an organization approved by the State Insurance Department. Part I, the Workmen's Compensation section, did not become effective until July 1 the following year. At the heart of the statute, Part I required coverage of medical expenses due to work-related injuries and compensation

for time off work, disability, burial, and survivors' benefits.

While some states enacted state or competitive state plans in which private insurers could compete with the state program, Iowa passed a private plan. Provisions in the law made it almost compulsory for employers to insure their compensation risk through private companies. Although they could opt out of the Workmen's Compensation Act, they would be presumed negligent, and common law defenses would not be available to them if they did so. This was a victory for IMA and the take-off point for Employers Mutual Casualty Association.

The Founding Fathers

John A. "Jack" Eddy was a general agent for the Casualty Company of America working in Iowa. Although stories about his exact role vary, he and IMA found common vision and self-interest in the creation of a company that would sell workmen's compensation insurance, and he joined forces with leading members of the manufacturers' organization. Key among them was John A. Gunn, who at that time was president of the Gould Balance Valve Company in Kellogg, Iowa, a director of the National Travelers Benefit Association, and vice president of IMA.

· · ·

George A. Wrightman, one of the six men who signed the EMCA Articles of Incorporation in April 1911, served on the EMC Board of Directors from 1911 to 1917.

· · ·

1914 letterhead of John A. "Jack" Eddy, one of EMC's founders.

LYMAN A. SPALDING
CHAIRMAN OF THE BOARD

EDWIN W. DE LEON
PRESIDENT

EDWARD L. HEARN
VICE-PRESIDENT

JOHN S. JENKINS
SECRETARY-TREASURER

GEORGE E. BARRETT
ASSISTANT SECRETARY

Casualty Company of America

Home Office 133 WILLIAM STREET New York.

JOHN A. EDDY
GENERAL AGENT FOR IOWA
708 CROCKER BUILDING

DES MOINES, IOWA

From Scotland to America

John A. Gunn's journey can be traced from his
family's roots in Scotland to his birth in Hamilton,
Ontario, on June 26, 1861, and then to Dakota
Territory and Nebraska before he arrived in Iowa.

John A. Gunn could
be called a self-made
man. He was of imposing physical stature,
a well-proportioned 6' 4" and 280 pounds in his
mature years. His formal schooling had ended
with fourth grade when the family moved to
Dakota Territory, but his mother homeschooled
her brood. By the age of 17, he had tired of
farm life and left home. That is probably when
he rafted down the Missouri River to Council
Bluffs, Iowa, and worked as a section man for
the Union Pacific Railroad. A couple of years later,
he put his penmanship to work writing policy
forms for the Pottawattamie Mutual Insurance
Association, a county mutual formed in 1876 in
Oakland, Iowa, 30 miles east of Council Bluffs.

After about four years, young John was ready
for greater adventures and, in 1885, moved west
to Plum Creek, Nebraska, where he took a job
selling windmills that could capture the prairie
winds to pump water. One day he stopped by
the 10,000-acre ranch owned by James Robb and
left saying, "I'll be back." He had met the spirited
Carolyn Robb, and selling windmills would not
be the main reason for his return. Carolyn and
John A. Gunn were married in 1886.

Following his wedding, John and a partner, Tom Hallen, started an implement dealership in Plum Creek, which changed its name to Lexington in 1889. The store building had been an opera house, and John and Carolyn established their home upstairs where they converted the stage into a bedroom. The first two children were born there — Anne Carolyn in 1887 and Susan Josephine in 1890. Carolyn gave birth to their first son, Royal Eugene, in 1892.

John next found work as a general agent selling farm machinery for J. I. Case Company, which made steam engines. Based in Des Moines, he commuted home to Lexington on weekends for several months, probably by rail, until he could move his family. The family grew, adding Hoyt Chapman in 1897 and John William on August 27, 1903.

John advanced to general manager at Case where he had an office in a large warehouse and the opportunity to make many contacts. Among them was a Mr. Gould who had invented a balance valve used on steam engines that cut wood on farms. An idea for a new venture began to hatch in John's mind. About 1907, he purchased Gould's patent rights and formed the Gould Balance Valve Company with Mr. Powers, a former Case employee.

An extant price list shows the company produced 59 different valves for 26 different manufacturers of steam engines. The company was located in Kellogg, about 45 miles east of Des Moines, and John again commuted from his business to his home on the weekends, this time for several years. Finally, about 1911, the family moved to Kellogg.

Unfortunately, as times changed, internal combustion engines began to replace steam engines. By 1917 the company's substantial inventory was causing a severe cash flow problem. Efforts to raise funds failed and the family moved back to Des Moines, where the youngest son, John W., graduated from West High School three years later. In 1922, the company went into receivership and then closed after about five years.

During his career with the Gould Company, John A. Gunn had become involved in insurance activities. He joined the board of the Iowa State Traveling Men's Association, then became vice president and chairman of the Executive Committee of IMA in 1911, and president in 1912. Thus, he was in a key position to help found Employers Mutual Casualty Association. ▪

■ ■ ■

Spectacles and case of John A. Gunn, who was known for smoking large cigars.

**Employers Mutual
Casualty Association**
of Iowa
Crocker Building, Des Moines

· · ·

On April 28, 1911, Iowa's
Secretary of State officially
recognized the incorporation
of Employers Mutual
Casualty Association.

Launching Employers Mutual Casualty Association

Whether IMA or Jack Eddy provided the initial impetus to form EMCA is not known, but it was Eddy who appears to have implemented its actual incorporation following a special authorizing committee meeting of IMA. On April 21, 1911, he gathered together five men who signed Articles of Incorporation, becoming both incorporators and the first provisional board of directors. All were housed in the Crocker Building at the southwest corner of Fifth and Locust Streets in Des Moines, where Eddy also had his office. George A. Wrightman, a business associate of Eddy in various ventures, was secretary of IMA. The other four were from the Miller and Wallingford law firm: IMA General Counsel Jesse A. Miller and his brother Oliver H., who were Eddy's cousins; their partner, J. D. Wallingford; and their stenographer, Christopher C. Christopherson.

The following day, Attorney General George Cosson and State Auditor John L. Bleakly approved the Articles of Incorporation. Two days later, the first provisional board meeting was held, at which Oliver Miller was elected president and Eddy, although not a board member, was named secretary with general management responsibility, as was the practice of that time. The articles were filed by Jesse Miller the next day, April 25, and were certified by Secretary of State W. C. Hayward on April 28. Employers Mutual Casualty Association was now a legal entity "for the purpose of mutual insurance" under Chapter 4, Title IX, of the 1897 Code of Iowa. The new corporation's business would be conducted from offices in the Crocker Building.

Upon its formation, "Mr. Eddy's corporation" was immediately confronted by competing stock liability companies, and actions were taken to strengthen ties with IMA. At the second provisional board meeting, held at the Miller and Wallingford office on July 14, 1911, Oliver Miller resigned as president and Wallingford and Christopherson resigned as board members to allow greater IMA presence on the board. They were replaced by John A. Gunn and another IMA member, B. J. Ricker, president of Morrison & Ricker Manufacturing Company, which produced gloves in Grinnell. Gunn was elected president, Ricker vice president, Wrightman treasurer, and Eddy remained as secretary.

Two additional provisional board meetings dealt with organizational matters to be carried out by Eddy. Chief among them was meeting

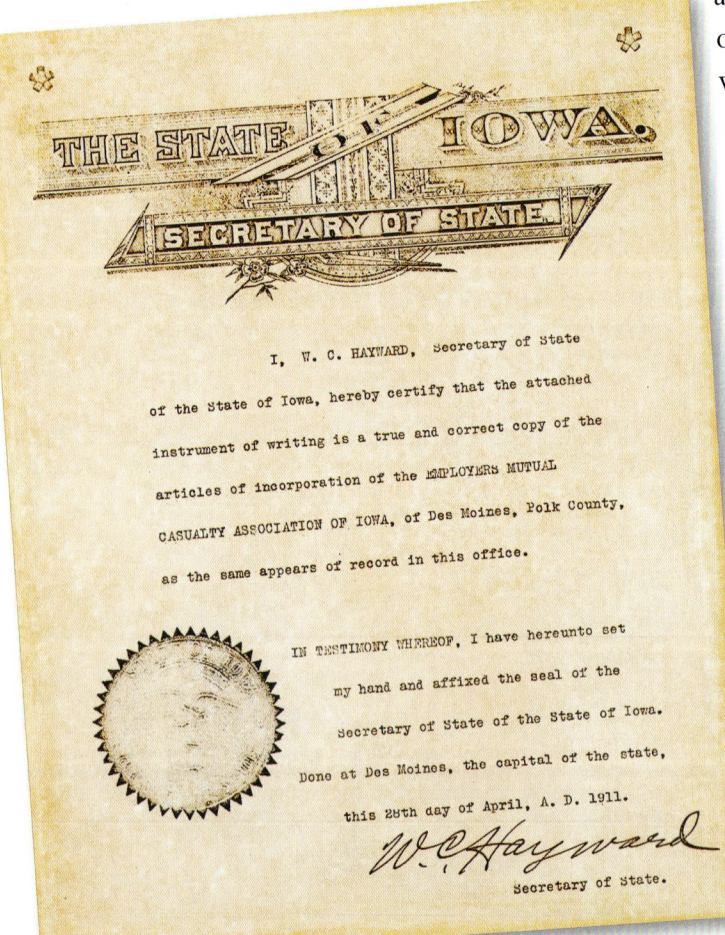

the requirement to obtain 200 bona fide applications for insurance with premiums totaling at least $25,000 in order to secure authorization from the State Auditor to do business. Many companies submitted more than one application, and the criteria were met. Premiums ranged from $5 to $2,400. Officers from several of the companies eventually became EMCA board members: Charles A. Rawson of Iowa Pipe and Tile Company and Brick and Tile Company in Des Moines, J. R. Mulroney of Mulroney Manufacturing Company in Fort Dodge, Gunn, and Ricker.

CROCKER BUILDING — 5TH & LOCUST — SOUTHWEST CORNER — 1ST OFFICE

. . .

EMC's first office was located in the Crocker Building on the southwest corner of Fifth and Locust in downtown Des Moines.

Eddy's Reinsurance Plan

From the beginning, EMCA, unlike most mutuals, chose to offer more predictability by charging fixed premiums based on payrolls and the rates of "standard liability companies" rather than by assessing members. Like all mutuals, it would pay dividends based on year-end profits. How could EMCA do this as a start-up company without a capital base and no experience of its own for determining rates? Jack Eddy provided a way.

Beyond premium dollars received, EMCA would reinsure its risk. This simply meant that it would insure its insurance by ceding liability to another insurance company, so that claims could be covered if premium income fell short. On June 22, 1912, a five-year reinsurance treaty, or contract, was executed with Eddy's employer in New York, Casualty Company of America (CCA),

"for all Liability risks of every description assumed by the Association." The limit of what CCA would pay for each claim was $10,000 per person or $20,000 for two or more persons. EMCA's premium would be 70% of that listed in CCA's manual of rates for Iowa and the two companies would share net profits on a fifty-fifty basis beginning on March 1, 1913. The treaty required claims to be reported to EMCA and delivered to a CCA representative who would have direct charge and control of all claim investigations, settlements, and suits, as well as inspection of all elevators. This would be highly efficient since Jack Eddy was to be the operative representative for both companies. ▪

Handwritten minutes of EMC's first annual meeting on July 10, 1912, held in the Crocker Building.

At the first annual meeting on July 10, 1912, it was announced that the organizational process was complete. By-laws were adopted, and a permanent nine-member board was elected by 121 members present or represented by proxy: Gunn, Ricker, Wrightman, and Jesse Miller were re-elected, and Jack Eddy, Charles A. Rawson, Frank J. Hanlon (Mason City and Clear Lake Railroad Company and Peoples Gas & Electric Company), A. E. Matless (Huiskamp Brothers, Keokuk), and Henry Phillips (Phillips Coal Company and Ottumwa Box Car Loader Company) were added in staggered terms. At the first permanent board of directors

meeting immediately following, the officers were all re-elected and Jack Eddy was named general manager, to be under contract to conduct the business and pay expenses. EMCA now had full operational status.

The young association had not waited for such status to begin operations, however. As early as January 1912, advertisements began appearing in IMA's *Iowa Factories*. They listed nine types of liability coverage being offered: manufacturers' employers, contractors' employers, public, vehicle or teams, automobile, elevator, general, owners' and contractors' protective, and contingent. In addition, a form of workmen's compensation insurance was available directly to workers, collectively or individually. EMCA must have begun writing policies about that time. A letter dated December 10, 1912, from Douglas and Company, America's largest independent starch plant located in Cedar Rapids, Iowa, commends EMCA for their "first year's experience" in "Liability Insurance." They had "no complaints" about the way their "injury claims of every nature" were handled at "less cost than could be secured in any other way" and they credited EMCA with bettering conditions to eliminate accidents of a serious nature in their plant.

Early advertisements took pains to establish the new association's sound standing by listing its officers and directors as well as emphasizing its reinsurance protection, fixed premiums, and low cost. Established competition charged that EMCA's "cut rates" did not offer reliable protection. EMCA's rejoinder educated the

Left: A letter from a pleased policyholder, Douglas & Co., the largest starch manufacturer in the United States in 1912, located in Cedar Rapids, Iowa.

Center: A bulletin from the Iowa Manufacturers Association.

Right: A letter from EMC's first policyholder, The Adams Company, a gear manufacturing company in Dubuque, Iowa.

IOWA FACTORIES

BULLETIN

SWALD SCHMIDT, Davenport, Pres.
Chairman Cereal Mfrs.

ARTIN C. JOHNSON, Sioux City, Vice-Pres.
Chairman Confectionery Mfrs.

GEORGE WRIGHTMAN, Sec'y-Treas.
EDW. A. KIMBALL, Asst. Secretary

Iowa State Manufacturers Association

EXECUTIVE COMMITTEE
J. W. HILL, CHAIRMAN
Chairman Silo Mfrs.

Term Expires 1915
H. BERGMAN, Newton
Chairman Washing Machine Mfrs.
J. RICKER, Grinnell
Chairman Glove Mfrs.
R. MULRONEY, Ft. Dodge
Chairman Men's Garment Mfrs.
F. MOREY, Ottumwa
Chairman Brick Mfrs.
S. WALKER, Des Moines
Chairman Vehicle Mfrs.

Term Expires 1916
F. E. KEELER, Mason City
Chairman Tile Mfrs.
J. M. McFADDEN, Dubuque
Chairman Coffee and Spice Mfrs.
JOHN A. GUNN, Kellogg
Chairman Agl. Implement Mfr.
S. W. MERCER, Iowa City
Chairman Publishers
STEPHEN IRWIN, Keokuk
Ch'n Mfg. Dept. Wholesale Dry Goods

Term Expires 1917
KIRK STEWART, Waterloo
Chairman Printers
O. M. BURRUS, Burlington
Chairman Monument Mfrs.
J. C. HAMILTON, Sioux City
Chairman Launderers
F. R. CHILDREN, Council Bluffs
Chairman Implement Mfrs.
GEO. M. KERRIHARD, Red Oak
Chairman Founders

Term Expires 1918
CEPHAS HARRISON, Keokuk
Chairman Box Mfrs.
J. L. MATTSON, Cedar Rapids
Chairman Motor Impl't Mfrs.
A. O. COLE, Clinton
Chairman Mill Work Mfrs.
E. F. CONSIGNY, Avoca
Chairman Millers

HELP ! !

Ever since this Association was formed it has been supported by certain "dues" paid once a year by interested manufacturers.

If a manufacturer paid his dues July 1st, one year, he paid again July 1st, the next year, if still interested.

Members came in at all times of the year; this made dues to support the Association come in at all times of the year.

When the Association was small, not doing much and with small expense, this was not so bad. But when the Association began to occupy its field and do things, plan things, start things, assume obligations, this was an impossible way.

It was impossible because the membership is very inconstant. If 60 ... ps fall due July 1st, say, ... pay very tardily and 20 ... xpensive drumming for ... much more expensive ... e the place of the third ... s for an institution that ... obligations.

... though, because to ... ge was almost as im-

... authorized to change ... would come in at the ... st. To do this some ... forward to May 1, ... but more members

Is the Association worth my money and efforts?

If he cannot answer that with a big capital YES! let him wire me immediately; there is something wrong with him.

Are my own dues paid up to May 1, 1915?

If they are not there is one helpful thing he can do at once.

Where can I get two new members for the Association within the next thirty days?

If he cannot tell where he should write me at once; I will tell him where. He should then go and absolutely get them.

That's the kind of work that wins and the kind we must have.

The office force is working full blast to pull through; but the office force cannot do it. The ASSOCIATION must help pull itself through.

After May 1, 1915, we shall be a business institution, not a begging institution. For twelve years it has been beg, beg, beg; squirm, fret, worry and hope. That is not business. Hereafter we shall know at the beginning of every year just what we can do that year and we shall go at it man fashion, not fretted to death by the fear of non-support and the constant torture of unpaid bills; we shall not waste two-thirds of our effort, time and money begging for support for a work we have undertaken on hopes.

This is worth working for and suffering for; worth while for every manufacturer in the state to get out some day and hustle for. But it is never necessary for any Iowa manufacturer to hustle for this Association; ... able he only has to write a letter or speak a

---

22

IOWA FACTORIES

Liability Insurance

ALL ORDERS ARE ACCEPTED SUBJECT TO DELAYS OCCASIONED BY ACCIDENTS, STRIKES, FIRES OR CAUSES BEYOND OUR CONTROL PRICES ARE MADE FOR PROMPT ACCEPTANCE AND ARE SUBJECT TO CHANGE WITHOUT NOTICE.

Douglas & Co.
Manufacturers of Starch
for Laundry, Table and Manufacturing Purposes.

Corn Oil, Germ Oil Meal and Gluten Feed.

Cedar Rapids, Iowa.   Dec. 10th, 1912.

Employers Mutual Casualty Assoc. of Iowa,
Des Moines, Ia.

Gentlemen:-

We have now completed our first years experience on our Liability Insurance in your Company and we are pleased to say that we have no complaints whatsoever as regards the way our injury claims of every nature have been handled and especially the prompt action taken whenever an injury of importance occurs. With the cooperation of your Company, conditions have been bettered in our Factory and our records show a gradual elimination of accidents of any serious nature.

Last but not least, this insurance has been furnished us, as well as other Members of the Iowa State Manufacturers Association, at a less cost than could be secured in any other way and this statement is based before receiving any of the benefits of the mutual part of the agreement.

We can heartily recommend your Company and trust the coming year will be met with the success due to the efforts which have been put forth by the Company's managing officers.

Yours very truly,

E-K   Douglas & Co.
                    Per

THE PROOF OF THE PUDDING.

Just to let our members know the quality of the liability insurance furnished by our Association, we take especial pleasure in reproducing above a letter received from the largest independent starch plant in the United States, commending our plan.

This member employes about four hundred (400) workmen of all nationalities and some time ago was

experiencing a great deal of ann ... damage suits. With our plan w ...
Douglas & Co. have seen the ... their workmen and we claim th ... the very safest in Iowa. Ever ... by us has been cheerfully com ... see the proof.

EUGENE ADAMS, President
HERBERT ADAMS, Secretary

THE ADAMS COMPANY

ESTABLISHED 1883

DUBUQUE, IOWA, U.S.A.

CABLE ADDRESS
"ADAMS DUBUQUE"
LIEBER'S STANDARD CODE
LIEBER'S FIVE LETTER CODE

Phone 441

June 18, 1942

Employers Mutual Casualty Company
210 Seventh Street
Des Moines, Iowa

Gentlemen:

Having been your company's first policyholder, we take this opportunity to express our appreciation for the fine way in which you have handled our insurance over this period of time.

Very truly yours

THE ADAMS COMPANY

By Eugene Adams
Eugene Adams, President

EA:MLB

public about its "unquestionable" reliability. Its rates were determined by funding requirements for (1) loss payments using the industry standard and (2) expenses and profits. Extra savings resulted from the secretary writing policies "wholesale" or directly, eliminating the cost of "middle men" or agents.

Insurance Department records show that EMCA wrote $9,723.98 in premiums in 1912. The next year, premium income increased to $13,728.27. Other activities included lobbying for its own interests in the workmen's compensation bill and changing board membership due to term ends, death, and resignations. New members were Cephas Harrison, E. E. Manhard, M. F. Black, C. C. Deering, J. F. Leefers, and A. R. Sale. Perhaps most significant was Jesse Miller's resignation as a director when he was named general counsel on June 13, 1914.

With passage of the Iowa Employers Liability and Workmen's Compensation Act on April 18, 1913, plans to implement the workmen's compensation section when it became effective in July 1914 could now be made with assurance. Eddy was instructed by the board to proceed with arrangements to issue insurance to the applicants already on file, and he and Gunn were sent to New York to negotiate new reinsurance contracts.

In the last weeks before the law became effective, final preparations were in place. IMA gave its stamp of approval in mid-May when it adopted, upon Gunn's presentation, an endorsement resolution that recommended EMCA as having a "safe, sound, and economical plan" for its members. New by-laws were adopted that made the secretary responsible for daily management and specified executive committee powers: to fix rates, determine forms, enter contracts, conduct regular business, pay claims, employ and discharge persons necessary to conduct business, and fix their compensation. The president's and secretary's annual salaries were set at $2,000 and $3,600, respectively, beginning May 1, 1914. Premium income was divided, allowing 70% as a reserve fund to be deposited in the Des Moines National Bank for paying losses and 30% as a general fund for operating expenses.

EMCA was ready to hit the ground running as a workmen's compensation insurer on July 1, 1914, at just the right moment for young George Mundy Jr. ■

Employers Mutual Casualty Association
of Iowa
Crocker Building, Des Moines

JOHN A. GUNN, Kellogg, Iowa, President
GEORGE A. WRIGHTMAN, Des Moines, Iowa, Treasurer
JOHN A. EDDY, Des Moines, Iowa, Secretary

DIRECTORS

JOHN A. GUNN, Kellogg, Iowa
CHARLES A. RAWSON, Des Moines, Iowa
B. J. RICKER, Grinnell, Iowa
HENRY PHILLIPS, Ottumwa, Iowa
FRANK J. HANLON, Mason City, Iowa
JOHN A. EDDY, Secretary, Des Moines, Iowa

❡ This Association was organized solely for the benefit of the Manufacturers of Iowa, to furnish them with the best of Liability Insurance at the lowest possible cost.

❡ It deserves your support.

❡ The standing of its Directors and Officers is a guarantee that the interests of the members will be fully protected.

❡ The liability of a member is limited to the premium charged. There are no assessments, dues or other fees.

❡ The liability of the Association is fully protected by re-insurance contracts with the very best Standard Stock Liability Insurance Companies

❡ There could be no stronger combination, as the full Capital and Surplus of the reinsuring Companies are back of our contracts.

❡ Our rates are a great reductive below the rates of the Standard Companies.

❡ We have no agents. Our plan, as worked out by the officers and committees of the Iowa State Manufacturers Association, cuts out the middle man; the manufacturers themselves get the saving. All business is done with the Secretary direct, or through the Secretary of the Iowa State Manufacturers Association.

❡ Write for full information at least thirty days before your present liability insurance expires.

How to Save Money on Your Liability Insurance

Here's something worthy of your immediate attention. First Class Liability Insurance at COST. Get the full benefit of your association by insuring in your own company.

No! We are Not Cutting Rates

It is being charged by our competitors that the EMPLOYERS MUTUAL CASUALTY ASSOCIATION OF IOWA is cutting rates and therefore its insurance is not safe because it will take your risk at lower rates than Stock Companies. While it is true that the rates named by the ASSOCIATION are low, the saving is made entirely upon the selling agents expense. You buy your insurance at wholesale and deal direct through the ASSOCIATION with the largest and best Casualty Companies in the United States.

Some Points Worthy of Your Attention

❡ The liability of a member is limited to the premium charged. There are no assessments, dues or other fees.

❡ It deserves your support.

❡ The standing of its Directors and Officers is a guarantee that the interests of the members will be fully protected.

❡ This Association was organized solely for the benefit of the Manufacturers of Iowa, to furnish them with the best of Liability Insurance at the lowest possible cost.

❡ Our rates are a great reduction below the rates of the Standard Companies.

❡ The liability of the Association is fully protected by re-insurance contracts with the very best Standard Stock Liability Insurance Companies.

❡ We have no agents. Our plan, as worked out by the officers and committees of the Iowa State Manufacturers Association, cuts out the middle man; the manufacturers themselves get the saving. All business is done with the Secretary direct, or through the Secretary of the Iowa State Manufacturers Association.

❡ Write for full information at least thirty days before your present liability insurance expires.

Employers Mutual Casualty Association
OF IOWA

JOHN A. EDDY, Des Moines, Iowa

OFFICERS

JOHN A. GUNN, Kellogg, Iowa, President
GEORGE A. WRIGHTMAN, Des Moines
JOHN A. EDDY, Des Moines

DIRECTORS

FRANK J. HANLON, Iowa
JOHN A. EDDY

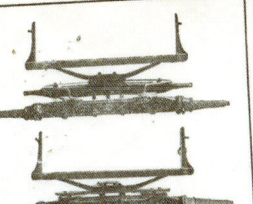

Done

The J. H.

Malleable

D. R. SPIEKER, President
H. A. SCHNECKLOTH, Secretary

Nevada Manufacturing Company
Manufacturers of the
Only Four Wheel Gear Drive Truck Made in the U. S.

Manufacturers of the Famous
"Even-Up-Equalizers"

Nevada, Iowa,

THE BAKWEL BRANDS A

DERBY MILLS CO.
BAKWEL
STANDARD QUALITY
BURLINGTON, IOWA

THE DERBY MILL
MANUFACTURERS OF
BAKWEL BRANDS
FLOUR, GRAHAM, CORN MEAL, BUCKWHEAT
RYE FLOUR AND ALL KINDS
OF MILL FEED

BURLINGTON, IOWA, Sept. 28, 14

C. E. FORKNER, President   P. F. ARNEY, Vice-President   J. C. WILLIAMS, Secretary   H. S. LAWRENCE, Treasurer

The Light Draft Harrow Co.
EXCLUSIVE MANUFACTURERS OF
"FORKNER"
"LIGHT DRAFT" TILLING MACHINES

MARSHALLTOWN, IOWA.

Employers Mutual Casualty Co.
DES MOINES, IOWA

• • •

Top: Two advertisements placed in the Iowa Manufacturers Association bulletins.

Center: Letterheads from original policyholders in 1914.

• • •

Right: A paper weight magnifying glass advertising specialty item.

•••

CHAPTER TWO

A stereopticon card of downtown Des Moines — the birthplace of EMC — as it appeared in the early 1900s.

•••

Mattie P. "Peg" Burroughs, EMC's first employee, worked from 1913 to 1943. She retired as superintendent of the automobile policy writing department.

Up and Running: 1914 – 1920
Entering New Territory

In the first six months after July 1, 1914, when the workmen's compensation section of the Iowa Employer's Liability and Compensation Act was enabled, EMCA wrote over $55,000 in workmen's compensation premiums — nearly two and a half times its total liability writings in 1912 and 1913. Workmen's compensation was now the main focus, although more than $8,000 in liability premiums was also written in 1914.

To handle this burgeoning business, a permanent employee was now on board. One day in May 1913, when Secretary Jack Eddy was going out of town, he had needed someone to answer the office phone. He called a friend, Mattie P. "Peg" Burroughs, and asked if she

would fill in for him. She agreed to help, never anticipating that she would remain for 30 years.

As EMCA's first employee, Burroughs learned quickly and proved herself indispensable. Two weeks after the association entered the workmen's compensation field, she was named chief clerk by the board of directors and was given a salary of $65 per month. Over the years, she would serve in various departments, advancing to become superintendent of the Automobile Policy Writing Department for both new and renewal policies. Upon her retirement in 1943, her service was so valued that the board, which had not yet adopted a pension plan, made her the first employee to receive a pension.

Assets Dec. 31, 1915.

Cash in Office and Banks	$16,974.11	
Cash in Banks on Interest	30,059.39	
		$47,033.50
Compensation Premiums in Course of Collection	$ 5,658.42	
Liability Premiums in Course of Collection	1,141.67	
Bills Receivable	447.96	
Due from Reinsurance	78.81	
Interest Accrued on Deposits	719.49	
		$55,079.85
	$17,598.14	
	21,332.88	
	4,701.66	
	103.13	
	800.00	
	61.03	
	1,382.10	
		$45,978.94
		9,100.91
		55,079.85

1915

FOURTH ANNUAL STATEMENT

OF

Employers Mutual Casualty Association of Iowa

SUITE 708 CROCKER BLDG.
PHONE WALNUT 2589
DES MOINES - IOWA

John A. Gunn, President
B. J. Ricker, Vice-President
John A. Eddy, Secretary
George Wrightman, Treasurer

BOARD OF DIRECTORS

John A. Gunn, Kellogg
President Gould Balance Valve Co.
B. J. Ricker, Grinnell
Vice-President Morrison-Ricker
Manufacturing Company
Chas. A. Rawson, Des Moines
President Iowa Pipe Tile Co.
Des Moines Brick & Tile Co.
George Wrightman, Des Moines
Secretary-Treasurer Iowa State
Manufacturers' Association
John A. Eddy, Des Moines, Secretary
C. C. Deering, Des Moines
Secretary-Treasurer Iowa Independent
Telephone Association
J. F. Leefers, Cedar Rapids
Building Contractor
M. F. Black, Creston
Proprietor Laundry
A. R. Sale, Mason City
Secretary Retail Hardware Dealers'
Association

The 1915 annual statement listed the EMCA Board of Directors, four of whom represented the Iowa Manufacturers Association: one each represented the Master Builders Association, the Independent Telephone Association, the Hardware Dealers Association, and the Laundrymens Association.

By 1914, staff included a bookkeeper, Mr. Farmer; two inspectors, Mr. Ribble and Mr. Sweeney; and two stenographers, Miss McIntire and Miss Klingler. As premium volume increased, so did expenses. In addition to Peg Burroughs' salary, the bookkeeper and inspectors each received $100 per month and the stenographers $60, on top of the $2,000 and $3,600 annual salaries of John A. Gunn and Jack Eddy. Furthermore, Secretary Eddy, Treasurer George Wrightman, and Bookkeeper Farmer had to be bonded for $2,500 each, in addition to the $50,000 guaranty bond for claims indemnification. Office rent, supplies, and reinsurance premiums also had to be factored in.

Within a couple of months the operation began to feel what President Gunn termed the "condition existing." Finances were tight, and it was reported that there were "no prospects of securing the business of the coal operators." Not only was this a blow to anticipated premium income, but it also meant that only one inspector would be needed. In mid-October, the young company responded by releasing Inspector Sweeney and relinquishing three rear rooms of office space in the Crocker Building. Gunn offered to dispense with his salary because his major income was from the Gould Balance Valve

Company, but instead the board changed his compensation to $15 per day for actual time spent.

To remedy the "condition," the association augmented its sales effort. Gunn chose George E. Patterson, whose career at EMCA would last three decades, to head the endeavor. Patterson reminisced about the earliest sales. "In those days we sold direct, not through local agents. Selling insurance direct is very much different from selling through agents. Direct selling has local agency influence to combat, and the local agents were all good, competent, and experienced insurance men."

Soon EMCA changed its approach. Patterson said, "We found out the best way was to write through local agents, thus getting the benefit of [their] influence, contacts, and service." Able to roll with any changes in the sales environment, Patterson became EMCA's first field supervisor, as his role changed from direct sales to working with agents. In addition to his field activities, Patterson would serve on the board of directors from 1937 to 1944 and be the first employee to retire under EMCC's proposed pension plan even before it took effect in 1945.

The value of using agents was first recognized by the board on April 21, 1915, when it authorized hiring them at commission rates not to exceed 7.5% of premiums collected. But it would not be until November that A. Richards was hired as a special agent on what appears to be a trial basis — $100 a month plus traveling expenses for two months. Richards, in fact, remained in that position until April 30, 1916, when he was discharged

Sales with a Smile

George E. Patterson, former schoolteacher, county attorney, and newspaper publisher from northwest Iowa later recalled, "I was the first man and the only man then devoting his entire time to soliciting business." He remembered that business was not handed to him on a silver platter, but also how "interesting and pleasant" his experience was as he traveled by train and found the great outdoors to be a tonic. A born sales and public relations man, he always had candy bars and gum in his pocket for receptionists. His admonitions were abiding: never get mad, never be defeatist but come up fighting, make friends of everyone to whom you sell, be loyal to your company, never run down the competition, know your product, and keep talking. Finally, "Always smile whether you make a sale or not. There is something about a smile that — well, it is a stimulant to all of us." ▪

as special agent and placed on a 10% commission contract. The seeds of the company's dedication to the independent agency system had been planted. Over the next decade, the association converted completely from direct sales to the agency system. Field supervisors, such as George Patterson, and other salaried employees took on the role of orienting agents to EMCA and providing sales assistance. The working relationship between the company and its agents has remained close and successful to the present day.

Prior to adoption of the agency system, direct sales were promoted by IMA. From October 1915 through March 1916, it ran a full-page ad in its official publication, *Iowa Factories*. Directed to the IMA membership, it noted that all employers except farmers were required by law to carry compensation insurance, and EMCA was touted as having the "Most RELIABLE Insurance on Earth" while charging only "about ONE HALF what

outside companies charge." Additionally, the company promoted and educated the public about its inherent advantages as a mutual company: its underwriting philosophy and principles of service, still held today.

As 1915 neared its end, the association was feeling prosperous enough to purchase, for $119, the furniture Jack Eddy had loaned them. At the IMA Executive Committee meeting on December 15, 1915, several complaints were made about Eddy. During the summer, IMA sent letters of inquiry to EMCA Board members, policyholders, ex-policyholders, and non-policyholders. Of the 389 answers received, only 45 objected to EMCA's management and Eddy. John A. Gunn defended Eddy saying that all adjusters have enemies but that does not necessarily mean they are wrong. He stated that all EMCA directors knew and approved of all of Eddy's acts and that the files did not disclose any just reason for opposition to Eddy. In December, the EMCA Board voted to retain Eddy.

IOWA FACTORIES

May, 1915

BULLETIN

CEPHAS HARRISON, KEOKUK, PRES.
Chairman Vehicle Mfrs.
J. W. HILL, DES MOINES, VICE-PRES.
Chairman Nurserymen

GEORGE WRIGHTMAN, Sec'y.
EDW. A. KIMBALL, Asst. Sec'y.

Iowa State Manufacturers Association

OFFICE OF THE SECRETARY, DES MOINES,

EXECUTIVE COMMITTEE
OSWALD SCHMIDT, DAVENPORT, CHAIRMAN
CHAIRMAN CEREAL MFRS.

TERM EXPIRES 1914
F. H. KEYS, COUNCIL BLUFFS
Chairman Vehicle Mfrs.
C. A. RAWSON, DES MOINES
Chairman Sewer Pipe Mfrs.
JOHN H. TAFT, CEDAR RAPIDS
Chairman Women's Garment Mfrs.
IRA W. SHAMBAUGH, CLARINDA
Chairman Millers
G. L. CURTIS, CLINTON
Chairman Mill Work Mfrs.

TERM EXPIRES 1915
F. H. BERGMAN, NEWTON
Chairman Washing Machine Mfrs.
B. J. RICKER, GRINNELL
Chairman Glove Mfrs.
J. R. MULRONEY, FT. DODGE
Chairman Men's Garment Mfrs.
D. F. MOREY, OTTUMWA
Chairman Brick Mfrs.

TERM EXPIRES 1916
F. E. KEELER, MASON CITY
Chairman Tile Mfrs.
J. M. McFADDEN, DUBUQUE
Chairman Coffee and Spice Mfrs.
JOHN A. GUNN, KELLOGG
Chairman Agl. Implement Mfrs.
MARTIN C. JOHNSON, SIOUX CITY
Chairman Confectionery Mfrs.
STEPHEN IRWIN, KEOKUK
Ch'n Mfg. Dept. Wholesale Dry Goods

TERM EXPIRES 1917
KIRK STEWART, WATERLOO
Chairman Printers and Publishers
THOMAS WALPOLE, CEDAR RAPIDS
Chairman Ice Cream Mfrs.
O. M. BURRUS, BURLINGTON
Chairman Monument Mfrs.
J. C. HAMILTON, SIOUX CITY
Chairman Launderers

THE CONVENTION.

Our 12th Annual Convention meets at Mason City May 13, 14 and 15.

The first day will be separate group conferences. Different rooms are provided for meetings of the Clay Industry, the Millers, the Printers, the Vehicle Manufacturers, the Glove Manufacturers, the Foundry & Machine Industry, etc. The plan is that, from this beginning, the various Manufacturing organizations of the state will regularly hold an annual meeting on the day before the State Convention of all Manufacturers.

This is to be a DISCUSSION Convention. The questions that the Manufacturers of the state feel can be advanced toward solution by co-operation will receive attention. The most prominent of these is undoubtedly our Status under the Workmen's Compensation law. We will give that subject full time.

The question next in importance is preparation for the 36th General Assembly and our legislative work in general.

By no means the least important of our questions will be a full discussion of our organization, showing the actual value and the work required to maintain and increase that value.

Subjects now presenting no vital issue but always of importance to Manufacturers, will be overhauled and up-to-date information given on them by experts. These subjects include, Labor Conditions; Financing; Fire Insurance; Freight, Express and Mail; Selling; Advertising; Taxation; Highways; Factory Schools; Management; the Panama Exposition; questions of National importance, such as Currency and National Defence.

Mason City is one of Iowa's most interesting industrial centers. There is plenty of good hotel accommodations. Fellowship and pleasing entertainment have been provided for.

It is the universal comment at all our conventions, "Every manufacturer in Iowa ought to be here." It pays well to come.

GET YOUR COMPENSATION INSURANCE NOW.

The compensation insurance provided by the organized employers of Iowa in the Employer's Mutual Casualty Association of Iowa is ABSOLUTELY SOUND, RELIABLE insurance.

It costs about ONE-HALF what outside companies charge;

It has NO assessments or obligations;

It is strong as Gibralter and is here to stay.

The private stock companies trying to hold our business for their profit, are flooding the state with literature and speeches grossly misleading the people. They will fleece thousands, but no manufacturer should fall for their tricks and give up his good money needlessly.

The scare the stock companies are throwing into our people is:

"That the subject is so hard that no one but a stock jobber can handle it. The fact is that insurance requires good business ability and management the same as any other line of business; we have as much of that in Iowa as anywhere; co-operative insurance well managed is a thorough success in all parts of the world today, especially under the compensation law.

The 6000 manufacturers of Iowa can easily save $2,000,000.00 to enrich and extend their business, by buying their insurance of their own company, the Employers Mutual Casualty Association of Iowa. Apply at once; the rush for policies is on. Don't wait until the last days of June and then grab the first thing that comes along, PAYING DOUBLE. Write this office and get your rate now.

Remember this company is not a money making affair; it is a mutual economy carried on by the employers' organizations of the state.

It will issue all kinds of compensation and liability insurance, workmen's compensation, employers liability, public liability, general liability, teams and auto liability as well as property damage liability, elevator and boiler insurance.

See advertisement elsewhere in this issue.

Attacks on EMCA: Mutual v. Stock Companies

When George Patterson began to solicit business for EMCA, part of his job was selling the public on mutual companies in the face of competition from local agents, who usually represented well-entrenched stock companies, often called "private companies." Mutual insurance historian John Bainbridge wrote, "Foxy underwriters and indefatigable propagandists, [the stock companies] harried the mutuals on a wide front. One of their most popular, and entertaining, charges was that the mutual insurance business was in the hands of Bolsheviks."

Almost from the time it was organized, EMCA had been under assault by stock companies. Besides making charges of Bolshevism, attackers identified mutuals, among them EMCA, as assessable companies, which were increasingly out of favor. A 1912 *Iowa Factories* article defended EMCA, explaining that "mutual" simply means there is neither capital stock nor stockholders and that the organization is operated by members for their own interests.

The attacks continued. An August 1913 article stated that "only 150" IMA member companies were participating in EMCA due to "ingenious, voluminous and persistent lies put out by those who want the business."

IMA members were urged to counter "the combine of private companies" that was "carrying on a campaign of the grossest deception all over the state," conducted by 400-500 agents through lectures and the mail. "Unless the employers in each locality get busy at once and spread the truth about the

Employer's Mutual Casualty Association among their fellow employers, ... another million good Iowa dollars is going to take wings for New York," was the warning.

In October, EMCA Treasurer George A. Wrightman wrote about "a vicious campaign" by agents to poison IMA members' minds against "getting reasonable insurance rates for Iowa." He said, "These men make it a point to be strong in commercial clubs and similar organizations and that is where they are doing their dirty work, though they are also carrying on a house-to-house campaign."

The year ended, and a 1915 article stated, "The private stock companies ... will fleece thousands, but no manufacturer should fall for their tricks and give up his good money needlessly." Another added, "Last year you were dastardly and grossly deceived on the subject. You were told that the EMPLOYERS MUTUAL was illegal, unauthorized, incompetent, and other things. The hundreds of men who told you these things knew at the time they were absolutely false."

By July 1915, when EMCA had completed a year of writing workmen's compensation, an objective report was made that all claims had been paid despite "several hundred persons scattered all over the state [who] have industriously, ingeniously, and constantly, labored to mislead the manufacturers of Iowa in regard to this co-operative fund ... This whole raft of deceit should now be absolutely thrown into discard."

The *Iowa Factories* defenses were reinforced by IMA's identification of EMCA as its own creation. At the 1912 IMA annual meeting,

The executive committee
and manager of the IMA
encouraged all members
of the IMA to consider
EMCA for workers'
compensation insurance.

President B. J. Ricker had stated "very clearly and specifically" that the association was organized "after a careful investigation with the approval of the Executive Committee." Two years later, the message was reinforced: "The EMPLOYERS MUTUAL CASUALTY ASSOCIATION OF IOWA was organized under auspices of the Iowa State Manufacturers Association" — by unanimous vote of the executive committee. After yet another year, the refrain was the same, and IMA called the association one of its "three leading service departments."

In 1920, IMA officially recognized EMCA as a "Service Division" and suggested that its board be increased with at least four interlocking directors from the two organizations. EMCA complied, and the board was increased from nine to 12 members with the addition of three new manufacturing representatives: E. J. Wallen from Sioux City Tent & Awning Company; J. H. Fisher from Fisher Governor Company; and Howard W. Power from National Household Devices Company, H. F. Brammer Manufacturing Co., and Order of United Commercial Travelers. Defense of mutuals was gaining ground, but the battle was far from over.

EMCA's Legislative Role

From the time IMA had lobbied for the creation of a workmen's compensation law, legislation had been a concern of EMCA's founders. Part of EMCA's initial purpose was to work with IMA and all Iowa employers to "look after legislative matters covering Workmen's Compensation"

and to "keep out State Insurance with all its attendant evils." Iowa's passage of a private plan at the biennial General Assembly in 1913 had been a victory for IMA and EMCA, but that was not the end of the issue.

Within a year after the workmen's compensation law went into effect, the Iowa Federation of Labor proposed a plan for state insurance. IMA and EMCA opposed such a plan in the 1915 Iowa General Assembly and claimed that it "was defeated solely by and from information furnished the Legislature by the Employers Mutual Casualty Association thru the Iowa State Manufacturers Association."

Seeing that cooperation with employers was necessary, the Federation of Labor initiated a Joint Committee in 1916 to propose changes in the law at the 1917 legislative session. As a committee member, John A. Gunn "put in many weeks time" and EMCA would again claim it furnished most of the data. The law was liberalized, but EMCA took credit for maintaining limits on medical attention and payment amounts, as well as for preventing creation of a state insurance plan. The 1917 scenario would be repeated in 1919 with similar results, and a bill that included creation of a state fund along with numerous other measures was "indefinitely postponed" in 1921. EMCA commended the General Assembly for the "sane and sensible manner in which they disposed of the needless acts proposed" and contended that blocking this, and other such "obnoxious" similar bills, saved the industry millions of dollars.

C. S. WALKER, Des Moines, President
Kratzer Carriage Co.

F. P. MILLER, Marshalltown, Sec'y
Victor Heater Co.

F. S. FAWKES, Dubuque, Vice-Pres.
H. B. Glover Co.

H. C. McCARDELL, Newton, Treas.
The Parsons Company

EDW. A. KIMBALL, Manager
Des Moines, Iowa

MADE IN IOWA

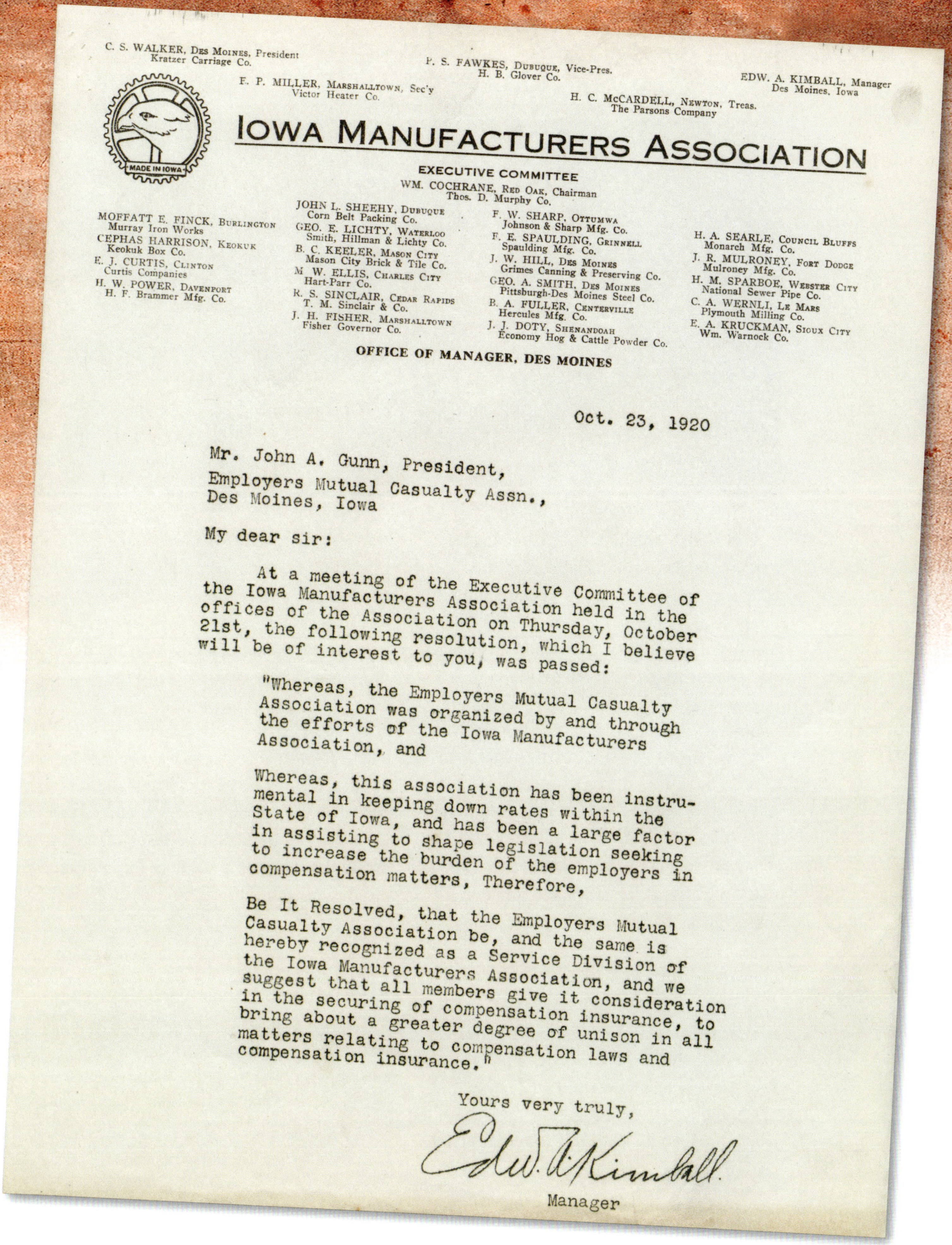

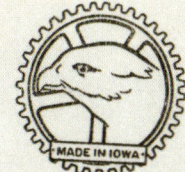

IOWA MANUFACTURERS ASSOCIATION

EXECUTIVE COMMITTEE
WM. COCHRANE, Red Oak, Chairman
Thos. D. Murphy Co.

MOFFATT E. FINCK, Burlington
Murray Iron Works
CEPHAS HARRISON, Keokuk
Keokuk Box Co.
E. J. CURTIS, Clinton
Curtis Companies
H. W. POWER, Davenport
H. F. Brammer Mfg. Co.

JOHN L. SHEEHY, Dubuque
Corn Belt Packing Co.
GEO. E. LICHTY, Waterloo
Smith, Hillman & Lichty Co.
B. C. KEELER, Mason City
Mason City Brick & Tile Co.
M. W. ELLIS, Charles City
Hart-Parr Co.
R. S. SINCLAIR, Cedar Rapids
T. M. Sinclair & Co.
J. H. FISHER, Marshalltown
Fisher Governor Co.

F. W. SHARP, Ottumwa
Johnson & Sharp Mfg. Co.
F. E. SPAULDING, Grinnell
Spaulding Mfg. Co.
J. W. HILL, Des Moines
Grimes Canning & Preserving Co.
GEO. A. SMITH, Des Moines
Pittsburgh-Des Moines Steel Co.
B. A. FULLER, Centerville
Hercules Mfg. Co.
J. J. DOTY, Shenandoah
Economy Hog & Cattle Powder Co.

H. A. SEARLE, Council Bluffs
Monarch Mfg. Co.
J. R. MULRONEY, Fort Dodge
Mulroney Mfg. Co.
H. M. SPARBOE, Webster City
National Sewer Pipe Co.
C. A. WERNLI, Le Mars
Plymouth Milling Co.
E. A. KRUCKMAN, Sioux City
Wm. Warnock Co.

OFFICE OF MANAGER, DES MOINES

Oct. 23, 1920

Mr. John A. Gunn, President,
Employers Mutual Casualty Assn.,
Des Moines, Iowa

My dear sir:

At a meeting of the Executive Committee of the Iowa Manufacturers Association held in the offices of the Association on Thursday, October 21st, the following resolution, which I believe will be of interest to you, was passed:

"Whereas, the Employers Mutual Casualty Association was organized by and through the efforts of the Iowa Manufacturers Association, and

Whereas, this association has been instrumental in keeping down rates within the State of Iowa, and has been a large factor in assisting to shape legislation seeking to increase the burden of the employers in compensation matters, Therefore,

Be It Resolved, that the Employers Mutual Casualty Association be, and the same is hereby recognized as a Service Division of the Iowa Manufacturers Association, and we suggest that all members give it consideration in the securing of compensation insurance, to bring about a greater degree of unison in all matters relating to compensation laws and compensation insurance."

Yours very truly,

Edw. A. Kimball

Manager

Why were EMCA and IMA so opposed to a state plan? They believed that employers banding together privately to create a mutual fund was the "easiest, simplest, and best method of handling compensation insurance." If a state plan replaced mutuals, they asserted, rates would double, causing many companies — stock as well as mutual — to go out of business.

Contemporary literature further contended that a state plan would be funded from assessments on manufacturers and distributed by "a coterie of politicians, without regard to the interests of those who furnished the money." EMCA also feared "a continual labor political interference with the details of our factories." Since no state plan was ever instituted in Iowa, these charges were neither proved nor disproved.

Another issue that confounded the founders was the lack of uniformity in state laws related to regulation of corporations. In January 1912, *Iowa Factories* had printed an article by John A. Gunn in which he made a case for federal regulation of incorporation. Citing conflicting laws of various states that were sometimes

"farcical" or "ridiculous," he pointed out how they placed strains on smaller companies that were required to comply with more than one state's laws and fees. "We have gone daft on the subject of regulation of corporations by each state," he asserted, continuing, "The only sane remedy for this multiplicity of corporation laws is the enactment of a federal law that will enable a corporation ... to transact business with the same rights as an individual." In time, EMCA would make an about-face and support state regulation of insurance, just as it would change its initial promotion of direct sales.

Life Goes On

Within the swirl of attacks, defenses, and legislative concerns, EMCA's daily work continued. When Bessie Newell began working for EMCA as policy writer and general office clerk on December 1, 1916, she was one of four employees. They worked with Secretary Jack Eddy, who managed the young association and served as claims supervisor. After a year, claims had grown to the point that Newell was moved to the claims desk where she worked for many years. Since most vehicles were horse-drawn at that time, many of the cases she handled were for wagon accidents.

Helen V. Mulligan was hired as bookkeeper in 1918 to fill the gap after two employees were called into World War I military service. Another example of professional progress and longevity at EMCA, her career would advance from managing accounting single-handedly to becoming assistant treasurer and superintendent of the accounting and statistical departments.

Other than loss of staff, it appears that the major impact of World War I on EMCA, as an organization, was to facilitate the creation of an investment portfolio. On May 17, 1917, John A. Cavanaugh, who had just replaced George Wrightman as treasurer in January, was authorized by the board to purchase $10,000 of Liberty Bonds. Two months later, Cavanaugh was instructed to dispose of the bonds and take out certificates of deposit. No reason is given in the minutes, but it could be surmised that the move was prompted by pursuit of a higher rate rather than a lack of patriotism. That view is substantiated by the fact that EMCA authorized four more purchases of Liberty Bonds: $28,000 on October 17, 1917; $12,000 on March 13, 1918; $20,000 on October 16, 1918; and $25,000 on September 21, 1919. After that, bond investments would increase steadily and would always dominate the company's investment portfolio.

■ ■ ■

Helen V. Mulligan was hired as a bookkeeper in 1918 to help fill in during World War I. At her retirement, she was assistant treasurer and superintendent of the accounting and statistical department.

One other effect of the war was discussed by the board. Workmen's compensation costs had increased, attributed to the "employment of old men and less skilled labor in many lines of business," which resulted in more accidents. Their more able-bodied counterparts had joined the armed services.

As part of his management responsibilities, Jack Eddy did all of the adjusting. Eventually, as the company grew, he needed help. One day, he asked Bessie Newell to call Mrs. Felix Hynes to see if her "little boy" who was running around the house would like "to come on down and go to work." That little boy was John F. Hynes, a practicing attorney past his mid-20s. He began as EMCA's first claims adjuster and claims attorney in 1918. In May 1920, he was named secretary and soon became claims manager.

where John later became a trustee. John then took degrees in literature and law at Notre Dame University in 1914 and 1915. Upon graduation, John was immediately admitted to the Iowa bar and joined the Miller and Wallingford firm that had played such a significant role in the organization of EMCA. It was three years later, in 1918, that he came to EMCA.

William studied law at Drake University for two years before completing his degree at Notre Dame in 1917. He then entered the 4th Infantry Regiment stationed in the Panama Canal Zone, where he served as first lieutenant and commander of Army Military Police during World War I. His experience would give him a special empathy for Employers Mutual personnel who served in World War II. Following the war, William practiced law in Red Wing, Minnesota, for a year and then sought "greater happiness" working in the coal wholesale and field leasing business in Des Moines. Before coming to Employers Mutual as a claims adjuster in 1933, he was also an independent insurance adjuster.

Enter the Hynes Family

John F. Hynes and his brother, William J., who would also play an important role in EMCA, were both born in Avery, Iowa — on June 26, 1891, and October 29, 1893, respectively. Their father's family had immigrated to America from Roscrea, Tipperary County, in central Ireland. The boys completed high school and college at St. Ambrose Academy in Davenport,

Early Workmen's Compensation Claims

The primary career focus of both John and William Hynes would be claims. When John came to EMCA in 1918, claims processing was still rather primitive. Before guidelines, procedures, and forms were established in the new workmen's compensation field, Jack Eddy and Bessie Newell had found themselves navigating uncharted regions. Correspondence from policyholders reflects both confusion and willingness to cooperate with EMCA.

Although EMCA recommended doctors, procedures for seeking medical treatment were not yet established. Sometimes recommended doctors were not available or injured persons sought out physicians on their own, thinking any doctor could be used. Policyholders raised questions about how much lost time should be covered and at what rate injured employees should be compensated.

William J. Hynes started his insurance career in claims during the 1930s, moved to Chicago as branch manager, and then to the Home Office as head of claims.

Early Case Files

The details of a claim by Great Western Remedy Co. reflect the period. "Mr. Arnold informed us that he hired a single horse livery rig with driver and that he believed the driver was slightly intoxicated. The horse managed to get the lines under his tail and then started on a dead run, left the road, run [sic] up an enbankment [sic] and upset the buggy. The driver fell on top of Mr. Arnold and was not injured, but Mr. Arnold's ankle was broken and he is unable to explain how the ankle was broken as the top was still up when the buggy upset. He was not thrown out, but simply upset. In this case it seems that the liveryman should be responsible." President C. T. Block asked if treatment was to continue with Dr. Fairchilds or EMCA's doctor, as EMCA's doctor was going on vacation and "acted rather indifferent about the case."

Sometimes it was unclear exactly what was covered by insurance. Tom Idso's arm was burned by a gasoline torsion burner at Light Draft Harrow Co. Although the accident was not serious and he was able to return to work after a week, he thought he should be compensated for both his medical expenses and lost time. President C. E. Forkner requested advice about the company's responsibility in the case and if they should make an allowance in wages although they had recommended treatment by a physician.

Issues extended beyond what doctor to use, how to compute claims, and what was covered. On May 21, 1915, Mrs. Reuben Mann reported to Green Foundry & Furnace Works that her husband had been taken to the Clarinda asylum for a mental condition she claimed was caused by a fall at the foundry on August 18, 1914. Correspondent R. E. Taylor from the foundry asked that EMCA "give this your immediate attention" because the Manns would probably "try to get damages." ▪

Signs of Maturing

Primitive though the early practices may have been, after several years of operation, EMCA was showing signs of becoming established. On February 21, 1917, the company declared its first dividend. Although dividends to members had been anticipated from the beginning, the Iowa Insurance Commissioner had advised that, before any were declared, EMCA should allow sufficient time to elapse for "fairly completed experience" to show that the dividends had been earned. Now EMCA had met the test and was able to declare a dividend of 10%. Benefits from the company's success

extended to the board of directors. Effective October 1, 1918, each director was to receive $15 per meeting attended, plus travel and hotel expenses.

Also on the financial front, the association had expanded its banking operations in 1916. While Des Moines National Bank remained the company's reserve fund depository, the general fund was placed in Century Savings Bank, while Commercial Savings Bank became the disbursing fund bank. New measures were adopted in 1919 to maintain solvency. First, the original $50,000 indemnification bond from Interstate Casualty Company of Birmingham was replaced by a new $50,000 Guaranty Fund using Liberty Bonds derived from the portion of premiums not legally required for reserves to pay losses and expenses. It was to be held intact until all other funds for payment of liabilities were exhausted. In less than a year, this fund was doubled to $100,000. Second was cancellation of a reinsurance contract with Interstate Casualty Company of Birmingham and execution of a new contract with American Reinsurance Company, Princeton, New Jersey, to reinsure all public liability policies of the association.

On the organizational front, EMCA made its foray into the larger insurance world as early as 1915 by joining the Employers Mutual Casualty Federation of America, which had been organized in October 1912. In November 1917, the federation was reorganized and incorporated as the National Association of Mutual Casualty Companies, and the EMCA Board voted on December 12 to become a member of the new organization. EMCA Secretary Jack Eddy had served on the executive committee of the original organization and was elected vice president in May before the reorganization.

A Changing of the Guard

As EMCA's confidence and stature grew, John Gunn was increasingly able to devote more time to the business. The Gould Balance Valve Company was now in decline, and he had moved back to Des Moines. On January 14, 1920, his $15 per day arrangement was

discontinued, and he was given chief executive powers with a salary of $5,000 while Secretary Eddy's salary increased to $7,000. General Counsel Jesse Miller's retainer fee was set at $500 per year and executive committee members were allowed $15 per meeting. Then, on May 12, B. J. Ricker resigned as vice president and Eddy was elected to replace him. John F. Hynes was elected to fill the secretary's slot while retaining his claims responsibilities. He would head claims until he became president in October 1947.

On July 23, John A. Gunn reported to the board that the insurance department had informed him of "irregularities" in Eddy's accounts based on their examination of company records for 1914 through 1918. Eddy submitted his resignations as both vice president and director. B. J. Ricker was immediately re-elected vice president. On October 13, the board vacancy was filled by J. W. Hill, whose résumé included president of the Des Moines Nursery Co., Iowa State Traveling Men's Association, and IMA; chairman of the Grimes Canning Co.; and director of the Central State Bank.

EMCA was now poised to enter a new era. ▪

...

Check signature plate belonging to John F. Hynes.

STATE OF IOWA

OFFICE OF
THE SECRETARY OF STATE

I, W. C. RAMSAY, *Secretary of State of the State of Iowa,*
keeper of the corporate records of the State,
Do Hereby Certify *that the attached instrument in*
writing is a true and correct copy of

AMENDMENT TO ARTICLES OF INCORPORATION

OF THE

EMPLOYERS MUTUAL CASUALTY ASSOCIATION OF IOWA

changing above said name to

EMPLOYERS MUTUAL CASUALTY COMPANY

of

Des Moines, Iowa

As appear of record in this office.

In Testimony Whereof, *I have hereu*
set my hand and affixed the official sea
of the Secretary of State, at the Capitol,
Des Moines, this 4th *day of* Februa
A.D. nineteen hundred and Twenty-fo

On February 4, 1924, W. C. Ramsay, the Iowa Secretary of State, officially recognized the association's name change to Employers Mutual Casualty Company.

CHAPTER THREE

Above: Employers Mutual Casualty Company's first logo.

Right: The first building the company purchased in 1937 in downtown Des Moines on Seventh Street.

Embracing Opportunities: 1920 – 1960

Part 1. EMPLOYERS MUTUAL CASUALTY COMPANY: CHANGES, CHALLENGES, TRANSITIONS

Roaring In

The Roaring Twenties ushered in numerous social changes that subsequently affected the insurance industry. Within EMCA, the Eddy era ended and John A. Gunn was in charge full time, and confidence was growing as the association gained experience.

In 1924, the Employers Mutual Casualty Association (EMCA) changed its name to Employers Mutual Casualty Company (EMCC). The name change was both symbolic of maturing status and a preemptive action.

The immediate impetus for the name change was a bill before the Iowa General Assembly that would allow only companies to write fixed premium policies and limit mutual associations, including EMCA, to writing only policies for which association members were assessed proportionally as losses occurred. If the bill passed, EMCA would have to change its philosophy and practice of charging fixed rates for its policies. EMCA's best recourse was to change its name from "Association"

and the board grew from 12 to 15 members. The name change also heralded a physical change. In the spring, the office moved from the Crocker Building to the sixth floor of the Equitable Building at Sixth and Locust Streets.

The company saw new opportunity in the burgeoning automobile phenomenon, particularly in the face of a national downturn in workmen's compensation business, and EMCA entered the automobile liability field in 1920.

Coming in on the ground floor of the new auto operation was John A. Gunn's youngest son, John W. Gunn. He had worked as a paper carrier, soda jerk, hotel clerk, warehouse laborer, cattle tender on a trans-Atlantic cattle boat, stenographer for R. J. Reynolds Tobacco Company, and as an EMCA policy writer and errand boy during high school and college. Following a year at Drake University, John W. worked full time as a stenographer and automobile underwriter at EMCC before continuing his education at the University of Michigan, where he received an A.B. in 1925. Upon graduation, John W. returned to EMCC, first as a stenographer in 1925, and then as a salesman in 1926 and sales manager in 1928.

During the interlude between Drake and the University of Michigan, the young auto underwriter had been sent to the field with George Patterson and Frank Berlin to introduce the company's first garage liability policy to automobile dealers. Ironically, Iowa's mud roads made it wise for the trio to travel by train. Their target was Ford. Not only did Model Ts outsell all other cars, making those dealers the most prosperous, but Henry Ford himself

to "Company" to assure its ability to keep writing fixed premium policies if the law changed.

EMCA officially became EMCC at the Annual Meeting on January 9, 1924. The Articles of Incorporation were amended accordingly, emphasized that liability insurance was highly desirable. When John W. returned to the sales field in 1926, he was responsible for writing both workmen's compensation and auto. At a board meeting on March 7, 1930, President John A. Gunn noted the need for an additional board member who was familiar with underwriting the expanding auto line. John W. Gunn's accumulated expertise made him the obvious choice, and he was duly elected.

EMCA's first auto coverage was for commercial fleets driven by the insureds' traveling employees. Premiums written in 1921 totaled $1,485.10 for general auto liability and $504.05 for auto property damage and collision liability. Also, as owning automobiles became more popular, a new risk emerged — theft. To meet increasing hazards, the Iowa legislature passed the Rutledge Bill in spring 1929. It allowed full auto coverage — fire, theft, tornado, and hail in addition to liability, property damage, and collision. By May, EMCC had a policy containing all of the new coverages allowed under its charter. Here was an opportunity to "put money in the pockets of every Iowa automobile agent." Only 20% of cars registered in Iowa were covered at that time. The remaining untapped 80% of the market translated to about 500,000 cars. A strong selling point was the law's provision that liable parties' licenses and motor vehicle registrations could be suspended if they did not have insurance or were unable to pay for injuries and property damage caused by accidents.

Harold A. Watson arrived at the company in 1927. The Illinois native graduated from East High School in Des Moines in 1925. Following insurance and public speaking classes and a brief stint in advertising and accounting, the young man soon found himself working his way through supply and printing, accounting, collections, and underwriting positions at EMCC. The Great Depression turned him into a service station operator for several months, but he became EMCC's supervisor of auto underwriting in the early 1930s. He remained in that position until his retirement at the end of 1971, although he would have the duties of assistant treasurer added in 1939 and assistant secretary in 1946.

Watson immediately faced an underwriting dilemma. Automobiles were considered more of a menace than a necessity in the early days. Among their dangerous features were top-heavy bodies set on high wheels, making upsets frequent. The ordinary window glass in use shattered easily, causing serious injury and even death on impact. And these dangerous vehicles were being operated by an increasing number of inexperienced and untrained drivers on increasingly crowded roads. Claims related to the multiplying accident rate were eating up a larger portion of premium income, while heightened competition was driving

•••

Harold A. Watson joined EMC in 1927 and was supervisor of auto underwriting, assistant treasurer, and assistant secretary.

Death Took the Wheel

A Grim Reminder to Drive Carefully. This Driver's Life Was Snuffed Out by Carelessness . . . A Tragic Story All Too Frequently Told. Play Safe! Obey the Rules of the Road!

DRIVE WITH CARE

t the Wheel . . . Collision! . . . Police Ambulance . . . A Ride to the Morgue. That's the story repeated . . . ften of how Death Stalks the Highways. afe. Obey All Traffic Laws! And . . .

E WITH CARE

• • •
Posters with graphic images of auto accidents were sent to agents as part of the 1930s Drive With Care campaign.

down premium rates. Furthermore, the Depression was causing cancellation of a number of policies, and EMCC's capacity to write automobile insurance was reduced by termination of a reinsurance contract with Capital Fire Insurance Company.

To deal with this squeeze, Watson placed emphasis on safe driving and support of drivers' education. His mid-1930s "Drive Carefully" publicity campaign featured headlines such

as "Worst Massacre in History," "Public Enemy No. 1," "A Blood-Curdling Tale," and "Death — 4 Times an Hour." Under these headlines, chilling auto accident statistics were given for 1935: 35,500 dead and 1,000,000 injured (one out of every 124 people in the country); a life claimed every 13 minutes and a person injured every 30 seconds by reckless drivers; one out of every 16 cars involved in an accident.

A Mutual Fights Back

Legislative, legal, economic, and competitive challenges continued at full tilt, and the battle with competing stock companies raged on. The ongoing defense was frequently a promotional offense carried out in print. EMCA's first newsletter, *The Employer*, promoted the company, and mutuals in general, to all Iowa employers. The lead article — "Who Is Your Friend?" — in the first issue on November 1, 1921, introduced EMCA as a friend who looks out for employers' interests through its realistic rates and non-assessable premiums. The article maintained that rate undercutting, exercised by stock companies, would eventually lead to their collapse, that non-assessable premiums assured there would be no additional assessment, and that EMCA's lobbying efforts with the Iowa General Assembly prevented "injurious legislation." The premise was that doing business with a business friend like EMCA was much more advantageous than with a personal friend who did not offer such benefits. The newsletter would expand on these themes through its eighth and final issue in June 1922.

The brochure, "EMCA: The History of a Service," distributed about 1922, stated that the mutual company saved Iowa insurers over $7 million through legislation, keeping rates down, and preserving the rights of employers. It also described the $100,000 guarantee fund that backed all claims, the practice of setting aside funds as soon as the cost of each claim was determined, and the reinsurance coverage for catastrophic claims.

In 1925, when the company, now EMCC, and IMA were lobbying against legislation that would have increased compensation costs, EMCC produced a pamphlet for Iowa employers. It touted EMCC's unique lobbying service, which, over ten years, had prevented millions of dollars in increased costs to employers by providing accurate information to the state legislature. Other states, it was pointed out,

The Employer

ISSUED MONTHLY BY THE EMPLOYERS MUTUAL CASUALTY ASSOCIATION OF IOWA

Volume 1   DES MOINES, IOWA, NOVEMBER 1, 1921   Number 1

WHO IS YOUR FRIEND?

Quite frequently in talking with certain employers in this state the explanation is given to us by the employer that owing to the friendly relationship existing between himself and the local agent of a stock company, he is compelled to give his insurance to that local agent. The explanation is made that the agent is a personal friend. They both belong to the same lodge—or perhaps to the same church—or the same club—and they meet every week or two and the employer thinks he cannot turn the agent down.

Again, the agent may be the banker in the home town, and that is offered as another reason why the employer thinks he cannot get away from him, as he feels under personal obligations to his local banker to give him his insurance business.

When we explain to him that we can make a saving for him, and that it is his duty to himself, as well as the business he represents to come with us, he comes back with this explanation: "I know you could save me a little money, but the agent for the X-Y-Z company is a personal friend of mine and I cannot get away from him. I know the splendid service that the Employers Mutual is rendering and I know that we ought to support it. I know it is our duty to support it and I furthermore know that every employer in the state ought to support the Employers Mutual. I am coming to you some day, but not this year. The local agent is a good friend of mine and I cannot refuse him."

What would you think of a business man who put all of his business on that basis? It is not our purpose to minimize the importance of friendship. A friend is a man whom you can trust and who seeks at every opportunity to favor his friend, but what would you think of the friendship of a merchant from whom you were buying a suit of clothes and who offered you a suit for $60.00 and when you explained to him that you could go down the street and buy a similar suit, or perhaps a better suit for $40.00, that he would turn to you and say—"Yes, you can do that, but I am your friend, and I ought to have a little more money"?

What would you think of a groceryman who sold you your groceries and charged you from twenty to twenty-five per cent more on your

grocery bill every month than you could buy the same goods for from a competitor and when you remonstrated with him he would say—"Yes, I know you can buy goods for less money, but I am your friend and you ought to patronize me even if it does cost you more"?

These two examples can be multiplied a thousand times in the ordinary transactions of business. Usually when the seller is a friend he gives the benefit to the buyer, but in the insurance business the buyer is the one who is expected to be generous and pay more to a friend than he could buy it for elsewhere. Furthermore, if you went to your friend and said to him—"I am seriously afraid of injurious legislation being passed, and I am further afraid that it will seriously increase my insurance premiums, and I wish that you would help me to keep them down"—what would your insurance friend say to you? Would he help you reduce the premiums by assisting the organizations of the state that were fighting for your rights, or would he be wholly indifferent?

In other words, is he your friend as much as the one who looks after your interests at all times, and not the one that is only interested when your insurance expires in hopes of getting a renewal?

Or again, the agent may be representing an assessment organization who takes on the risk for less than he should take it on, knowing that if it comes to the worst that he can again assess you for additional premiums. Is such a man your friend, or is he working against you?

What would you think of a man who sold you a bill of goods for less than he could replace the goods for, and afterwards you found that the reason he could make such a low price was because he was permitted by law or by agreement to collect another amount from you equal to the amount that he charged you for the goods? Would you consider such a man your friend, or would you consider the man your friend who gave you the goods at a reasonable price and guaranteed to you that this would be all that you would be charged therefor? Would not such a man be your friend in place of the one who pretended to be and yet sought to mislead you? That there are such friends whose interest in you is purely

...

The first issue of *The Employer* newsletter was published for Iowa businesses on November 1, 1921.

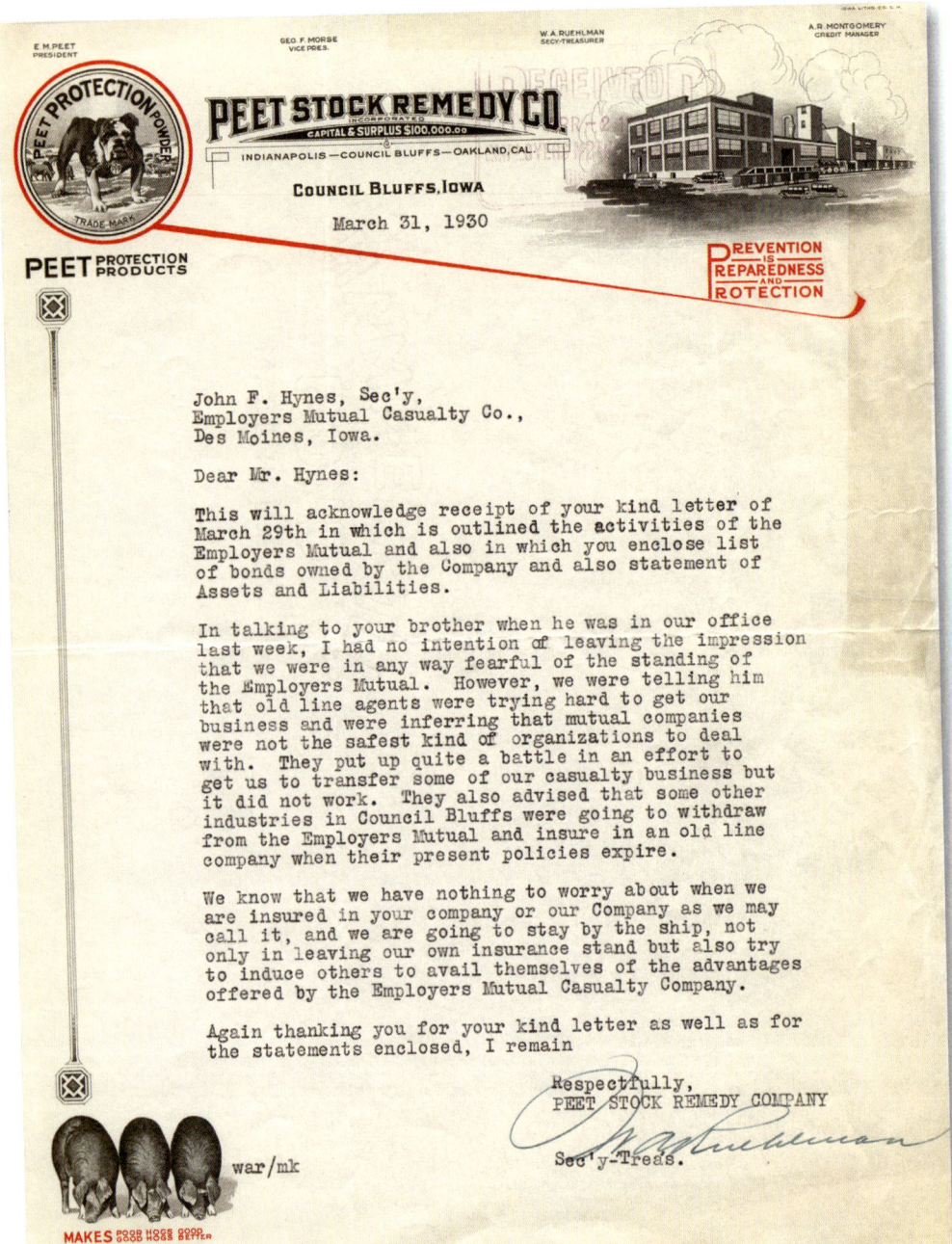

it reported, were trying to get its business by implying that mutual companies were not safe to deal with and that other industries in the area were going to withdraw their business from EMCC. Peet promised not only to "stay by the ship" but to induce others to avail themselves of EMCC's advantages.

In another instance, at an EMCC adjuster's request, a Wichita law firm assured a potential client that "there is no company that I represent or deal with with whom I would rather have business transactions either from an underwriting standpoint or from the claim adjustment end." That statement appears to have taken some courage because the firm added that their position might be considered "heresy on the part of some clients who feel that the only safe insurance company is a stock company."

Competition with stock companies lingered and the battles were not over, but some immediate issues abated as mutuals proved their worth.

Workmen's Compensation

While the auto business developed, workmen's compensation remained EMCC's basic line. To counter the national downturn in the line and to support its legislative efforts, the company adopted an educational promotional strategy in the early 1920s. For example, a brief article in the first issue of *The Employer* explained current Iowa law, which eliminated earlier confusion about claims procedures. Now, it stated, all employees were covered, except household and domestic

had higher rates than Iowa because they had no entity to lobby for employers' insurance interests. EMCC called on its constituency to support the lobbying effort by electing legislators who would be "free from the spirit of class legislation against the employer of labor."

By the 1930s, EMCC had won the loyalty of many policyholders who pled the company's case. The Peet Stock Remedy Co. of Council Bluffs is one example. "Old line agents,"

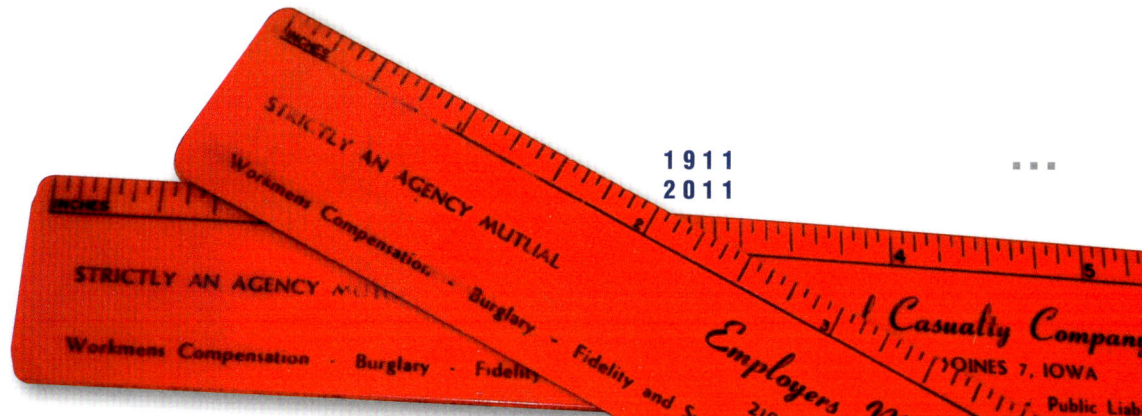

servants, agricultural and farm employees, casual employees, and clerical employees. Injuries were covered only if they arose in the course of employment. An employee must be incapacitated for at least two weeks in order to receive compensation for time lost from work, after which the payment would be 60% of the average wage with a $15.00 maximum and $6.00 minimum per week. The specified number of weeks that compensation could be received for partial permanent disabilities, such as the loss of a hand or arm, was determined according to a fixed schedule of benefits.

EMCC corrected confusion about care providers by specifying approved doctors for most cities and towns where industrial establishments were operating. Standards of competency were set for selecting physicians. Those chosen were familiar with handling compensation cases and knew reporting requirements. The doctors submitted standard forms immediately after the first examination and kept EMCC advised about the condition of injured employees, allowing prompt compensation payments. Thus, EMCC gained confidence that the most simple and inexpensive means was being used to give employees the best possible treatment to enable them to get back to work as soon as possible.

Over time, pressure developed to expand what workmen's compensation insurance should cover. Costs rose as the affected categories of workers broadened and benefit levels increased. Throughout the 1920s, EMCC "vigorously opposed" adding occupational disease to injury coverage and commended Iowa Manufacturers Association Manager Ed Kimball

for his part in helping defeat "bad parts" of proposed legislation, such as unlimited medical coverage. In 1925, EMCC and IMA lobbied successfully to defeat two bills that would have increased compensation costs by broadening benefits in Iowa. But, by the time Iowa's first Occupational Disease Law became effective in 1947, EMCC was ready to comply.

In the meantime, EMCC paid its 250,000th workmen's compensation claim in the fall of 1941. It was to H. Deets, a workman at Ted Cutler Plumbing Company in Des Moines, who fractured his arm. The policy had been written by Jester and Sons, which was to become one of EMCC's major agencies.

With changes in coverage came the question of appropriate rates. During the early 1920s, there was pressure to keep rates low — from IMA to benefit their constituency and from the competition of some stock companies that cut rates to obtain business. On the other hand, the National Council on Compensation Insurance (NCCI) attempted to raise rates to maintain the solvency of insurance companies.

President John A. Gunn participated in NCCI, although he made no commitment for the company to become a member. He believed that decision belonged to the board and, in January 1923, made a detailed report to them about NCCI and its positions, which included a history of rate making. Following discussion, there was consensus that the company was "created to keep workmen's compensation cost at as low a level as is consistent with sound underwriting" and that it should "go slow" in joining any organization that might increase rates to a higher level. Two years later, the

board voted to increase rates to a level adequate to meet rising costs, even if it meant losing policyholders. By early 1927, EMCC had concluded that sound underwriting meant some increase in rates. The company had joined NCCI and was receiving tabulated statistical material from them.

Insuring Insurance

From the beginning, the company had transferred, or ceded, part of its risk to reinsurance companies. Ceded reinsurance provided two benefits. First, in the face of adverse claims experience, the obligation to pay claims could be met, and the surplus would be protected. Second, the capital backup extended the company's ability to expand its business. In 1925, EMCC took steps that led

it into the other side of reinsurance — assumed reinsurance, or reinsuring insurance written by another company.

During the 1940s, EMCC also participated in another form of reinsurance by joining several specialty coverage risk pools. In these pools, each participating company ceded its risks to the pool and received back, as assumed business, a fractional portion of the total business assumed by the pool. EMCC began ceding insurance to the Mutual Reinsurance Bureau (MRB) in 1951 and then became an assuming member in 1957. Organized in 1921 by 16 small- to medium-sized mutual companies, in response to a study by two national mutual associations, MRB was an association of assuming companies that shared joint liability for risks accepted. Thus, if one member company failed, the liability would be shared proportionally by the remaining

Sharing the Risk

EMCC's entry into the assumed reinsurance field was rooted in the turn of the century when druggists maintained significant stocks of highly flammable naphtha gas to sell to customers for cleaning clothes. A large number of drug store fires resulted, making it difficult for them to obtain adequate fire insurance coverage. When Murtaugh's Drug Store in Algona, Iowa, became a victim, Mr. Murtaugh took the matter into his own hands. He banded together with other druggists in Iowa and Minnesota to form their own property insurance company, Druggists Mutual Insurance Company of Algona (now Pharmacists Mutual Insurance Company). Druggists Mutual made steady progress despite the naphtha gas

hazard, but the druggists still needed liability coverage and the law allowed the mutual to write only property coverage.

EMCC provided a solution in 1925 when it made Druggists Mutual an agent to sell EMCC liability policies to Druggists' members. That arrangement continued until 1949 when the law changed, allowing companies to write both property and casualty insurance. Druggists Mutual then wrote its own liability coverage, but EMCC continued the relationship by reinsuring Druggists' liability risk. Thus, EMCC entered the field of assumed reinsurance, and the relationship with Druggists Mutual has continued to the present. ▪

members. But this never happened. Able managers, adequate rates, high standards for membership, and additional accounting and reporting services made it a highly successful operation. Lessons learned from MRB membership helped EMCC's assumed reinsurance activities grow and prosper.

Branching Out

As new types of coverages were added to its business lines, EMCC turned its eyes toward geographical expansion. In 1921, shortly after entering the auto line, the board had begun exploring entry into other states but postponed the effort due to an "unsettled financial condition" and the possibility that meeting other states' requirements might lower the company's reserves. Two and a half years later they were ready to move forward. Officers looked at qualifications for being admitted in Illinois; yet another two years would pass with no action. Then, in 1925, EMCC entered Nebraska when arrangements were made to work with the new Turk-Somerville General Agency formed by Thomas Turk and Robert S. Somerville in Omaha. By 1928, Turk-Somerville was leading all EMCC agencies in volume of written premiums.

The company continued to explore entering Illinois, along with investigating Tennessee and South Dakota. But EMCC would enter only two more states — Kansas and Missouri — before the decade ended. Even though Missouri's workmen's compensation law became effective in 1927, EMCC chose to enter only the auto line

in both states because Missouri's compensation field "was not satisfactory." Beginning in 1928, EMCC worked through several Missouri agencies located in St. Louis and Kansas City. All underwriting was done at the Home Office in Des Moines. Claims were handled by a law firm that had a good relationship with rising star Maurice J. Wilkinson, who had joined EMCC's field staff in 1925 when he was 22 years old.

As soon as it was admitted to Kansas in 1927, EMCC contracted with State General Agency, owned by Farmers Alliance Insurance Company. Located in McPherson, it was listed as EMCC's fourth largest producer within two years. Writing a large fleet of highway construction trucks for the Kansas State

...

An original postal scale from the Turk-Somerville offices.

...

Maurice J. Wilkinson was instrumental in establishing the Wichita Branch and later became superintendant of agents at the Home Office in Des Moines.

In 1934, the Wichita Branch found its home in the downtown Ellis-Singleton Building (later known as the Petroleum Building).

Highway Commission in 1931 continued the production boom. The boom with State General Agency did not prove to be profitable, however. It was time to explore closer supervision of policy writing through organizational expansion. In 1933, President John A. Gunn sent M. J. Wilkinson to McPherson, Kansas, with directions to open a branch operation and promote business in Kansas.

In 1934, Wilkinson relocated the office to the Ellis-Singleton (later Petroleum) Building in downtown Wichita and then set the stage for profitability by trimming production from $400,000 to $80,000. Competency in this pioneering effort, as well as loyalty, earned the young manager a position on the board of directors in 1937. By 1941, he had built the branch's profitable production back up to $400,000 and was reassigned to the Home Office as superintendent of agents. Wilkinson was succeeded in Wichita by Iowa Field Supervisor Harold C. Dabler, who would serve as branch manager until 1970. During Dabler's tenure, premiums grew to over $6 million, staff from 14 to more than 80, and, in 1948,

the branch was first to have its own office built according to EMCC specifications.

In 1934, EMCC received approval to enter Minnesota and contracted with Citizens Fund Mutual Fire Insurance Company of Red Wing to serve as general agent. W. J. Hynes had one year under his belt as an Iowa claims adjuster when he was sent to Red Wing to open a claims office that serviced business produced by Citizens Fund. Citizens Fund was authorized to write property insurance but, as EMCC's agent, was able to write liability as well. The two companies made an arrangement in which the underwriting title "National Citizens Mutuals" was used to issue joint policies that covered liability, property damage, collision, fire, theft, and comprehensive lines.

Entry into Illinois was also finally accomplished in 1934. Gordon Nelson and a stenographer began underwriting operations from an office in Chicago, reporting directly to the Home Office in Des Moines. Two years later, Safety Engineer Lawrence "Larry" Pye was added to the staff. By 1937, Illinois business had grown to the point that a branch service office to handle underwriting, claims, and inspections in the Chicago area was desirable. W. J. Hynes was called from Red Wing to act as Chicago manager and was replaced in Red Wing by Joe Elliot, who had worked with EMCC as an adjuster since 1930. In Chicago, J. J. Faith was named claims manager and Chief Engineer Lu E. Byerly headed a staff of four safety engineers.

Chicago production was handled by two local independent agencies, Allied and Magill, who were conveniently located in the Insurance Exchange Building across South Wells Street from EMCC's office in the Insurance Center Building. The agencies obtained business through a brokerage system that represented insureds and placed their business with EMCC. Unlike general agencies, which were licensed to have full underwriting power and to pay subcommissions to agents, Allied and Magill had only limited underwriting authority and reported directly to the Chicago Branch and EMCC's Home Office.

While the Wichita and Chicago Branches were getting off the ground, the Turk-Somerville General Agency in Omaha maintained its place as a leading EMCC agency. Founders Thomas Turk and Robert Somerville were described as a "team of Mutual go-getters ... from eye-teeth to toenails" who had "landed in Omaha with a ... determination to show the Cornhuskers that a Mutual general agency could succeed." And they were proving themselves. It was even rumored that they had "designs on all the business in Nebraska."

By 1928, they were representing Mill Owners Mutual and Grain Dealers National, in addition to EMCC. A decade later, they had 300 agents writing for EMCC and were on course to become EMCC's third branch operation. In 1939, EMCC purchased the agency, converting it into the Nebraska Branch with offices in the Service Life Insurance Company building. Quickly dubbed EMCC's "mighty husky baby," its slogan was, "Watch Employers Mutual's Cornhusker business grow!" Upon conversion, Thomas Turk retired and Robert Somerville remained as general manager until he retired in 1955, a year after moving the office to the second branch

building built to EMCC's specifications. During his watch, Somerville built EMCC's Nebraska business to over $1.7 million, while branch staff grew to about 35 and agency force to 200.

The Wichita, Chicago, and Omaha Branches were complemented by contracts with several large general agencies that further broadened EMCC's geographical reach. Working through general agencies was a quick and economical way to open new territories and states. Besides having established business relationships with local agents and insureds and knowledge of the territory, they covered the costs of salaried employees, office rent, and travel expenses. The general agencies had oversight of the local agents, and EMCC's only production cost was local agents' commissions and general agencies' "override commissions," usually 2.5% to 7.5% of written premiums. The Home Office handled underwriting and claims service, and claims were investigated by independent field adjusters. The role of general agencies would grow as an integral part of EMCC's operations until about 1960.

...

Robert Somerville, cofounder of the Turk-Somerville General Agency in Omaha, later became the general manager of EMC's Nebraska Branch.

Wichita personnel in 1937. Back row: M. J. Wilkinson, branch manager; H. W. Tharp, claim adjuster; Cecil Mayer, underwriter. Front row: Mary Wilkinson, claim stenographer; Louise Huber, stenographer; Muriel Merdian, bookkeeper; Patricia Coleman, stenographer. (left to right)

Managing the Great Depression

EMCC was not unaffected by the Great Depression. The sound base on which it was built enabled it to grow, both geographically and in business lines, from the 1920s right through to World War II. EMCC felt little impact until mid-1930, when policies started to be cancelled and American Mutual Liability Insurance Company began cutting rates to take large risks away from EMCC. After that, President John A. Gunn's annual meeting reports anticipated "difficulties ahead" for several years.

As 1930 came to a close, banks had begun to fail, causing a panic in 1931. It was difficult to find a surety company that would issue bonds on bank deposits. Nevertheless, EMCC was able to purchase a bond to cover $50,000 deposited in the Iowa-Des Moines National Bank & Trust Company that fall. Fortunately, the bank remained solid. In fact, all of the company's bank deposits, in that bank and others, remained safe, escaping the swirl of bank failures that continued through 1932.

In May 1931, note was made in the minutes that the U.S. Chamber of Commerce was calling attention to the great number of unemployed, which might result in "considerable revision of workmen's compensation rates upward." Indeed, both workmen's compensation and auto rates did increase during the next few years. As rates went up, volume came down. Audits for 1932 showed the largest number ever of returned premiums due to diminished industrial activity, and there was "considerable difficulty in making collections from agencies."

EMCC experienced its first premium volume declines, from $964,198 to $915,608, in 1931 and then to $847,676 in 1932. The decrease in company income caused belt-tightening in 1933. Reinsurance contracts were renegotiated to save $7,000 a year. The office was moved from the top floor of the Hubbell Building, where it had been located since 1928, to the third floor of the Valley National Bank Building for a savings of 40% in rent over five years.

Thanks to its conservative financial management, EMCC was able to withstand the setbacks and, ultimately, to flourish. Long before Black Tuesday, the board had chosen to invest in "safe and marketable" securities, giving precedence to the safety of principal over a large return. Bonds were seen as the best investment, although there was shifting within the bond portfolio.

...

During the Depression in 1931, the average income was about $1,850 a year. A new automobile cost around $640. A gallon of gas was ten cents. The average house could be rented for $18 a month, and a ticket to a movie was a quarter. The daily paper was only two cents, a candy bar was a nickel, and a mere penny could buy a stick of candy at the store.

Bleak Times

John W. Gunn later remembered one case of trying to collect an agent's balance in Jefferson, Iowa, a prosperous town with three banks that, backed by wealthy citizens, had weathered many storms. The agent was sitting at his roll-top desk, head buried in his hands, when Gunn arrived. A check payable to EMCC was lying on the desk. With a wintry smile, the agent said, "Here's your check for all I've been able to collect. But it may be some time before it will be good. All three of our banks failed to open this morning." The bank on which the check had been drawn never reopened. ▪

As the Depression began, all holdings in federal and most state bonds were transferred into investments in county and municipal bonds, with smaller amounts going into railroads and public utilities. Matured Liberty bonds were sold, and proceeds from the sale of a foreclosed farm owned by EMCC in Greene County were invested in bonds. Bonds issued by smaller communities that were "going backward" were sold and the proceeds invested in larger and more stable municipal units. After a three-year hiatus, EMCC began purchasing U.S. government bonds in 1933, although the bulk of its investments would remain in counties and municipalities until World War II.

EMCC's financial position was enhanced by other measures. Reinsurance contracts were carefully managed, and the company reached outside itself for evaluation. In 1930, the first audit of the company's records and financial standing by an outside firm was conducted by Joseph Froggatt & Company, Insurance Auditors and Actuaries, of New York City. Their recommendations indicated how needed the audit was: keep general ledger entries in sequence, make sure petty cash vouchers and actual cash agree, maintain a standard payroll book and a premium-in-force register, and do not sign another officer's name on company checks. Other advice was given for recording bond dispositions, underwriters' and agents' processes, and other records maintenance

A Little Relief

While EMCC was able to provide adequate coverage to many throughout this period, a unique situation related to county and municipal relief workers arose. Employees of the federal and state governments and some relief organizations were not eligible for workmen's compensation coverage, and it was unclear who actually employed the relief workers. Even if eligible, they did not receive wages, per se, and were generally not included in the payroll base when premiums were calculated. EMCC's response was judicious. A 1934 communiqué from Secretary John F. Hynes instructed field and claims representatives to pay due compensation on two conditions: if the policies issued contained "definite coverage applicable to relief workers" and if they were included in the payroll audit for setting premiums. Where these conditions were not met, compensation for each claim was to be "handled upon its own merits." ▪

matters. Froggatt continued to serve as outside auditor for many years.

As late as the January 1935 annual meeting, the "present economic situation" was referenced. By September, the board's discussion of increased business volume led to an assessment that conditions were showing improvement and would continue to do so. Already, confidence had allowed the establishment of a $100,000 guaranty fund required to do business in Minnesota when the Red Wing office opened in 1934. The next year, EMCC took a step into other new territory with its first investment in common stocks — 100 shares each of General Electric

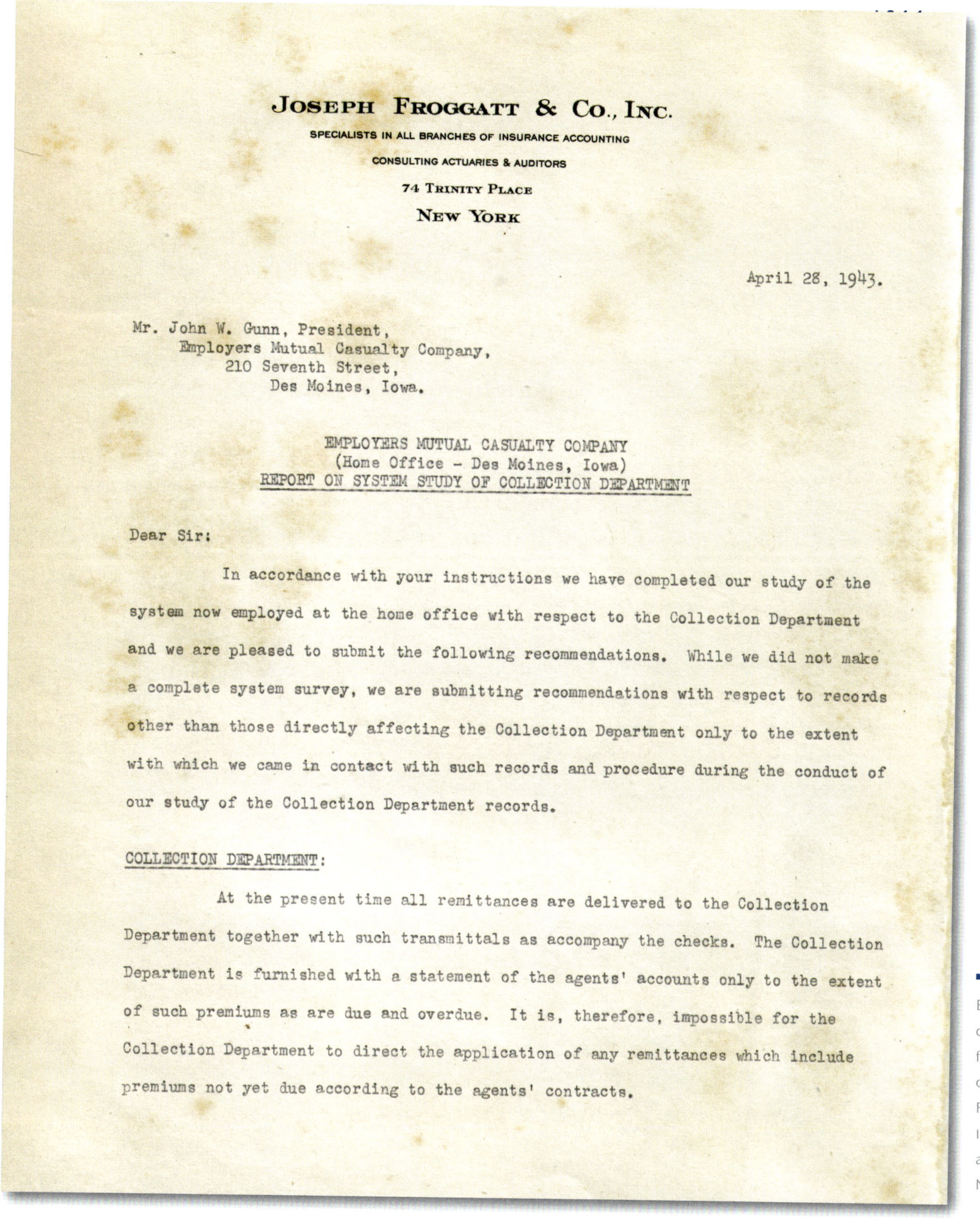

JOSEPH FROGGATT & CO., INC.

SPECIALISTS IN ALL BRANCHES OF INSURANCE ACCOUNTING

CONSULTING ACTUARIES & AUDITORS

74 TRINITY PLACE

NEW YORK

April 28, 1943.

Mr. John W. Gunn, President,
    Employers Mutual Casualty Company,
      210 Seventh Street,
        Des Moines, Iowa.

EMPLOYERS MUTUAL CASUALTY COMPANY
(Home Office - Des Moines, Iowa)
REPORT ON SYSTEM STUDY OF COLLECTION DEPARTMENT

Dear Sir:

In accordance with your instructions we have completed our study of the system now employed at the home office with respect to the Collection Department and we are pleased to submit the following recommendations. While we did not make a complete system survey, we are submitting recommendations with respect to records other than those directly affecting the Collection Department only to the extent with which we came in contact with such records and procedure during the conduct of our study of the Collection Department records.

COLLECTION DEPARTMENT:

At the present time all remittances are delivered to the Collection Department together with such transmittals as accompany the checks. The Collection Department is furnished with a statement of the agents' accounts only to the extent of such premiums as are due and overdue. It is, therefore, impossible for the Collection Department to direct the application of any remittances which include premiums not yet due according to the agents' contracts.

EMC's first audit of company records and financial standing was conducted by Joseph Froggatt & Company, Inc., insurance auditors and actuaries from New York City.

and International Harvester stock, worth about $10,000 total.

Following its low in 1932, premium volume rebounded to $906,250 at the end of 1933, rose to $1.54 million in 1934, and to nearly $2.2 million in 1935. Between 1929 and 1935 assets climbed steadily from $915,244 to over $2.2 million and, except for a dip in 1931, the surplus also increased from $204,573 to $503,654.

TRANSITIONS

The Great Proxy Fight

The period around 1940 was a time of transition that saw a new board, a new president, new competitive relationships, and a world war. The transition perhaps began with what became known as "The Great Proxy Fight of 1937," which resulted in the severing of the relationship that had recognized EMCA as a "Service Division" of IMA and created interlocking boards.

A conflict arose about the composition of the board. The election to fill nine expired and vacant positions on the 15-member board was at stake. Some had perceived that an attempt was underway to move control of the company from John A. Gunn to former U.S. Senator Charles A. Rawson. President of the Iowa Pipe & Tile Company, Rawson had been a director since 1912 and treasurer since 1922. The question of his control became moot when he died September 2, 1936. But a campaign still ensued to obtain enough proxies to elect a slate submitted by Gunn supporters to replace four IMA members whose terms had expired. Some felt so strongly about the issue that they were having policy records copied. It was rumored they were prepared to leave

··· Charles A. Rawson, owner of the Iowa Pipe & Tile Company and a former U.S. senator, was on the EMC Board of Directors from 1912 until his death in 1936.

EMCC and start a new company, using the contacts, if the proxy effort failed.

The record indicates that the effort was probably overkill. Vice President J. H. Fisher nominated John W. Gunn, then assistant secretary and a board member since 1930, and the four IMA members with expiring terms. John W. Gunn nominated himself, his brother-in-law Dr. Lawrence E. Kelley, retiring Field Supervisor George Patterson, General Agent O. B. McKinney, and W. Z. Proctor, who would become EMCC's general counsel in 1941. Gunn was unanimously reelected with 1,080 votes, and the rest of his slate each received 1,069 votes, while Fisher's slate (H. C. McCardell, Howard W. Power, C. C. Deering, William Cochrane) received only 11 votes each. W. W. Wise, director since 1917, also left the board at that time.

Also nominated by John W. Gunn and elected to fill vacancies were Wichita Branch Manager M. J. Wilkinson; Des Moines businessman Anselm Frankel; general agent Thomas Turk; and Hjalmer Hjermstad, president of Citizens Fund Mutual Fire Insurance Company, EMCC's general agency in Red Wing, Minnesota, (eventually renamed Citizens Security Mutual Insurance Company). Hjermstad had played a large role in obtaining proxies for the Gunn slate. At the same meeting, Gunn was elected vice president of the company.

Written records do not tell the entire story, but it is thought that a question of underwriting policy might have been involved. Oral tradition suggests that IMA members wanted to write more business, while

management preferred restraint. Thus, the quarrel could have been, in part, about EMCC's desire to create a more cautious board. Later conjecture also indicates that a larger consideration than immediate control of the board was the company's changing nature. As new business lines were adopted, the IMA members' direct business was no longer the backbone of EMCC's volume, business was written in other states, and most production came from an independent agency force. The commissioner's growing concern about interlocking boards may also have been a consideration. It was time for the company's governance to reflect changing conditions.

After the new board was elected, the Articles of Incorporation were amended in 1938 to address evolving management issues. Although the IMA manager made an ineffective charge of non-cooperation by EMCC, little rancor is recorded on the part of IMA members. Upon his defeat, William Cochrane expressed his regrets but complimented the company and its officers and returned his director's fees for 1936. The 1938 annual meeting completed the removal of IMA members. They were replaced by other representatives from business and industry the following year. Over the years EMCC and IMA, now the Association of Business and Industry, have exhibited a deep mutual respect.

Leadership Transferred

John A. Gunn was 77 years old when the board changeover was completed, and his health began to fail shortly afterwards. On December 11, 1940, he submitted a letter of resignation to the board saying, "This is the first Board meeting I have missed since I was elected President of the Company nearly 30 years ago … I hope to be able to be present at the Annual Meeting next month … I no longer have the strength or desire to continue to do very much work. I am afraid the time has come for me to relinquish some of the responsibility which you … have entrusted in me." He then

requested that he be named to the position of chairman of the board, which had been created with the recent changes in the Articles of Incorporation.

Gunn went on, "As you all know, it has long been my wish that John W. Gunn, my son, become my successor as President … I believe that I have trained him to perform with satisfaction the duties." Gunn also expressed his wish that John F. Hynes be elected vice president while continuing as secretary. All of his wishes were granted and he continued as treasurer. John W. Gunn's assumption of the presidency on December 11, 1940, was confirmed.

On August 22, 1941, John W. reported that his father would be unable to give further consideration to business problems. EMCC's founder died November 23, 1941, and services were held two days later with John F. Hynes, William Z. Proctor, Maurice J. Wilkinson, Harold A. Watson, George E. Patterson, and Robert S. Somerville serving as pallbearers.

Present at the August 1941 board meeting, where President John W. Gunn reported his father's inability to handle business problems, was Jesse A. Miller, who had shepherded the company's birth and served from day one, first as a board member and then as general counsel. It would be his last meeting. When the board next convened on November 18, Gunn called attention to the "severe loss" due to Miller's "unfortunate death." His "valuable contributions … to the life and progress" of the company were noted in the minutes. His successor as general counsel, Director William Z. Proctor, was then named.

The new general counsel and John W. Gunn had been school chums. Born nine months apart, the boys graduated from high school in 1920, attended Drake University one year, and then went on to the University of Michigan, where Proctor received his LL.B. in 1925. He was immediately admitted to the Iowa Bar and became an attorney with Bradshaw, Schenck & Fowler. In 1935, Proctor was named partner, two years before his election to the EMCC Board. Renamed Bradshaw, Fowler, Proctor, and Fairgrave, the firm's office was located in the Crocker Building where EMCC had its origins.

Proctor remained on the EMCC Board until 1992. Very active in industry and civic organizations, he gained wide respect as general counsel. Upon his retirement in 1985, Proctor was made general counsel emeritus, a position held until his death on February 22, 1995.

As John W. Gunn assumed the presidency, the challenges presented by stock companies were changing. Facts and experience had made them unable to discredit mutuals with charges of financial instability or claims of "socialism" and "communism." In a 1942 speech to agents, Gunn described stock companies' new competitive tack. To reduce costs, they had drastically lowered their producers' commissions, which allowed them to reduce rates substantially. Gunn did not see any way agency mutuals like EMCC could lower their overhead enough to compete with stock companies on the basis of rates. Service would become the new watchword.

To retain agents and policyholders, it would be necessary to surpass the service of stock companies. "It seems imperative that we abandon our emphasis upon saving," he said. "We must overcome the feeling that mutual insurance is necessarily cheaper. The policyholder must be sold on the principle that a mutual company is just as sound and stable as a stock company and can give him *better* service." By "better service," he meant that handling of claims, selling and delivering policies, collecting premiums, auditing payrolls for workmen's compensation, and accident prevention inspections should all be prompt, courteous, and tactful. His slogan was "Never forget a policyholder and never let a policyholder forget you." The emphasis on service would continue to the present.

Another World War

World War II came to America with the bombing of Pearl Harbor exactly two weeks after the death of John A. Gunn. As in the rest of the country, life at EMCC was altered, but its growth did not stop. Written premiums increased from $4,059,931 in 1941, the year of America's entry into the war, to $6,347,895 in 1945, the year the war ended. During the same period, assets grew from $5,044,899 to $9,154,193 and surplus from $1,100,000 to $2,122,835.

Superintendent of Agents M. J. Wilkinson claimed that it was easy to write

...

An army officer's cap from the World War II era (1939–1945).

Uncle Sam urged citizens to buy war bonds in this World War II era poster.

Buy Bonds!

The practice of buying U.S. government bonds, established during World War I, was continued as a safe way to invest and a patriotic act. During the first four months of 1943, over $500,000 in bonds were purchased. Cash income was higher and general disbursements lower than for the same period the previous year. By September, EMCC held over $3 million in government bonds and expected to "make a substantial commitment" in the third of eight war loan drives. The commitment continued through succeeding drives. By the 1945 annual meeting in January, EMCC held $4.3 million in government bonds and purchased an additional $700,000 by midyear. Throughout the war, employees were also encouraged to buy defense stamps and bonds. •

business "over the counter" for walk-ins who did not have to be solicited and that insurance companies had all the business they could handle. In fact, war activities provided some new opportunities. For example, EMCC insured the Des Moines Ordnance Plant. Then the company entered Alaska in 1943 and insured war contractors such as the Green Construction Company, which was building military barracks and bases there.

The biggest problem was service to policyholders. At the same time that President John W. Gunn was espousing service as EMCC's primary competitive tool, it became more difficult to maintain because of the diversion of human and other resources to the war effort. Many employees and potential employees left to join all branches of the military on both fronts. Commendatory recognition was given to those

in the service, but there were fewer qualified people at home to carry on the work.

M. J. Wilkinson later wrote, "During the war years, try as we did, and we did try, we were unable to maintain our service at the high level we desired. Personnel problems were varied and difficult." Nevertheless, he continued, "We never thought of discouragement, although at times the problems seemed almost insurmountable. We never faltered in our course. We always knew that every problem would be solved." Among the problems for those still writing insurance and handling claims were gasoline rationing and other privations. To counter heating oil rationing limits, which were only two-thirds of what was needed at the Home Office, a coal stoker was installed to replace the oil heating unit.

When peace returned, Wilkinson expected it would be necessary to work harder for business after the war. The task ahead, he said, was "picking up the loose threads and beginning anew weaving our tapestry of life."

EMC NEWS LETTER -- ISSUE NUMBER ONE

FOR ALL EMC MEN IN SERVICE
November 25, 1942

We're going to do better by you from here on, in the matter of correspondence. To start the ball rolling, the guy known as Simon Legree is writing the first letter; and if he can crack his whip hard enough, you'll get one every week from some other civilian in the office.

The Employers Mutual gang is really scattered now. I think we ought to start advertising "World-Wide Claim Service," with McGruder in England or Africa, White in Trinidad, and others from San Diego to Washington, and Camp Dodge to Mississippi. No doubt by the time some of you get this humdrum message from the uneventful paper works on Seventh Street, you will be even farther away. "The sun never sets on an Employers Mutual Representative" would be a good punch line for our next folder; but, of course, Conner had that reputation years ago.

I am attaching a list of the last known addresses of all the men in the service. The next time we print it, we may have a couple of women to add to it, as two of the gals have applied for the Waves. If the addresses are incorrect in any case, please let us know where you are. Particularly we want to know what your mailing address will be after December first, as the kindhearted Board of Directors has a lithographed message for you with figures and $ signs displayed in a prominent position.

Speaking of Waves, something brings to mind the Waacs, of which there are one or two hereabouts. There being no single men left in the office, very little of an intimate or detailed nature is known about them; but as a purely disinterested observer, I could venture the opinion that Beauty will not Win the War. Of course, I don't get around much.

Furthermore, they don't let me in on much of the dirt, so you'll have to wait for later editions of this news letter for really interesting information. All I know is what some of you have written, and having found it interesting to me, I will pass it on.

Robb Kelley, one of our latest recruits, you will remember as being over six feet seven. They finally allowed Robb to enlist; but apparently no one ever thought he would need a uniform, so he is currently equipped with a set of undersized coveralls and a fatigue cap, and is spending his days making beds at Fort Leavenworth.

Another recent addition to the armed forces is K. L. Pearce, who was inducted at Camp Dodge last Friday. Immediately, the war began to go much better, and Eisenhower is reputed to have said that his troubles were over. Ken worked day, night and Sundays getting his organization in shape to perform during his absence, and army life ought to give him a real rest.

Russ Englemann writes that he has been doing a colonel's job on a captain's pay, and is thinking of asking for a raise. He has been in charge of a battalion at Camp Shelby, and has the distinction of being the only officer to bring in his men after a day's forced march with full equipment, all walking on their own feet. Something tells me that Russ is a

-2-

...cer, and I'll guarantee he doesn't ask his men to do anything that he can't do better himself.

Max Smith was home on leave the other day. He is now Lieut. Smith, having gone right up the ladder -- private, corporal, sergeant, and now lieutenant. Max likes the army, and the army likes him. I doubt if we'll ever get him back to collecting past due accounts.

Pete Lemley's last letter from Lakehurst, where he is taking Aerographer's training, told us that if he failed to pass the course, he would spend the rest of the war hanging on the ropes of blimps. If Pete's remarks under such conditions wouldn't deflate any blimp that ever flew, then they must be making them out of cast iron. We're not worried, however, as Pete will pass the course, and before long will be predicting dire weather and cyclonic disturbances with the same insight as he used in forecasting trouble ahead on a comp. risk.

Ron White has been in Trinidad since about five weeks after he enlisted; and unless his letters are rose-colored, he is having a whee of a time, enjoying the tropical weather and the strange sights of that jigs' paradise.

The only other correspondent to the Home Office has been Bud Mantz, now a marine at San Diego; but it takes a solid hepcat to interpret his jive. It's distinctly out of this world, and too strong on the boogie for an old man who's not on the beat.

There has been plenty doing in the automobile department these last few weeks. To put it mildly, the rate situation has been chaotic. For a few days we didn't know ourselves what our rates were, and we changed them twice between Watson's morning coffee and the afternoon mail. The Bureau finally made a slash to end all slashes, and we have ended up at about 25% less than formerly, only a few cents below our stock chums in all categories. Competition is going to be plenty tough; and the situation became so serious that they even got me out of the office to visit the agents. We have had seven agency meetings over the state. After a big meal, I passed them the cigars, Wilkinson and Dick Owens put them to sleep, and Mr. Hynes woke them up and sent them home feeling good. It is still too early to tell what effect gas rationing and the new rates will have on our business; but those of us left are in there pitching, and we expect to have an institution still here at the old stand when you come back.

Write us when you can; we want to hear from you and will pass the news around to others in the service.

Good luck and an early return!

J. W. Gunn

COMING ISSUES OF THE NEWS LETTER

Next week: Eleanor Newell -- all the news that's fit to print.

Week after next: Web Hawkins -- straight from the composing

The Home Front

For 165 weeks, W. J. Hynes, who was Chicago branch manager at that time, mailed a mimeographed weekly bulletin, written by various staff members, to the approximately 30 EMCC employees on the front. It was filled with information, compassion, and humor. At the end, he called it a "hobby" that helped the office staff feel they were contributing to the war effort, and he thanked the many women who would be "blessed at least in Heaven for their patience in working with our old mimeograph machine." Management was thanked for materials and postage. But most important, the "fellows" were thanked for the "many nice letters." In appreciation, they provided him with an ample supply of cigarettes.

Hynes had created a community in which the participants got to know and care for each other as they shared experiences and information. And he gave them food for thought, as he asked for their input. Their contributions were sometimes funny or cheerful, but just as often poignant, sad, philosophical, or informative. ▪

...

The first issue of the weekly newsletter mailed to EMC employees in the service was penned by EMC President J. W. Gunn and mentions Robb Kelley's recent enlistment.

T. V. Ransford, SK3/c
USS Sheliak, AKA-62
c/o Fleet Post Office
San Francisco, Calif.

Employers Mut
330 South
Chica

PASSED BY NAVAL CENSOR
ald.

T. V. Ransford, SK3/c
USS Sheliak, AKA-62
c/o Fleet Post Office
San Francisco, Calif.

Dear Mr. Hynes:

For the past few days I have been receiving the Bulletins right on time and they sure are good to read. I am also glad that you have my new address and thank you for the write up.

In one of the bulletins were the names and addresses of those in the service. Reading thru them, I came upon Jack M. Daly, 1st. Lieut. Marine Corps. Navy 128, c/o Fleet Post Office, San Francisco, Calif. I have never met this fellow nor did I ever hear his name mentioned in the office but he is one a short walk from where I am now.

I am going to try and see if I can get in touch just for the sake of meeting each other. I am sure you would like that. I also have an idea where Ed Schultz is and if I ever get there I'll be sure to look him up.

As for myself, I am feeling fine. This is so much different from the old Atlantic it makes one feel like a million. I am sorry to hear about Lieut. Appaia being injured and I hope that he is well soon. Maybe they'll send him back to the States for a while.

I'll close for now but I promise to drop a line soon again. Say hello to the gang at the office and I hope this finds all in good health, happiness and God's blessing.

Sincerely,

Tom

Two of the many letters sent to W. J. Hynes by service men and women who were EMC employees.

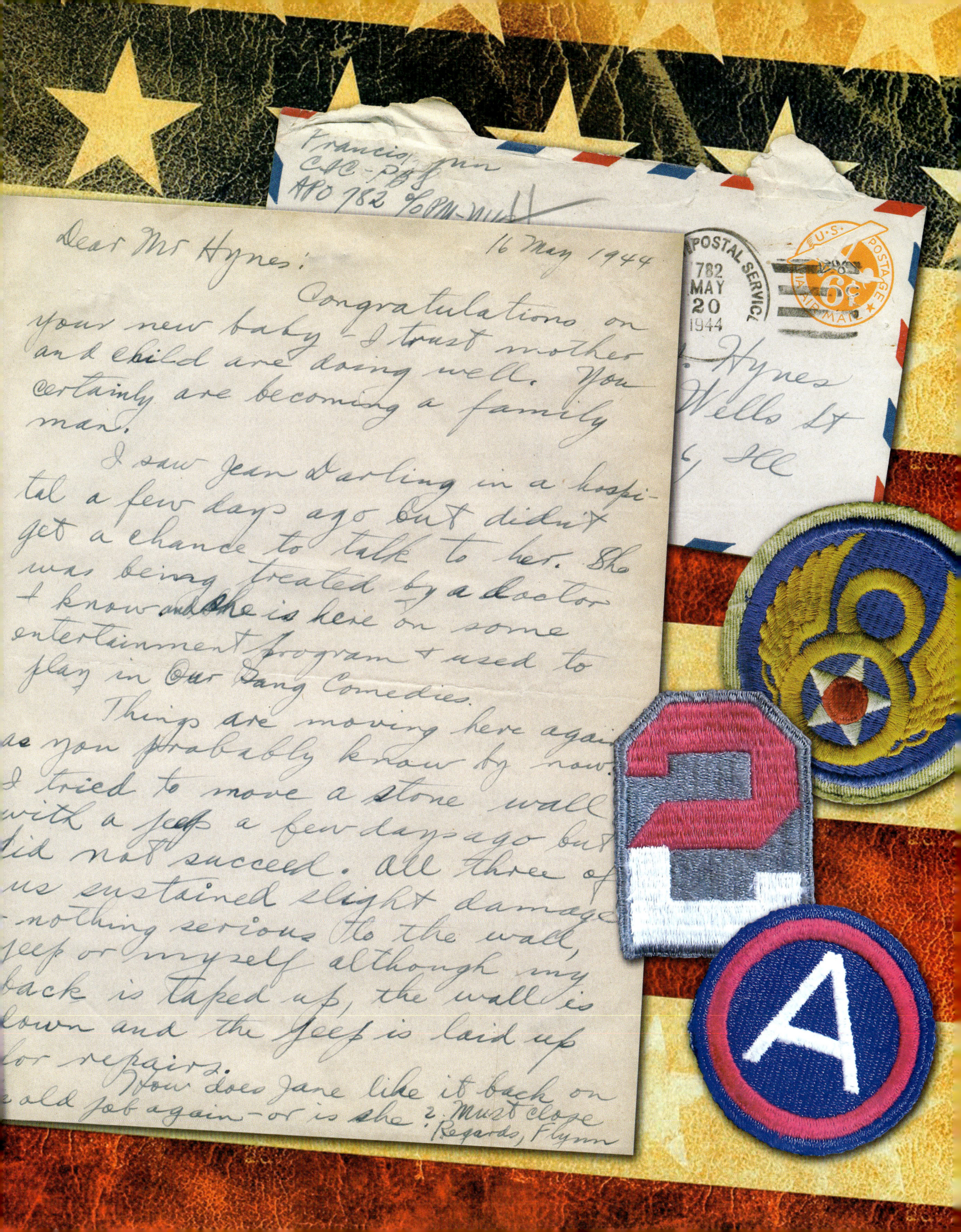

Dear Mr Hynes:

16 May 1944

Congratulations on your new baby – I trust mother and child are doing well. You certainly are becoming a family man.

I saw Jean Darling in a hospital a few days ago but didn't get a chance to talk to her. She was being treated by a doctor I know and she is here on some entertainment program & used to play in Our Gang Comedies.

Things are moving here again as you probably know by now. I tried to move a stone wall with a jeep a few days ago but did not succeed. All three of us sustained slight damage – nothing serious to the wall, jeep or myself although my back is taped up, the wall is down and the jeep is laid up for repairs.

How does Jane like it back on old job again – or is she? Must close

Regards, Flynn

Part 2. ENDURING PRINCIPLES, NEW PRODUCTS AND METHODS

An Underwriting Culture

In 2003, retired President George Kochheiser wrote, "Our company's underwriting style and consistency was the product primarily of a management that recognized from day one the importance of a strong underwriting component that must never be subordinated to pressure from competition or any of the sales, agency, claims, or investment sectors of our business." He defined the company's underwriting discipline as "the accumulation of leadership, protocol, style, history, environment, and who knows what else." In short, underwriting was the heart of EMCC's business.

Underwriting began to take shape as a department when Harold Watson was named supervisor of auto underwriting in the early 1930s. It developed further when R. J. "Pete" Lemley joined EMCC as underwriter for workmen's compensation and public liability in 1937 and then became chief underwriter in 1941. These two men laid the groundwork for a modern department with the dual responsibility of risk selection and product development.

Born in a country store in southeast Iowa in 1901, Pete Lemley brought with him a career as a grocery clerk, shoe fitter, undertaker's assistant, tomato picker, rock buster, service station attendant, and positions in various companies as auditor, special agent, field assistant, and underwriter. Considered "a very strict, but very good teacher" in the fundamentals of insurance and underwriting, Lemley spelled out clearly what he expected

of the people he supervised. A bachelor for life, he reminded them that if he could get up, shave, fix his own breakfast, and be at work on time, they could do the same.

Lemley's commitment to professional excellence could be seen as he trained his staff, better known as "Pete's boys." Former Underwriter and Milwaukee Branch Manager William "Bill" Young, who joined EMCC in 1958 under Lemley, particularly remembered Jack Roehr, Ed Olson, Wayne Goettsch, Jack Everett, Gordon Jorgenson, Fred Schiek, and Dick Fraser, all of whom began with the department from the late 1940s through the 1950s. One of their assignments came when rates were being changed. The "boys" were assigned to figure out the new rate using a hand-cranked calculator while Lemley did the same calculation by hand. Although time consuming, the process uncovered discrepancies and proved its worth.

The art of good writing was Lemley's trademark skill. He was given a carbon copy of all memos and letters written each day. Often they came back to the writer with a red ballpoint instruction, "See Me Pls." Bill Young remembered responding to that request many times, but he was always helped by Lemley's constructive criticism. And sometimes that red ballpoint wrote, "Bill — good letter, R.J.L." Besides teaching communications skills, the reviews kept Lemley on top of what risks were being written and declined, thus

A Solid Foundation

Underwriting would be EMCC's primary marketing tool for years to come. George Kochheiser wrote, "Our elders from the days of Pete Lemley and Harold Watson would hew to solid conservative underwriting principles, knowing that management would always back them up. They mentored a cadre of professional underwriters who passed on that culture, instilling it in those who followed. Succeeding generations of our underwriters realized that this was the style endorsed and expected by their top management. That underwriting culture and our continuity of like-minded management (and not just the management) is what produced a consistent marketing strategy that was appreciated by our corps of loyal agents and resulted in underwriting ratios that stood the test of time and erratic cycles." ▪

enabling him to further train employees to make good decisions.

At least one of Lemley's own letters was circulated to "All Who Dictate Letters" as a sample to be studied for writing effective answers to letters of complaint or criticism. In speeches throughout his career, he stressed the importance of conveying information and establishing good will. For him, communicating clearly and concisely took precedence over rules of grammar and sentence structure learned in school. He spelled out how to organize thoughts, set a cheerful tone, show that the recipient is understood, and use a straightforward style. Negative instructions were "do nots": do not write hurriedly or in anger, do not use irritating or stilted phrases and clichés, do not sign letters without reading them.

Lemley's language was often colorful, as when he instructed that the repeated use of the word "I" does not leave the impression that the writer is a big shot. "To the contrary," he said, the reader's "conclusion will very likely be that the writer is simply an egotistical peewit who is trying to work off an inferiority complex. Personally, I would find no quarrel with this conclusion." Recognizing that not everyone is a born letter writer, he taught that everyone can learn satisfactory composition by picking apart their own letters and getting friendly criticism. Sometimes he ended his instructions humorously with a sample he said was designed for entry in a worst writing contest.

After being named chief underwriter in 1941, Lemley worked with M. J. Wilkinson, who had just returned to the Home Office from Wichita, and John S. "Jack" Roehr to establish the company's early underwriting policy and philosophy. A Kansas native born in 1906, Roehr had come to EMCC as a workmen's compensation underwriter in 1940. Previously, he had worked his way up from messenger boy to traveling car auditor for the Santa Fe Railroad after high school. He earned his mechanical engineering degree from Kansas University in 1931, and then worked with a wholesale grocery concern

...

Tools of the insurance trade in the 1920s and 1930s: a Monroe adding calculator and *The Underwriter's Book of Forms*.

and the Kansas Compensation Rating
and Inspection Bureau. A student of
insurance, he was known for his work with
agents and his excellent understanding
of casualty language.

In 1942, Roehr's EMCC career was
interrupted by military reserve training at
the American Television Institution in Chicago
and a radar installation in Naperville, Illinois.
Active duty followed in the U.S. Army Signal
Corps on the Pacific front and as a U.S. Navy
aerographer's mate on the escort carriers
Pybus and *Wake Island*.

After the war, Lemley, Wilkinson, and
Roehr continued their policy development

work, establishing criteria for determining
risk characteristics and creating a review list
of what to accept or avoid when writing
business. Complementing their work was the
company *Digest*, initiated by President John
W. Gunn for the benefit of sales and operations.
An "encyclopedia" of the company's services
and organization, it included comprehensive
underwriting guidelines. The *Digest* took
the form of a loose-leaf notebook in which
all employees and agents could add material
as it was produced from November 18, 1941,
through September 1958.

Five months before the *Digest* was initiated,
the first annual Conference and School for

Home Office and branch technical employees was held in Des Moines. Company leaders and occasional outside speakers presented topics covering the wide range of company operations and current developments affecting the industry. Attendees were introduced to new themes and products, participated in workshops, and socialized at dinners in clubs or hotels around Des Moines. These meetings set a precedent for other branch personnel, such as underwriting, claims, and accident prevention managers, to hold annual meetings in Des Moines. The Conference and School continued until 1970, when it had become so large that it was replaced by an annual branch managers meeting.

New Lines for a Casualty Company

Like John W. Gunn, Lemley, Roehr, and Wilkinson emphasized service. Wilkinson wrote, "The difference between our service and that of anyone else is solely in the extra service we perform." In the underwriting area, that meant meeting the emerging needs of policyholders as their businesses evolved and new hazards developed, as well as adjusting to legislative mandates, court decisions, and changing public expectations. Because the law allowed companies to write only one classification of risk, EMCC was restricted to liability,

...

Home Office and branch technical employees attended the first Annual Conference and School in Des Moines in 1941.

Left: C. Leonard Williams was promoted to bond manager in 1945 after joining EMC two years earlier as an underwriter.

Right: Thomas X. Wright, named manager of surety bonds in 1959, was promoted to assistant vice president in 1960.

or casualty, insurance. But it was able to add a number of new lines within that classification during the 1940s.

First were plate glass, burglary, and fidelity and surety bonds in 1942. Plate glass premiums that year amounted to over $15,000. The bond business began as a service to construction contractors, most of whom were doing war work. EMCC was already writing liability and workmen's compensation for them, but they needed bonds to cover their bidding process. To meet that need, J. R. "Dick" Owens, who had 22 years of experience in the bond business, was brought on board to organize a bond and burglary division. In 1945 he was replaced as bond manager by C. Leonard Williams, who had 18 years of experience in the bond

business and had first joined EMCC in late 1943 as an underwriter and worked part-time in the bond division.

Because most construction during World War II was war-related, there was a huge pent-up demand for commercial construction when it ended, and a period of profit and growth in the construction industry followed. By the late 1950s, Williams had built EMCC's contract surety book to be the largest of any Iowa company. Unfortunately, when the construction backlog was caught up in the mid-1950s, there were more contractors than available work. At one point EMCC had 23 contractors in loss, which contributed to the surplus dropping from $12,642,214 to $11,838,179 in 1957.

Williams became despondent over these results and offered to resign in 1959. His offer was not accepted, but surety bonds was made a separate department and Thomas X. Wright, a decorated B-24 navigator during World War II and attorney in EMCC Claims since 1948, was named manager. Burglary and plate glass were placed under Williams until his retirement in March 1966. As bond manager, Wright cut volume 75% and discontinued surety bonds in all states but Iowa and those of one Missouri agent. The department began to turn around, and Wright was promoted to assistant vice president in 1960.

Other lines followed plate glass, burglary, and bonds. In 1943, a travel policy that covered residences and outside theft, and another for aviation, were announced. The next year saw a new personal comprehensive liability policy, and a money and securities policy was added in 1947. That year workmen's compensation policies were affected by a new national wage and hour law. In Iowa, the legislature passed an occupational disease law that covered employment-related diseases such as silicosis, lead, mercury, and other metallic poisoning.

After World War II, huge polio epidemics occurred in the United States into the 1950s. In response, EMCC began offering a polio and dread disease policy in 1949, and the first claim was filed in September. The policy covered nine diseases — polio, leukemia, rabies, scarlet fever, diphtheria, smallpox, spinal meningitis, encephalitis, and tetanus. Over the next five years, 52,400 policies would be issued. When the Salk vaccine became available in 1955, mass immunizations resulted in near

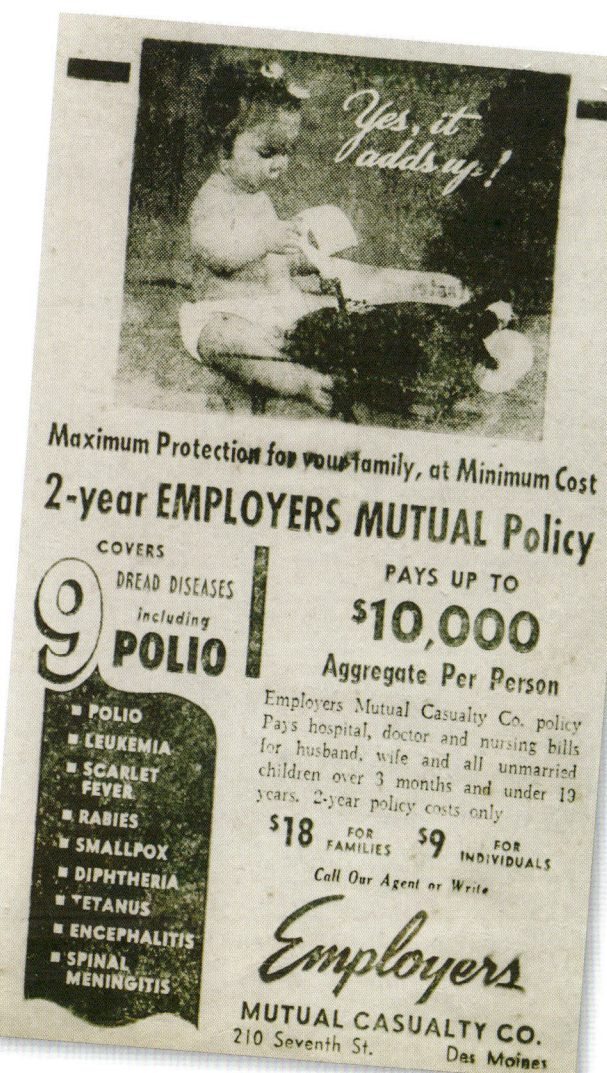

This 1950s newspaper ad shows some of the benefits of the polio and dread disease policy, which EMC began offering in 1949.

eradication of polio in the U.S. within two years, and some impetus for the policy was lost. It was then converted into a perilous disease policy with the addition of cancer, typhoid, and tularemia. This policy was phased out by nonrenewal and was dropped in 1980.

For all of these additions and changes, the Underwriting Department had to identify the specific need and create forms that contained correct wording and accurate pricing. Appropriate rates were set, aided by membership in the National Council on Compensation Insurance. Then the forms had to be filed with state insurance departments, the products marketed, and the experience monitored.

New Classifications Are Allowed: Property and Specialty

Opportunities to develop new lines expanded dramatically during the late 1940s, as states began to lift restrictions that allowed companies to write only one classification of insurance. The rationale for allowing only one classification per company had been that premiums for any classification should be used to pay the claims for that classification only. Now, that concept was dissolving. Passage of an Iowa law in 1949, and one in Nebraska in 1951, allowed EMCC to add property insurance to its offerings, but it would not do so until 1955.

When it did enter the property business, EMCC was well prepared. In November 1954, Frederic M. DuBois was recruited to form a division to write fire and inland marine insurance. Born in New Jersey, DuBois was educated in Connecticut schools and graduated from Harvard University. He had worked as a field man, underwriter, branch manager, and vice president for several stock and mutual companies, most recently at North Star Reinsurance Corporation of New York City, a subsidiary of General Reinsurance Corporation. During World War II, he had spent four-and-a-half years in the Army Infantry, including 18 months in France and Germany, and rose from private to captain. At EMCC, he would be promoted to assistant vice president and general manager of the fire and inland marine division in 1957 and to vice president in charge of property underwriting operations in 1960.

Under DuBois's direction, the division expanded rapidly. Writing fire and allied lines commenced in Iowa, Nebraska, and Minnesota on January 1, 1955, and the premium goal for the first year was set at $500,000. By mid-year, Illinois, Michigan, Missouri, Pennsylvania, New Jersey, and Maryland had been added to the fire business territory, and the division was writing in 12 states by year's end. The 21st state was entered a year later.

Premiums the first year totaled $434,000 — $416,000 for fire and $18,000 for inland marine — not quite the goal, but significant. The next year total premiums had increased to $1,576,000 — $1,496,000 for fire and $80,000 for inland marine. During the same time period, losses rose from $56,000 to

$260,000 for fire and from $4,000 to $17,000 for inland marine.

Early policies included a home protector "package" (fire, burglary, personal liability, personal property, and other scheduled articles) and a standard homeowners policy. In January 1956, a $3.5 million policy was written on Iowa State College's dormitories and Memorial Union, and that line quickly expanded into at least ten more states. Reinsurance arrangements allowed sizeable contracts to be written as preferred risks in residential, mercantile, and nonmanufacturing classes. By the fall of 1958, business had grown to the point that John L. Barnett was added to the staff to handle inland marine and commercial multiple peril policies and to assist with fire underwriting.

EMCC soon discovered new ways to expand its property offerings. For some time after its initiation in 1956, a canine shield policy was available to cover pets in Iowa, Kansas, and Missouri. The brainchild of agents Richard R. Nelson and Gordon J. Reabe from Kansas City, Missouri, its first claim was for the hospitalization of a dog that had been attacked by a swarm of bees. The men had studied veterinarian records for 10,000 pets and set

...

These advertisements from 1955 showcase new insurance products from EMC.

the annual premium at $15 for up to $150 coverage. Included were hospitalization, surgery, X-rays, laboratory fees, and drugs for dogs between the ages of six months and ten years.

Advancing technology brought another opportunity. An atomic-powered generator at the U.S. Reactor Testing Station in Idaho first produced electricity in 1951, and ground was broken in Pittsburgh, Pennsylvania, for the first U.S. atomic power plant in 1954. Two years later, EMCC joined the $12 million capacity Mutual Atomic Energy Reinsurance Pool with a $150,000 commitment. Later renamed MAERP Reinsurance Association, it was created by mutual companies to reinsure bodily injury liability and property loss to the general public resulting from a release of nuclear material or radioactivity from atomic energy plants.

Some specialty lines turned out not to be EMCC's cup of tea. Such was the case with

accident insurance. In the early 1950s, aggressive Chicago broker G. Shannon Grover had brokered reinsurance with Lloyd's of London for EMCC travel accident policies. Unfamiliar with this specialty and wanting to expand accident writings, EMCC contracted with Grover in 1953, to underwrite accident and health policies as general agent.

Grover produced some accident business with "unusually liberal and variable amounts of coverage" and pushed to add new lines such as medical malpractice. A man with his own ideas about how to conduct business, he tended to ignore EMCC's procedures, despite the company's diplomatic attempts to obtain his compliance. At one point Grover wrote to M. J. Wilkinson, "We are sincerely sorry if our simplified method of handling these group cases does not fit in with your established home office procedure ... but if a procedure becomes so burdensome in detail that overhead eats up all of our overriding commission, then we would be better off without the business." In time, EMCC agreed that they would, for their part, be better off without Grover, and the relationship, as well as accident coverage, ended about 1958.

A Subsidiary Opens New Options

Competition from "captive" agency companies in the auto and homeowners lines led to expanding operations beyond EMCC's traditional limits. "Captive" agents wrote business exclusively for one company, and this created some efficiencies. For example, independent agents had to obtain rate quotes from a number of companies, whereas captive agents received them directly from only one, requiring only one set of paperwork. Reduced duties translated into smaller commissions, or less expense for the carrier, which allowed rates to be lower. In turn, lower rates gave a competitive edge to agents as well as to the insurer.

Stock companies also had certain advantages. Mutual companies were limited to filing rates by class of business, while stock companies could break down rates into categories within a class. Thus, EMCC, as a mutual, could not, for example, give preferred rates to low-risk drivers.

EMCC addressed these competitive disadvantages by forming a wholly-owned subsidiary stock company — EMCASCO

Insurance Company — to write low risk personal lines at preferred rates using direct billing. Incorporated in late 1958 and reinsured by EMCC, its enabling resolution called for the adoption of "some or all of the methods used by competitive companies, such as reduced commissions, continuous policies, home office billing, and collection."

EMCASCO provided new competitive products for EMCC's independent agents, but this advantage was offset by two disadvantages. First, the lower premiums meant a lower commission base. Second, loss of billing responsibilities further reduced commissions for various products. The alternative, however, was to lose business to companies such as State Farm and Allstate. President John W. Gunn wrote, "EMC is not pushing EMCASCO. It is offered as a competitive weapon to be used to retain good risks and to gain back good risks, which have been lost to the low-cost carriers." He left it to the agents to choose whether to sell EMCASCO or higher premium EMCC policies. With either choice, Gunn emphasized, the agents' time and work would be fairly compensated.

EMCASCO's operations began in April 1959 with writing auto risks in Iowa. By June, the first claim had been paid to Fred E. Shewmaker, a Younkers Department Store floor manager

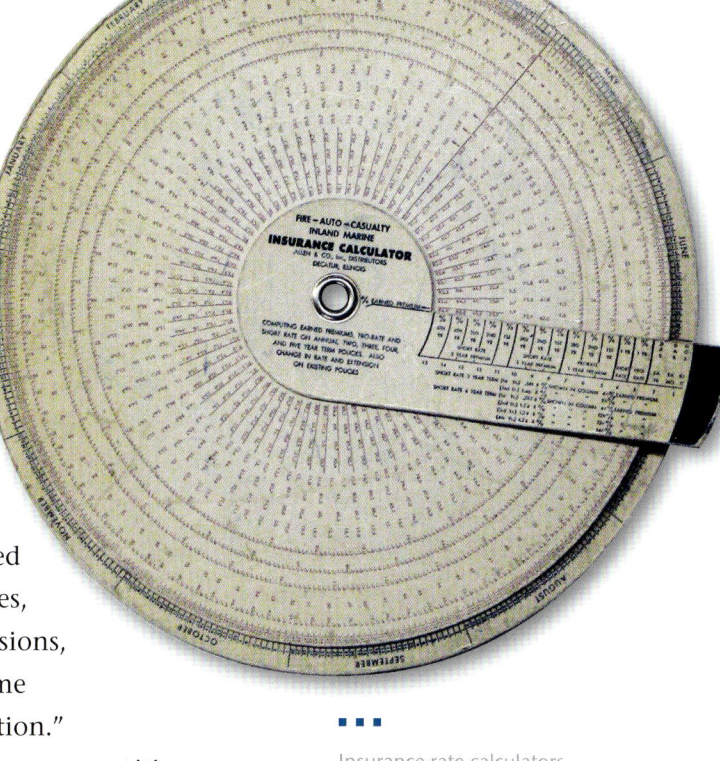

...

Insurance rate calculators, like this one from the 1950s, were used to determine insurance rates.

who had obtained his policy from local agent Ernie Borgen. An article in the July 26, 1959, *Des Moines Register* outlined eligibility limits for EMCASCO auto policies: Class 1 owners of private passenger automobiles, no male drivers under 25, and only occasional business use. The preferred rates for these limits on a 1959 four-door sedan were $74 annually, as opposed to $95 for typical coverage, and $94 instead of $117 for the greatest coverage.

The agents gradually adapted. Milwaukee Field Supervisor Ray L. Russell's experience was typical. He found most agents to be cooperative, but some almost threw him out of their offices before matters "got back to normal" after nearly a year. Eventually, agents began saying either choice paid equally well.

By the end of 1959, EMCASCO had met requirements to extend business into Kansas and Illinois. Rapid expansion into more and more states would contribute to double-digit annual increases in premium volume throughout the 1960s, bringing it to $9.4 million in 1969. The subsidiary company expanded through the 1970s, and EMCC and the branches have continued to use EMCASCO Insurance Company to the present.

Auto Moves Ahead

After World War II, there had been a brief, alarming trend in auto accidents. As young men returned from the service, more drivers were on the road, and they drove more miles as wartime driving restrictions were lifted. Return to a domestic economy also resulted in a surge of

new and faster car models. All contributed to a rising accident rate. But by late 1947, EMCC's auto experience was improving and a profit was thought possible. Iowa's new assigned risk plan and a visual test requirement to obtain a driver's license were contributing to an improved accident frequency rate. By 1952, auto accidents had been reduced 7% in Iowa, and premium volume was up 19% at EMCC. It seemed wise to expand the auto line.

... This advertisement from 1954 urged drivers to use caution in icy winter conditions.

During the 1950s, auto insurance overtook workmen's compensation as EMCC's top line. This evolution in the company's business reflected a national trend. In 1953, the *National Underwriter* reported that auto was the largest segment of the casualty business — $3.3 billion, up from $2 billion in 1948. EMCC was in the top 10% of auto writers, rating 70th of 772 total companies and 13th of 266 mutuals.

By 1955, auto had grown to approximately 60% of EMCC's business, with $15 million of the company's nearly $26 million total premiums, and growth continued with new auto products. Uninsured motorist and extended medical liability coverage had been introduced in 1954. The next year, EMCC insured all of the Iowa State Highway Commission's 4,000 units of rolling stock, and a safety program was prepared for the 2,500 drivers. In 1956, a new family automobile policy for private passenger cars was made available, and uninsured motorist coverage was added to those policies in 1957.

EMCC attributed its success to its management of rating and loss ratio issues and to the standards set for agents. Changes in American life were bringing changes in rate setting, as well as giving rise to new lines. Rating by weight, horsepower, and cost of different brands of automobiles had become outdated, but new standard safety features resulted in some surprises that had to be accommodated. For example, bumpers were causing a rise in whiplash injuries. Because bumpers reduced damage to vehicles, there was less crushing metal to absorb impacts, which were passed on to injure the vehicles' occupants.

Cars had become an indispensable means of transportation as people moved to the suburbs. Many families had two cars with varied uses and exposures to hazards, ranging from business to personal to teenage drivers. Financial responsibility laws were changed from rating the automobile itself to requiring coverage of all drivers regardless of age, occupation, or physical condition. This forced insurers to set broad classifications based on average use rather than the rating of individual drivers. For about a decade, EMCC was able to stay ahead of these new conditions.

Then, the positive trend began to reverse, and the causes of accidents came under the microscope. Underwriting was tightened, and auto business dividends were eliminated in some states. In a late 1957 speech to agents, Claims Vice President W. J. Hynes noted that, nationally, 360,000 people had been killed and 12.5 million injured in the previous ten years. Speed, he pointed out, was involved in 70% of fatal accidents and drinking was a factor in 50%. The period from Thanksgiving to New Year's was the most dangerous, with

■ ■ ■

At the turn of the 20th century, driver's licenses were not required; however, safety concerns prompted states to begin testing a driver's skills before issuing a driver's license.

COMES AN ACCIDENT!

And then he realizes that he waited too long!

He finds himself likely to be sued for every cent he is worth. He has to hire a lawyer, pay court costs, spend time and money in costly litigation. His property, his savings, and his business are at the mercy of a jury!

And then the Verdict—
$10,000!

To him who waits may come Heavy Loss and Poverty

One car in every three in the United States met with an accident last year.

Not all of them were serious; but the difference between a minor collision and a death **is only a matter of luck.**

When your turn comes, are you prepared? Or will you still be waiting?

For a few dollars a year, you can be safe—why wait?

A policy in the Employers Mutual is complete assurance against loss.

A non-assessable, iron-clad contract—prompt, intelligent and satisfactory service—years of experience in handling claims.

Over a million dollars paid in losses.

Employers Mutual Casualty Company

JOHN A. GUNN, President

LIABILITY IN...

AUTOMOBILE INSURANCE

AUTOMOBILE driving is dangerous. Thousands are injured and killed by automobiles every year.

The streets are full of careless drivers. Pedestrians are injured and killed. It's easy to injure some one.

AUTOMOBILE LIABILITY INSURANCE protects you against lawsuits and claims on account of injuries to the other fellow.

AUTOMOBILE PROPERTY DAMAGE INSURANCE protects you against lawsuits and claims for damage to the other fellow's property.

We can save you money on your automobile liability insurance.

EMPLOYERS MUTUAL CASUALTY COMPANY, Equitable Bldg., Des Moines, Iowa

---

BUT HOW ABOUT THIS YEAR?

You intend to drive your car. The thought of an accident will not keep you indoors when you want to be out in the fresh air. If you use your car in business, or to drive to and from your work, you cannot afford to dispense with it.

Yet—

CHILDREN ARE PLAYING IN THE STREETS CONSTANTLY, AND YOU ARE ALWAYS IN DANGER OF INJURING ONE—

PEDESTRIANS ARE ALWAYS WITHIN A FEW INCHES OF YOUR CAR AT BUSY CORNERS, AND THE LEAST MISHAP MIGHT CAUSE A DEATH OR SERIOUS INJURY—

CARELESS AND INEXPERIENCED DRIVERS ARE ON EVERY STREET AND HIGHWAY, AND SMASH-UPS ARE ALMOST INEVITABLE — AND

JURIES AND JUDGES ALWAYS FAVOR THE INJURED PARTIES IN AN AUTOMOBILE DAMAGE SUIT.

It doesn't always matter who is to blame. Witnesses can always be found to testify that YOU were in the wrong. THE VERDICTS RENDERED LAST YEAR IN AUTOMOBILE DAMAGE SUITS AVERAGED MORE THAN TWO THOUSAND DOLLARS! MANY WERE FOR FIVE THOUSAND AND SOME AS HIGH AS TWENTY AND THIRTY THOUSAND DOLLARS!

Are The Cards Stacked Against The Automobile Owner?

They are. But there is one way, and only one way, to protect yourself against loss—

THAT IS A PUBLIC LIABILITY AND PROPERTY DAMAGE INSURANCE POLICY IN A COMPANY STRONG ENOUGH TO PROTECT AND REPAY YOU IN THE EVENT OF LOSS OR DAMAGE.

The Employers Mutual Casualty Company

Has written Automobile Liability insurance since 1911

Our Rates Are Reasonable   Our Protection Is Complete

Write us or see our agent in your town for particulars regarding coverage, and protect yourself against the greatest possibility of heavy loss that the auto owner incurs.

EMPLOYERS MUTUAL CASUALTY COMPANY
ORGANIZED IN 1911 BY THE MANUFACTURERS, BUILDERS AND OTHER EMPLOYERS OF IOWA

⋯

EMC used advertisements, posters, and brochures to promote safe driving and auto insurance.

the rush of the holiday season, icy road conditions, and liquor consumption.

Hynes asked the agents what they were doing to cut down on the number of accidents in their territories: Promoting driver education in high schools? Using mail folders designed by themselves or national and state safety organizations? Placing posters in their office windows? He added suggestions. Agents could send postcards to their insureds with a different message each week during the holiday season. They could give local newspaper editors information for weekly articles and ask the ministerial association to issue statements about the problem. Individual creativity was encouraged. "Your idea is as good as the other fellow's!" he said.

Another problem for EMCC during the early 1950s was a re-emerging concern that stemmed from proposals made in 1929 to legislate compulsory auto liability insurance. At that time, the company had feared its ability to select and rate risks would be curtailed if a law passed. It sketched out several doomsday scenarios: state insurance replacing private companies, "an endless amount of litigation," and questions about remuneration handled by a commission or the county treasurer. EMCC's agent newsletter, *The Co-Operator*, told them on February 15, 1929, "The whole thing is too visionary to be enacted into law … Such a law would, if passed, destroy your Automobile Insurance business." Agents were advised to inform their state representatives and senators about the defects of such legislation.

The February 1953 *Co-Operator* again encouraged agents to lobby against compulsory

insurance bills. Now the arguments were that most cars on the road were already insured, the rate of insured drivers was increasing every year, and current financial responsibility laws were working very well. "This is the way of free enterprise … and for producers of automobile insurance, it is also the alternative to extinction."

Agents were told that, if insurance became compulsory, they would become mere order clerks, rather than producers who needed salesmanship ability and knowledge of insurance, and their commissions would likely be reduced. Consumers, EMCC claimed, would demand lower prices as the product was forced on them and they lost their free will to choose. Political pressure would result in the government dictating rates that would make it impossible for agents and companies to stay in business. The only alternative, state insurance, would "give employment to thousands of ward heelers and party hacks and take a loss on every policy, making up the deficit through taxation."

By this time, however, average policyholders saw no reason why everyone should not be required to carry auto liability insurance. *The Co-Operator* article reluctantly accepted this fact, stating, "Whether we like it or not, the idea of everyone being required to have financial responsibility as respects every automobile accident is one which appeals to almost everyone — except those who have to write and service the insurance." Insurance agents and companies would eventually discover that fears about compulsory insurance were overblown.

■ ■ ■

Throughout the 1950s, engine power and vehicle speeds rose, design and technology became more integrated and artful, and car sales boomed across the world. This increase helped contribute to EMCC's shift in growth, with auto insurance becoming approximately 60% of the company's business by 1955.

Commitment to Independent Agents

Because agents were the frontline sales force, most of EMCC's promotional activities were directed toward them rather than policyholders. *The Co-Operator* was a major tool, first published, nameless, on October 15, 1928. The four 6" x 9" pages of the first issue emphasized two-way communication between the company and agents: "This monthly paper is being sent to you for the purpose of promoting a more friendly feeling between us ... We can learn much from each other ... This is your paper, and we want you to help us write it." Humor abounded. Agents could write about their old flivver, a dry cow, or falling heir to a fortune. It was reported that Mrs. Mae Taylor from Neosho, Missouri, had written a policy for EMCC every day in July. "Who says a woman can't write insurance?" was the query. A list of six "do nots" was titled, "How to be an Unsuccessful Agent."

In a more serious tone, changes in the field force were noted, and 24 new agents were listed, increases in premium writings and assets were reported, and information about available policies was given. Finally, a $10 prize was offered for naming the paper. But most important was a tribute to the agents: "Our agency force is our greatest asset. The agent's success is ours, and our success means much to the agent." EMCC, in turn, had responsibility: "The greatest service a company can perform for its agents is simply to do its job well — to pay all just losses promptly, fairly, and cheerfully."

Response was positive. The next month

The Co-Operator was selected from over 100 "excellent" names submitted, and H. W. Jensen, an agent from Audubon, Iowa, pocketed the prize. Twenty-two more new agents were welcomed. Over the years, articles continued in the original vein with a great deal of information about available products, promotional resources, and company guidelines and developments. Pertinent current events were reported, and agents were urged to focus on certain kinds of insurance. Motivational material suggested selling techniques and offered prizes.

For a number of years, *The Co-Operator* was edited by Forrest E. Ginn, who assumed field supervisory and management duties for Iowa and Missouri after World War II. A twice-wounded U.S. Army veteran from World War I, he had come to EMCC as a field supervisor in 1942, following experience in retailing, real estate, and insurance. He used *The Co-Operator* to link field supervisors and agents in relationships of confidence and trust and was recognized for his success. Another part of *The Co-Operator's* mission was advertising. From 1938 to 1941, gory pictures of auto accidents were printed on the back page to be displayed in agents' offices. These were supplemented by folders for general distribution and ads in newspapers. During the 1940s, calendars and matchbooks appeared. After that, little would change in promotional approaches until the 1960s.

The superintendent of agents position, created in 1941 and filled by M. J. Wilkinson, signified the increasing importance of EMCC's agency relationships. Wilkinson

WHAT SHALL ? WE CALL IT?

PUBLISHED MONTHLY BY THE EMPLOYERS MUTUAL CASUALTY COMPANY

VOLUME I — OCTOBER 15, 1928 — NUMBER 1

$10.00 FOR THE BEST NAME!

Here's a chance to use [your] talent for calling people names. C[...] call this paper a name—[...] dollars!

We are starting this [...]tious sheet for you. Get [...] by christening it. For [...] submitted by any agent [or em]ployee of the Company, [...] will be paid in cash. Co[...] the insurance policies) [...] November 1st, 1928.

CHANGES IN F[...]

If you haven't seen [...] quite a while, let us [...] agency force has recen[...] and our plan is to ma[...] tion of service to you[...] you get business, bu[...] other assistance they[...]

John S. Kerper is[...] Western Iowa. If y[...] yet, you will. He's[...] if there is any bus[...] he'll help you scare[...]

M. J. Wilkinson h[...] as far west as For[...] used to be Credit[...] last spring to the[...] find him ready and[...] any way that he c[...]

Jim Garner, the[...] force, works North[...] years of experience[...] ness, both as a sp[...] gives Jim a viewp[...] help the local ma[...] is a valuable as[...] Southern Missouri[...] Brown & Spicer[...] Spicer is putting[...] in developing loc[...] tory.

The value of a[...] [a]s the means sor[...] people[...] get it.—Street [...]

This monthly paper is being sent you [fo]r the purpose of promoting a more [fri]endly feeling between us.

We can learn much from each other; [a]nd it is our intention to feature in this paper, articles by our agents, and about our agents. Your experience is worth a good deal to us, and to other agents. Let us have the benefit of it.

Our agency force is our greatest asset. The agent's success is ours, and our success means much to the agent. We publish frequently our financial statement, setting forth our assets and liabilities, but the greatest asset which we have, and the one on which we place the most importance, is the good will and support of our agents.

The greatest service a company can perform for its agents is simply to do its job well—to pay all just losses promptly, fairly, and cheerfully. That is why we are all in the insurance business, and by working together to do our job better, we can all succeed.

J. A. GUNN.

THE CO-OPERATOR

PUBLISHED MONTHLY BY THE EMPLOYERS MUTUAL CASUALTY COMPANY

VOLUME I — NOVEMBER 15, 1928 — NUMBER 2

H. W. JENSEN WINS THE TEN!

The $10 Prize for the best name submitted for the bulletin goes to Mr. H. W. Jensen, agent at Audubon, Iowa. "The Co-Operator" was chosen out of a list of more than 100 names submitted. Many submitted names similar in thought and form, but the prize-winner was chosen because of its simplicity, ease in remembering, and because it expresses exactly the ideal upon which the bulletin is founded.

Many excellent names were submitted, and the choice was a hard one for the editors. We wish to take this opportunity of thanking everyone who submitted a name.

Now that we have a name, let's co-operate in making it a paper of real co-operation! Give us your help.

EMPLOYERS MUTUAL LEADERS

We list below the leading ten agencies, in total volume of business written, in three classes, for the year 1928. Division is made according to size of the town in which the agency is located, using the last official census as a basis. Is your name on the list? Beginning next month, monthly leaders will be listed. Make an extra effort during November, and get your name on the Honor Roll.

Class "A"—Cities Over 25,000

Turk-Somerville Company
Omaha, Nebraska
O. B. McKinney Ins. Agency
Cedar Rapids, Iowa
Charles M. Young
Waterloo, Iowa
Brown & Spicer
Joplin, Missouri
T. M. Prall
Sioux City, Iowa
Geo. M. Dwight
Burlington, Iowa
F. L. Reinhard & Son
Ottumwa, Iowa
Cecil F. Cook
Davenport, Iowa
Chambers & Chambers
Des Moines, Iowa
Paul L. Stempel
Fort Dodge, Iowa

In Cedar Rapids, when they think of [a]utomobile and dwelling insurance, the [inh]abitants think of O. B. McKinney. [M]ac is one of our leading producers, [an]d now stands as one of the leading agents of Cedar Rapids—a standing gained only after ten years of hard work. Coming to Cedar Rapids at that time with only his knowledge of insurance and the desire to work, he rapidly built up a large dwelling-house business for the Town Mutual Fire. He then went into the mercantile and automobile lines with the same vigor, and soon became one of the leading producers for the Mill Owners and the Employers Mutual.

Mr. McKinney is a mutual man, through and through. He believes in the principles of mutual insurance, and in consequence, has no difficulty in selling it. He is a director of the Town Mutual Dwelling House Insurance Association.

Being a modest man, he did not give us all the facts of his career; a picture was all we could elicit from him. He has four brothers—all in the insurance business at various locations in Iowa.

Left: The first issue of the new, but yet unnamed, monthly agent newsletter published by EMC.

Right: *The Co-Operator* was selected from over 100 submissions as the name of the newsletter, and is still the name of the newsletter in 2011.

gave considerable credit to the "loyal force of agents" for the company's growth from "a small but sound company to one of the largest, if not the largest, *agency mutual* casualty company in the field." He particularly noted the understanding, cooperation, and patience of the reduced agency force during the war years.

New field duties were created by the post-war rash of new policies, especially after EMCC was allowed to write property insurance. It was an ongoing educational process to equip agents with specific knowledge about new policies and lines as well as sales approaches, and a number of returning veterans were added to the field staff to work with them. Display booths at annual National Association of Mutual Insurance Agents (NAMIA) conventions supplemented information in *The Co-Operator*. Sales meetings at the Home Office for agents from all over the country, begun before the war, continued for years. Speakers were provided by EMCC for meetings and clinics sponsored by agents' associations, and the relationship was reciprocal.

Throughout the 1940s and early 1950s, profitability was almost certain in the casualty insurance business. Rates were stable and adequate, and "any financially conservative company with decent management could automatically grow if it wasn't greedy or too careless in its underwriting," reflected retired President George Kochheiser in later years. But stability and profitability began to diminish as competition increased from both stock and mutual companies that used either salaried direct writers or captive agencies that wrote

for only one carrier. These companies were supplanting traditional stock companies as EMCC's primary competitors. The line-up was no longer stock vs. mutual but agency vs. direct writer and independent agent vs. captive agent.

EMCC declared that direct writer and captive agency companies were "going after the business ... with a vengeance" and charged that they were "skimming off the cream of business" with preferred rates while avoiding higher risks. Those left with the "skim milk, curds, and whey" were under pressure to lower rates below sustainable levels, even though their risk was greater. An imbalance in competition was the result.

Nevertheless, EMCC remained committed to the independent agency system. The advantages of using agents who had knowledge of their territories had been discovered soon after the company started writing insurance. By the Great Depression, EMCC was known as an "agency mutual." Then, general agencies had provided an efficient and economical way to help the company grow, and the expertise of agents continued to be valued.

Casualty insurance was thought to be a product that, for the most part, was not bought by potential policyholders, but rather had to be sold to them. Agents who understood the particular circumstances and needs of their regions could accomplish this task most effectively. The close and long-lasting relationship with their constituencies allowed them to give seasoned advice and counsel and to review and update accounts regularly. They had a vested interest in writing policies that were tailor-made to fit clients' needs and pocketbooks and in settling claims fairly and rapidly.

For EMCC, staff was one hand and agents were the other. As producers, agents were called "the foundation of our business," who do "a most remarkable and successful job of selling," while field staff were known as "diplomats without portfolio," who mediated among "claim men," "underwriting men," and local agents. The competition of the 1950s only served to draw EMCC and its independent agency force closer together in the common struggle for survival.

A Safety Pioneer

EMCC's First Recognized Department

As EMCC became more diverse and complex, a need for specific definition of organizational functions developed and departments began to emerge. While designations tended to be rather informal, the first function to be called a "department" was accident prevention, which grew out of the underwriting process. Safety and prevention had always been central motivating forces in American insurance from Benjamin Franklin's organization of the Philadelphia Contributionship to the creation of workmen's compensation legislation. Reduction of risk benefited both insurer and insured. Because the primary function of underwriting was to evaluate and select risks to be covered, it was only logical that accident prevention would be an important component of the process.

"Safety engineers" had been employed by insurance companies since the days when little more than practical "horse sense," good mechanical aptitude, and experience were prerequisites for the work. The country's first mutual liability company, American Mutual Liability Insurance Company, founded in Massachusetts in 1887, employed a safety engineer from the day it opened business. From the time Employers Mutual Liability Insurance Company of Wisconsin (later Employers Insurance of Wausau) issued one of the first American workmen's compensation policies in 1911, it stressed "reduction of hazard." Since then, mutual casualty companies have consistently been pioneers and leaders in the area of loss prevention. They have conducted research into the causes of industrial accidents and diseases and set high preventive standards for policyholders.

EMCC was no different. Before the passage of Iowa's workmen's compensation law, Jack Eddy had written in IMA's November 1912 issue of *Iowa Factories*, "The fast spreading sentiment that 'THE TRADE MUST BEAR THE BURDEN OF THE RISK,' strongly advocated by Theodore Roosevelt and echoed by many public men, makes it imperative that employers of labor give the safety of their employees more attention ... If we had only taken up the prevention question in earnest and had reduced our accidents to the lowest minimum, we wouldn't be racking our brains over the subject of Workmen's Compensation." IMA claimed it had preached the necessity of prevention "day after day, year after year, but with little success."

You Lose the Most Through Accidents

Do Your Part to Make This Place **SAFE** For Everyone

Always **B**e **C**areful

Published by the Accident Prevention Department of the Employers Mutual Casualty Co., Des Moines, Iowa

No. 504—Please Post Conspicuously.   Extra Copies on Request

BE CAREFUL NOW Tomorrow May Be Too Late

YOU PROFIT MOST

Published by the Accident Prevention Department of the Employers Mutual Casualty Co., Des Moines, Iowa

Bulletin No. 505—Please Post Conspicuously.

THE BEST SAFETY DEVICE KNOWN IS A CAREFUL MAN

Always Be Careful

Published by the Accident Prevention Department of the Employers Mutual Casualty Co., Des Moines, Iowa

Safety posters distributed by EMC's Accident Prevention Department, 1926.

By the time the company was writing workmen's compensation, IMA stated that the money consideration was slight in comparison to the humane consideration, but that the business end was not ignored. "The more injuries we prevent, the more money we leave in the treasury of the Employers Mutual for return to the policy holders," they wrote. "We now, by safeguarding against injury, can reduce the business burden to the lowest human possibility."

In 1921, the first issue of the company's first newsletter, *The Employer*, listed 13 accident prevention suggestions in the form of "don'ts." They included such concerns as guarding elevator shafts and floor openings, guardrails on stairs, machinery safety guards, use of goggles, eliminating protruding and sharp objects from walls and floors, proper lighting and "danger" signs, designating fire exits, keeping explosives off of the premises, and not retaining careless employees.

A 1922 brochure, "EMCA: The History of a Service," noted that inspection of plants and extending safeguarding of employees was part of EMCA's service, and, in 1926, a safety engineer was hired. By then reference was already being made to the "Accident Prevention" or "Safety Engineering" Department, which essentially functioned as "the eyes and ears of the Underwriting Department." The engineer's job was to inspect and report on newly insured policyholders and to provide recommendations and safety training for their foremen and supervisors. Safety posters were given to policyholders to display in their work places.

The next decade witnessed a broadening of safety awareness programs. Here EMCC was a leader. When the Iowa Safety Council was formed in late 1935, as an affiliate of the National Safety Council, EMCC was a charter member, and President John A. Gunn was elected treasurer. Auto safety, as well as workplace safety, began to be promoted. EMCC's "Safe Driving Program" awarded hundreds of thousands of windshield stickers to drivers with two consecutive years of safe driving.

The effort was promoted through *The Co-Operator,* as well as the *Des Moines Register* and local radio station WHO. Agents were given, for follow-up, the names of sticker recipients, who were not EMCC policyholders, and were encouraged to organize safety committees and promote safer driving in their communities.

By 1941, EMCC's safety program had expanded so rapidly and was providing such great benefits to the company that a supervisor was needed to oversee and guide the work. That August, Oscar M. Nanfeldt was hired as chief safety engineer to head a new Accident Prevention Department. He came well prepared. Born in Wallingford, Connecticut, in 1902, he had a B.S. in chemistry and bacteriology from the University of Connecticut. Before coming to EMCC he had gained a broad base of experience: work in industrial plants, research in cattle disease and tuberculosis, as a chemist with U.S. Rubber Company and the Connecticut State Water Commission, and as a safety engineer for three insurance companies. His membership in the American Industrial Hygiene Association and the American Society of Safety Engineers gave him additional knowledge and expertise for the new position.

Shortly after his arrival at EMCC, Nanfeldt outlined the need for industrial safety programs in a talk titled "How to Set Up a Safety Program." He cited National Safety Council statistics for 1940: $700 million paid for lost wages, medical expenses, and insurance overhead; 17,000 lives lost; 60,000 permanently disabled; and 1,350,000 temporarily disabled. The complete dollar loss to the industry was three to four times greater due to lost production time, spoilage of materials, and damage to machinery and equipment. Crucial to successful accident prevention, he said, were four criteria: management's interest and education, education of supervisors and employees, prevention through engineering, and ongoing enforcement of the program. For almost seven years, until Nanfeldt's death in 1948, these were the guiding principles for developing the department's services as it grew to seven individuals handling field inspection and engineering duties company wide.

Upon Nanfeldt's death, Raymond T. Sanders filled the chief safety engineer position until his retirement in 1972. A Massachusetts native, born in 1911, Sanders had a degree in industrial engineering from Northeastern University in Boston and did post-graduate work in business administration at Babson Institute in Wellesley, Massachusetts. At 6' 2", he played both college and semipro basketball before becoming manager of the Safety and Payroll Audit Department of Glens Falls Indemnity Company, working in Boston, Chicago, and Glens Falls, New York. During World War II, he served as lieutenant commander and assistant safety officer at the Brooklyn Navy Yard and officer in charge of safety at the Bayonne Annex.

...

Safe Driving Award windshield sticker, 1935.

...

Oscar M. Nanfeldt was hired as chief safety engineer to set up the Accident Prevention Department.

Raymond T. Sanders was chief safety engineer from 1948 until his retirement in 1972.

At EMCC, Sanders' duties expanded with the Accident Prevention Department, and he was promoted to assistant vice president in 1957 and vice president in 1966. During his tenure, premium audits of insured companies, conducted by field staff, were added to the department's responsibilities. Premium audits had been used to determine workmen's compensation premiums since EMCC began writing the line. A number of factors had to be considered in the calculations, which were based on payroll — number of employees, length of employment, exposure time on the job, type of work done, and salaries or hourly wages. New hires, terminations, retirements, and changes in positions during the year complicated the process, and it was the premium auditor's job to include all of these factors in calculating final premiums at year's end. Placing premium audit with accident prevention was a practical matter. The same field employee could handle both functions, which was sometimes necessary to sustain a full-time position.

Another duty assigned to the Accident Prevention Department was procurement and maintenance of EMCC's fleet, which grew from zero to over 200 vehicles used by traveling employees during Sanders' tenure. The other major responsibility was oversight of construction and remodeling of all company properties. Within two years of Sanders' arrival in 1948, the field safety engineering staff grew to 12. Six more were on board by 1953, with an additional three added the next year.

Safety Is Recognized and Promoted

Safety was promoted to both insureds and EMCC employees through a variety of new activities. One of the most popular technological innovations was 35mm filmstrip presentations with accompanying commentary on vinyl records, provided by the National Safety Council. Covering a wide variety of topics, the filmstrips usually contained 60 to 100 frames, and the commentary contained beeps that signaled when it was time to advance to the next frame.

EMCC worked with two National Safety Council programs to recognize and promote driver safety. The windshield stickers of the 1930s evolved into award pins for five-year accident-free records issued to EMCC fleet drivers and policyholders, beginning in 1949. This program has continued into the present, with little change in the appearance of the pins, although in 2005 prizes were added for successive five-year intervals. In 1953, EMCC employees played a prominent role when the Insurance Women of Des Moines cosponsored the city's first free, one-day driving clinic for women. Chief Claims Clerk Ildra Hennies was president, and over a dozen EMCC employees were members of Insurance Women.

Also in 1953, EMCC began giving awards to large client companies with outstanding safety programs and records. First to receive the award was Lennox Furnace Company of Marshalltown. Other recipients in those early years were the Des Moines Register

Announcing . . . .

SECOND ANNUAL
EMPLOYERS MUTUAL
SAFE DRIVING
AWARDS

The m___ful safety idea
—and ___

1. To help red___
2. To help Em___
   SALES in ___

DEATH STALKS THE HIGHWAYS!

In 1935—
35,500 Dead
1,000,000 Injured

In 1936—
? ? ? ?

To help reduce this terrible
toll on Iowa's highways, Employers Mutual Casualty Co.
announces its

2d Annual
SAFE DRIVING
AWARDS

**Badge of distinction for every Iowa driver who
has driven two years without an accident**

A great, new humanitarian
campaign is starting in 800
Iowa communities today, to
curb highway accidents in
1936.

Will you join—do your part—
to help reduce Iowa's mount-
ing toll of highway deaths and
injuries?

Basis of the campaign is the
new 1936 SAFE DRIVING
AWARD—an emblem of safe-
driving, to be presented to
every driver who has not had
an accident in two years. In
800 communities, local Safety

Campaign committees, co-op-
erating with agents of Employers Mutual Casualty Co.,
will start presenting these
emblems this week. If you can
qualify, through a two-years'
safety record, see your committee, get your windshield
emblem, join in the campaign
—and help reduce accidents.

Somehow, some way, we
MUST curb Iowa's growing
highway fatalities. The appeal
is to every Iowan—to every
community. The time to start
is Now!

Civic clubs, women's groups, employers and public
spirited individuals are urged to see the local Employers Mutual representative or write us for free
Safe Driving campaign manual and suggestions on
conducting local safety campaigns.

If you can qualify for the Safe
Driving Award, you are entitled to
the advantages of Employers Mutual protection—in a company
which insures only selected drivers.
If you are a careful driver, why

help carry the load for the careless, vicious driver? Insure with
Employers Mutual, where you get
complete coverage at lowest net
cost—backed by assets of over
$2,200,000.00.

Employers Mutual
IOWA'S LARGEST CASUALTY COMPANY

John A. Gunn, President   Valley Bank Bldg., Des Moines

If you have not had an auto accident in two years, write our Des Moines office for your
Free Safe Driving emblem, in case emblems are not being issued in your community.

Reprint of Ad Ap___ Moines Sunday Register, Sunday, January 12, 1936

SAFE DRIVER CERTIFICATE

This Certifies that **Phylis Bull**
Marysville, Kansas
Insured under Policy No. **347887** Expiring **11-3-40**
is considered by the undersigned, by virtue of experience and moral character, a SAFE & CAREFUL DRIVER
pledged to every careful driving standard
under the laws of the state.

**EMPLOYERS MUTUAL
CASUALTY COMPANY**

J. A. Gunn President
(OVER)

The actual emblem is twice
this size, lithographed in
colors—a striking badge for
your windshield.

As A REWARD
For Safe Drivers

If you have not had an accident with your
car in two years, you have earned this Safe
Driving Award for 1936 — now being presented free to those who can qualify. • If
you have earned one, stop in or call our
office. You can be proud to display it on your
car. And you will be doing your part in a
great state-wide campaign to reduce auto
accidents in 1936.

AGENT'S NAME
AND ADDRESS
AND PHONE

Certificates, badges, and pins were
used to promote the Safe Driving Award
to agents, policyholders, and the public.

and Tribune Co.; Hager and Sons Hinge
Manufacturing Co. and Stupp Bros. Bridge
and Iron Works, both in St. Louis; Service
Transport Co. (fleet safety) in Racine,
Wisconsin; and the Charlotte Workshop
for the Blind, Inc., in North Carolina.

Into the Branches

As the Accident Prevention Department grew,
it began to move out into branch operations.
For example, Dale C. Fry, a Navy veteran from
the Pacific front, who joined the Home Office
as a safety engineer in January 1947, was sent
to the Minneapolis Branch as a field engineer
in August. Two years later he advanced to
manager of the Accident Prevention Department
of the Chicago Branch where he would become

an underwriter in 1956, a field supervisor
in 1957, and branch manager in 1958.

For about a year, Fry was joined in Chicago
by Safety Engineer George W. Kochheiser.
Kochheiser was a World War II Army infantry
veteran, who had enlisted after graduating from
North High School in Des Moines, and served
three years as a staff sergeant in the European
and Pacific theaters, earning a Purple Heart
and a Bronze Star. He began working in EMCC's
File Department in the Home Office basement
upon receiving an A.B., cum laude and Phi Beta
Kappa from Drake University in 1949. Within
weeks he was up and out, traveling in eastern
Iowa as an accident prevention engineer
trainee until his transfer to Chicago. He later
recognized his "escape" from the basement
as the beginning of a career filled with a broad

...
George W. Kochheiser
started with EMC as
a safety engineer and
ended his career as
president and COO.

range of experiences that eventually led to becoming EMCC president and chief operating officer in 1982.

Kochheiser delighted in what he gleaned from his inspections, knowing the information would be used by underwriters to evaluate whether the potential insured's risks and the premium rate being charged would produce a reasonable profit. He learned the type of work that bridge contractors were doing and how punch presses and other machinery might cause accidents in manufacturing operations. He learned what questions to ask: Did meat markets use proper guards on machines that ground lamb? Were the surrounding sidewalks full of holes that could trip people? Did stairwells have handrails? Were there guards on printing presses and factory belts?

What was the impact of a skid row saloon and a flophouse on a business in the Chicago Loop, or the liability related to a decrepit tenement in a heavy industrial area?

Each site, each industry, each geographical region was different. Kochheiser added to his understanding of risks when he left Chicago to serve as a safety engineer in the St. Louis area until he transferred to Iowa as a field supervisor in 1952. Around St. Louis, a post-war boom in highway and airport construction was underway. The number and kinds of hazards continued to grow, including the addition of fire inspections when EMCC began writing property insurance in 1955. Several short-lived attempts were made to incorporate the word "fire" into the department's name, but it remained Accident Prevention.

On Course Under John F. Hynes

Personal matters intervened in the company's administration in 1947. On October 15, John W. Gunn took a pay cut and stepped down as president so that he could give more care to his daughter, Madge Carolyn, who had cerebral palsy. He remained as chairman-treasurer and, for a number of years, returned to chair meetings while wintering in Florida. John F. Hynes assumed the presidency and stayed in that position until March 13, 1957, when he reached retirement age. Then Gunn returned as president-treasurer, and Hynes became chairman of the board until he retired from that position after the company's 50th anniversary when he was 70. In 1962, Hynes was named honorary chairman for life. When he died on May 17, 1968, his service record was the longest to date — 44 of the company's 51 years.

Favored by John A. Gunn, Hynes had earned his way. As secretary from 1920 to 1947, he was responsible for the company's books and records and supervised the accounting function, in addition to managing the claims operation. At Gunn's request, he was named vice president in 1940 and was promoted to senior vice president half a year before becoming president. After his election to the board in 1925, he never missed a meeting until his death.

Hynes was known not only as a fine lawyer and brilliant executive but also as a warm and understanding man to whom anyone could go for solutions to their problems, a trait grasped by employees since his early card-playing days

in the office. His oldest daughter, Joan, remembers how, as a child, she and her siblings visited him at work where they lay on the filing stools and shot "rubber runners" — large red rubber bands — the length of the office. This introduction encouraged her to work a summer under Claims Clerical Supervisor Ildra Hennies.

...

John F. Hynes, president of EMC from 1947 to 1957.

A hard worker, Hynes was in the office most evenings and weekends. During his decade as president, the company experienced its greatest growth to date and became known as one of the outstanding companies in its field. At the beginning of his presidency, EMCC was a small, conservative regional insurance company in which the complexities of the present-day market could not be imagined. In those days, a "packaged" policy might mean combining auto damage with liability or adding extended coverage to a fire policy. Rates were maintained in manuals, usually less than a half-inch thick, and changes seldom were made more than once a year.

This all began to change with the burst of economic growth as the GIs returned home. They took advantage of education through the G.I. Bill, entered the work force, started families, and built homes served by new businesses, often in the suburbs. Wearied by the Great Depression and war, they wanted quiet, security, and material prosperity. These conditions presented opportunities to EMCC as it expanded its lines of business and geographic reach.

Under Hynes, investment in common stocks grew along with confidence in the stock market. In 1950, the board authorized $1 million to be invested in high-grade common stock, and the

Harris Trust and Savings Bank of Chicago was contracted as the depository to manage a common stock portfolio with a beginning balance of $500,000. U.S. government and municipal bonds were still heavily favored, but the relative amount invested in common stocks kept increasing. In 1958, a year after Hynes left the presidency, the board increased the limit on common stocks from 5% of assets to a cap of 10%, and a plan was approved to bring the amount of stocks up to 7.5% of assets by adding $200,000 a month for five months.

Events confirmed the importance of reinsurance as part of the company's financial protection and growth. It provided substantial relief when a large department store fire loss occurred shortly after the Fire and Inland Marine Division was formed in 1955. Adding to the need for reinsurance was the multiplication of lawsuits, which made it necessary for the company to write higher limits.

Even more important than investments and reinsurance were the sound underwriting practices supporting EMCC's financial health. The first year of Hynes's presidency, EMCC wrote $1 million in one month for the first time, and total premiums passed the $12 million mark. By the end of his term, in 1957, nine branches and over a half dozen service offices were doing business in 32 states, the District of Columbia, and Canada. Approximately 4,000 local agents were writing about 400,000 policies for total premiums of over $31 million. Assets had grown from $13 million to almost $44 million, surplus had grown from $2 million to about $12 million, and the A. M. Best rating had been upgraded from A to A+ in 1952.

EMC now writes all **3**

Fire... Casualty... Bonds

Addition of Fire and Inland Marine marks a new milestone in the growth of EMC... a growth made possible, in great degree, by our more than 600 Iowa agents. Now, more than ever before, it pays to represent EMC. Write for full details of our money-making agency plan.

A NATIONAL INSTITUTION

Employers MUTUAL CAS[ ]
DES MOINE[ ]

43 Years of Service and Savings • Assets Over $[ ]

Employers
MUTUAL CASUALTY COMPANY
OF DES MOINES

CASUALTY • FIRE • BONDS

1752

Advertisement announcing the availability of fire and casualty insurance and bonds.

Left: "Green Tree" fire mark plaque presented to EMC by Mutual Assurance Company in honor of EMC's 50th anniversary.

Middle: Logo highlighting the products the company could write: casualty, fire, and bonds.

Right: "Hand-in-Hand" fire mark given to EMC on its 50th anniversary by the Philadelphia Contributionship.

Although 125,000 claims totaled a record $15 million in 1957, which was considered the worst year to date for insurance companies generally, EMCC would keep growing in all areas through John W. Gunn's second term, during which assets topped $50 million in 1959.

Keeping Up With Complexity: Claims and Adjusting

Time Changes Everything

Little had changed in the administration of claims during the first two decades of the company's history, when the secretaries — Jack Eddy and then John F. Hynes — were in charge, assisted by staff, such as Bessie Newell. Field conditions, also, were not much different. As late as 1933, when W. J. Hynes came to EMCC as an adjuster, Iowa's mud roads still made travel by train a frequent necessity. Because many small towns did not have hotels, he often stayed in private homes. Improvement of Iowa's road conditions and overnight accommodations was a slow and gradual process as motor vehicles replaced horse-drawn equipment into the 1940s.

Change in administration of claims came sooner under the leadership of John F. Hynes as he moved toward assuming the presidency in 1947. It would continue under his brother, W.J., who had transferred to the Home Office from Chicago the previous year to phase in as superintendent of claims.

As business grew, the brothers witnessed a continuing increase in the number and cost of claims. A report from Central Trust Company of Des Moines at the end of 1922 stated that reserves had been deposited for 30 claims ranging from $5 to $3,049.80 for a total of $31,889.75. Seven years later, 1,100 claims, mostly workmen's compensation, were being disposed of each month, and the company was pleading with agents for understanding about delays caused by a backlog. A jump ahead to 1956, as John F. Hynes's presidency reached its conclusion, shows 100,898 claims filed and an average of $105.19 paid out each minute of every working day. The total of $13,127,317 that year was slightly more than total claims paid by EMCC from 1914 through 1940. At the end of 1956, over $110.4 million had been paid out since the company's founding.

Claim adjustment expense was $2.5 million in 1957, the year claims reached a record $15 million. The high numbers were due, in part, to the trend of higher jury awards for personal injuries and increased auto repair costs. To EMCC's advantage was its reputation for not being a "chiseling" insurer, validated by its low number of lawsuits. In 1956, *The National Underwriter* reported that EMCC had the best score among 68 companies with premiums of $15 million or more, doing business in Illinois from 1953 to 1955. EMCC's average was two lawsuits per $100,000 of premiums, while the overall average was six.

The growing sophistication of the claims and adjusting staff, which now operated out of the branches and claims service offices as well as the Home Office, could be credited for this record. As the 1950s drew to a close, the investigation and settlement of claims and losses was seen as "much more complicated than it was 15 years ago." John Hynes had laid the foundation for development of a multifaceted claims process that was prompt, liberal, and fair, and W. J. Hynes built on that foundation. Information about claims management was continually added to the company *Digest*. Courses offered by the Insurance Institute of America, seminars, talks at industry meetings, and other materials increased staff expertise. In addition, the knowledge of architects, engineers, photographers, medical specialists, and defense counsel was drawn on.

Automobile damage was one of the major problems. More than ten claims people from the Home Office and branches received concentrated special training at the Vale Technical Institute of Blairsville, Pennsylvania. There they learned car identification, flat rate manuals, damage analysis, frames, steering geometry, suspension, steering linkage and gears, sheet metal, cooling, engines, transmissions, and many other aspects of automobiles. They learned whether to repair or replace parts and how to recognize overlapping charges in estimates. Their "bible" was a parts and labor manual that was updated every three months.

Finally, they learned about the "eternal triangle" in adjusting. One side of the triangle is the policyholder who wants proper and prompt repair of the damaged vehicle. The second side is the repairman who wants top dollar profit and sees insurance as a means to enhance that profit. The third side is the insurance company, which wants to satisfy the policyholder, treat the mechanic fairly,

and save every dollar possible. The adjuster's task is to reconcile these three sides to ensure savings, service, and satisfaction.

...

Ads like this one from 1955 promoted EMC as a trustworthy company.

The Life of an Adjuster

John P. Strother remembered keenly his introduction to adjusting, which, despite one aberration, prepared him well for a claims career that lasted from 1953 through 1992 in the Texas and Charlotte Branches. In preparation for practical training, he spent a week reading claims files and learning the importance of claimants' statements. Next, he took statements, using a pad, carbon paper, and a clipboard, and he copied reports on automobile accidents "verbatim et literatim" at the police station. Most of Strother's initial training was with automobile accidents, because workmen's compensation claims were considered too complicated for a trainee to handle.

In those days, payment of claims required execution of a release from every party privy to the claim. Calling on claimants without notice was the best way to obtain truthful statements. This meant adjusters did a lot of driving. EMCC issued new cars every 25,000 miles to prevent maintenance problems and added costs. This policy usually allowed two new cars a year in Texas, where distances were great. Strother was thrilled with his first car, a 1953 two-door, six-cylinder, stick shift Chevrolet Styleline. There was little chrome and no ashtray, but it had an armrest, a sun visor, a heater, black rubber floors, and black tires.

An automotive innovation of the 1950s was seat belts, and EMCC's concern for driver safety extended beyond its insureds to its own drivers. By 1955, the company's entire fleet of 120 vehicles, driven by field and claims

Cool Fleet

Chevrolet did not introduce air-conditioning until 1957. That summer, W. J. Hynes chose Texas for one of his famous visits to the "front lines" to "get down in the trenches with the adjusters fighting the wars." One hot, humid day he accompanied Dallas Claims Supervisor Charles C. O'Dell on a working trip to Austin. They stopped to see an attorney in Waco. Hynes waited a half hour in the car and shed his hat and coat. After other stops and taking care of business in Austin, Hynes's necktie was gone, his sleeves were rolled up, and he was fanning himself with file papers. He told O'Dell to take him directly to the airport; the heat was too much. The next cars delivered to Texas were 1958 Bel Air Chevrolets, fully loaded with Hydramatic Drive, radio, heater — and air-conditioning. ▪

Three Who Believe

Herb Beier

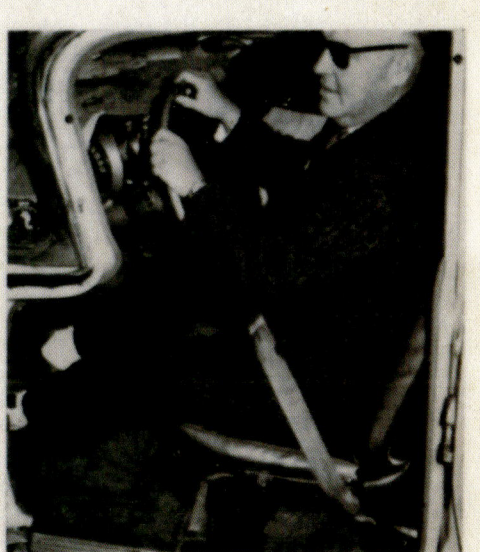

Fred Thomas

Glenn Newell

personnel in 30 states, was equipped with safety belts in the front seat. Since 1953, annual recognition had been given to those drivers who had no chargeable accidents. The first year, 71 full-year and 27 part-year drivers were recognized. For the 2.5 million miles driven and 150,000 gallons of regular gasoline consumed, there had been only six accidents. Each year the number of awards increased, as did the number of miles driven. In 1960, 156 safe driving awards were given for 5.2 million miles driven with 18 accidents. With the exception of 30 accidents in 1959, there were never more than 20 accidents in any year of the program.

• • •

These photos in the 1962 employee newsletter encouraged seatbelt use by EMC employees. EMC began installing safety belts in the company's fleet vehicles in 1955.

Strange but True Claim Stories

Adjusters could expect surprises and unusual experiences. A few examples illustrate. During the Great Depression, a farmer from Wright County, Iowa, thought he had received a "very satisfactory settlement" after some of his cattle died from drinking paint at a bridge construction site. The construction company assured EMCC that they would do their best "to see that we do not have another claim of this nature in the future." It is doubtful that cattle drinking paint was ever specified as a liability in any of EMCC's policy forms.

Mary Jane Kamm, who worked as a claims clerk in Wichita, Dallas, Kansas City, and the Home Office from the mid-1940s through the late 1980s, tells a more gruesome tale. One day around 1950,

a claimant on crutches came to Claims Manager Russell Engelmann's office at the Wichita Branch. Shortly after, Forrest Mercer, then an adjuster, entered the office. After seeing the claimant's injuries from an oil field burn, Mercer staggered back out and fainted in front of Kamm's desk. Kamm tended to Mercer, and Engelmann confessed that he didn't help because he was not sure he could stand up himself.

In another case, EMCC received a worker's compensation claim for some employees who were cut by flying glass in Kansas City. It seems two elderly ladies had stopped at a gas station and decided to switch drivers. But it was raining so they crawled over each other in the car while the engine was running. One accidentally shoved the gearshift into forward while the other stepped on the accelerator. The car shot out of the station, across four lanes of traffic, down a grade, and smashed through the plate glass window of a shop, injuring several employees. The ladies survived, and the shop employees received compensation. •

The W. J. Hynes Legacy

By the mid-1950s, the Claims Department, under W. J. Hynes, included six supervisors who would have long careers with the company. J. Earle Miller and Harry E. Wishard were in charge of claims reserves with responsibility for assuring that reserves for outstanding claims were "neither insufficient nor excessive." Hillis W. Noon and Addison Hayne had oversight of all claims offices east of the Mississippi River, while Russell B. Wellman and Forrest C. Mercer handled the western region. The branches and claims service offices had authority for most claims matters, but when that authority was exceeded or there were problems, claims were referred to the Home Office.

Working with the supervisors were 22 women supervised by Chief Claims Clerk Ildra Hennies as they made reports, did filing, and carried out "a million and one clerical duties." Hennies was known for having correct answers to almost any question. Assisting all of these people were three men working full time and some part-time Drake University law students who worked with storage and files. Fire claims were handled separately by the newly created Fire and Inland Marine Department.

An increase in production in the Midwestern states in the late 1950s, along with the approaching retirement of W. J. Hynes, led to reorganization of the territory and realignment of personnel in 1959. A new Central Division consisting of Iowa, Kansas, Missouri, and Nebraska was carved out of the

Western Division, and Iowa Claims Manager Clarence E. Johnson became superintendent. Forrest Mercer continued responsibility

■ ■ ■
W. J. Hynes, 1960.

Abe Shapiro, superintendent
of claims for the Eastern
Division, 1956.

for what remained in the Western Division, and Abe Shapiro became superintendent of claims for the Eastern Division, working out of Chicago. At the Home Office, overall claims management responsibilities were transferred from W. J. Hynes to Russ Wellman. Hillis Noon stayed on as overall claims supervisor with Addison Hayne as his assistant. This new team was lined up to face the challenges of the 1960s.

After transfer of responsibilities to Wellman, W. J. Hynes served five more years as claims counsel. He had earned his honorific title, the "Dean of Claims Men." It was under his direction that EMCC's claims facilities in branch and service offices were established

across the country. He made major contributions to organizing an insurance information bureau and an insurance speakers bureau to educate the public about "who really picks up the tab" for insurance claims. His reputation as an engaging speaker at industry meetings brought him national notice. He used a question and answer format with intriguing titles such as "Is the Sun in Your Eyes?" in a presentation on public relations, or "I Would" on how to be a successful agent, or "You and I" on auto accidents. The literary quotations that peppered his speeches revealed his wide reading. One of his recurrent themes was excessive jury awards that caused increased rates for casualty insurance.

An instructive speech to potential adjusters at Drake University's law school in 1954 was reprinted for the company's employees and gives insight into Hynes's thought and character. For him, the adjuster was the face of the company upon which the insured's opinions were based. Among adjuster's qualifications that he outlined were legal background, mechanical knowledge of automobiles, medical knowledge, and ability to sell the company.

Through examples, Hynes portrayed the successful adjuster as a detective, able to ferret out false claims. He contended that the smartest people in the world were formed in an environment of "courthouse square common horse sense." Modest personal appearance and the use of witnesses' exact language — even swear words — in statements were advised. The adjuster should be curious, he said, but should not go so far as the man who bit off chunks of 32 caterpillars to determine that they taste like leaves and learned the same way that ants taste like lemons. He advocated the humor of pianist and comedian Victor Borge and the compassion of Father Flanagan, who offered chocolates from his desk drawer to his wards at Boys' Town. Talking to people about what was important to them was essential, and he found a little flattery or coin tricks for children helpful. Strength of character to say "no" to temptations plus honesty, fairness, and love of people were Hynes' guiding values.

Hynes was known as cordial, open, easy to approach, and quick with a compliment. Just as he had kept in touch with servicemen during World War II, he tended to those at home. For example, Casey, Iowa, native Richard E. "Dick" Haskins worked part-time for EMCC five years while in school and became a full-time adjuster after receiving his law degree from Drake University in 1951. But after about a year, he wanted to try practicing law and went to work for an insurance and real estate abstract firm in Vinton, Iowa. When he left EMCC, Hynes told him, "If it doesn't work out for you, you've got a place back here." A year and a half later, Haskins' boss died and he could not afford to buy the business and establish a law practice. Word got back to EMCC that he was "looking around." Hynes made sure he was brought back into the fold, where his career in claims, bonds, and reinsurance lasted 38 years.

Keep a Keen Sense of Humor

W. J. Hynes could laugh at himself. One of his habits was strolling with his hands clasped behind his back for exercise at noon. Afterwards, he was not to be disturbed for 45 minutes while he napped on a leather divan in his office. One year, a skit by the Claims Department was performed at the company's Christmas party. The script had everyone leave the office because "Hynes" had an important appointment. He then loosened his tie, lay down, slept, awoke with an alarm, tightened his tie, and let the troops back in. The executives roared with laughter, and the real Hynes was delighted that impersonator Dick Haskins had loosened his tie exactly right. Hynes kept on with the daily walks until his death on June 25, 1972. ▪

Rae Punelli, Jo Boehm
and Kenneth Doudna.
(left to right)

Sally McCarthy (left)
and Katie Juliano.

Employee cafeteria.

Mail room.

1950s office scenes.

Norma Holland using
a keypunch machine.

• • •

Philadelphia Branch Office
staff in 1954: Front row:
Mary Russell, Patricia Jones,
Josephine McGill, Maryann
Naplacic, Ruth Baumgartner,
Annette Dubin, Alice Mattern,
Elsie Luce, Janet Petersen,
Ann Riley. Second row: Mary
Hickey, Margaret Dean, Doris
Buehler, Nellie Hawthorne,
Jean Hoke, Loretta Cichonska,
Evelyn Yoos, Phillis Payne,
Elizabeth Cipollone, Dorothy
Hullar, Dorothy Zukowski,
Thomasina Scaife, Eleanor
Walker, Rosemary Andrulonis,
Virginia Morris, Regina
Conklin. Back row: Joseph
Speiser, Johnson Payne Jr.,
Frank Mattucci, Richard
Forster, Gordon Coulter,
M. R. Feller, Robb B. Kelley,
Giles K. Riley, G. Herman
Burne, Byron Hoke, Joseph
Torsella, Alexander Hudson.
(left to right)

Part 3. EXPANSION

Branch Development Continues

The general agency relationship worked well to expand operations and, in 1954, the company was represented by ten general agencies. During the 1940s and 1950s, branch development and use of general agencies operated in parallel. In addition, about 20 claims service offices were opened across the country and were used for as long as needed to service general agencies or to extend the service of branches or the Home Office.

As the 1950s drew to a close, however, the insurance industry grew more complex, and working through general agencies became less desirable. Proliferating regulatory and bureau statistical requirements forced EMCC to duplicate the clerical work of general agencies in addition to servicing the agencies through claims offices. It made sense to operate with branches rather than general agencies. To retain the original advantages of the agencies and to obtain efficiency through standardization, EMCC began purchasing

general agencies and converting them into branch offices after 1960. From then on, branches would take priority over general agencies in the company's operating structure, and most additional branches would be developed from general agencies or affiliates.

In the meantime, six new branches were created between 1940 and 1960: Lansing (1940), Minneapolis (1942), Philadelphia (1946), Milwaukee (1956), Polk County (1947, which became Iowa Branch in 1958 and Des Moines Branch in 1971), and Phoenix (1958). In 1953, another office opened in British Columbia to service the British Columbia Automobile Association. (Additional information about the EMCC branches is in the "At the Branches" section in the back of this book.)

At two of the new branches, two future presidents of EMCC served as the first branch managers: Robb Kelley in Philadelphia and George Kochheiser in Milwaukee.

• • •

The Western Savings Society
Building in Philadelphia,
where the branch was
located on the sixth floor.

Robb Kelley in Philadelphia

While some branches were started from scratch and others were "converted" general agencies, others were a sort of hybrid. Such was the case in Philadelphia, EMCC's sixth branch. In 1939, EMCC contracted with the R. A. Downes General Agency in Philadelphia to represent the company in Pennsylvania and Maryland. Seven years later, EMCC purchased the agency's business relationships as the base for starting a branch office, which was opened by Robb B. Kelley, and Downes was retained as an independent agency to write insurance in the Philadelphia area.

The son of John A. Gunn's daughter Susan and Lawrence E. Kelley, who joined the EMCC Board in the "Great Proxy Fight" of 1937, Robb Beardsley Kelley was born in Des Moines on January 21, 1917. Upon earning a degree from Dartmouth College (1938) and a year of law studies, Kelley joined the company in 1939 as an underwriter trainee in the Wichita Branch. A year later, he transferred to Credit and Auto Underwriting in the Home Office and, in 1941 and early 1942, traveled in northeast Iowa as a field supervisor. War then intervened. After graduating as a first lieutenant from the U.S. Army Officer's School at Camp Davis, North Carolina, he was stationed with an anti-aircraft artillery unit at Santa Ana, California. Upon returning home in 1945, he became a field supervisor in the Omaha Branch. Next came Philadelphia.

Kelley began operating the branch out of a one-room office on the sixth floor of the Western Savings Fund Society Building in June 1946 and, by fall, had a staff of one adjuster and two office assistants. Over ten years, he built up the Philadelphia Branch to serve Pennsylvania, Maryland, and New Jersey. Philadelphia was a particularly difficult area to underwrite because of the concentrated population, and he was proud to achieve a losses-incurred-to-premiums-earned ratio of 47.2% in 1955 and 49.8% in 1956. About that time, he also oversaw relocation of the office to a building several blocks away.

Romance Revived

While he established the Philadelphia Branch, Kelley revived a relationship that had begun just before he joined EMCC. While working at a youth camp near Minoqua, Wisconsin, in summer 1939, he met Winifred Murray, a doctor's daughter. She was working at a neighboring camp, and they had two dates. Kelley followed up, somewhat belatedly, with a letter in 1941, but gave no return address. Winifred continued her education, receiving a B.A. from Coe College in Cedar Rapids, Iowa, and a master's degree in music education from the University of Michigan. With degrees in hand, she then taught elementary, junior high, and junior college in New Jersey and Michigan and served in the WAVES in San Francisco during World War II.

Little known to Winifred, Kelley still thought of her a decade after their dates. In August 1950, he posted another letter. This time it had a return address and Winifred responded. They began corresponding every day by special delivery. Meetings in Philadelphia, Chicago, and Iowa for holidays and an EMCC annual meeting furthered the romance, and they were married June 21, 1951. ▪

Kelley's success with the branch could be traced, in part, to the innovative relationships he established with agents as well as to his own professional development. Recognizing his achievements and potential, the board elected him a director in 1955 and returned him to the Home Office in 1956 as assistant superintendent of agencies. He became full superintendent the next year when M. J. Wilkinson was promoted to executive vice president. Kelley progressed to assistant vice president in 1957, secretary in 1959, and vice president and secretary in 1960, before becoming president in 1963.

When Kelley returned to the Home Office, R. Gordon Coulter, a Pennsylvania field supervisor since 1953, replaced Kelley as branch manager. Coulter, whose insurance career had

begun in 1933, had experience as an auditor, underwriter, and brokerage manager with five different companies before he arrived at EMCC. He remained in Philadelphia for ten years until he was transferred to Phoenix in 1966.

George Kochheiser in Milwaukee

EMCC established its seventh branch, in Milwaukee, in 1956. Its story began in 1945 when the company entered Wisconsin and executed a general agency contract with the Wylie C. Sampson Agency in Milwaukee. The Sampson Agency was so productive that EMCC opened a supporting claims office in 1947. Business kept increasing until

· · ·

Above: Wisconsin Branch staff in 1958: Seated: Joyce MacBride, Arlene Rahlf, Patricia Adkins, Gwendolyn Schaefer, Mary Kutka, Dolores Thomas, Betty Ostrowski. Standing: Darlene Wolff, James Boren, Patricia Watson, George M. Higbee, Ray Russell, Charles Murray, George Kochheiser, Thomas Mattson, Eugene Reese, Charles Olive, Robert L. Young, Ruth Ziemer. (left to right)

Right: George W. Kochheiser was sent to Milwaukee in 1956 to start a new branch office.

EMCC purchased the agency in 1955, and Superintendent of Agents M. J. Wilkinson sent 32-year-old Iowa Field Supervisor George W. Kochheiser to Milwaukee the next year to form a full branch office. Kochheiser recognized the promise of Milwaukee's excellent business environment — well-written workmen's compensation laws, good rating bureaus, and a sophisticated and sensible industrial commission. His optimism was justified. By 1958, premium volume had increased from over $600,000 the first year to $1 million, led by workmen's compensation and then auto business. Other early business included a small book of fire and homeowners policies and other types of risks. The claim load was 3,000.

...

Lansing Branch staff in 1955. Front row: Neurldean McKillop, file clerk; Elizabeth Kintz, compensation claim clerk; Myrle Bruce, accountant; Irene Sparkia, production secretary; Frances Hummel, junior underwriter; Earlean Hicks, file clerk; Katherine Miles, endorsement clerk; Charlene Hone, claim clerk. Second row: Joylynn Angell, junior underwriter; Eleanor Branson, receptionist; Barbara Beystrum, claim secretary; Judy Casper, Jackie Reed, and Joyce Collins, policy writers. Back row: F. E. Baker, manager; Edward J. Pilon, claim supervisor; W. Darrel Biggs, Richard Long, and James C. Olin, adjusters; Keith Card, automobile underwriter; Lee Spitzbergen, adjuster; Glen Dutcher, compensation underwriter; Bob Kelley, chief underwriter. (left to right)

After the Milwaukee Branch was formed, it remained in the claims office's two rooms above a Walgreen's store at a mall. The office was staffed by a close-knit group. One small room was occupied by Branch Manager George Kochheiser, Branch Secretary Isabel Baker, Claims Manager John Bliss, and Auditor Ray Russell. All other personnel and functions filled a slightly larger second room.

By 1958, the staff had grown from the original seven to 23, and there were 160 agents producing business. A move was essential. On July 1 the office relocated to the second floor above a five-and-dime store and a music store located about two miles north of the former mall location.

The Other New Branches

Lansing and Phoenix:

Two of the remaining branches established before 1960 — Lansing and Phoenix — were organized by John S. Kerper from his home in each city. An Iowa special agent since 1928, he was sent to Lansing to open the Michigan territory in 1940. Because of World War II gas rationing and other privations, he traveled with a marketing representative from another company to appoint agents throughout the middle of the state. By 1946, he was able to open a full branch office with five employees — underwriter, claim man, secretary, and two clerks — in a converted dwelling. A year later the office moved to

...

First branch office location in Lansing.

a commercial building, and the branch
kept growing.

Kerper transferred to Chicago as branch
manager in 1951 and was succeeded by former
Kansas State Agent Francis E. Baker. By 1955,
there were 24 employees, with engineering
services provided by the Chicago Branch.
At that time, Michigan law did not allow
companies to write both casualty and property
insurance, so EMCC worked out an arrangement
with Michigan Millers Mutual Insurance
Company similar to those with Druggists

Mutual in Iowa and Citizens Fund Mutual
in Minnesota. Until Michigan law allowed
companies to write both types of insurance in
1957, EMCC referred agents to Michigan Millers
for property coverage, and Michigan Millers
referred agents to EMCC for casualty coverage.

There were two other significant events in
Lansing in 1957. First, Robert E. Kelley was
promoted from chief underwriter to branch
manager when Baker transferred to Oklahoma
as state manager under the Wichita Branch.
Second, the staff of 32 employees moved into
a new office, the third branch office built to
EMCC's specifications.

That same year, John Kerper took mandatory
retirement as Chicago branch manager. But,
he had barely retired before he only too gladly
accepted a special assignment to open Arizona
on a part-time basis and moved to Phoenix
as state manager in 1958. There, he appointed
a nucleus of agents to write personal lines.
The operation grew and moved into its first
office in 1962. The next year, Kerper permanently
retired when the office was recognized as a
full branch, former Iowa and Phoenix adjuster
Rex L. Davis became branch manager, and
the office moved to the building next door.

Minneapolis:

Business expanded from Red Wing, Minnesota,
across the state as EMCC continued the
arrangement begun in 1934 with Citizens
Fund Mutual Fire Insurance Company and the
claims office. By 1942, the board determined
that a centrally located, full-service office
was needed. EMCC took over Citizens Fund's
general agency functions and opened a branch

...

Left: R. Gordon Coulter
first served as manager
at the Philadelphia Branch,
then managed the
Phoenix Branch.

Right: LeRoy E. Bruce
headed up the Polk County
Office in 1947.

office in the Northwestern Bank Building
in Minneapolis to serve Minnesota, the
Dakotas, and western Wisconsin.

M. H. "Jim" Jamar, an Iowa underwriter
and field supervisor since 1939, was named
branch manager, and he built up complete
underwriting, claims, engineering, and field
supervision services. Staff grew to about 30,
requiring a move to larger space in 1954.
Jamar retired in 1956 and was succeeded
by James T. Larson, who had served in several
underwriting and field capacities at the
branch since 1946.

Polk County, Iowa:

Iowa business had always been handled by the
Home Office, but a more specific Iowa operation
became necessary as the company expanded
into new lines and geographic areas. In 1947,
a separate Polk County Office was set up in the
Home Office building to provide underwriting
and claims assistance to agents and policyholders in Des Moines and six other towns
in the county. It was headed by LeRoy Bruce,
who became an Iowa field supervisor in 1944,

teaching himself the insurance business at
night after two decades at Flynn Dairy. A year
later, Clarence E. Johnson, a lawyer who had
worked with claims in Iowa, Denver, and
Charlotte since 1940, became claims manager
until named superintendent of claims for
the central division in 1959.

As the new office was taking shape, M. J.
Wilkinson recommended that an Iowa Branch
be formed. By 1955 the Polk County Office had
a premium volume of $1.2 million and a claim
load of 6,500. All lines but fire and bonds were
being serviced, and business kept growing.
Furthermore, the high volume of all Iowa
business dictated that a new branch absorb the
Polk County Office and expand its jurisdiction
across the state. In 1958, the Iowa Branch
opened with 21 employees in separate quarters
at the Home Office facility. To help with the
transition, a group of high school students
copied all Iowa policies, making them readily
available to both the branch and the Home
Office. The next year staff more than doubled
and handled well over 20,000 claims.

MN

Minneapolis, Minnesota

AZ

Phoenix, Arizona

Omaha, Nebrask

NE

Polk County, Iowa

Lansing, Michigan

A Canadian Venture

As the post-war economy grew in the 1950s, EMCC was challenged to expand beyond its U.S. boundaries. During the decade, the company contracted with several auto clubs in Wyoming, the Carolinas, and New Mexico to write auto insurance for them. In Seattle, D. K. MacDonald & Company, EMCC's general agency since the company entered Washington in 1940, appointed EMCC lead underwriter for auto clubs in Seattle, Spokane, and Coeur d'Alene, Idaho. Then, in May 1953, MacDonald proposed that EMCC write auto insurance in Canada through the Vancouver-based British Columbia Automobile Association (BCAA). Following investigations of the Canadian market, EMCC contracted with the BCAA, and the BCAA incorporated A.A.A. Insurance Agency, Ltd., to write business for members. In December, licensing and financial requirements were completed.

President John Hynes's son, John F. Jr. (who had begun as a Denver adjuster in 1947 and joined Omaha's Accident Prevention staff in 1952) was appointed chief Canadian agent. Ross E. MacKinnon, a Home Office accountant since 1947, joined the office as chief accountant. Under the ongoing supervision of Superintendent of Agents M. J. Wilkinson, Hynes Jr. frugally set up an office in rather cramped space in the BCAA headquarters and received additional helpful counsel from Thomas Telfer of Seattle's Farwest General Agency.

Before the first ad appeared in the *Vancouver Sun* on April 19, 1954, 30 policies had been issued. Six inches wide and a full page long, the ad was answered by 300 people. Other advertising and application forms subsequently appeared regularly in the BCAA's newsletter, *The Headlight*, and A.A.A. Agency published a brochure. Because the BCAA's underwriting approach was more liberal than EMCC's, Hynes Jr. reviewed all applications to ensure that excessive limits of liability were not written. He was relieved when no claims came in from the "plague" of pits in windshields caused by regular road use, which were popularly attributed to recent atomic experiments in the Pacific.

Even though profits were offset by commissions and operating expenses in the early years and there were rate wars similar to those in the United States, the Canadian venture showed promise. But, after five years, Hynes Jr. requested a transfer back to the United States. He first reported to Minneapolis Claims Manager "Barney" Barron in 1959. Then he served as superintendent of claims in the Lansing office from 1964 until his death at age 45 on February 10, 1970.

Before Hynes left Vancouver, Ross MacKinnon was named chief agent and branch manager. Walter Waskel, adjuster and claims supervisor in the Denver Claims Office since 1952, transferred to Vancouver to supervise claims handling. Under the direction of MacKinnon and Waskel, the British Columbia venture progressed. Oral tradition holds that EMCC became the number one writer of private passenger auto insurance. Documentation shows that, by 1967, EMCC was recognized as the second largest writer

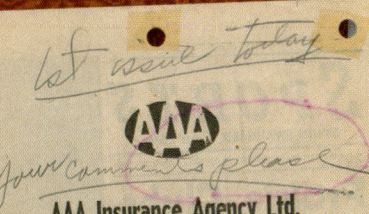

AAA Insurance Agency Ltd.

offers an

Exclusive New Automobile Insurance Plan

For BCAA Members

The AAA Insurance Agency offers members of the B. C. Automobile Association a unique new Car Insurance Plan whereby policy holders become eligible for savings dividends at the end of each policy year. The plan is made possible by the high, accident-free record which B.C.A.A. members have chalked up in past years.

Under the plan, every mem* - insured through the AAA Insurance Agency will become eligible for a share of the total savings effected by the Company during his or her policy year.

This new plan is similar to Automobile Club Insurance plans which are enjoying a distinguished record of success throughout the Western United States. In the States of Washington and Idaho last year, Automobile Club members earned a 10% dividend — while in California the dividend paid out was 22%.

RATES BASED ON B.C. ONLY – NOT CANADA

- B.C.A.A. Members who have a 3-YEAR Accident-free record will be given special concessions in their premium rate.
- High School Driver Training Graduates with AAA diplomas are eligible for SPECIAL RATES.

PROMPT, COMPLETE SERVICE

- The AAA Insurance Agency handles automobile club members' insurance only. Claims are settled promptly and efficiently with a minimum of red tape.

Before you reinsure—compare rates offered by AAA Insurance Agency. Find out how you can "earn while you insure"—and enjoy substantial savings in your automobile insurance costs.

PHONE TAtlow 5811 or Mail Coupon Today

AAA Insurance Agency Ltd.,
303 West Pender Street,
Vancouver 3, B.C.

Yes, I am interested in the new Car Insurance Plan offered by AAA Insurance Agency Ltd. Please send me full details.

Name
Address

BRITISH COLUMBIA AUTOMOBILE ASSOCIATION

PENDER AND HAMILTON STREETS, VANCOUVER 3, BRITISH COLUMBIA CANADA • TELEPHONE TATLOW 5811

World wide affiliations

Safety First

E. J. IRWIN: PRESIDENT
CHAS. E. THOMPSON: VICE-PRESIDENT
Z. K. ESTEY: HONOURARY TREASURER
H. FRANK BIRD: SECRETARY-MANAGER

SECURITY

Employers Mutual Casualty Company and its agents offer a nation-wide claims service to serve the needs of the policy-holder, wherever he may be. Each claim, large or small, is handled promptly, courteously, efficiently.

Assets of more than $32,000,0... offering financial...

GOOD NEWS!

for

ALL MEMBERS
of the

BRITISH COLUMBIA AUTOMOBILE ASSN.

SAVINGS **AAA** SAVINGS

ON YOUR AUTOMOBILE INSURANCE

TURN THE PAGE AND FILL IN THE QUESTIONNAIRE

...te:
A.A.A. INSURANCE AGENCY LTD.
...r St. Vancouver 3, B.C.

TA. 5811

BRITISH COLUMBIA — CANADA

...OMOBILE UNDERWRITING GUIDE

...PLOYERS MUTUAL CASUALTY CO.

Des Moines, Iowa

Effective January, 1954

A.A.A. Insurance Agency, Limited

Pender and Hamilton Streets

Vancouver 3, British Columbia, Canada

Telephone — Tatlow 5811

Has Any Insurer ...
Refused to Renew or Issue Auto ...
Are You Now Insured? ... Expiry Date
Have You Owned & Driven a Car for Last 3 Years?

Particulars of All Accidents, Losses or Claims from Ownership, Use or Operation of Any Automobile During Last 3 Years

| Injury to Persons | Damage to Property of Others |

Damage to Owned or Operated Automobile by:
A. Collision
B. Other Causes

What Cover Are You Interested in?
Check ∆

Public Liability—Amount
Property Damage—Amount
Passenger Hazard
Medical Expenses
Collision: Deductible $
Comprehensive
Fire & Theft

A.A.A. INSURANCE AGENCY LTD.
...11 303 West Pender St., Vancouver 3, B.C.

BRITISH COLUMBIA AUTOMOBILE ASSN.

HEADQUARTERS:
845 BURRARD STREET
VANCOUVER 1, B.C.
TATLOW 5811

MEMBERSHIP NUMBER

...R WALKER
...30 SMELTERITES
...TIMAT B C

58-21818-98-2

218

...MBER IN GOOD STANDING

EXPIRATION DATE
JAN 1 1959
For Services in Greater Vancouver Call MA. 8181 or TA. 5811

SECTY MANAGER

••• Advertisements, brochures, insurance cards, applications, and underwriting guide for the EMC and British Columbia Automobile Association program.

of auto premiums in the province, with a volume in excess of $4 million handled by 29 employees.

At the Home Base

Physical Expansion

At the Home Office, EMCC kept bursting at the seams and, over the years, moved several times to accommodate the growth. The company stayed in its original home in the Crocker Building until 1924. Although three rooms there had been relinquished shortly after organization in 1911, the company's subsequent growth necessitated leasing two additional rooms for $150 a month in 1920.

In early 1924, offices were leased on the sixth floor of the Equitable Building at the southwest corner of Sixth and Locust Streets. Rent there was $317 a month for five years with a five-year renewal option. Before the Equitable lease expired, EMCC moved in 1928 to the tenth floor of the Hubbell Building at the southwest corner of Ninth and Walnut. Even as this move was made, the board began discussing possible purchase of other buildings for use as a Home Office. While considering relocation, they added space in the Hubbell office to accommodate a Hollerith tabulating system in 1929 and occupied an additional room in 1931. After the economy move to the Valley National Bank Building in 1933, office space was expanded 50% by moving to the entire fourth floor. By this time,

EMCC was able to give serious consideration to owning its office building.

In 1937, the three-story Brinsmaid Building, which housed a china shop at 204-210 Seventh Street, was purchased. EMCC took possession on January 1, 1938, and, in April, began a $65,000 remodeling project with elevator repairs. The design by Tinsley, McBroom and Higgins retained the high ceiling and balcony that stretched across the rear of the building on the first floor. General contractor, Weitz Company, had the facility ready for occupancy by October, when separate open houses were held for the public and agents.

After World War II, useable space was expanded when functional areas were rearranged throughout the building and the third floor was extensively remodeled into executive offices and a board room. A 1948 appraisal just before the $100,000 renovation was completed, valued the property at $275,000.

While the Brinsmaid renovations were underway, EMCC purchased the Seventh Street Realty Company building at the northwest corner of Seventh and Mulberry Streets. Owned by A. H. Blank and S. Marx, this $80,000 facility was intended for future expansion and storage, and the current lessees could provide income to EMCC in the interim. Next, possession of the adjacent Hotel Madrid on Mulberry Street, owned by the Dorothy Goldberg Trust, was obtained in 1951 through a lease-purchase arrangement.

With these properties assembled, the board appointed a committee in the fall of 1952 to

The Brinsmaid Building
at 210 Seventh Street,
the first property purchased
by EMC in downtown
Des Moines, 1937.

plan for a new Home Office facility. A contract was executed with Chicago architects Childs & Smith, following a conference with them in June 1953. The new structure was to replace the recently acquired properties at Seventh and Mulberry and incorporate the Brinsmaid Building. The company's address would remain 210 Seventh Street.

Plans were approved at the end of 1954, and Weitz Construction was hired to build the $1,250,000 three-story steel and concrete structure. Construction began in March 1955, and the cornerstone was laid in October. The red granite and Indiana limestone building of 67,000 square feet included a 32'x40' reception lobby, a new board and conference

room, a 200-capacity auditorium/recreation room, aluminum reversible windows, and under-floor ducts for phone and electric connections.

First to be occupied was the third floor, housing the Bond, Workmen's Compensation, Underwriting, and Fire Departments. Next was the second floor, with Personnel, Accounting, Audit, Statistical, Accident Prevention, and IBM storage. Last was the first floor, where Home Office Claims, Filing, and Iowa Claims were located. All three floors were fully occupied by November 1956. When the Iowa Branch was created in 1958, it operated out of the first floor. Still, space was inadequate, and storage space was leased in three additional buildings.

...

Construction of this red granite and Indiana limestone EMC Home Office building was completed in 1956.

There was also a need for parking facilities. EMCC's eye kept roving, this time across Seventh Street to the News Arcade Building owned by the Thomas H. Stoner and Ruth Hamilton Stoner Trusts. It was purchased for $75,000 and leased to Davidson Company until April 1963. Within a year, however, the unheated facility proved to be too integrated with the Davidson Department Store operation and did not serve EMCC's purposes well.

The solution was a trade. EMCC purchased the Bolton and Hay Building located next to the new office on Mulberry Street, giving the six individual Bolton owners the News Arcade Building in exchange. Already, EMCC had been leasing two floors in the Bolton and Hay Building for supply and printing operations and storage. With the exchange complete in December 1957, EMCC connected its heating plant to the new purchase and expended $5,000 making repairs. Nearly a decade would pass before pressure for further expansion would be felt.

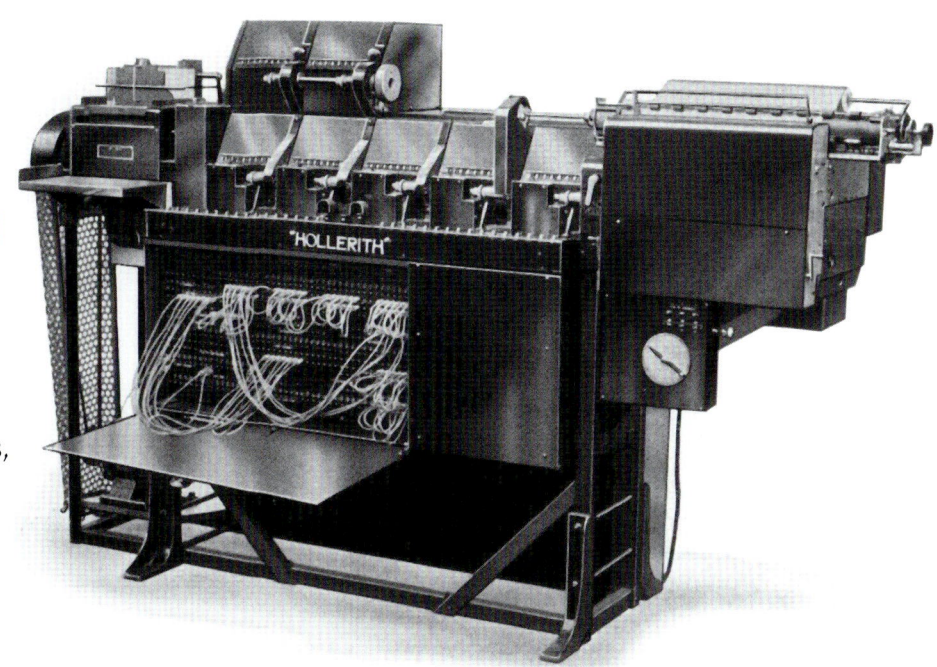

Technology Leaps Forward

Entry into the computer age began shortly after Harold Watson and the Multigraph machine arrived at EMCC in 1927. In late 1928, a contract was made with IBM for two Hollerith punched card tabulating machines, and Dorothy Lowman was transferred from claims to operate them. EMCC's first use of tabulating equipment was primarily for accounting purposes, and a full-fledged keypunch operation was in place by 1933. When EMCC moved into the Brinsmaid Building five years later, four keypunch operators and a tabulating supervisor were enclosed in a separate space under the balcony because the machines were so noisy. Among the operators was Merle Kesler, who had come to EMCC as a file clerk in 1930. She became a keypunch operator about 1936 and then took charge of coding some years later. She would also work with premium services before her retirement in 1963.

Kesler saw many changes during her career. At first the tabulating operation was used to process data such as policy numbers, dates, and premium or expense amounts. Very strong fingers were required to mechanically punch holes into columns on cards about the size of business envelopes. To obtain desired numerical information, a hand-cranked tabulator sorted the cards according to where the holes were placed. The first cards used by EMCC had 45 columns, but a switch was made to 80-column cards in 1936 and, by then, electric motors powered the machines.

By the spring of 1944, over 150,000 items were being processed each month. In the early 1950s, the section became known as Data Processing, when key punch, tabulating, coding, programming (and later, systems analysis and design), and methods and procedures functions were brought together under Personnel Director Darrell B. Southern. Southern had become familiar with punched card operations when he specialized in data processing for movement of war materials with Army Ordnance and the Quartermaster Corps during World War II. As personnel director, this University of Iowa graduate was responsible for oversight of most areas now considered general administration.

Under Southern's direction, the key punch, coding, and tabulating functions were combined in 1954 into a Statistical Department supervised by Jack H. Wagstaff, an EMCC accountant and statistician since 1945, who had worked for the company's first auditor, Joseph Froggatt & Company. This department produced about 112,000 statistical card records each month. Most were forwarded to statistical bureaus such

•••

The Hollerith tabulating machine was invented by American statistician Herman Hollerith (1860-1929), who developed the mechanical tabulator based on punched cards to rapidly tabulate statistics from millions of pieces of data. He was the founder of one of the companies that later merged and became IBM.

as the Mutual Insurance Rating Bureau (MIRB) and the Transportation Insurance Rating Bureau (TIRB) to provide premium and loss data for determining rates for the industry.

Other changes occurred within Data Processing after two recent employees switched from underwriting to computer programming and systems analysis in the late 1950s. James J. Stansell became supervisor of the Tabulating Department in 1959, and Donald E. Andrew was the first supervisor of the Methods and Procedures Department, created by Darrell Southern in 1960. In 1963, Stansell was promoted to manager of Data Processing, which encompassed all of these departments.

In 1957, EMCC installed its first mainframe computer, an IBM 650, leased for $60,000 a year. Executives estimated that its replacement of other machines saved about $12,000,

reducing the effective net annual cost to about $48,000. First produced and marketed in 1954, the computer used vacuum tubes that allowed electronic technology to become widespread and practical, making mechanical tabulating machines obsolete. Programming consisted of manually wiring program boards and setting function switches, reminiscent of a telephone switchboard. Totals were punched into cards that the tabulating machine used to print paper reports. A new operations section within Data Processing would evolve around this computer.

In 1958, an IBM magnetic drum data processing system was leased and installed in the Statistical Department. It increased processing speeds through use of a computer, power unit, and card input-output unit. At the end of the year, it was reported that, despite the increased speed and efficiency,

...

Left: Jack H. Wagstaff
supervised the Statistical
Department in 1954.

Right: Catherine "Katie"
Juliano uses keypunch cards
and an IBM machine to issue
pay checks in the late '50s.

no one had been displaced by computers. Indeed, what was now the Coding and Tabulating Department had grown to 48 and the entire Home Office staff to 355, thanks in part to increasing business volume and centralization of operations done by computers.

Another big step in 1958 was purchase of an IBM Cardatype payroll machine that employees dubbed Nellie. Her operation was overseen by Catherine "Katie" Juliano. She had come to EMCC as a key punch operator upon graduation from high school in 1943, when all operations were manual, including the individual typing of about 400 checks. By the time Nellie arrived, payroll had grown to 700. Nellie transferred data from punched cards to one typewriter that typed checks and another that typed the payroll register. She required

two operators, manual handling of the cards, and left much to Katie: computing overtime and undertime, entering new employees and discontinuing those who had left, and taking care of daily general disbursements. Nevertheless, what previously took a full month to accomplish could now be completed in a few days. During Nellie's first year, payroll increased to 775, and the only mistake discovered in the $2.5 million disbursed was a $10 underpayment.

While punched card machines and computers were making their debut, old mainstays were still necessary to office operations. Royal, L. C. Smith, and Underwood manual typewriters were standard. They were used for typing correspondence, policy forms, reports, and stencils for mimeograph machines, the main method of duplication. Forms, letterheads, and other business papers were printed in-house

on the Multigraph machine and, then, the Multilith that replaced it. Overseeing this transition was Webster F. Hawkins, a World War I veteran who had worked in the printing business in Des Moines and Peoria, Illinois, before coming to EMCC in 1935.

Dictaphones had appeared in the 1940s. They used a "cutting" needle to record dictation on six-inch wax cylinders that were then placed on a machine with a "listening" needle for transcription. Once transcribed, the dictation was shaved off. After 15 to 20 shavings, the cylinders became so narrow they had to be discarded. The cylinders were followed by flat disks until reusable plastic belts replaced both. By 1958, EMCC's outside adjusters were being given thin plastic belts that could be used once and then attached to the files. But most executives still preferred their secretaries' Gregg shorthand skills.

In July 1956, EMCC announced that its new telephone number would be CHerry 4-4254 as part of Bell Company's move to meet the growing demand for service with a "two-letter, five-number plan." Half a year later, the number was again changed to ATlantic 8-3671, this time to accommodate the ten incoming and outgoing trunk lines that were being connected to the switchboard in the new office building.

Personnel Matters

Wages and Benefits

When Hynes became president in 1947, there were 221 employees in the Home Office and 167 in 11 service and branch offices. He would oversee tremendous changes and growth in personnel matters during his tenure. At the end of Hynes's decade as president, the number of employees had increased by approximately 75%.

New ideas about employee benefits began to emerge along with this growth. Workmen's compensation, of course, had been available in Iowa since 1914, and Social Security was enacted in 1935. Mention of employee benefits first appeared in EMCC's minutes in the mid-1920s when a decision about vacations was left to the officers, $1,000 life insurance policies were secured for all employees through John Hancock Life Insurance Company, and a $10/year service bonus was added. Merle Kesler remembered receiving a $10 bonus the year she started, and then working up to $50 before the amount was cut back to $5 during the Depression.

The idea of retirement income began to be explored in 1935, but it was 1942 before President John W. Gunn's recommendation to consider instituting a pension plan stimulated serious discussion. Although $20,000 was immediately set aside for employee pension annuities, long deliberations ensued with outside consultants, and a plan did not become effective until 1945. It was while these discussions were underway that first employee Peg Burroughs and Field Supervisor

Employees enjoy
a company Christmas
party at the Kirkwood Hotel
in Des Moines in 1949.

George Patterson were granted pensions in 1943 and 1944, respectively.

After the plan was adopted, the inadequacy of the projected total annual cost of $23,000 to $30,000 was illustrated when Claims Clerk Bessie Newell requested special consideration. Upon her retirement at the end of 1947, after 31 years of service, she requested a $20 pension allowance on top of her monthly annuity to bring her total monthly income to $50. EMCC agreed to her request until she became eligible for Social Security. In 1956, Burroughs was receiving $70.64, Patterson $145, and Newell $26.58. They would receive annual increases until their deaths, and the board gradually instituted new pension options and improved employees' insurance coverage.

When setting a mandatory retirement age was explored in the 1940s, the idea was dropped because only one in ten of the Company's oldest males favored it. Even when retiring at 70 became mandatory in 1956, many exceptions were made, and the provision was eliminated as President Robb Kelley approached the benchmark in the 1980s. More popular were a reduction in employees' contributions to the pension fund with the company paying a larger portion, disability remuneration beyond workmen's compensation benefits, and a comprehensive major medical plan.

Christmas brought cash gifts. In 1935 every employee received $20. Nine years later, Christmas gifts based on length of service were instituted and ranged from $5 to $25. Military service personnel received $50. In 1948, the gifts were doubled and would remain constant for many years. What became more meaningful were the annual Christmas buffets at the

Employers Mutual
Annu
AUGUS

• • •
Employees gather at Riverview Park in Des Moines for the summer picnic in 1950.

Kirkwood Hotel, attended by nearly 200 in the mid-1950s.

Social time did not end with Christmas. A summer picnic for Home Office personnel at Riverview Park in 1944 turned into an annual event. Planned by employees, it was attended by about 250 revelers during the 1950s. The agenda featured serious consumption of fried chicken and corn on the cob, prizes for guessing the number of candies in a jar, ballroom dancing to Don Hoy's ten-piece orchestra, and thriller rides on the Rock-O-Plane, Tumblebug, and roller coaster. Another annual tradition started in 1955 when the company treated 300 Home Office employees and spouses to State Fair grandstand

performances. More selective was sponsorship of employee participation in sports activities. These began in 1948 when EMCC first competed in the Des Moines Golf League. A long history of company competitions in golf, bowling, softball, and other sports would follow.

Administrative Accommodation

Growth in staff size, various benefits, and employee activities made development of a distinct personnel function within the general area of administration necessary. Shortly after Darrell Southern came to EMCC as personnel

sualty Company
ienic
1950

director in 1946, he was joined by Claude Baker as assistant personnel director and Keith Card as personnel clerk. These were not yet full-time responsibilities; Southern was also in charge of General Administration and Baker of Office Services.

Another step was taken in 1953 when Baker and Card moved to other functions and Dean Price was hired as employment manager. Price had served as employment manager at the Des Moines Ordnance Plant during World War II and was staff supervisor at the Iowa Employment Security Agency before coming to EMCC. An excellent judge of character and intellect with significant knowledge and relationships in the personnel field,

he was known as "Mr. Personnel" among his contemporaries in Des Moines. Under his direction, a Personnel Department with specified tasks began to take shape at EMCC.

One task was formalizing the employee recruitment process. In the early days, recruiting had been conducted by word-of-mouth at neighborhood, church, social, and family gatherings and through newspaper advertising. Price introduced background checks and interviews to determine educational and work experience, indications of character, and social values. Personnel staff had oversight of attendance, work rules, dress codes, wages, and benefits, while the hiring departments, which were more familiar with their specific needs,

NOVEMBER • 1953
VOLUME 1   NUMBER 2

THE EMPLOYERS MUTUAL
CIRCUIT

This is our CIRCUIT—our periodical journey 'round the Home and Branch Offices of Employers Mutual Casualty Company; a monthly visit with all our friends and associates in Des Moines, Chicago, Minneapolis, Omaha, St. Louis, Kansas City, Denver, Charlotte, Philadelphia, Lansing, Wichita, Jackson, Dallas, Milwaukee, Seattle, Houston and the territories they serve.

Chicago Girl Names Our Magazine

'Accidents' Can Be Expensive!

Comprehensive Personal Liability Coverage Protects!

The price of negligence runs high.

And if it harms another it can be disastrous; at best, it's costly in proportion to the harm done.

But there's protection for those who want it—through Employers Mutual Comprehensive Personal Liability insurance.

* * *

Look at these real situations:

Thinking he'd entertain the children at a small party, one of our policyholders set off some firecrackers. It was a thoroughly exciting display until the very last one exploded. That one took the sight of a 3-year-old girl. The policyholder thought he had exercised due caution . . . but the unforeseen happened, and because of our coverage, the claim was satisfied without loss to the policyholder.

While fishing, a policyholder's hook tore into the back of his companion. Result: great pain, hospital and doctor bills, loss of income . . . and a claim for damages. Under provision of the policy, Employers Mutual paid the claim.

A policyholder's dog tore the trousers off a milkman. EMC paid for the pants.

A visitor at the assured's home tripped on a toy on the sidewalk and sprained her ankle. EMC paid.

A 15-year-old daughter of an assured dove from
(Continued on page 4)

Mrs. Dale Fry Wins $50 For Suggesting 'Circuit'

Employers Mutual is pleased to announce that Mrs. Doris Fry of the Chicago Office wins the $50 U. S. Defense Bond for suggesting the name of our new magazine.

She suggested *The Employers Mutual Circuit,* because the magazine "serves as a connecting link for all our offices, thus making a 'circuit' for the exchange of information and items of interest to Company personnel."

As you might guess, the choice was not an easy one for the judges, because they had to choose from a list of 165 names. Contest judges were Chairman of the board John W. Gunn, Vice-President M. J. Wilkinson, Secretary W. J. Hynes and Director of Personnel Darrell Southern.

Prior to the judging, a list of all the names was prepared and each was coded by number. Each judge then, individually, studied the list and picked the five names he preferred. At a meeting of the four judges, each "candidate" title was discussed and eliminated or kept for a final vote. When it came time for the final vote, the judges' opinion was unanimous; each felt confident that *The Employers Mutual Circuit* was a name our readers would like. The "master list" of suggested names was then con-
(Continued on page 4)

Doris Fry

evaluated particular job skills. Highly valued were penmanship, typing and spelling ability, oral communication skills, and mathematical knowledge. Before he retired in 1972, Price would develop increasingly sophisticated personnel practices.

For Employees

Coinciding with Price's arrival at EMCC was publication of an employee newsletter in October 1953. Temporarily called *E.M.C. News*, it received its permanent name the next month by way of a contest. Doris Fry, who worked in the Chicago Branch with her husband, Dale, was the winner. Fry's title, *The Employers Mutual Circuit,* was selected unanimously from 165 entries because it described the new organ's purpose of serving "as a connecting link for all our offices, thus making a 'circuit' for the exchange of information and items of interest to company personnel." Her prize was a $50 U.S. defense bond.

Edited by President Hynes's secretary, Elizabeth Berens, who had come to EMCC in 1935, the new monthly featured articles about the company's processes, events, and the branches. A "Personal Items" column established a "family feeling" among the rapidly growing and scattered staff. Employees reported engagements, weddings, births, deaths, trips taken, people visiting back and forth, the baby sleeping through the night, parties attended, funerals and condolences, falling asleep in church, illnesses and operations, flowers raised at home, hobbies, cars purchased, fish caught, bowling and golf scores, and much more. Input about employees' personal and professional lives continued to be solicited, but printing of personal information became more selective after December 1958, when the column title was changed to "Around the Personal Circuit." Typography and layout were changed, and cartoon-type illustrations added

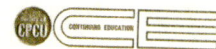

In Recognition of his many years of faithful service to the

Society of Chartered Property and Casualty Underwriters

this Certificate is presented to

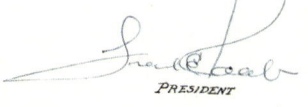
Robb B. Kelley, CPCU

October 12, 1971

For his outstanding contribution toward the furtherance of the Society's purposes and objectives; for his local, regional and national leadership as the president of two chapters, regional director, national officer, and most recently as President; for his encouragement of colleagues to obtain the CPCU designation, and for his outstanding personal contributions to the industry and the public. His leadership in the Society has lent strength to its continuing redevelopment into a more viable entity and brought credit to the designation. His influence on the Society will be lasting.

William G. Pritchard Jr.
SECRETARY

PRESIDENT

spice. Essential to the *Circuit*, and all of the company's publications, were good writing and vocabulary.

Another benefit that bound employees together in a very practical way was the Home Office Credit Union formed under the Federal Credit Union Act of 1934. It was organized in 1936 by John W. Gunn, John Kerper, Webster Hawkins, and Russell Engelmann, with Harold Watson as the first president. Early growth was rapid. Assets of $520.18 at the end of 1937 multiplied to $2,822.84 by 1940. Then little was heard about the organization in the company's publications for nearly 15 years, during which assets rose only to about $7,500.

After that, driven by growth throughout the company, the numbers increased steadily. Membership grew from 66 in 1953 to 280 in 1958. Assets jumped from $7,500 to $16,000 in 1955 and to $48,835.42 in 1958. In 1956

nearly 1,000 loans totaling over $88,000 were made, with a net uncollected loss of only $560. Among 1958 loans was one for $5,000 to finance a new car. A 4% dividend was declared in 1958 and reached a new high of 4.5% in 1959. By 1976 membership had grown from about 100 to over 900. Assets stood at over $735,000 and dividends paid to members were over $33,000.

EMCC's strong emphasis on continuing education, certifications, and professional designations was kicked off in 1952 when Philadelphia Branch Manager Robb Kelley became the first at EMCC to earn certification as a Chartered Property and Casualty Underwriter (CPCU), the "Cadillac" of professional insurance designations. Before he left Philadelphia in 1956, Kelley became president of the Philadelphia CPCU Chapter. Next to earn the designation at EMCC were

...

Left: 1969 Credit Union Board: John Larsh, president; Ruth Short, vice president; Ed Olson, treasurer; Karen McCarthy, secretary. (left to right)

Right: Special recognition certificate for Robb B. Kelley for his service to the CPCU Society.

The 18 charter members of the 20-Year Club started in 1958. Seated: F. E. Baker, H. C. Dabler, W. J. Hynes, John F. Hynes, Ann Shannon, Merle Kesler, John W. Gunn, M. J. Wilkinson, Abe Shapiro. Back row: R. J. Lemley, Harry Wishard, Russell Engelmann, Earle Miller, John Kerper, Harold Watson, Eugene Meyers, Lawrence Pye. (left to right)

Chicago Branch Underwriter Dale C. Fry in 1956 and Omaha Branch Underwriter Maurice O. Cooper, Milwaukee Branch Manager George W. Kochheiser, and Claims executive Forrest C. Mercer in 1959.

In 1954, Elizabeth Berens was one of three Des Moines women, and one of 360 women in the United States, to be certified as a Professional Secretary (CPS) by the Institute for Certifying Secretaries, organized in 1950 to upgrade the status of secretaries. Certification required passing a 12-hour exam that covered stenography, accounting, business law, personal relations, general office procedures, principles of economics and management, and general business administration. The next decades would see a proliferation of employees earning

a wide variety of designations and of educational courses and events, both in-house and industry-sponsored.

As EMCC neared its half-century mark, a sense of history was beginning to develop. In 1958, a 20-Year Club with 18 charter members, who had served at least 20 years with EMCC, was organized. Honored at the Annual Conference and School with presentation of membership pins, these members' total years of service was an impressive 469. Topping the list were John F. Hynes, with 40 years, and five others with 30 or more years. Over time, branch clubs would be formed, and recognition of employees' service at five-year intervals would become a prominent feature in the *Circuit*.

Approaching the Fifty-Year Milestone

The careers of John W. Gunn and John F. Hynes were roughly contemporaneous, spanning four decades that witnessed EMCC's transition from a small one-line Iowa company into an increasingly complex and diversified player in many insurance markets. As the two men interchanged positions as president and chairman, they shepherded the company through the big events of war, geographical expansion, and entry into multiple lines.

By the time John W. Gunn returned to the presidency in 1957, the company's identity had again been expanded, and a resolution was passed at the Annual Meeting to change the name to Employers Mutual Insurance Company because "Casualty" was "undesirably restrictive." However, investigation revealed that a company in Denver had a similar name and that Employers of Wausau would object to the change in all states. Furthermore, it was difficult to secure a new name that contained "Employers" because there were so many other companies with similar names. Thus, no further actions were taken, and the resolution was rescinded at the 1958 Annual Meeting.

Employers Mutual Casualty Company would remain the company's name as it spawned other companies and subsidiaries through its second half-century. It would become the longest standing independent "Employers" insurance company in the nation, as others went broke or ceased to exist for various reasons.

When John F. Hynes retired as president at the 1957 Annual Meeting, he was given

...PROTECTING BUSINESS AND INDUSTRY

A half century ago, in 1911, a group of Iowa business leaders founded Employers Mutual Casualty Company especially to provide a non-profit institution for meeting the requirements of the newly-enacted Workmen's Compensation laws. Through the years, Employers Mutual has kept pace with the needs of business and industry . . . affording complete insurance protection, always with up-to-date policies . . . developing and increasing the services so important in commercial coverage. For over 25 years, as Iowa's largest fire, casualty and bonding company, Employers Mutual has written more Workmen's Compensation for Iowa employers than any other company.

For complete protection, competitive rates, prompt nationwide claim service, accident prevention engineering . . . for PROTECTION IN ACTION . . . call the professional independent agent who represents us in your community . . .

A NATIONAL INSTITUTION

Employers

MUTUAL CASUALTY COMPANY
HOME OFFICE
210 SEVENTH STREET, DES MOINES

FIRE • CASUALTY • BONDS
750 AGENTS SERVING IOWA, 4,000 SERVING THE NATION

special recognition. He had seen EMCC grow from assets of approximately $105,000 in 1918, when he joined the company, to $42 million in 1956 at the end of his presidency. Assets would be $60 million in 1961 at the end of his active chairmanship. For those same dates, premiums increased from $110,000 to $27.6 million to $42 million and surplus from $58,000 to $12.6 million to $15 million. A strong foundation had been constructed for the next stage of the company's development. ▪

EMC reached its 50-year milestone in 1961.

50 years of SERVICE

1911-1961

Employers

MUTUAL CASUALTY COMPANY
DES MOINES
FIRE · CASUALTY · BONDS

Below: Chicago Branch Manager Dale Fry (center) and Vince Bergquist, field supervisor (right), celebrated EMC's 50-year anniversary with costumes and cake.

Above: Carolyn Spaw, in vintage costume, lit the candles on EMC's 50-year celebration cake at the Home Office.

Charting New Territory: 1960 – 1980

Part 1. REORGANIZATION AND EXPANSION: DECENTRALIZATION

O'Toole's Retooling

EMCC celebrated its golden anniversary on April 24, 1961, 50 years to the day after its first provisional board meeting. Employees in 24 cities celebrated simultaneously with coffee, cake, and period costumes. President John W. Gunn wrote, "This 50th year is only a milestone. While we may pause for a few minutes to commemorate it, we will waste no time in either mourning or praising the past. Today the present is important. Here each of us can do our best;

and what we make of the present is our best guide to the future." For two decades, Presidents John W. Gunn and John F. Hynes had been leading the company rapidly into the future. Since they had come on board over 40 years before, the reins held by John A. Gunn had been converted into a steering wheel, and "giddyup" was replaced by an accelerator. Soon both men would step down, knowing Robb Kelley was poised to take command.

When the "father of modern management," Peter Drucker, published *The Practice of Management* in 1954, he popularized the concept of "management by objectives," a highly influential organizational method that would remain in vogue through the next several decades. As its own complexity increased, EMCC became increasingly interested in organizational structure and management styles. In 1959, the board approved hiring E. F. O'Toole Associates, Inc., a business consulting firm based in New York City, to do an efficiency review of EMCC.

O'Toole was well schooled in Drucker's principles of setting objectives and goals, monitoring and measuring achievement, instituting performance incentives, identifying interrelationships and erasing hard boundaries between disciplines, and involving all levels of employees in strategic planning and implementation. Key to the process were decentralization and simplification, supported by SMART criteria — **S**pecific, **M**easurable, **A**chievable, **R**elevant, and **T**ime-Specific.

Conducted during 1960, O'Toole's study changed both the organization and its management philosophy. Staff input was incorporated into 150 recommendations for consolidation and streamlining of functions, forms, procedures, organizational structure, and physical office arrangements. By the 50th anniversary, implementation was underway. In mid-June, 38 recommendations had been completed, 51 were in process, and nine had been rejected. Because decentralization was a major component, the Iowa Branch was included in the initial study, and the Philadelphia Branch operations were reviewed

■ ■ ■

Employees at the Home
Office replicated what
a standard office may have
looked like when EMC first
opened its doors in 1911;
Judy Mecham, personnel;
Carolyn Spaw, receptionist;
and Bill Young, workers'
compensation. (left to right)

in 1961. This information guided the conversion of branches into separate regional profit centers with authority for integrated operations of production, underwriting, and claims.

At this time, Robb Kelley, as superintendent of agents, vice president, and secretary, was instrumental in creating the position of marketing administrator to oversee implementation of the reorganization. In 1962, he called George Kochheiser back from Milwaukee to fill the position. Kelley believed Kochheiser's excellent memory, organized mind, ability to articulate, and proficiency in judging the character and capabilities of others equipped him well for the task. When Kelley became president on March 13, 1963, he and Kochheiser formed a highly effective, visionary team that would carry the company into the 1990s. With

characteristic modesty about his own role, Kochheiser later said of Kelley, "He reached out to seize the future."

One of Kochheiser's and Kelley's first tasks, as they took the next step forward, was to attend management schools "back East." Particularly helpful were those of the American Management Association, which taught the fundamentals of developing plans that could be measured. Instructive books were added to the company's library. One of them discussed long-range planning for the company's growth in a rapidly changing and highly competitive environment. Another promoted the concept that the primary responsibility of field sales managers was to develop salesmen rather than to be supersalesmen themselves.

Kochheiser said, "It was an exciting time to put programs together and involve all levels

of management." He observed that, until recently, plans had existed only in the minds of CEOs and chairmen. Even though American business was seen as the "machine that changed the world," he believed that activities added in the early twentieth century, particularly in finance, marketing, and "image-making," had merely enhanced what already existed and did not create "endemic changes." Now, however, he saw new opportunities.

Kochheiser embraced his own experience, which had expanded his vision as he advanced in the company. He had learned about commercial operations as a safety engineer, gained insight about agencies and marketing as a field supervisor, and acquired management skills as a branch manager. Together, they created the "big picture" he needed as marketing administrator.

As the O'Toole recommendations were developed into a reorganization plan, annual goals were established and progress was measured by regular reviews of results. Organization charts appeared. All employee positions were classified and given descriptions and salary ranges. Future COO and Board Chairman Fred A. Schiek, who joined EMCC as an underwriter trainee in 1959 after army service during the Korean Conflict and graduation from Drake University, later remembered his enthusiasm for the raise the new salary ranges gave him. Recommended annual salaries for executives and key personnel ranged from $5,500 to $22,000. Schiek had not yet attained that level, so he had no quarrel with the $15 increase beyond his $320 a month starting salary.

These, and other components of the plan, began to take shape under the umbrella of "marketing." In his first speech as president, to the Annual Conference and School in 1963, Robb Kelley spelled out the vision. It was rooted in what he called "The Marketing Concept." Originated by General Motors around 1950, it emphasized producing maximum corporate profits. Kelley modified this emphasis by stating that EMCC's overall goal and purpose was "to sell and to provide a service of protection against loss to policyholders in a modern enlightened way and, in the process, produce a maximum of long-range corporate profits." The approach required broad perspective and teamwork — seeing beyond narrow functions to complex organization.

Speaking to the conference theme, "Take the Positive Approach to the Future," he observed, "The tempo of competition has stepped up in staggering proportions, but so has the effectiveness of the weapons and tools with which we are provided by the company." Marketplace forces were bringing about dramatic changes for business. Among the problems Kelley cited were weakening of the bureaus' ability to uphold rates, thin or nonexistent underwriting profits, high loss ratios, company mergers, rapid changes in forms and endorsements, negligence laws moving toward favoring the plaintiff, and workmen's compensation "slipping dangerously close to federal government intervention through the Social Security program."

The antidote, for Kelley, was decentralization — using the branches to meet local conditions and subsidiaries to provide new opportunities. EMCC's new subsidiary, EMCASCO Insurance Company, was already combating the rate

cutting of direct writers. Employers Modern Life Company, a subsidiary then in the process of formation, would allow property, casualty, and life insurance to be purchased in "one stop." EMCC's size — small enough to keep in touch with branch and general agency problems and large enough to have the capacity to withstand shocks — also boded well for the company's future.

· · ·

Robb Kelley gave his first speech as EMC president at the Annual Conference and School in 1963.

The Branches Become Unified Profit Centers

Significant attention was given to converting the branches into individual functional entities as the reorganization plan moved forward. Authority was gradually transferred from the Home Office to the branches as each developed into a unified profit center, encompassing the sale, underwriting, and servicing of all lines — property, casualty, and life. The primary link with the Home Office was the branch manager who coordinated the work of field supervisors, underwriters, and claims and administrative personnel. In consultation with the Home Office, each branch determined premium and profit goals for its territory, the nature of the agency force, and what kind of accounts to write. Quarterly reports and financials were submitted to the Home Office and returned with feedback. Profit-sharing bonuses were given as incentives toward reaching goals and managing within budget.

Kochheiser maintained a close working relationship with the branch managers, and branch personnel expressed appreciation for his guidance. He was ably assisted by Richard Q. "Dick" Fraser, who was hired as an underwriter in 1960 and was named marketing analyst when Kochheiser became marketing administrator in 1962. An army veteran with degrees from the University of Northern Iowa and Drake University, Fraser would continue his career in marketing analysis and administration after his early retirement in 1995 and until his death a year later. Some of the management reports he developed have remained in use to the present.

Though the branches were assuming greater autonomy, their claims representatives, often skilled lawyers, had always reported directly to the Home Office. Western Division Claims Supervisor Russell B. Wellman, an attorney and Army Intelligence veteran of World War II, probably spoke for many when he said that claims was "a good line for a lawyer because you still practice law in a sense, without being a practicing attorney."

Wellman succeeded W. J. Hynes as Home Office claims manager in 1959. Shortly after, reorganization placed all branch functions under the general supervision of Executive Vice President M. J. Wilkinson. Branch claims managers were now to report to their branch managers rather than directly to the Home Office, thus separating them from Wellman in daily conduct of operations. Wellman tendered his resignation in March 1963, but the board responded by voting that he continue on a monthly basis for up to six months.

T. X. Wright was heading the Surety Bond Department. When Wellman departed, Wright was named manager of the Home Office Claims Department and headed claims operations until his retirement in 1989. His successor in the Surety Department was Dick Haskins who had stayed in Vinton, Iowa, as an adjuster until becoming a claims supervisor at the newly formed Iowa Branch in 1958.

In the Claims Department, Wright immediately began to turn things around. Known for his ability to communicate ideas through public speaking and his persuasive skills, he also had astute management skills.

Implementation of the O'Toole-generated plan became a positive experience, as Wright introduced goal-oriented and measurable duties that were outlined in a claims manual created by company personnel. He established biannual evaluations of branch operations by Home Office personnel. Their written reports were delivered with an oral critique to the branch managers, who shared them with the claims managers, who, in turn, shared them with their staffs.

A Uniform Architechural Plan

Branch restructuring was not limited to operations. Attention was also given to physical location, and a uniform architectural plan was adopted for new branch offices as operational reorganization stabilized. EMCC had already joined the movement to the suburbs with the Wichita Branch in 1948 and the Milwaukee Claims Office in 1951. In the ensuing years, EMCC would locate strategically near the best agency markets in business parks and along interstate highways where there was ample parking and expansion room. Convenience to shopping, other businesses, residential areas, and scenic and recreational facilities were other considerations.

EMCC had begun building new branch offices according to its own specifications with Wichita (1948), Omaha (1954), Milwaukee (1956), and Lansing (1957). Then, between 1967 and 1980, the company more efficiently constructed ten new branch offices in the preeminent modernist style of the

New Suburban Convenience For Chicago Branch Office

The artist's rendition above shows the new Chicago Branch Office building to be constructed in Oak Brook. In three words—it's spacious, luxurious, convenient!

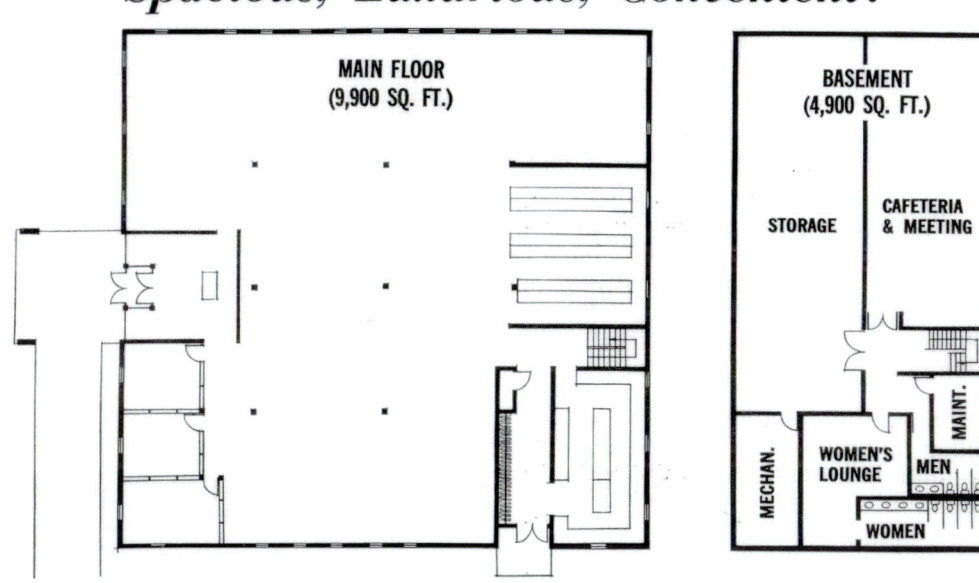

Spacious, Luxurious, Convenient!

MAIN FLOOR (9,900 SQ. FT.)

BASEMENT (4,900 SQ. FT.)

STORAGE

CAFETERIA & MEETING

MECHAN.

WOMEN'S LOUNGE

MEN

MAINT.

WOMEN

The new building in Oak Brook will provide almost three times more space than now occupied in the old downtown Chicago Branch Office. Offices, conference and working areas will be located on the main floor.

mid-twentieth century. Modeled after a prototype designed by Illinois architects Keys and Hestrup for the Chicago Branch, the simplicity and functionality of these one-story, box-like structures reflected values of the operational reorganization. They had flat roofs, narrow floor-to-ceiling windows, and were positioned in attractive landscaped settings.

····

The 1966 floor plan and exterior rendering used in construction of several branch offices, including the Chicago Branch.

Some branches used local supervising architects who made modifications to the prototype, which were suitable to the specific locations.

The uniform plan buildings generally housed executive offices, open work areas, conference rooms, and meeting facilities in a 10,000-square-foot main floor with cafeterias, lounges, tiled restrooms, storage, and utility areas in a 4,800-square-foot basement. An expansion option of 7,000 square feet was often part of the design. The latest heating, air conditioning, and lighting systems were installed, and fixtures and amenities were "ultra-modern," incorporating decorator colors and carpeting.

EMCC's uniform building program began with its original three branches — Wichita, Chicago, and Omaha. First to open was the prototype Chicago office, relocated to the Central Industrial Plaza subdivision of suburban Oak Brook in 1967. Owned by the Oak Brook Development Company, the structure provided three times more space than the previous downtown office. The relocation was determined, in part, by a strategy to de-emphasize the Chicago focus and to increase business in northern and central Illinois. Under Branch Manager Dale Fry, production in the Chicago metropolitan area was allowed

to decline, and the contract with Allied Agency was terminated. Because there was no public transportation to the new location, over 15 new employees were hired to replace those who could not move with the office.

In December, Omaha relocated to similar space among numerous other insurance offices in the Center Street Plaza subdivision, ten miles from downtown. The next year Wichita, already relocated to the suburbs, moved even farther out to an 80,000-square-foot lot five miles northeast of downtown. The $350,000 facility opened in November 1968 with 93 employees.

Philadelphia, like Chicago and Omaha, moved from downtown to the suburbs when it opened its new uniform plan building in 1971. Located on a 2.25-acre plot near Valley Forge National Park in King of Prussia, the building's completion coincided with the branch's 25th anniversary, and both were celebrated with an open house in September.

The Lansing uniform plan building, located in Midway Industrial Center No. 2 on the south side of town, opened in 1974 with an open house for 90 agents, a luncheon for 130, and an education program. President Robb Kelley presented 25-year agency recognition plaques.

Creative Real Estate Management

Because Iowa law did not allow a casualty company to own real estate outside of its home office state, EMCC developed creative financing arrangements that resulted in advantages over time. The financing plan called for EMCC to choose locations and for owner/developers to construct the buildings. With five of the buildings, Employers Modern Life Company, a stock subsidiary formed by EMCC in 1962 to sell life insurance, served as construction lender or mortgagee. EMCC determined specifications and worked with the owner/developers to select contractors. Then EMCC leased back the property, usually

for ten to 15 years, with optional extensions, usually ten years. Rent was based on each project's total development costs, prorated annually. While operating costs, taxes, and other expenses for which EMCC was responsible increased over the years, the base rent remained the same. By the end of the lease's terms, EMCC was sometimes paying less than half of the going rate for comparable space. For example, a decade after it opened, the Omaha lease was only $4.75 per square foot, while the market rate for comparable space was over $10 per square foot. ▪

The building still houses the Lansing Branch, now enhanced by renovations that included new furniture in 1995 and the addition of the adjoining building with an enclosed walkway in 2002.

During the 1970s, the Minneapolis office made two moves unrelated to the building program. While the branch occupied its second office near Franklin and Nicollet Avenues in the central city, an explosion occurred a block away causing concern for employee safety. The branch relocated to Bloomington in 1972. Crime followed the branch there, when a thief unlocked the back door with a credit card and absconded with a number of claim drafts. Fortunately for EMCC, the intruder made out the drafts in his real name and was easily tracked down by the police. Finally, in 1976, a uniform plan building was constructed on a 500-acre rolling, wooded industrial office complex in the western suburb of Minnetonka. Completely renovated to provide more efficient work

flow in 1995, this structure has served the branch to the present.

Four more branch offices followed the uniform plan: Milwaukee (1970), Providence (1970), Kansas City (1971), and Bismarck (1980). Today, the Milwaukee, Lansing, Minneapolis, and Bismarck Branches still occupy their original prototype buildings.

Expansion: New Branches

EMCC's decentralization process extended well beyond the branches already in operation in 1960. In an era of property and casualty company failures, mergers, and acquisitions, EMCC carefully sought possibilities for territorial diversification and growth. Between 1962 and 1983, the company opened nine more branch offices, most growing out of general agencies or becoming part of EMCC through affiliation or as subsidiaries. The other branch EMCC would open after 1983 would be Cincinnati in 1997.

Branch offices built using the uniform architectural plan. Top to bottom: Lansing, Bismarck, Minneapolis, and Milwaukee.

Kansas City

The first branch to be organized under the restructuring plan was Kansas City in 1962. It brought together fragmentary Missouri operations that had begun with opening the Kansas City Claims Office in 1946 to support three agencies: George Eric Williamson Agency, Bernard Thompson Agency, and Western General. Subsequently, claims offices had been opened in St. Louis (1949), Springfield (1957), and Jefferson City (1958). Arkansas operations were also placed under the branch's jurisdiction. The state had been entered in 1954 through the Lewis and Norwood General Agency in Little Rock, and a claims office was opened there five years later. Miles R. "Dick" Barnhart, who had been a field supervisor in Nebraska, Kansas, and Missouri since 1946, was named branch manager to bring together underwriting, production, claims, engineering, payroll audit, and other essential company services.

Four years after the Kansas City Branch was formed, two factors caused EMCC to withdraw from Arkansas. First, there was a loss of key personnel at both Norwood Agency and the claims office. Second, the action was part of a larger strategy to modify the impact of market fluctuations following a string of companywide underwriting losses that began in 1961. This experience gave impetus to creating a long-term solution — forming a holding company that could raise additional capital through stock offerings to counter losses. Through a long process, EMC Insurance Group Inc. evolved as the holding company and made its first

stock offering in February 1982. Half a year later, EMCC was able to re-enter Arkansas as part of the Kansas City servicing territory, and the Little Rock Claims Office was re-opened.

Jackson

Next to open was the Jackson Branch, EMCC's first fully staffed branch office in the South. It was part of the emerging pattern in which general agencies and claims offices were combined and converted into full branch operations. EMCC had begun to do business

Miles R. "Dick" Barnhart was named the first branch manager of the Kansas City Branch in 1962.

Russell A. Engelmann was named southwestern divisional claims superintendent in 1952.

in Mississippi in 1935 through the Southern Underwriters general agency, which was founded in 1929 by the same George Eric Williamson with whom EMCC worked in Missouri. EMCC became Southern Underwriters' dominant company. Beginning in 1946, the company provided some local claims services to the agency, but it was not until 1956 that a full claims office opened in Jackson. When premiums had grown to over $1 million in 1966, EMCC purchased the agency and turned it into a branch, staffed by personnel from both Southern Underwriters and the claims office.

One unique feature of the Jackson office was its reinsurance business. Southern Underwriters had handled the fire business of Millers Mutual Fire Insurance Company of Harrisburg, Pennsylvania, and the branch reinsured that business. Then in 1968, EMCC purchased Union Mutual Insurance Company of Providence, Rhode Island, and the Jackson office began to reinsure their Mississippi fire business. This purchase also brought Tennessee business into the Jackson fold through one of Union Mutual's general agencies in Knoxville.

Dallas

Expansion continued in the South for another year with the Dallas Branch opening in 1967. Like Kansas City, it brought together scattered operations, and like Jackson, it began with purchase of a general agency. As with both of these offices, its roots could be traced to George Eric Williamson. In 1939, he and Richard R. Nelson Sr., from Kansas City, had opened the Williamson & Nelson General Agency in Houston in order to write business

for EMCC as it entered Texas. Production the first year totaled $8,000. In 1941, State Agent William J. Kent joined the agency, and it moved to Dallas as Williamson, Nelson & Kent. When Williamson sold his interest to his partners four years later, the agency became Nelson & Kent. By 1946, production had increased to $457,995, and EMCC opened the Texas Claims Office in Dallas.

Business was flourishing enough by 1952 to create a southwestern divisional claims superintendent position filled by Iowa native Russell A. Engelmann to oversee business in Texas, New Mexico, and Arizona. He replaced the Texas Claims Office with regional offices. The Dallas Office, headed by Charles C. O'Dell, moved to Nelson & Kent's headquarters in the Corrigan Tower and served northern Texas. The Houston Office, headed by Roy H. Schaller, served the southern part of the state. Nelson & Kent handled underwriting, accounting, and production functions, while the EMCC offices conducted claims, audit, and risk improvement services. By 1954, Nelson & Kent was producing $2.2 million in premiums for EMCC.

As business grew, satellite offices were opened in San Antonio and Austin, and service personnel were located in Fort Worth and New Braunfels. Two key people in these operations were John P. Strother, who held claims positions in Texas and became Charlotte claims manager, and Franklyn Y. Wright, a Nelson & Kent field supervisor who became Dallas branch manager. The final claims satellite in the Southwestern Division was in Albuquerque, opened by Harry Wishard in 1959 to process production of the New Mexico Motor Club.

In 1967, EMCC purchased Nelson & Kent Agency and combined it with the claims service operations to form the full-service Dallas Branch. Most Nelson & Kent employees became part of the EMCC staff, and former Lansing Branch Manager Francis E. Baker became the first Dallas branch manager. The branch relocated to a new office north of downtown where 28 employees serviced over 300 agents.

Providence

EMCC headed northeast to Providence, Rhode Island, to open its next branch in 1968. This time, the Providence Branch was created by affiliation with another company, Union Mutual Insurance Company of Providence. Union Mutual traced its history to 1863, when it was organized as Union Mutual Fire Insurance Company of Providence, an affiliate of Firemen's Mutual Insurance Company.

Although business grew slowly during Union Mutual's first 50 years, advancement came during the next half century under the leadership of Frederick Taft Moses and his son, Harlan Taft Moses. By its 100th anniversary in 1963, Union Mutual had become the second largest writer of homeowners policies in Rhode Island and had added automobile, comprehensive and general liability, multiperil, replacement costs, and excess of loss policies to its writings. The agency force had grown to 700, operating in 30 states and Puerto Rico. Premiums had increased to over $2.5 million, and assets stood at over $3.2 million. Governor John Chafee issued a special citation honoring Union Mutual for its "distinguished service" and "notable achievements."

Dramatic change came four years later. Firemen's Mutual, with which Union Mutual was still affiliated, eliminated personal lines, the primary business of Union Mutual. At the same time, EMCC was looking for a way to enter the New England market. One day in 1967, the door was opened during a conversation between Robb Kelley and Franklin N. Folsom, senior vice president, secretary, and a director of Union Mutual. If Union Mutual changed its affiliation to EMCC, it would have a way to continue, and even expand, its business, and EMCC would have entrée into New England. Within weeks, the two men, along with Union Mutual CEO Harlan Moses and others, worked out details.

In April 1968, EMCC acquired Union Mutual as an affiliate with assets of $4.15 million, surplus of $1.65 million, and annual premiums of over $4 million. Harlan Moses resigned as CEO and became an independent consultant to both organizations. Robb Kelley became chairman, CEO, and treasurer of Union Mutual, and Frank Folsom became president, making him the effective EMCC branch manager. EMCC reinsured its new affiliate and made expanded lines and amounts of coverage available to agents, who were to service all of New England. In 1970, the Providence Branch moved to a new uniform plan building owned by the Springdale

...

Union Mutual logo, 1960.

Employees gathered around President Robb Kelley as he cut the ribbon in front of the newly constructed Providence Branch in 1970.

Franklin N. Folsom, senior vice president, secretary, and a director of Union Mutual, in front of the Providence Branch.

Enterprising Corporation in suburban Warwick and remained there until 2008 when it moved to another new facility.

Charlotte

In 1972, the Charlotte Branch grew out of a general agency founded by an Iowan. During the 1933 Chicago World's Fair, Iowa native Don J. Kelleher worked in the fair's insurance department. Later, Kelleher traveled in various capacities for insurance companies in North Carolina. There he was struck by the need for strong companies with varied expertise. To fill this need, he organized a general agency, Kelleher & Associates, Inc., in Charlotte in 1943, to act between agents and strong, small specialty companies. He staffed it with three people, and his first business for EMCC proved profitable, developing mutual respect between the two organizations. Although most of Kelleher's agents were in North Carolina, the agency also wrote South Carolina Auto Club business for EMCC for a time. Two years after Kelleher opened, Iowa Adjuster Clarence Johnson was sent to Charlotte to open a claims office, housed with Kelleher, and Chicago Safety Engineer Larry Pye joined him a year later. Early in the 1950s, an Accident Prevention and Premium Audit Department was added.

In 1972, EMCC purchased Kelleher & Associates, Inc., and continued operating under their name, with Don Kelleher as manager, until he retired in 1975. The agency was then dissolved, and the office was converted into a fully decentralized branch. Former Kelleher Underwriter and Field Supervisor Robert N. Holden became the first branch manager.

Don J. Kelleher, founder of Kelleher & Associates, which was purchased by EMC in 1972.

Bismarck

The last branch to open in the 1970s was EMCC's first branch subsidiary, Dakota Fire Insurance Company of Bismarck, in 1973. Incorporated as a stock company in 1957, its initial purpose was to enhance North Dakota's economy by bringing back some of the $25 million in fire and casualty premiums being paid annually to out-of-state companies. Dakota Fire opened its doors in 1958 with five employees, over 200 agents, and 1,200

•••

The founders of the Dakota
Fire Insurance Company
of North Dakota, 1957.

IN HONOR OF OUR FOUNDERS

W.E. KELLEY

EDGAR AGNEW

EVAN LIPS

PROSPECTUS

April, 1957

THE DAKOTA FIRE INSURANCE COMPANY
OF NORTH DAKOTA

NORTH DAKOTA'S OWN

Keep Your Insurance Dollars in North Dakota

Because these securities are believed to be exempt from registration, they have not been registered with the Securities & Exchange Commission, but such exemption, if available, does not indicate that the securities have been either approved or disapproved by the Commission or that the Commission has considered the accuracy or completeness of the statements in this communication.

These securities have been registered with the Securities Commissioner of the State of North Dakota. Such filing, however, is not to be construed as approval or disapproval by the Commissioner of the merits of these securities or any other selling literature.

UNDERWRITERS
DAKOTA SECURITIES COMPANY

SECURITIES DEALER REGISTERED AND BONDED WITH THE SECURITIES COMMISSION OF NORTH DAKOTA
Dakota National Bank Building – Bismarck, North Dakota

DR. VJ FISCHER

C.A. WILLIAMS

JOHN W. CARLISLE

RECEIVING COMPANY CHARTER

Organized By North Dakota People
For North Dakota People

EMC Insurance Companies

FIRST POLICY PURCHASED

stockholders. Because the stockholders represented a strong nucleus of potential insurance customers and agents with a vested interest, it began with an operational status most companies do not reach for five years.

During the 1960s, premiums grew to over $2 million, and Dakota Fire was operating at a profit by the end of the decade. Success brought both hostile and friendly attempts to take control of the company through purchase of large blocks of stock, attempts to gain seats on the board of directors, threat of proxy fights, and proposals for merger and stock transfer. The last offer came from EMCC in 1973. EMCC already owned 159,007 shares of stock and, now, made a tender offer to purchase all outstanding 569,144 shares. Dakota Fire accepted EMCC's offer after EMCC indicated there were no plans to merge the two companies.

EMCC gained controlling interest through a $1.7 million stock transfer, and a new board was elected with Robb Kelley as chairman. Dakota Fire Manager Bob J. Jones stayed on as president of Dakota Fire and EMCC branch manager. Dakota Fire assumed responsibility for sales, underwriting, and servicing of all of EMCC's North and South Dakota business, which allowed it to expand its product lines while receiving EMCC's corporate support. Through a series of complicated transactions, EMCC completed its ownership in 1981. Only then was EMCC able to execute a reorganization that made Dakota Fire a wholly owned subsidiary of EMCC's holding company, then called EMCASCO, Inc.

EMCC built its last uniform plan building in 1980 when Dakota Fire relocated across Interstate 94. While the structure was typical, its ownership was unique. The land and improvements were owned by the City of Bismarck, financed through municipal bonds, and leased to Employers Modern Life Company, which sublet the property to Dakota Fire. A 7,000-square-foot addition and major remodeling in 1997 allowed the facility to meet present needs.

Denver

The Denver Branch could trace its history back to 1918 when O. B. "Mac" McKinney opened an agency in his name in Cedar Rapids, Iowa, to write residential fire insurance for Town Mutual Dwelling Insurance Company. He began writing for EMCC in the early 1920s and, by 1928, was one of its strongest producers of auto and casualty business. In 1935, he moved to Denver and opened the McKinney Fire Insurance General Agency, writing for EMCC and four other mutuals. Within two years, the other companies severed their connections with the agency because EMCC had become dominant and was perceived to be getting the best business. McKinney's loyalty was recognized when he was named to the EMCC Board during the Great Proxy Fight of 1937. To service the agency, EMCC established the Denver Claims Office in 1940.

Mac McKinney died in 1943 and left the agency to his wife. When Mrs. McKinney died in 1981, EMCC was able to buy the agency and combine it with the claims office to form the Denver Branch with five employees and Roger L. Ford as branch manager.

...

Bob J. Jones was Dakota Fire manager in 1961 and continued to work for EMC after the purchase of Dakota Fire.

Orange County

August 1981 marked the opening of the Orange County Branch, created to open new territory south of Los Angeles and to establish EMCC as a national company with business from coast to coast. Its initial staff of three was Branch Manager Kent Kochheiser, son of George Kochheiser; Field Supervisor John R. Kelley, nephew of Robb Kelley; and Administrative Assistant Debora Barnhart, daughter of Des Moines Branch Manager Dick Barnhart.

Bringing in family and friends whose qualities were known has been a long and productive company practice. In fact, hundreds of spouses, children, siblings, cousins, in-laws, and friends have worked at all levels within the company over the years.

Alpel Insurance was appointed as the branch's first agency, and business began with a focus on commercial lines. Claims were handled by the Phoenix Branch until Ron Foglesong's arrival. EMCC believed it had something unique to offer California's high volume, low service market in which most business was conducted through large brokers. Midwestern values of providing "high touch" service and establishing long-term, personal relationships with producers was at the heart of its philosophy.

Birmingham

On the last day of 1982, EMCC purchased controlling interest in the American Liberty Insurance Company of Birmingham. The next day it was recognized as an EMCC subsidiary, known in-house as the Birmingham Branch. Owned by four members of the Statesman Group, American Liberty was doing business in Alabama, Florida, Georgia, Louisiana, and Mississippi at the time of the transaction. It had about 300 agents writing premiums of approximately $18 million. American Liberty President and CEO Robert L. "Bob" Stewart was retained as president of American Liberty and Birmingham branch manager.

The Remaining Established Branches

The Milwaukee and Phoenix Branches continued to grow as they implemented the changes that came with decentralization. The British Columbia office also grew until the relationship with the British Columbia Automobile Association was terminated, and EMCC withdrew from Canada in the early 1970s.

The Iowa Branch, which changed its name to Des Moines Branch in 1971 to conform with the practice of naming branches for their metropolitan areas, developed two programs that had great impact on EMCC's expansion. A special risk underwriting unit was created in 1968, and the safety dividend groups were initiated in 1974.

The special risk underwriting unit was unique to the Iowa/Des Moines Branch. It began with John Wesley "Wes" Sticken, who had a 16-year insurance career. He wanted to develop a risk management program to work with large account

EMC CIRCUIT

JANUARY, 1983

DES MOINES

American Liberty Insurance Joins EMC

Employers Mutual Companies has concluded negotiations and agreed to the purchase of American Liberty Insurance Company whose home office is in Birmingham, Alabama.

Written premiums in 1981 for American Liberty were $18,480,000, written in the following states: Florida, Alabama, Louisiana, Mississippi and Georgia.

300 independent agents representing American Liberty Insurance write business in fire, allied lines, homeowners, commercial multi-peril, inland marine, workers' compensation, miscellaneous liability, auto liability, auto physical, surety, and other forms of insurance coverage.

R. L. Stewart is currently president of American Liberty, and he will remain in that position along with his management team.

"We believe this acquisition will plant our foot firmly in the southeast," commented Robb B. Kelley, Chairman of Employers Mutual Companies. "The sun belt has long been an attractive goal for EMC. Experts say much of the future growth in the U.S. will extend along the southern tier of states from Florida to California and we expect to be a part of that growth."

Although American Liberty was a company in the Statesman Group, it should be clearly understood that EMC does not plan to buy any more companies from that group.

We'd like to take this opportunity to welcome American Liberty Insurance Company to EMC.

R. L. Stewart, President, American Liberty Insurance Company.

First impressions are important! The main entrance of American Liberty Insurance in Birmingham.

Meet some new EMC faces. American Liberty employees gather in Birmingham to talk with visiting Home Office representatives.

...

The January 1983 issue of *Circuit* featured an article on EMC's acquisition of American Liberty Insurance.

...

John Wesley "Wes" Sticken
was instrumental in forming
the special risk underwriting
unit in Iowa.

production and unusual risk features
in the city of his choice — Des Moines.

Robb Kelley saw Sticken's potential, and
the two met in Des Moines in early 1968.
They hatched EMCC's special risk underwriting
operation in which Sticken would implement
his dream. Iowa Branch Manager Dick Barnhart
quickly assigned Sticken to work with
Underwriters Wayne Goettsch and Carrol Cline
to develop the program. Risk management was
added when a safety supervisor, four auditors,
six risk improvement men, and one clerk were
moved to the branch in 1969. Until that time,
all safety services in Iowa had been provided
from the Home Office.

The first large account opened in 1973.
Hy-Vee, a Midwest supermarket chain, was
having difficulty getting property insurance
coverage for its large non-sprinklered grocery
warehouse in Chariton. EMCC began working
with them on risk management and was able
to provide coverage by obtaining reinsurance.
The relationship grew as EMCC helped Hy-Vee
develop measures to prevent losses, partnered

in the design of new stores, and provided
the best coverage at the best price available.

Such practices, along with innovations
and productive personnel, secured a number
of large accounts with major Iowa companies
over the years: Lennox Industries, Pella
Rolscreen, Maytag, *Des Moines Register* and
Tribune, Drake University, Casey's General
Stores, Brenton Banks, Anderson-Erickson
Dairy, Weitz Construction Company, Garst
and Thomas Seed Company, Pioneer Hi-Bred
Seed Company, and many others. Similar
accounts would be developed by a few other
branches, but the Des Moines Branch would
remain EMCC's leading writer of large accounts.
When Sticken retired in 1992, the special risk
unit was producing $80 million annually,
more than half of the branch's total premium
of nearly $145 million.

The Des Moines Branch expanded further
in 1973 when it opened a Davenport Claims
Service Office to extend claims service in eastern
Iowa. Today it has grown from its initial adjuster
and secretary to over a dozen employees.

Diversification: Subsidiaries

Along with branch development in the
1960s and 1970s, EMCC's organizational
structure grew as it created and acquired
a number of subsidiaries. No longer a single
company, it began calling itself "Employers
Mutual Companies." That trade name would
be used until January 1, 1993, when the
board took action to change the title to
"EMC Insurance Companies."

Employers Modern Life Company

On January 15, 1961, Robb Kelley wrote a note to himself, "Things to do today — develop a Life Co." If EMCC could not be all things to all people, he reasoned, it could certainly become a "one-stop" facility for offering a complete package of insurance: property, casualty, and life. Provision of life, health, and accident products through a life company would round out EMCC's lines.

Life insurance was the largest private business in the world, and underwriting profit was considered "practically guaranteed." Furthermore, the economy of operations in an all-line company allowed more competitive rates, and the spread of risks through greater diversification enhanced financial soundness. Finally, Kelley thought that the enthusiasm and sales power of a life program would "rub off on the fire and casualty operation." Twenty-four of the top 25 property and casualty (P&C) groups were in the life business, which was a survival measure for many in the face of fierce competition.

Kelley did not accomplish his goal in one day. In fact, serious discussions about organizing a life company did not begin for over a year, and organization was not authorized until June 1962. After that, matters moved quickly. Employers Life Company was incorporated in August. Owned by EMCC, which invested an initial $1 million for capital and surplus, it was housed in the Home Office. License to do business was obtained at the beginning of 1963, and the operation began "very cautiously," using Iowa as a pilot program.

Robb Kelley's memo pad with the note about forming a life company.

Edward W. Bird, first director of agencies, Employers Modern Life Company.

Education about the new line and selling the program began immediately through in-house publications and presentations at meetings.

Kelley was named president; John W. Gunn, chairman and treasurer; and John F. Hynes, honorary chairman. Edward W. Bird, a highly decorated World War II Infantry veteran who had eight years of management experience with other life companies, was hired as director of agencies, with responsibility for sales and developing the company. John E. "Jack" Carlson, who had prior underwriting experience, became director of life services with responsibility for new business, underwriting, issuing policies, policyowner service, and other functions.

Carlson purchased the first policy, a "Junior Estate Builder" insuring the life of his son. Nicknamed the "Jumping Juvenile," it was a policy for children aged 0-14, that would quintuple in face value and remain in force until age 100. Other policies offered were a homeowners term life and the "Challenger," a whole life policy with a $25,000 minimum face value. Until 1966, only nonparticipating policies were offered in which insureds did not receive dividends because they did not participate in the company's underwriting and investment success or failure. Their premiums, death benefits, and cash surrender values were determined when the policies were set up.

In 1964 the name was changed to Employers Modern Life Company (EML) to avoid confusion with companies that had similar names and to show a fresh and creative approach to marketing by using the word "modern." Challengers said a P&C agency force was not equipped to write life products. Undaunted, Bird appointed salaried life managers to the branches to help P&C agencies develop marketing programs for life products. The life managers encouraged professional development through training courses, meetings, seminars, and earning LUTC (Life Underwriters Training Course) and CLU (Certified Life Underwriter) designations, which gave both knowledge and status.

In 1964, EML was licensed to do business in South Dakota, Nebraska, Arkansas, and

Illinois, as well as Iowa. Six years later, it was operating in 28 states with 37 employees, and it would eventually be licensed in 48 states, working with 2,400 agencies. The number of products also kept increasing. Among them were an annuity for Koegh plans and participating policies, which paid the first dividends a year after being introduced. Although pension planning products and partnering with mutual and annuity funds were most helpful to premium growth, the best sales results came from two other marketing programs. Bank marketing allowed bank presidents to endorse life policies for their customers. Payroll deduction marketing used an employee advisory service, inaugurated in 1969, to inform employees about the benefits of paying premiums through payroll deductions and how their benefits might be supplemented.

The most crucial issue, as EMC entered the 1970s, was that surplus was not increasing in proportion to the rapid growth. Additional capital was needed to support further growth. In 1971, Robb Kelley proposed a merger with National Travelers Life Company in which he would handle casualty insurance, and National Travelers' President and CEO Virgil J. Nutt would handle life. But no action resulted, and consequently EMCC invested another $1 million in EML, bringing its total investment to $3 million.

To help manage growth, Loren D. Littrell was named EML marketing manager in 1973. Drawing on his wide range of life marketing and management experience at EML and other companies, he organized an EML Home Office Marketing Department that had oversight

The new name and logo
for the life company, 1964.

of the branch life managers and seven regional life managers. Efficiency was also added by installation of EML's first computer system, used for paying dividends and processing retirement plans and endowment policies.

The 1970s concluded with a change in management. In 1978, Philadelphia Branch Manager John W. Button, who held CLU and FLMI (Fellow, Life Management Institute) designations, transferred to Des Moines to serve as Ed Bird's executive assistant and vice president of EML. Two years later, Bird retired, and Button became COO, and then president and COO in 1982.

EMC Premium Services Company

Premium Finance Company, incorporated in 1972, was a wholly owned subsidiary of EMCC. It provided premium financing plans to insureds — both individuals and companies — at interest rates preferable to the high commercial rates of that time. All policies written for companies having an A. M. Best rating of "B" or better were eligible for installment payment plans, and terms could be tailored to the needs of each client. By early 1974, the company was operating in all but six states and, in April it was renamed EMC Premium Services Company.

In 1975, Patricia E. Spowart (Meyer by marriage in 1978), a former supervisor in Account Services and Office Services, was named manager. When she took charge, more than 2,000 agreements with total premium value of nearly $2.4 million had been processed, and the milestone of $1 million on loan was reached within several months. Five years later,

premiums financed totaled over $5.6 million, even though the number of accounts had not increased significantly.

EMC Underwriters, Ltd.

"Abnormal business is normal for us!" commented former Home Office Property Underwriting Manager Robert J. "Bob" Ruby after he transferred to president of EMC Underwriters, Ltd. in 1980. Although his work had been with EMCC's standard lines, he shared a fascination for uncommon coverages with Robb Kelley. The merging of these two men's enthusiasms resulted in incorporation of EMC Underwriters, Ltd., in 1975, and business formally began the next year.

Until that time, EMCC had been primarily a standard lines, or admitted, carrier. This meant that wherever it did business it was licensed by the state department of insurance, was bound by rate and form regulations, and was required to contribute to the state guarantee fund that was used to pay claims of insolvent carriers. As property underwriting manager, Ruby had made some forays outside the box and began acting as an agent to place unusual business with other companies.

At the same time, Kelley had become interested in "markets of the world." Next in line to become president of the National Society of CPCU, he was intrigued by the Society's engagement with the excess and surplus lines market. Although under the oversight of state insurance departments, excess and surplus (E&S), or nonadmitted, carriers were exempt from the licensing, rate and form regulations, and contributions to guarantee funds required

...

John W. Button served as executive assistant and vice president of Employers Modern Life Company before becoming COO and then president and COO in 1982.

...

Patricia E. Spowart was named manager of the Premium Finance Company in 1975.

...

Above: Robert J. "Bob" Ruby was named president of EMC Underwriters in 1980.

Right: Commemorative button from Pope John Paul II's visit to Des Moines on October 4, 1979.

for standard line carriers. Thus, they had flexibility to provide coverage to those who had one-of-a-kind risks or who could not meet standard guidelines for qualification such as age, location, or loss history. In exchange for entrée into an alternative market, additional capacity, and innovative underwriting opportunities, E&S carriers were restricted from writing standard business, were not protected by state guarantee funds, and paid higher taxes.

Building on what Ruby had begun rather informally, Kelley and Ruby worked with Underwriting Manager M. O. Cooper to develop a "facility" to handle E&S business: EMC Underwriters, Ltd. It would serve as both a broker and managing general agent for E&S business, using the newly acquired Dakota Fire Insurance Company of Bismarck as its nonadmitted carrier, reinsured by EMCC.

The purpose of the new company was to improve opportunities for agents in EMCC's network and to relieve pressure on EMCC underwriters by using other companies, such as Lloyd's of London, to carry risks not ordinarily written by EMCC. The new company was not intended to set the world on fire. Kelley warned that it should be a bootstrap operation, built step-by-step and financed by commissions. Staff time to develop the company was to be EMCC's investment. Three people, reporting to Cooper, composed the initial staff: Ruby, Carole Gudehus, who handled accounting, and Ron D. Hallenbeck, who handled underwriting and brokering.

At the end of the first year, EMC Underwriters operations had expanded to a nucleus of Midwestern states, reached to Texas and Rhode Island, and were producing over $1 million of business. In 1978, an "amazing volume of surplus lines" was reported, and premium growth was well above expectations. Risks written included a big-frame birdhouse for parakeets, worm farms, a manure drying plant, pumpkin festivals, a model of Big Foot, and a fishing Hovercraft. Seven different policies, managed by Carole Gudehus Hallenbeck, covered Pope John Paul II's visit to Des Moines in October 1979, among them physical damage on the portable restrooms, event cancellation (no show), and premises liability coverage. Agents were encouraged to write special events liability, such as town Fourth of July celebrations; specified substandard classes; and personal lines, such as jewelry and furs. By 1980, Ruby was named president of EMC Underwriters, Ltd., and the subsidiary came of age.

EMC Risk Services, Inc.

EMC Risk Services, Inc. was formed in 1981 to handle third-party administrator (TPA) accounts. These were arrangements with large companies that were self-insured or had very large deductibles and outsourced administration of their insurance programs. The TPA could manage claims and provide other services, either within its own operation or by utilizing various EMCC functions such as risk management, audits for cost containment, medical management, or additional insurance coverage.

EMC Reinsurance Company

EMCC had used reinsurance since its origin to protect its surplus, ensure funds for payment of claims, and increase capacity to write business. Throughout the company's first half century, treaties were negotiated with reinsurers by the president and top management as needs arose. Payment of ceded premiums and claims collections were accounting functions. This informality was possible because policy limits were low and severe losses were infrequent. During the presidencies of John W. Gunn and John F. Hynes in the 1940s and 1950s, the addition of new lines made business more diverse and complex, particularly as legislation allowed companies to write both casualty and property insurance. Concomitantly, reinsurance needs became more sophisticated.

EMCC was among companies that began asking, "With all the ceded premium going out the door, why shouldn't we let some assumed business come in?" The relationship with Druggists Mutual, as well as membership in risk pools and the Mutual Reinsurance Bureau in the 1950s, had opened the door. But, like other companies, EMCC had little capacity to reinsure entire blocks of other companies' business. Action began with moving some reinsurance responsibilities from top management to staff in 1966. Fred DuBois was transferred from the Property Division to serve as manager of reinsurance activities for EMCC and EMCASCO Insurance Company, as well as reinsurance consultant to Employers Modern Life. Already, his ceded reinsurance acumen had been utilized at

EMCC as he negotiated reinsurance treaties related to property risks.

As reinsurance manager, DuBois originated EMCC's Reinsurance Assumed Department and worked with colleagues from eastern reinsurance brokerage firms with which EMCC had strong ceded relationships. Focusing on property reinsurance offerings, DuBois established a particularly long and warm relationship with Towers, Perrin, Forster & Crosby in Philadelphia. With them, he initially wrote 35 to 40 retrocessional cases in which EMCC reinsured reinsurance risks. Thus, the company's share in any given risk was small and several layers removed from the primary risk. The result was minimal losses, even though risks extended as far as Australia and Africa.

Two years into this activity, the Iowa legislature passed the Iowa Basic Property Insurance and Placement Program, implemented through the FAIR (Fair Access to Insurance Requirements) plan, to provide affordable insurance to owners and tenants in high-risk areas. In 1969, DuBois was given "loaned executive" status by EMCC to manage the plan and remained there until 1974. Thereafter, he became EMCC's first "historian in residence" and compiled a body of materials that eventually helped inform this narrative.

Assistant Vice President Dick Haskins replaced DuBois as manager of Assumed Reinsurance, while retaining his position as manager of the Surety Bond Department. For a decade, he continued the modest assumed business, keeping it loss free in a soft market. Haskins and Underwriting Vice President

M. O. Cooper worked together as "point men" on ceded reinsurance. Their work convinced them that a broker-placed program was superior to a single reinsurer because it spread risks among a number of companies. Their consultation with department heads in the later 1970s led to gradual formation of a Reinsurance Ceded Committee, composed of executives from Underwriting, Actuary, Accounting, Claims, and Reinsurance.

Then, in 1980, at management's request, Haskins conducted a survey to determine why companies that wrote assumed reinsurance were incorporating separate reinsurance companies. The reason, he discovered, was to create visibility in the reinsurance marketplace. Because EMCC's assumed business was profitable, President Robb Kelley deemed it advisable to create a separate reinsurance company as another subsidiary profit center

under the EMCC umbrella. "It's time to really get into the reinsurance business. Let's incorporate," he said. So they did — in 1981, as EMC Reinsurance Company (EMC Re).

EMCC capitalized the new company with a $6 million investment. Haskins was named president and chief operating officer where he remained until his retirement in May 1992. He was succeeded as surety manager by David L Hixenbaugh, who had served in bond underwriting and supervisory positions at the Home Office and Chicago Branch since 1974.

EMC Insurance Group Inc.

Formation of a downstream holding company had begun with EMCC's desire to file a consolidated tax return with three of its wholly owned subsidiaries — Kelleher and Associates, Inc.; EMCASCO Insurance Company; and

EEMSEE Corporation, created in 1969 as a vehicle for financing construction of the new Home Office building. The law, however, required a parent company to be part of the filing and, as a mutual, EMCC was not eligible to file a consolidated return. EMCC's executive committee approved a solution in 1972 — create a holding company between EMCC and the subsidiaries. The holding company would own the stock of the subsidiaries and could file a consolidated return with them, and EMCC would own the stock of the holding company.

Creation of what eventually became EMC Insurance Group Inc. was an eight-year-long tangle of complicated legal maneuvers handled by EMCC General Counsel W. Z. Proctor, with Robert E. Drey and Kent M. Forney from the Bradshaw law firm. It involved formation of a number of companies, dissolution of some, and stock transfers within the group. The names EEMSEE Financial Corporation, EEMSEE Service Corporation, Dakota, Inc., Bismarck, Inc., and EMCASCO, Inc. came and went.

As the organizing process progressed, the purpose evolved with changing needs. In 1974 and 1975, there were significant net underwriting losses, and surplus dropped. Although there was only a minimal under-writing loss in 1976 and the surplus turned back up, the need for capital overshadowed the simple desire to file a consolidated tax return. The primary purpose for the holding company now became to gain access to equity markets where capital could be raised through the sale of stock. EMCC could add this capital to its consolidated surplus, allowing acquisition of other companies or businesses and making

it unnecessary to withdraw from states, as it had done in Arkansas in 1966. It further allowed employees to participate in the benefits and growth of the company through stock ownership.

The articles of incorporation for EMC Insurance Group Inc. were filed on November 19, 1974. New responsibilities came with its formation. For example, independent directors, representative of the public stockholders, were named to its board. Records had to be maintained in generally accepted accounting principles (GAAP), required by the Securities and Exchange Commission for publicly traded companies, in addition to the statutory accounting used by insurance companies.

A prospectus was drafted, and a road show to potential investors in over ten U.S. cities culminated with an initial public stock offering on February 4, 1982. Four hundred thousand shares of common stock were issued over-the-counter on the New York Stock Exchange at $8.00 per share, and EMCC retained 92% of the total shares. Of these, 500,000 shares at $1.00 par value were reserved for a stock option plan for EMCC officers and key employees. The investment banking firm of Drexel Burnham Lambert, Inc., through which EMCC had bought bonds for a number of years, helped manage the stock offering.

The five subsidiaries held by EMC Insurance Group Inc. at its formation were EMCASCO Insurance Company, Illinois EMCASCO Insurance Company (Chicago Branch), Dakota Fire Insurance Company (Bismarck Branch), Employers Modern Life Company, and EMC Reinsurance Company. ▪

The COOPERATOR

In the Interests of Agents of the EMPLOYERS MUTUAL Companies

EMPLOYERS MUTUAL CASUALTY CO. • EMCASCO INSURANCE CO. • EMPLOYERS MODERN LIFE CO. • DES MOINES, IOWA

JULY - AUGUST, 1964

EMC Completes Marketing Clinic Series

The marketing clinic held July 20 in Des Moines for the Iowa Branch Office marked the final in a series of 14 branch office and general agency marketing clinics for 1964. A Home Office staff marketing team conducting the clinics was composed of President Robb B. Kelley, Executive Vice-President M. J. Wilkinson, Vice-President and Secretary D. B. Southern, Underwriting Vice-President R. J. Lemley, Underwriting Vice-President F. M. DuBois, Claims Vice-President T. X. Wright, Marketing Assistant Vice-President George Kochheiser, and John Hargett, Payroll Audit Supervisor.

In addition to the Iowa Branch meeting, the group traveled 10,700 miles between February and June, holding clinics in the Milwaukee, Omaha, Lansing, Minneapolis, Wichita, Chicago, Kansas City, and Philadelphia Branch Offices. Meetings were also conducted with general agencies and EMC service offices at Nelson and Kent, Dallas, Tex.; Lewis and Norwood, Little Rock, Ark.; Southern Underwriters, Inc., Jackson, Miss.; Kelleher and Associates, Inc., Charlotte, N. C., and McKinney Fire Insurance General Agency, Denver, Colo.

The purpose of these meetings was to analyze and discuss marketing and service problems and opportunities in the specific territories serviced by these offices. Round-table discussions were conducted with branch and general agency employees on fire, casualty, multiple-line underwriting, production, and claim service in each territory to assist these offices in better meeting the needs of EMC agents and attaining their EMC marketing goals for 1964.

In addition to the round-table discussions, a noon luncheon honored the ladies employed by our branch offices and general agencies. President Robb Kelley spoke at these luncheons, stressing the importance of service as the principal reason for which agents select their preferred companies. He emphasized that prompt and accurate response to agents' requests is the most important responsibility of all EMC employees.

In Little Rock, Jackson, Charlotte, and Denver, workshops on SMP underwriting, rating and selling were conducted jointly by EMC and general agency personnel for some 158 local EMC agents. The clinics developed many suggestions and ideas, as well as exchanges of information which will be of value in expanding EMC service and facilities throughout the country. The opportunity to discuss specific regional problems with the men responsible for EMC operations in each locality proved to be of distinct value.

EMC and general agency personnel meet with local agents in Arkansas clinic at Little Rock.

Home Office staff meets with branch personnel at Omaha branch clinic.

Part 2. "MODERN METHODS" ON A SOLID FOUNDATION

The Keystone: EMCC's Agents

When Superintendent of Agents and future President Robb Kelley observed his 20th anniversary with EMCC in 1959, he commented that he had seen the industry move from a "rather serene, slow-moving, tradition-bound business to a dynamic mutual operation, moving more and more to mass merchandising techniques." He believed that the next ten years would witness "a change in the American agency system to more streamlined operations, where the independent agent, though here to stay, will have to accept modern methods or face a declining operation." He further predicted that "companies that don't coordinate their modernization with the times will be curtailed in operations, and may even face merger or liquidation." Yet he was confident that "regardless of the intense competition," EMCC had a sound operation and was "moving to meet and overcome pressures that are behind the dynamic changes now occurring." History proved him prescient.

EMCC never wavered in its support of the American, or independent, agency system as the best way to serve the policyholder. It was the keystone of EMCC's regional distribution in developing the branches as separate profit centers. Agents were linked to the branches and the Home Office by the field staff, who encouraged mutual cooperation. During the 1960s and 1970s, field supervisors and Home Office staff received agents' feedback, suggestions, and requests, and they expanded on the sales service to agents that began in the 1940s. In addition to daily field supervision, EMCC staff held instructional, planning, and motivational events for agents in the branches, regions, and Home Office to deal with marketing objectives, production goals, new and improved products, and lines to be emphasized.

One example of field outreach was a series of marketing clinics held in 1964 when a group of Home Office personnel traveled 10,700 miles to conduct clinics in 14 locations. Round-table discussions explored specific marketing and service problems and opportunities in each territory. Many of the suggestions and ideas were put to use to expand EMCC's service and facilities throughout the country. Such was the success that, five years later, EMCC's Policy Committee, composed of top officers, conducted a similar venture. They spent two days at each of the branches. One day was a working session with branch staff. The other was a workshop for agents in which they dealt with technical aspects of commercial insurance.

In Des Moines, the first annual Commercial Lines School for agents was held at Drake University in 1965. Attended by approximately 50 agents, the week-long event was led by EMCC staff people and augmented by speakers from leading companies in various fields — accident and health, marine and inland marine, excess and surplus, and reinsurance. Younger agents, whose primary experience was in personal

Attendees at the first
Annual Commercial Lines
School for agents held
at Drake University in
Des Moines, Iowa, 1965.

lines, were targeted in the hope that they would develop commercial books of business for EMCC.

The first schools emphasized EMCC's all-lines capacity and its need to build the commercial book of business. Over the years, participants toured area industries to learn risk improvement and environmental safety techniques. They donned firemen's gear and used the latest equipment and techniques to beat down fires deliberately set in old buildings. They became familiar with the Home Office and enjoyed the night life of Des Moines. The week was capped off with a banquet and presentation of diplomas. The schools eventually became biannual and then evolved into sales conferences, but the same spirit of camaraderie and loyalty remains.

Another service was granting scholarships to an annual three-week insurance school sponsored by the National Association of

Mutual Insurance Agents (NAMIA) at Oberlin College in Ohio. It covered the full range of property and casualty insurance theory and practice. Beginning in 1964, eight years after the school was organized, EMCC sent some of its most promising agents from all over the country to the school. EMCC claimed the honor of having one of its own, Fred Schiek, on the faculty in 1977.

To enhance their ability to serve agents, field supervisors and other branch personnel were active participants and officers in 1752 Clubs, named for the founding date of America's first viable insurance company, Benjamin Franklin's Philadelphia Contributionship. Organized nationally at the 1935 National Association of Mutual Insurance Companies (NAMIC) convention in Des Moines, these statewide clubs, some known as "Sparks Clubs," were formed across the country to provide ongoing insurance education.

Left: A fire prevention display by EMC won first in its division in a city competition for Fire Prevention Week in 1972.

Right: Fire prevention for policyholders has been an ongoing focus for EMC.

Below: 1976 fire school.

Employers Mutual CO-OPERATOR
In the Interests of Agents of EMPLOYERS MUTUAL CASUALTY COMPANY of Des Moines

FEBRUARY · 1962 GE

22 WAYS
Your General Agency Field Man Can
HELP YOU

1. **He is a part of your agency — on your staff ready to work for you.** You pay him no salary, commission or expenses.

2. **He is a salesman and ready to make calls with you.** Your fieldman is out every day and keeps sharp by selling. He knows that nothing happens in the insurance business until a policy is sold.

3. **He is a survey man.** By working with EMC special survey forms, he can help you get good accounts, profitable to you and the company. Policies can be put up in EMC's attractive Commercial Insurance Protection package binder.

4. **He is a sales consultant in the practical sense.** He calls on many successful agents and has figured out how they tick. Where there is no disclosing of agency secrets, he can pass on to you practical down-to-earth ideas.

5. **He can analyze your competition.** For example, suppose you are up against a well-known direct writer in the hardware and implement field. They have quoted low rates for a Garage Liability policy. It looks as if the buyer is let-

(Continued on page 4)

(Continued on page 4)

•••

Co-Operator printed information and sales tips of interest to agents.

twenty national and agent-oriented magazines in 1969. A 90-day campaign, directed by George Kochheiser in 1973, filled billboards, newspapers, and the air with the theme, "When You've Got Misery, You'll Love Our Company." Sales were also promoted through incentives. For example, a President's Production Club was introduced in late 1961 to increase premium volume through competition. Each dollar sold by an agent was a vote for his field supervisor.

Probably the most popular incentive was kicked off by EMCC's 50th anniversary "Sellebration" in 1961. Agents set their own goals and earned points for new business for a grand total of $2.3 million in premiums. Prizes, based on number of points, were chosen from about 2,000 listed in a catalog of awards. Two hundred thirty-five points was enough to win a prize, but an autumn haze mink stole by Annis required 95,000 points. More common were items like a Victor 21-inch color television or various kinds of fishing reels. The most

Sales tips continued to be provided in the *Co-Operator*, and more assistance was given for advertising to the general public. In 1961, a flip-top projector with a film and accompanying record about homeowners insurance, was given to agents for client viewing. Promotion of "Mutual Insurance Week" was a highlight sponsored by NAMIC in 1964. At the urging of agents, ads began to be placed in about

When you've got misery, you'll love our company.

EMC

Employers Mutual Companies

50th Anniversary Trip and Prize Sellebration a $2,000,000 SUCCESS

All indications point to EMC agents having written over $2,000,000 in premiums in new business in lines other than Automobile. This figure includes EMCASCO Insurance Company new business not transferred from EMC. We believe many agents will be sharing handsomely in the 50th Anniversary when all the prize point checks are issued and cashed for prizes. A group of happy agents and their wives will be arriving in Nassau November 30 for six days of carefree vacation in the beautiful Bahamas.

The final calculations of over 8,000,000 points are now being made in the Home Office. Eligible business written before the July 31 deadline and effective that date or earlier is still in process.

Fire policies must be stamped by the rating bureaus by August 15. Cancellations of policies are to be deducted if a cancellation is received any time up to September 30. Agents' accounts must be checked to make sure they are paid up to date.

This means the final prize point checks will not be mailed until some time after the middle of October. This should explain why you have no prize point checks in your possession for points earned in July. It is a huge job clearing and balancing out over eight million points. We hope all agents will understand that EMC's staff aims to expedite this job as fast and accurately as possible.

EMPLOYERS MUTUAL CASUALTY COMPANY
50 years of SERVICE 1911-1961

coveted prize, for 60,000 points, was five days and six nights at the British Colonial Hotel in Nassau. The trip was touted as "a memorable holiday with other successful EMC agents" and "a grand opportunity to give your wife that glamorous vacation she has always wanted."

In Nassau, winning agents from towns of 2,600 to 16,000 joined with those from large cities to enjoy deep-sea fishing, golfing, swimming, shopping, dancing to calypso music, doing the limbo, sightseeing by boat and car, and just plain sitting in the sun. Since then, sales award trips have been an annual event — to numerous sites in Europe, Canada, the Caribbean, Mexico, South America, and the states of Hawaii and Alaska.

...

EMC entered into the special multiperil field in the early 1960s with policies for retail stores.

During the 1970s, more attention was given to streamlining processes that supported agency work. In 1972, EMCC joined 28 other companies in an Agency-Company Operations Study Project conducted by the National Association of Insurance Agents (NAIA). George Kochheiser led EMCC's participation in finding ways to improve claims reporting and policy transactions.

Two years later, Kochheiser was a founding member of Agency-Company Operations Research Development (ACORD), an organization sponsored by NAIA to permanently continue the streamlining work begun in 1972. A major focus was simplification and standardization of forms, which EMCC encouraged its agents to use as the documents evolved over the years. ACORD also promoted loss reporting by telephone and direct billing.

Audits were a unique service that provided added protection to agencies. Bankruptcies and changes in operations of commercial policyholders, which increased in the 1970s, required policy adjustments within coverage periods. For example, a slump in the residential construction market might cause contractors to enter the commercial market where premiums were higher. Or, the insured might expand into another state with different rates. Or, a change in personnel might throw payroll into a new rate classification. Periodic audits by EMCC could help the insured, the agent, and the company anticipate and prepare for such contingencies. Agents could be informed about what information was

needed from their clients, when "rush billing" was necessary, how state rates differed where companies were doing multistate business, or whether additional premium might be required before the policy expired.

Coupled with the audits was advice to agents to maintain up-front payments, called deposit premiums, at about 80% of the anticipated premium for insureds who had "moving targets." Monitoring for changes and maintaining sufficient premium deposits reduced the potential for unexpected large final payments, which were difficult for policyholders to pay and for agents to collect. Adequate premium deposits reduced carrier losses if insureds went bankrupt, and it was much better to reimburse overpayments or to apply excess deposits to renewals than to have uncollected accounts.

Among the most noteworthy benefits to agents was the agency profit sharing plan initiated by George Kochheiser in the 1970s to reward agents' increasingly strong progress in sales. Total payments increased 51.4% from $952,307 for 605 agents in 1973 to $2,468,396 for 722 agents five years later. Average payment from 1977 to 1978 jumped 43.1% to $3,419. Two years later, 62% of agents received a total of $3,195,856. In 1981, the distribution was $3,219,409, with 197 agents receiving over $5,000 each. Appreciation was mutual, and agents recognized the program as unique. In 1978, a poll of Iowa agents named EMCC the company that most effectively listened to agents' needs, and the Professional Insurance Agents of Nebraska gave EMCC their "Listening Ear Award" in 1980.

New and Expanding Product Lines

Multiline and Packaging

By the 1960s, the mass market was no longer making strict distinctions between types of insurance. Significant for EMCC, was the introduction of multiline and packaged policies that particularly aided growth of its commercial business. These unified coverages created efficiency, allowed more competitive premiums, and tied agents more closely to the company.

EMCC's entry into this field was a special multiperil (SMP) policy for apartment houses in 1961 and new SMP property and retail store policies the next year. The company also began to "package" different coverages into single accounts under the direction of Multiple Line Underwriter Harry E. Wolters, who had come to EMCC from Iowa Hardware Mutual Insurance Company in 1956.

Reinsurance was often utilized to make possible large coverages in the multiline instruments. One example was a commercial umbrella liability policy for manufacturers and businesses that responded to higher amounts being awarded by juries. Created by Underwriters Jack Roehr and Fred Schiek with Tom Kellogg of General Reinsurance Company, and announced to agents in 1964, it covered excesses beyond the limits of primary policies. By 1965, commercial multiperil was one of EMCC's fastest growing lines.

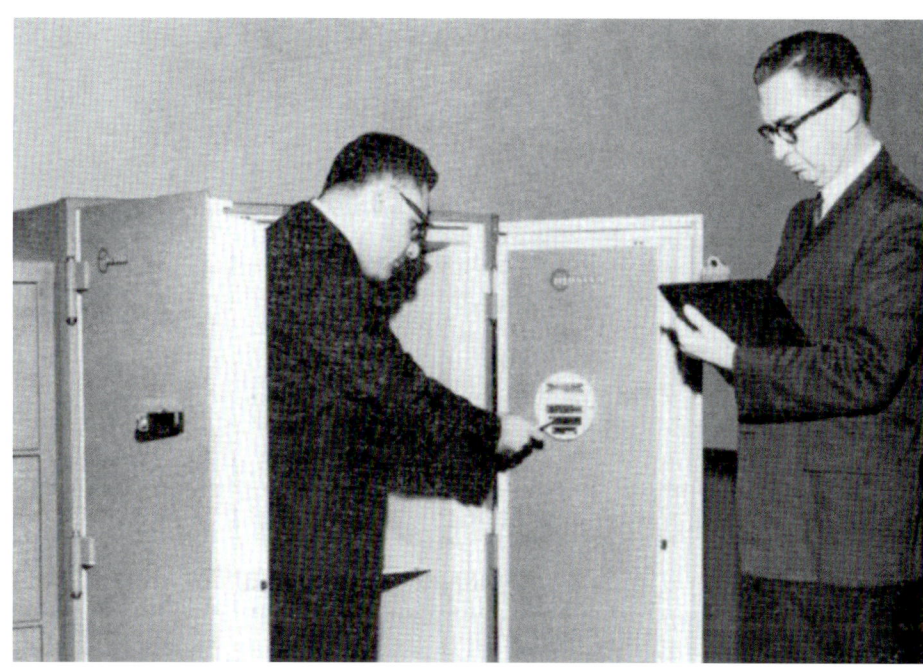

Commercial Lines

EMCC's commercial business covered a variety of urban risks: a 1963 "talk of the town" retail multiperil policy which evolved into the special mercantile program as wholesalers and storekeepers' burglary and robbery, business interruption, and contents coverage were added; a 3-D policy — dishonesty, destruction, disappearance — provided comprehensive crime coverage in 1964; and a business protection policy combined workmen's compensation with commercial coverages in 1972. The extremely popular volunteer fire department policies introduced many years ago received extra promotion following record fire losses in 1967. Another policy combined commercial and institutional risks in 1974. In 1982, a total insurance program package for religious institutions was promoted with the statement, "It's hard to believe, but churches and synagogues can be sued and suffer unnecessary financial loss because of exposure to risks of which they were totally unaware."

■ ■ ■

In 1963, EMC field men worked with agents to rate risks under the special multiperil policy, which included comprehensive crime protection.

Boiler and machinery coverage was also available as a part of the EMC special multiperil package in 1963.

reluctant to cover schools. Positive experience over time allowed expanding that coverage. Beginning in 1965, tuition fees insurance for camps, schools, and colleges that collected tuition fees reimbursed claimants if a loss prevented the institution from operating.

About that time, George Kochheiser spearheaded introduction of errors and omissions coverages for school boards and municipalities, utilizing the underwriting skills of M. O. Cooper and James E. "Jim" Williams and the reinsurance knowledge of Dick Haskins. Williams' previous experience as an underwriter and high school teacher uniquely qualified him for this assignment. He drafted the chief product, naming it the "linebacker" policy because it was a "second line of defense." Its broad definition of wrongful acts, combined with the legal defense and indemnity provided to school board members, made it an especially attractive component of EMCC's overall school offerings.

EMCC gave significant attention to educational institutions, and blanket coverage was introduced in 1960. Entry into the boiler and machinery business two years later took package form under the SMP program and was geared primarily to schools. It was supported by reinsurance contracts with Mutual Boiler and Machinery Company of Waltham, Massachusetts, and then Hartford Steam Boiler after 1974. EMCC also obtained other reinsurance for school coverages through General Reinsurance Corporation in the late 1960s, when most reinsurers had been

Unusual Lines

Another means of expanding product offerings was to associate with other organizations. Through industry contacts, for example, President Robb Kelley met John M. Blackman of the Mutual Marine Office (MMO), head-quartered in New York City. Their conversations led to EMCC becoming a one-sixth member of MMO in 1965. MMO retained sole authority for quotations, binders, authorizations, and policies, and EMCC participated by writing pleasure yachts, commercial hulls, ocean cargo, war risks, and various indemnities. About $968,000 in premiums was produced the first year.

Sea Witch Casts a Deadly Spell

A most dramatic loss occurred June 1, 1973. About midnight, the *Sea Witch*, a container ship, headed out of New York harbor where a tanker, *ESSO Brussels*, lay anchored near the Verrazano-Narrows Bridge, full of highly volatile Nigerian crude oil. When the *Sea Witch* was given the order to turn toward the sea, nothing happened. Steering control had been lost, and the ship was traveling at about 15 knots toward the tanker. Despite alarms and attempts to reverse the engines and drop anchor, the container ship rammed the tanker, piercing three cargo tanks, which released 31,000 barrels of oil. An instantaneous conflagration shot 3,000 yards in front of the vessels, radiated 200 feet out from both ships, and rose 228 feet to scorch the deck of the Verrazano Bridge. Fire-fighting efforts were almost impossible. Malfunctions with the *Brussels'* lifeboats and other complications caused its crew to jump overboard to escape the flames. Thirteen, including the captain, were lost and never found.

On board the now listing *Sea Witch*, aerosol cans of hair spray, shaving cream, and spray paint became lethal projectiles as entire containers caught fire and exploded. Breathing became an ordeal. Heroic efforts by the captain allowed most of the trapped crew to be rescued, but he and two crew members died. By dawn the fire was under control, and the boats were separated and docked. But it would be two weeks before the container ship could be brought back to even keel and all fires were extinguished. MMO's share of the $23 million loss was $246,000, and EMCC's loss was its small proportional share of that. EMCC's ocean marine line remained profitable until its relationship with MMO ended in 1984. ▪

By 1976, the $12 million capacity Mutual Atomic Energy Reinsurance Pool (MAERP), joined by EMCC in 1956, had increased to $300 million capacity. EMCC's participation had grown from $150,000 to $500,000 for any aggregate of losses — a meltdown, nuclear contamination, conventional perils — and Union Mutual (Providence Branch) had joined with a commitment of up to $18,000. Enthusiastic about the line, EMCC emphasized its low risk. An April 1976 *Co-Operator* article pointed out that most scientists agreed a nuclear plant could not blow up like a bomb and that a core meltdown would not be serious if well contained. Furthermore, insurance pools could influence future designs and operations to make plants even safer. Other risks of death to the individual were far greater — one in 4,000 by motor vehicle, one in 100,000 by air travel, and one in 2,500,000 by tornado, compared to one in five billion by nuclear reactor accident.

Then the unexpected occurred. The nuclear generating station on Three Mile Island, near Harrisburg, Pennsylvania, had a partial meltdown on March 28, 1979. About 140,000 people evacuated the area within days, but EMCC's loss was only about $300,000, or 0.2% of the

total. Reaction of the board appears to have been quite matter of fact, and the minutes merely indicate that there was "considerable interest" in the event.

The Oldest Line, A New Name

Workmen's compensation remained an important part of offerings. In the early 1960s, EMCC was the industry leader in written premiums in Iowa, fourth in Nebraska, and fifth in Kansas. Nevertheless, consistent underwriting losses were experienced into the mid-1970s, due primarily to increased benefits and broader coverages instituted by state laws. Death and disability benefits had roughly tripled, and medical benefits had increased nearly 1700% in the first five decades EMCC wrote the line. As the 1960s progressed, economic prosperity meant more hours worked, which gave rise to more on-the-job injuries.

Despite the underwriting losses and lower commissions for workmen's compensation as compared to fire and auto lines, agents were encouraged to keep writing the line as "a genuine opportunity to demonstrate service." Because of the personal nature of the claims, high-quality service could create a uniquely close relationship between agents and injured insureds. Promoting EMCC's safety engineering and premium auditing services to policyholders further emphasized the company's service.

In 1975, the National Council on Compensation Insurance introduced new terminology. "Workmen's" compensation became "workers'" compensation, in recognition that women, as well as men,

were part of the work force. EMCC endorsed the change and instructed agents that all references to "workmen's" in existing policies were to be interpreted as "workers'."

EMCC stressed the advantages of the private system to its agents: protection from lawsuits, more complete benefits, reduction in injuries and claims due to health and safety services, and prompt benefit payments. Particularly highlighted was physical and vocational rehabilitation, which enhanced the well-being of injured workers, reduced costs, and returned many to work. Efficiency was also noted. Between 1939 and 1964, benefits had risen 64%, while the rates paid by employers declined 9%.

The Safety Dividend Group Program

Sometimes new programs began quietly. Such was the case in 1973 when the Lansing Branch developed a new program — EMCC's first safety dividend group — with the Michigan Manufactured Housing, RV, and Campground Association. Opal Barrett and her husband, Clinton, of the Hempstead-Barrett General Agency in Pontiac, Michigan, had approached the branch with the idea of a trade association group program. It would give members special safety services leading to attractive premium rates as well as dividends. Coverage began with workers' compensation for mobile home park workers and gradually expanded into general liability, auto, and other lines for association members, becoming the branch's largest premium source.

The safety dividend group continued until 1990 when Barrett moved it to another carrier

....

Wes Sticken, M. R. Barnhart,
and Phil Jester of the Jester
Agency helped initiate
a school safety dividend
group. (left to right)

that was interested in developing a national safety group program. At that point, the branch opened the writing of manufactured housing coverage to all agents. Their success was proven in 2000 when Barrett returned all of the former safety group policyholders to the Lansing Branch because of its superior service and stability. The policyholders would evolve into a successful target market group that remains active today.

Expansion of the safety dividend group program perhaps grew out of a chance comment. One day in the early 1970s, following lunch with some regulars at the Des Moines Club, Robb Kelley casually mentioned to Philip E. Jester that his agency should do more business with EMCC. Phil Jester, with his son and associate, Robert E., decided to take Kelley's comment seriously. Their decision was aided by some previous nudging from Des Moines Branch Manager Dick Barnhart and Field Supervisor Ed O'Hair. They had urged Jester Agency, as early as 1967, to "avail yourselves of our many insurance services" in order to correct a rather high loss ratio from the auto business. Even they could not have anticipated what was to come.

Jester initiated a safety dividend group program for schools in Iowa similar in concept to the Michigan Manufactured Housing Association program. Through the school and other safety dividend groups added later, Jester's group business brought in millions in premium by 2009. It was an excellent example of cooperation among EMCC's Home Office, branches, and independent agencies to meet emerging needs.

The safety dividend group concept presented an opportunity for both consolidation and expansion of school coverages already in existence. Each school district could get a complete package, tailored to its specific needs. Furthermore, program participants could learn from each other, and there was a multiplier effect in developing safety and risk control measures. After several years, these measures had decreased losses to the point that substantial dividends, not possible with individual accounts, could be paid. As the program grew, the pool of school districts got larger, giving added advantages of economy. But this did not happen overnight.

Coverage was generally difficult to obtain in the "hard" insurance market of the early 1970s. Schools had the added disadvantage of being considered less than desirable risks due to the riots and burning that had taken place in the late 1960s. Jester had been retained by the Iowa Association of School Boards to develop a property and casualty insurance program for Iowa schools.

Jester developed and sent specifications to insurance markets all over the country.

Out of responses from a number of carriers, EMCC's proposal for inaugurating a school safety group with the Iowa Association of School Boards was the one accepted. Jester managed the program through its marketing company, Central Iowa Services, Inc. Implementation was overseen by Iowa Branch Manager Dick Barnhart, who utilized Special Risk Underwriting Supervisor Wes Sticken's sales ability and risk management expertise.

It was not an easy sell in the beginning. Introductory meetings with agents and schools in the spring of 1974 were not always friendly. A number of local agents feared they would lose control of their large school accounts and questioned general agency Jester's pledge to do business with them. Others, who had been strong stock company supporters, were skeptical of doing business with a "small" mutual company from Des Moines. But Jester and EMCC were persistent.

The first policy was issued to the Waukee Community School District in April 1974. Then, EMCC's coverage of a nearly $2 million fire at the Clear Lake Junior High School early in 1975, gave credence to the sales message better than any promotional campaign. The program grew to almost half of Iowa's school districts in the early years and eventually covered nearly 100% of the state's K–12 schools. Also covered were the regional Area Education Agencies created by legislation in 1974 to address resource inequities among various school districts as rural populations shrank.

...

Top: Accident and
sickness programs offered
by EMC in 1965.

Below: Innovation
and technology opened
up opportunities for
new personal line policies,
including the addition
of a credit card and
depositor's forgery
endorsement to the
homeowners policy.

Personal Lines

While EMCC increasingly emphasized commercial lines from the 1960s into the 1980s, innovations in technology were opening opportunities for new personal lines policies. Credit cards appeared in the 1960s, and, in 1965, EMCC added a credit card and depositor's forgery endorsement to the homeowners policy. Solar heating equipment was added in 1978, and the importance of insuring home computers was being stressed by the early 1980s. For those who were vulnerable to claims or who needed high limits for "jumbo lawsuits" in an increasingly litigious society, a personal umbrella liability policy was offered in 1967 to cover excess beyond primary and self-insurance.

For travelers, EMCC introduced its Tourguard policy in 1966. This travel accident and baggage policy provided short-term protection from three to 180 days in amounts from $5,000 to $50,000.

Motorcycle policy was introduced at the 1973 annual meeting with a display of motorcycles in the lobby. Premium grew to $114,000 by June. Soon, the policy was expanded to include other recreational vehicles. Snowmobiles were on display that winter, followed by a week-long display of 30 motorcycles the next spring.

By 1975, premiums had risen to $1.5 million, and the number of motorcycles on display kept rising — 50 in 1976 and 60 in 1977. Mopeds were incorporated into the program in 1978 when there were half a million on the road, and a National Highway Traffic Safety Administration study predicted there would be 2.5 million by 1984.

By 1968, the auto line was almost 60% of EMCC's business. Nationally, motor vehicle travel had increased since 1950 from 456 billion vehicle miles driven annually to 967 billion. Costs and death rates were escalating. Five million people were injured, and 46,000 were killed in auto accidents in 1975. Repair bills doubled between 1970 and 1976, and the cost of replacement parts soared to the equivalent of four times the price of a new automobile. At EMCC's 1973 annual meeting, Robb Kelley had analyzed the automobile insurance situation as "most threatening." He said, "Inflation is not going to go away, and its impact on medical, hospital, and auto repair costs and other elements that enter into insurance claims is continuing to be a dominant influence." Participation with national organizations informed his perspective.

INLAND MARINE BRIEF
CAMPING TRAILER AND EQUIPMENT FLOATER

More and more families are enjoying weekends and vacation camping trips in the 20th century style. This includes a camping trailer that is readily converted into a tent. Most of these are complete with all the necessary camping equipment, such as cooking apparatus, sleeping bags, etc.

The Employers Mutual Companies Camping Trailer and Equipment Floater covers all of these on an "All Risk" basis, anywhere in the Continental United States and Canada. The policy, of course, is subject to the normal exclusions. Sports equipment is excluded from coverage since it is insurable specifically.

The annual rate for this broad coverage is 2½% subject to a $10.00 annual minimum premium. There is a 25% theft of equipment deductible and a $50 deductible applying to collision, landslide and upset of the camping trailer.

Now is the time to obtain a list of purchasers of this equipment from dealers in your area. Expand your list of clientele by soliciting this broad coverage.

INLAND MARINE BRIEF
Camera and Projection Machines

COVERAGE: ALL RISKS, excluding wear and tear, inherent vice. Additionally acquired equipment provision included.

RATES: Amateur "camera bugs" enjoy a lower rate than pros; rates are lower as schedule limit increases. Manual contains details.

ALTHOUGH THE HOMEOWN[ERS] COVERS CAMERAS FOR [MA]NY PERILS, DAMAGE TO [FRA]GILE LENSES AND IN[TRIC]ATE MECHANICAL SYS[TEM]S BY DROPPING IS COV[ERED] ONLY ON THE CAM[ERA] FLOATER. PUT YOUR [CLIE]NTS IN THE EMC PIC[TURE] WITH THIS POLICY OR [BY AD]DING TO HOMEOWN[ERS] MINIMUM PREMIUM [APPLIC]ABLE ONLY ON SEP[ARATE] POLICY.

[IN]LAND MARINE BRIEF
[St]amp and Coin Collection Floater

COVERAGE: ALL RISKS, excluding fading, creasing, denting, mysterious disappearance unless scheduled; theft from unattended auto.

RATES: Manual contains rates. The unattended auto exclusion may be deleted for an additional premium. A rate credit given if some items are kept in fireproof safe.

MORE AND MORE PEOPLE ARE COLLECTING STAMPS AND COINS! AND THE HOMEOWNERS EXTENDS COVER FOR ONLY A LIMITED AMOUNT! PROTECT THE PHILATELISTS AND NUMISMATOLOGISTS! THEY NEED IT!

TOURGUARD

Profiling High Risk Drivers

Attention focused on predicting the risk of young male drivers in the early 1960s, and EMCC gave dividends to those who were accident-free. A Company Advisory Conference of the National Association of Mutual Insurance Agents (NAMIA), chaired by Kelley, researched psychological testing as a means of determining risk for youthful drivers. Results of their five-year study, published in 1966, showed that demographic and driving history variables were better predictors than psychological testing, but accident rates could not be predicted. ▪

The energy crisis of 1973–1974 saw gasoline prices skyrocket from 38.5¢ per gallon to 56¢. As a consequence, public demand rose for lower premium rates. The 1977 annual meeting of the Insurance Services Office (ISO) was addressed by ISO President Daniel J. McNamara. He spoke of the necessity of meeting public demands for affordable pricing in order to keep government interference at a minimum. "We have reached a point where we must, in our own self-interest, seek different ways to meet the demands of the public," he said, pointing out that adjustment was needed in the current system of classifying and rating private passenger automobile insurance.

In the mid-1960s, the creation of uninsured motorist coverage satisfied the public's need for protection from injuries caused by financially irresponsible drivers without absolving them from responsibility for the damage they inflicted. Under compulsory insurance, insurance companies are required to insure all drivers regardless of cause. With uninsured motorist coverage, the insurance company paid damages to accident victims, but could collect the costs from uninsured perpetrators.

No-fault insurance was the next issue, and initially, as with compulsory insurance, it absolved from responsibility the person who caused the accident. EMCC favored a "limited no-fault" plan endorsed in 1969 by the Iowa Insurance Institute. This plan allowed the injured party to be paid immediately, before fault was determined, but the right was retained to sue the party at fault to recover damages. Beginning in late 1974, EMCC joined the insurance industry at large to successfully oppose national no-fault legislation. They believed state control allowed quicker, location-friendly responses to changing conditions.

Further, EMCC supported state guaranteed protection plans, designed to protect motorists against lawsuits and pay injured parties quickly

• • •

Opposite page, clockwise from upper left: Thirty different makes and models of motorcycles were on display for a week in the Home Office lobby.

The TOURGUARD travel insurance kit contained the necessary tools to take advantage of the travel and vacation market.

President Robb B. Kelley climbed aboard one of the 1973 motorcycle models that were on display in the EMC Home Office lobby to promote the new motorcycle insurance program. Board members Blaine A. Briggs (left) and John D. Stoddard (right), joined him.

New personal lines coverage included camping trailers, cameras, and stamp and coin collections.

and equitably. These plans set limits on medical coverage, but allowed coverage options for income loss and payment of various damages. Provisions were similar to no-fault plans. In addition, stricter law enforcement, licensing controls, and more damage-resistant auto design were encouraged.

Ever Stronger Support for Underwriting

At the branches, underwriters gained expertise in writing multiple line policies. They gave particular attention to developmental needs and different types of property and casualty risks as their authority grew under the decentralization plan. In late 1968, under Fred Schiek's coordination, senior staff created a 12-section Branch Underwriting Guide. To monitor use of the guide, Schiek developed a branch underwriting audit system, which also helped determine training needs. He and M. O. Cooper performed the first audit at the Kansas City Branch, and it became a useful tool in developing Home Office-branch relationships and functionality. Because the underwriting audit worked so well, it was later extended to claims.

One program that benefited insureds and was a good "business-getting sales tool" for agents was the premium budget plan. A precursor to EMC Premium Services a decade later, it provided for installment payments on premiums. Established in late 1962, it financed 3,181 policies in the amount of $1,238,885 during the first two years. Sixty percent was

new business. By 1966, the plan had been used over 8,000 times for premium payments of $3.25 million. Besides benefiting insureds, the plan gave agents the benefit of full commissions while EMCC did the bookkeeping. In 1965, a similar successful program called personal accounts payment plan was instituted for EMCASCO clients.

As business grew and became more complex, underwriting staff duties became more specialized. In 1960, Fred DuBois was charged with expanding property underwriting beyond fire and inland marine. By 1966, other underwriters, among them Jack Roehr and Fred Schiek, were being assigned specific lines, grouped into administrative units. That change coincided with Pete Lemley's retirement and his succession by M. O. Cooper as underwriting manager, a position Cooper held until retirement in 1990.

Rates and Filings

Two EMCC functions that supported underwriting — Rates and Filings, and Actuarial — became recognized as departments at midcentury. Rates and Filings was established to help select rate levels, develop coverage forms, and take responsibility for satisfying state insurance department regulatory requirements. Until that time, these matters had been handled largely by the Underwriting Department.

The increased importance given to rates and filings stemmed, in part, from rate competition with direct writers. EMCC began using more specialized and discounted deviated rates that were lower than the stable "manual," or standard, rates traditionally used. This required more interaction with state insurance departments. Where state laws did not allow discounted rates, particularly with workers' compensation, EMCC paid dividends, which gave similar end results.

John L. "Jack" Holtzbauer, a World War II Air Force veteran whose EMCC experience was in accounting and accident prevention engineering, was named the first supervisor of Rates and Filings in 1952. A more distinct department emerged around 1965 when Dick Fraser was named to assist Holtzbauer, while continuing his analyst duties as marketing assistant to George Kochheiser. After Fraser was named market analyst in the Executive Department in 1970, a succession of assistants who had begun as premium audit reviewers followed him in Rates and Filings: Douglas J. Zmolek, who would become personnel director; Carl Evans; and Donald L. Coughennower, a Vietnam Army veteran who joined EMCC in 1969. Holtzbauer retired in 1985 and was succeeded by Coughennower.

The next year, Linda S. Samson, who began as a relief receptionist in 1977, was named assistant manager. She tells how agents' manuals were created when she arrived. The rules pages were typeset by Support Services in tiny eight-point type. Data was coded manually and then keypunched and processed by the Data Processing Department. Rates and Filings staff cut and pasted the listings onto rate pages. At one point, the Supply Department questioned why Rates and Filings requisitioned so much rubber cement.

Actuarial

The second support function was actuarial, which was needed for quick adjusting of rates to meet changing conditions. Its primary responsibility was setting premium rates and determining adequate reserve amounts for claims not yet reported and those that might occur later. One project was creating, with Data Processing, an average reserve system for medical, property damage liability, and physical damage claims against auto and motorcycle policies.

Formalization of actuarial as a separate function began in 1974 with the employment of Actuarial Trainee Lyle DeGarmo, EMCC's first actuary. But the Actuarial Department was not created until 1979 when Ronald W. Jean, a mathematics and physics graduate from the University of Wisconsin and Michigan State University, who had worked at State Farm Mutual Automobile Insurance Company, was hired to organize it. He was joined by Assistant Actuary Samuel P. Colvin, another State Farm alum, who had an actuarial science degree from East Carolina University.

Both men's backgrounds were in personal lines where EMCC was using the most nonstandard rates. Among their first tasks were initiating regular rate reviews and communicating rate change proposals to the branches. They subsequently moved into rate analysis of commercial lines, worked with the Insurance Services Office and National Council of Compensation Insurers to determine deviated rates, created dividend and rating plans for individual and group accounts,

...

Ronald W. Jean joined EMC in 1979 to form the Actuarial Department.

Roger Kilborn of the Risk Improvement Department (right) was instrumental in producing safety videos for EMC.

representatives gradually turned their focus toward reducing policyholders' risks through safety consulting, employee training, and evaluating accident potentials.

The first step was developing a self-inspection plan that used a checklist of plant or office hazards. Then, measures were implemented to eliminate hazards and promote safety procedures. Informational meetings for policyholders provided further guidance. These were augmented in the early 1960s by safety-oriented, black-and-white 16mm movies acquired by the Accident Prevention Department. One was a motivational film featuring the Green Bay Packers' famous coach, Vince Lombardi. By the end of the decade, two men from the Iowa Branch, Premium Audit Manager Fred Thomas and Risk Improvement Representative Roger Kilborn, collaborated in producing the in-house "Lulubelle's Building." A precursor of things to come, it was a manually synchronized tape and slide show on fire safety in which audio beeps indicated when to move to the next slide.

Educating employers about the importance of safety and planning was part of the field representative's job. Employees probably appreciated a break from the grind of the punch press or factory line to see a safety movie, but managers had to evaluate the cost of taking people from their jobs to attend meetings. They had to be convinced that the long-term benefits of increased safety overrode breaks in production. Sometimes the threat of policy termination was required to get management to participate in accident prevention programs.

and developed data bases for loss reserves. By 1982, there were three actuaries and an administrative assistant in the department.

Accident Prevention Matures

Accident Prevention continued to complement underwriting and played a significant role during the 1960s. The growing force of field

Safety inspections underlay educational programs, but EMCC's geographical expansion and increasingly varied and complex policies challenged its inspection capacity. Capacity was enhanced in 1967 by joining Improved Risk Mutuals (IRM), an underwriting and reinsurance pool for large commercial and manufacturing fire and allied risks, that provided engineering and loss prevention services to members. Membership helped EMCC cover its first large accounts and develop loss prevention measures for them. But as member companies, EMCC among them, developed their own capacities, they began to pull out. By 1993, IRM had served its purpose and was dissolved.

Risk Improvement: A New Name, A Developing Department

Two events occurred that caused EMCC to examine its perception of accident prevention and create a formal department. In the mid-1960s, an inspector for another insurance company, who identified himself as a "safety engineer," toured a multistory building construction site and expressed satisfaction with conditions there. A few days later, a "manlift" that carried materials and personnel from one floor to another dropped, causing a fatality. An ensuing lawsuit against the insurance company was based on use of the word "safety" in the inspector's title because the manlift he approved was evidently unsafe.

This situation gave pause to many companies, including EMCC. Perhaps the title "accident prevention" promised more than intended. The expectations of insureds had increased even more rapidly than the expertise of safety engineers. To clarify EMCC's capabilities in safety efforts, Marketing Administrator George Kochheiser changed

Safe From the Fallout

Fear of nuclear holocaust during the Cold War generated a unique project. In the early 1960s, the Seventh Street entrance to the Home Office sported a sign with three yellow triangles in a black circle pointing to a Fallout Shelter in the building's bowels. Able to accommodate 750 people for two weeks with 31,500 rations of emergency food and 2,500 gallons of drinking water, it allowed only 1/1000 of the outside atmosphere's exposure to radiation. Set up by Accident Prevention Manager Ray Sanders and Safety Engineer Fred Thomas, it was carefully planned. The duties of nine committees formed to administer the shelter included monitoring radioactivity, providing first aid, maintaining a log of all happenings, and keeping up morale with news, classes, and religious services. Sanders said the shelter was like buying insurance — you hoped you would never need it but it was good to have "just in case." ▪

Vice President George Kochheiser addressed the opening session of a three-day safety school for EMC employees focused on OSHA regulations and compliance in 1972.

...

Bill Duncan (left) and Norm Anderson review the operations manual of the Dodge appraiser system, while Kathy Chaplin punches information into the Home Office terminal.

the name to "Risk Improvement" in 1965, and the name stuck. After that, the title of "engineer" tended to be reserved for those with engineering credentials, while field staff were generally called "risk improvement representatives."

A second event that impacted EMCC's safety operation was enactment of the Occupational Safety and Health Act in 1970. It created the Occupational Safety and Health Administration (OSHA) to issue and enforce minimum safety and health standards in nearly every workplace in the United States. Prior to its enactment, EMCC had already adopted standards, based on its own experience as well as those published by the American National Standards Institute (ANSI), the National Fire Protection Association (NFPA), and other nationally recognized standards organizations. The company took pride that its operating standards were more stringent than those presented by OSHA.

Nevertheless, implementation of OSHA demanded not only understanding of what the law required but also greater technical knowledge, as workplaces became more and more hi-tech. In 1972, EMCC conducted a three-day safety school, at which an OSHA compliance officer spoke to about 60 employees. An educational kit called "EMC and OSHA, and YOU" was created for agents and policyholders to present provisions of the act, record-keeping requirements, and a checklist for meeting OSHA standards. It explained how EMCC's services could ensure compliance and that OSHA officers were called in only when there were safety violations.

The enactment of OSHA coincided with the retirement of Ray Sanders, who had helped make accident prevention a key EMCC strength. It was an opportune time for the reorganization and expansion of the vision of Robb Kelley and George Kochheiser to turn to risk improvement as a service that would make EMCC stand out. They created a formal Premium Audit and Risk Improvement Department, which operated out of the Home Office.

Once the department was formalized, Lloyd W. "Bill" Duncan was hired as manager in 1972. He brought high professional qualifications gained from earning a civil engineering degree from Montana State College and graduate work in industrial psychology, as well as a career in civil, construction, and safety engineering in Greenland, Texas, and California. His expertise with large industrial risks and loss control, combined with his philosophy and energy, became the base of the department's development. Evidence of his high standards was seen in his encouragement of professionalism. By 1979, five employees, in addition to Duncan, had earned the Certified Safety Professional (CSP) designation created by the Board of Safety Engineers in 1969. Over a dozen more from the department would follow suit in years to come.

Well aware of the burgeoning technical requirements in the field, Duncan set out to hire graduate engineers with special knowledge of fire protection, industrial engineering, and environmental health. When Duncan arrived at EMCC, Technical Services Supervisor Roger Kilborn, who had been assigned responsibility for field staff oversight under Ray Sanders, was the only technical employee in the department. Within six months, Duncan transferred Joseph T. "Joc" Lamb, Des Moines Branch risk improvement representative, to the Home Office as the second technical services supervisor. Both men would have long and innovative careers with EMCC's safety operations.

Next, Duncan created an industrial hygienist position and hired former university instructor William "Bill" Pendgraft to create an industrial hygiene section, often called the Environmental

Health Lab. About 400 square feet of lab space and a training room twice that size were laid out on the second floor of the office building at Seventh and Mulberry Streets. New equipment was ordered and installed, while a nearby steel fire door and freight elevator from the original construction were retained. A year later, in 1974, another former high school and college instructor, Dennis R. Lamport, replaced Pendgraft and was given the title manager of environmental health.

Specialty services were conducted from the Home Office within a 400–500 mile radius until 1979, when hiring and training new branch risk improvement representatives with degrees in safety became the "rule of the day." Roger Kilborn assumed supervision of all risk improvement field representatives.

As the concept of safety risks grew and technological devices were developed, the lab

....

Lloyd W. "Bill" Duncan was head of the Risk Improvement Department for more than 20 years.

...

Bill Pendgraft, industrial hygienist, explained some of the sampling and testing technologies of the new industrial hygiene laboratory to EMC branch managers in 1973.

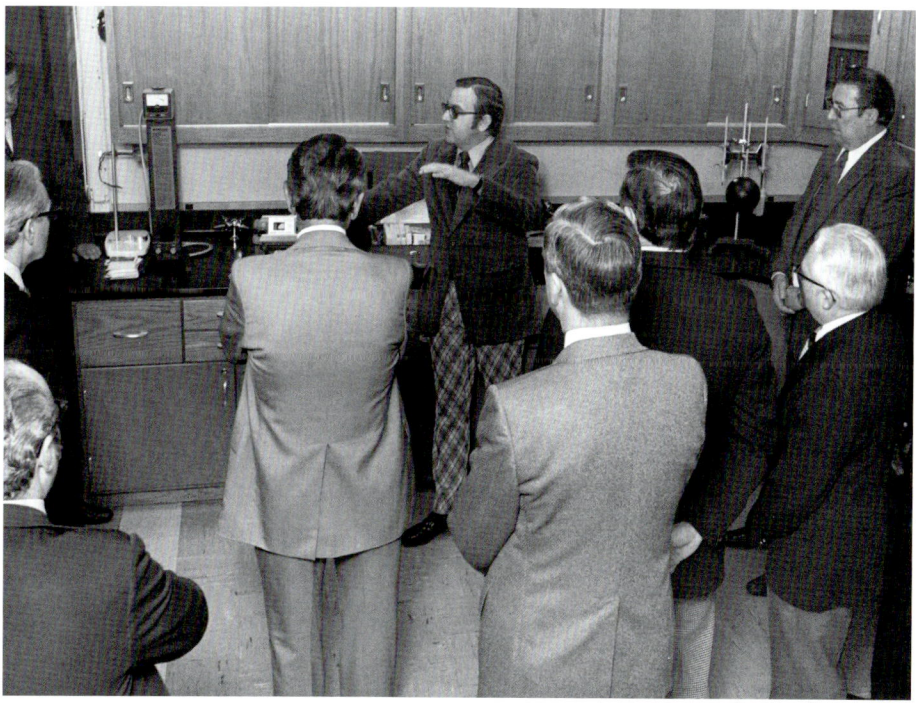

Risk Improvement Department staff
assembled kits to help policyholders
understand the new federal
Occupational Safety and Health Act
in 1972. Susan Amsberry, John Hargett,
Roger Kilborn, Sharon Bohach,
Mary Jo Battleson. (left to right)

expanded its activities to ensure both safety and the regulatory compliance of clients. Air quality was monitored to identify relative amounts of chemical compounds; evaluate particulates such as cotton dust, welding fumes, and silica; and test for gases such as carbon monoxide, methane, oxygen, and hydrogen sulfide. Dennis Lamport began a primitive form of noise monitoring to prevent hearing loss by using no more than a sound level meter and a stop watch. By the early 1980s, a Metrosonics noise dosimeter was used to measure the cumulative effect of noise over time. The data were downloaded on EMCC's first "portable computer," an HP-85, complete with a keyboard, screen, tape drive, and thermal printer. Its "Biorhythms" program was an attention grabber at convention promotional booths, where EMCC introduced noise monitoring as a policyholder service. Prime clients for this service were Lennox Industries, Pella Windows, Lowe Boats and Canoes, and Pioneer Hi-Bred.

As the new department took shape, training was strengthened through Red Cross First Aid courses and schools at the Home Office for fire protection, product liability, and loss control. Technical Services Supervisor Roger Kilborn and Property Underwriting Manager Bob Ruby organized loss control projects. Most exciting were the "house burnings" in which the rate flames spread, temperatures, and carbon monoxide production were recorded. A new portable gas chromatograph detected organic vapors of accelerants, and the effectiveness of smoke alarms and sprinkler systems were tested.

Top: A commercial kitchen deep fat fryer fire extinguishing system demonstrated by Dennis Lamport, EMC environmental health manager. The model was assembled by Roger Kilborn in the late 1970s and was used for training risk improvement representatives, as well as for Fire Prevention Week and ISU Fire Extension training sessions.

Bottom: EMC's first Type I Sound Level Meter with Octave Band Analyzer, used in the 1970s to check noise levels for commercial policyholders.

Home Office Underwriter Bob Ruby talked to school children who came to see EMC's Fire Prevention Week display in the Home Office lobby in 1977. The event also included displays of home fire detectors, home insulation, and professional firefighting equipment.

Throughout the 1970s, education extended to the public. EMCC trained local fire departments and Iowa State University's Fire Extension service. A session on arson investigation was offered at the Iowa State Fire Marshal's office. Safety shows were staged for school children, who received safety-themed coloring books as parting gifts. The spacious two-story lobby in the new office building at 717 Mulberry Street became the site of many meetings, demonstrations, and displays that attracted hundreds. During Fire Prevention Week in the autumns of 1972 through 1974, the company's fire prevention and safety display won the city's top award in the retail-industrial division.

In the late 1970s, Kilborn and Lamport moved beyond slide shows for safety presentations and developed EMCC's first safety video, "On Target," for Lennox Industries.

After the first production, the Environmental Health Lab found the video camcorder useful for a number of policyholder surveys and fire training exercises. Kilborn was named manager of a new audio-visual division in 1979.

Technology, combined with Duncan's vision of loss control services, not only changed the relationship between the field and the Home Office, but it also changed field processes. To help policyholders understand the true value of property they were having insured, replacement cost estimating, rather than current value, was promoted as the best way to determine adequate coverage. The point was made vivid by the Clear Lake Junior High School fire in 1975. Initially, the school's coverage was only 60% of the building's current value, but was increased upon completion of EMCC's review and replacement cost estimate. After the fire occurred a short

■ ■ ■

At the site of the burned-out junior high building in 1975, Clear Lake School Board President Crosby Ingersoll receives a check from EMC's Clear Lake agent Ken Coulter (left) and Des Moines Branch Manager M. R. Barnhart (right). In background: Superintendent Richard Lashier and school board members Don Neuberger, Roger Amosson, and Bob Halford. (left to right)

time later, the school district received over $2 million for the actual cash value of the burned building and construction costs and was able to rebuild the school without loss or extra expense.

Beginning in 1973, field representatives calculated replacement costs using pencils and the Marshall & Swift Manual (the industry standard for information about construction costs based on type of building, quality of construction, location, and depreciation). By 1980, need for the manual ended with introduction of the Dodge Reports cost estimating database system from McGraw-Hill Publishing Company. This system increased accuracy, drastically reduced turn-around time, and required half the field and technical support force.

By 1977, a punched card operation was being utilized for several large accounts.

Also, Systems Engineering Supervisor Norman H. Anderson, who had a background in both nuclear and industrial engineering before joining EMCC in 1974, worked with IBM to develop a commercial lines reporting system (CLRS). It could perform loss analysis for all of the branches. This system was also used in claims management.

Another significant interdepartmental relationship, related to risk improvement, was between the Des Moines Branch's special risk unit and the safety group program. The synergy between Bill Duncan and Wes Sticken lasted until their retirements in the early 1990s. They helped retain good business by making renewal of old accounts desirable and encouraged new accounts, which in turn stimulated development of additional services and set a standard for operations into the future. ■

■ ■ ■

Norman H. Anderson joined the Risk Improvement Department in 1974 and went on to become head of the department.

Some More Fire Risks Insured by EMC

University of Illinois
Champaign, Illinois
Schedule in EMC: $11,336,425

Douglas County Hospital
Omaha, Nebraska
Coverage in EMC: $1,141,600

...apacity for Big Fire Risks

New Assembly and Gymnasium
University of Illinois
Coverage in EMC: $1,375,000

Partial List of Educational and Governmental Schedules

... currently being insured by Employers Mutual Casualty Co., Des Moines

COLORADO ●
School District No. 1, Englewood ......$ 1,957,800
Sheridan School District 496,000

ILLINOIS ●
Augustana College 2,300,000
Belvidere School District 3,439,800
Effingham School District 2,027,490
Rolo Community Unit No. 22 1,869,577
University of Illinois 11,336,425
Marshall Community Schools.......... 2,178,200

INDIANA ●
North Manchester Township........... 1,573,173

IOWA ●
Cedar Rapids School District 6,398,494
Valley Community, Elgin 1,074,100
North Scott Community 1,125,000
Iowa State University 3,792,100
State University of Iowa 1,794,597
Storm Lake School District 1,618,500
City of Spencer...................... 1,878,723

MICHIGAN ●
Berrien County 502,594
Clio School District 1,827,000
City of Detroit 2,591,000
Flint School District 645,897
Grand Blanc School District........... 1,608,500
City of Lapeer 1,976,000
Mt. Morris School District 2,733,864

MINNESOTA ●
City of Duluth 1,994,230
Roseville Ind. School District........... 4,015,200

NEBRASKA ●
Douglas County (Omaha) 4,250,000

PENNSYLVANIA ●
Swathmore College 750,000
City of Pittsburgh 488,300
Logan Township Schools 942,000

WASHINGTON ●
King County School District 4,722,500
University of Washington 819,000

WISCONSIN ●
Campion College 2,084,000
Wood County 1,420,382

Bankers Life Company
Des Moines, Iowa
Coverage in EMC: $2,500,000

Apartment House
Kalamazoo, Michigan
Coverage in EMC: $210,000

Heights Hospital
Houston, Texas
Coverage in EMC: $655,000

Wood County Court House
Wisconsin Rapids, Wisconsin
Coverage in EMC: $1,420,382

...ge in EMC: $198,000

Memorial Union
Iowa State University, Ames
Coverage in EMC: $1,750,000

George Washington High School
Cedar Rapids, Iowa
Coverage in EMC: $1,165,195

Houston Title and Guaranty Co.
Houston, Texas
Coverage in EMC: $198,000

Coverage...

Part 3. ACTION IN THE FIELD, SUPPORT AT HOME BASE

Prompt and Fair Settlement, Imagination and Ingenuity

As large commercial risks became a greater portion of EMCC's business, the potential size of claims grew commensurately. By 1960, for example, many fire accounts were over $1 million. They ranged from business buildings to school and university complexes to hospitals to government facilities. There were numerous school districts in the $1-6 million range. Topping all was the University of Illinois at Champaign at over $11 million.

Even as accounts grew larger, EMCC's commitment to prompt and fair settlement of claims never changed, whatever the line of insurance, however large or small. Adjusters and claims personnel built reputations for timeliness, imagination and ingenuity. The annals of EMCC history abound with examples:

- John Hill, from the Vancouver office, won kudos for his prompt service. The 1968 Vauxhall Viva Sedan of one of his policyholders had been smashed at the airport by a crash-landing jetliner. Hill had a check in the insured's hand before the wreckage was cleared from the area.

- Dale Fronk, a Wichita Branch adjuster from Salina, was assigned a stolen car case shortly after the event. Closing time came before he could finish processing the paperwork, and he went home. But his work had not ended. As he settled back to watch television, it struck him that an unfamiliar car had been parked in front of his house since he left for work that morning. Sure enough, upon examination, it turned out to be the stolen car with $400 worth of carpenter's tools still inside. The insured got his car back the same day it was stolen, and Fronk saved EMCC a $1,300 claim.

- A workers' compensation case involved a 26-year-old man who became quadriplegic from a spinal cord injury. Imaginative settlement benefits created a win-win situation for everyone involved. Believing the man could once again become productive, an EMCC claims manager arranged for him to be treated at the Mayo Clinic in Rochester, Minnesota. There, he regained limited use of his hands and arms. Then, rather than take the usual path to a nursing home, he returned to his home, which was modified with ramps and an enlarged bathroom that could accommodate his wheelchair. Exercise weights and daily care from a visiting nurse were also provided. A physiotherapist prepared him to take a course in bookkeeping so that he could be gainfully employed. The man's spirits were lifted, and he was able to become productive and self-supporting. Without such claims handling, he might have suffered more severely. At the same time, EMCC's future medical costs from the claim were reduced, a factor that contributed to lower premiums for policyholders.

- Some unusual rewards came back to the company from satisfied insureds. A woman in Hutchinson, Kansas, received a check for $187.71 estimated damage to her car. When she paid the bill, it was only $185.66. She immediately returned the $2.05 overpayment to F & M Agency that had written her policy.

- In another case, a man did not act so quickly. In 1963, his car, purchased for $650 the previous week, was totaled, and EMCC paid him $950 book value. For nine years, the "fraud" bothered his conscience. Finally, to make things right, he sent a check for $408 to EMCC — $300 for what was "wrongly received" and $108 for nine years of interest. The check was returned to him, noting that fraud had not been committed and that the amount paid for the car was immaterial to the settlement. "We truly regret," the claims manager wrote, "that this matter has been of concern to you over the years."

Safety Engineer Fred Thomas reacted quickly to the Younkers Department Store fire in the winter of 1962.

On the Spot

One evening in the early winter of 1962, Safety Engineer Fred Thomas unexpectedly put his skills to good use to reduce a fire loss. As he headed home from work, he passed by two burning buildings in the block north of EMCC's Home Office. Looking up at Younkers Department Store across the alley, he noticed two open windows that offered a prime opportunity for the fire to spread, even though the building was protected by fire doors. He quickly notified store officials, but 30 minutes later noticed one of the windows was still open. Gaining entrance into the store, he and an employee got the window shut.

That did not end the problem. The fire was so intense the radiated heat set off Younkers' sprinkler system, endangering merchandise as the water pooled on the floor. Thomas then assisted Younkers employees in moving merchandise out of danger and using squeegees to push water down elevator shafts to be carried away by the shaft drains. The store, for which EMCC insured all contents, was safe, and Thomas's quick thinking and action probably saved EMCC a bundle of money.

The burning buildings and their contents, also insured by EMCC, did not fare as well. Both were totally destroyed, causing EMCC's greatest fire loss to date. Fortunately, Property Underwriting Manager Fred DuBois had reinsured a major portion of the risk, resulting in a low net loss. Thomas gave further credit for loss reduction to the Des Moines Fire Department's "superlative" containment of the fire and careful handling of well-maintained equipment to prevent damage. ▪

Following a 1967 hail storm in Des Moines, Claim Supervisor Wes Hirsch rented a vacant service station in western Des Moines to use as an automobile drive-in claim processing center.

Innovations for Better Service

After T. X. Wright became manager of the Claims Department in 1963, he introduced a number of innovations to improve service. Among them were annuity payments and lump sum settlements in workmen's compensation cases. Concern for insureds was particularly evident in the advance payment program, introduced in 1968 for cases in which expected settlement was delayed. In such cases, repair costs, medical expenses, and ongoing financial obligations caused hardship and nagging uncertainty while injured parties were unable to return to their jobs. Serious injury, prolonged disability, and death increased the economic and psychological distress for victims and their families. The advance payment program provided interim payments for out-of-pocket expenses, advances to pay other obligations, and guarantees to pay future expenses such as medical bills.

EMCC people were always looking for ways to enhance on-the-scene service. A tornado in Minneapolis in 1965 sparked one innovation.

A "storm crew" of agents, adjusters, Home Office and branch personnel immediately set up a temporary claims office in Minneapolis. They worked around the clock inspecting damage, covering buildings with plastic to prevent further damage, and paying claims on the spot. This service would be replicated at various sites. The Iowa Branch, for instance, converted a vacant gas station into a drive-in claims service in 1967 after a hailstorm in Des Moines. In nine days, 190 automobile claims, averaging $213, were processed, along with numerous collision and property damage claims. Agents settled many claims on the spot. From 1970 to 1974, the percentage of these immediate settlements rose from 8.69% to 14.9%.

Efficiencies reduced office support time and costs. Agents recorded statements and other investigative information by telephone. Adjusters used battery-operated dictating units to record claimants' statements, along with their written reports. Major cases, though, still required field adjusters to obtain medical reports, photographs, diagrams, estimates, and verification of facts.

All claims documents had to pass through the Home Office so that the data could be entered into reports for industry associations and statistical bureaus. Processing time was shortened by a new keypunch unit that updated the claims master file nightly, making current information available almost immediately.

Improved working relationships in the branches enhanced the settlement process. The claims manual introduced by T. X. Wright informed everyone of exactly what was

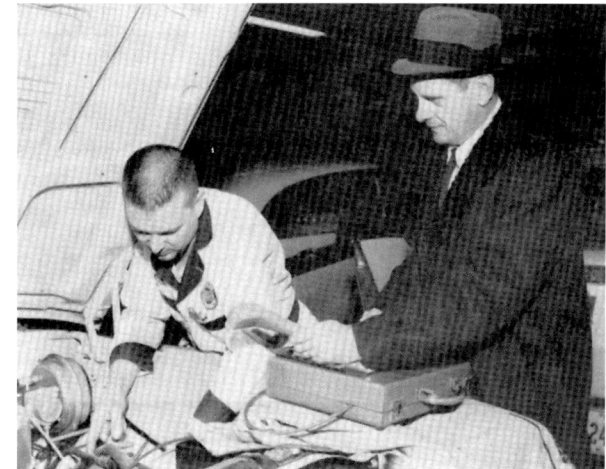

...

EMC Adjuster Hugh Mote took employee statements with portable dictating equipment so the employer did not lose very much time of valuable skilled workers who were paid on an hourly basis.

expected of them, causing work to flow more smoothly. Constant modification of the manual to adapt to changing practices and procedures kept all personnel up-to-date and "on the same page." When serious questions about coverage occurred, staff devoted many hours to intense case law study. Then, if they could not find adequate answers, outside counsel was hired.

Every effort was made to avoid the expense and delays of litigation, and the increasing size and unpredictability of jury awards was further incentive to keep out of court. Even though no-fault and uninsured motorist coverage provided some relief, the best way to prevent litigation was fair and reasonable settlement of all meritorious claims. EMCC earned a broad reputation for adhering to this principle as it tallied a below-average number of lawsuits. Nevertheless, it was sometimes necessary to draw on outside expertise. Most common was defense counsel, but medical specialists, architects, engineers, and photographers were also consulted on various types of claims, especially those made on more complicated multiline policies.

Arbitration

In the 1960s, EMCC began to take advantage of arbitration, which was gaining national popularity as an alternative to litigation. The success of a New York program in reducing litigation, improving inter-company working relationships, and making possible lower premiums resulted in development of similar programs nationwide. By the late 1950s, over 270 companies, EMCC among them, had signed on to a "Nationwide Inter-Company Arbitration Agreement." Instead of filing suit, participating companies submitted their statements and files to three-person arbitration panels in over 90 cities. Hearings were seldom an hour long, expenses were minimal, and decisions were final. Of over 14,000 cases filed for a total of $4.1 million in 1957, over 9,000 were heard and decided, while most of the rest were settled or abandoned without hearing. By the late 1960s, arbitration committees were hearing and closing almost 100,000 cases annually. A succession of administering organizations were finally replaced by the not-for-profit Insurance Arbitration Forums, Inc., created in 1981.

A number of EMCC employees donated their time to this "informal justice" process. First to serve was Hillis Noon, superintendent of claims for EMCC's Eastern Division. During his term from 1962 to 1964, about 560 cases were assigned to committee members who donated their time. Next from EMCC was Forrest Mercer, superintendent of claims, Western Division, who served as an arbitration committee chairman in 1967. That year, 670 cases from 49 companies were heard. Ten arbitrators were appointed from EMCC in 1968; eight participated in 1969 when Iowa Branch Claims Manager Jewell Crouch chaired the Des Moines Committee; and in 1978, EMCC's participation was 15, representing the company's geographical range. All had gained knowledge of what was involved in settling claims by working on the front lines as claims adjusters, supervisors, and/or managers.

Storms and Disasters: Mother Nature's Fury

EMCC is Exposed: 1965

Although EMCC added storm loss exposure when it began writing property insurance in 1955, there was little loss until 1965. That year, President Robb Kelley reported that storms "severely tested" EMCC's claim paying abilities. First came a series of 78 tornadoes that killed 261 people during an 11-hour period on Palm Sunday. Then the tornado that resulted in EMCC's on-the-scene claims office in Minneapolis struck in May. Most devastating was Hurricane Betsy in September, the first hurricane in America to cause over a billion dollars in damages. EMCC was hit by them all.

On Palm Sunday, an F4 tornado, defined as having winds of 207–260 miles per hour, touched down in Clinton County, Iowa, and moved on through southern Wisconsin and northern Illinois, killing ten people in a swath 200 miles wide. Hardest hit was north central and central Indiana, where numerous lethal twisters killed 138 people. Elkhart County alone suffered 62 deaths when hit by F5 winds of 261–318 miles per hour. Fifty-three people were killed in southern Michigan, and 60 died in Ohio, as tornadoes touched down from Toledo to Cleveland. The devastation finally ended in Cuyahoga County, Ohio, 450 miles from Clinton County, Iowa.

EMCC paid its share of claims promptly, and its agents and field staff provided personal support at the scene of the storms. Indiana

Above: Flooding in
the Lower 9th Ward
of New Orleans after
Hurricane Betsy in
September of 1965.

Photo courtesy of NOAA NWS

Left: In one of the
most incredible tornado
photographs ever taken,
monstrous double F4
tornadoes rip through
Indiana, between Goshen
and Elkhart, on Palm
Sunday, April 11, 1965.

Photo by Paul Huffman, courtesy
of NOAA NWS

Field Supervisor Jack R. Scharringhausen sent a moving report to the Home Office: Goshen agent Raymond Sala and his wife did not sleep for 48 hours after the tornadoes struck. They were too busy identifying the deceased, locating family members who had been separated, and setting up a first-aid station to handle overflow from hospitals in four neighboring communities. During the crisis period, this Mennonite couple took time away from their relief duties only to attend the funerals of three close friends.

In Russiaville, Indiana, which was almost totally obliterated, EMCC's Kokomo agent

Virgil Chandler was ushering at evening church services. Just as the electric power went off, outsiders came to the door and reported that tornadoes were approaching. Chandler warned everyone to go to the basement, saving the lives of all but three of the 111 congregants. Businesses on both sides of agent Howard Greenlee's office were destroyed. His windows and door were blown off and the back of his roof caved in, but his file cabinets and desk were untouched. He was able to provide claims service, in addition to working at a disaster center set up in the still intact Lions Club.

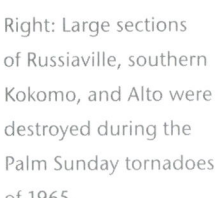

Right: Large sections of Russiaville, southern Kokomo, and Alto were destroyed during the Palm Sunday tornadoes of 1965.

Luckily, the storm skirted EMCC's most concentrated volume areas in Indiana — South Bend, Fort Wayne, and North Manchester.

When Hurricane Betsy hit later that year, 76 people were killed in the Caribbean's Windward Islands and the Bahamas. In the Gulf of Mexico, it destroyed eight oil platforms with winds up to 155 miles per hour. Betsy struck landfall in Florida and Louisiana before traveling up the Mississippi River Valley to Ohio. As it passed over Lake Pontchartrain, the surge breached levees. EMCC's share of the total $715 million claims paid was nearly $27 million for 126,302 claims.

Despite these losses, EMCC showed an underwriting profit before paying dividends to policyholders. Indeed, its surplus increased, in contrast to many companies that experienced significant reductions in their surpluses. In a report to employees, Robb Kelley attributed EMCC's good fortune to the concerted efforts of all. Loyal agents, fieldmen, and underwriters brought in $49 million in premiums on policies that resulted in good loss ratios. Auditors and risk improvement representatives maintained steady vigilance. Accounting, methods,

programming, data processing, and clerical people throughout the company "strove mightily to increase efficiency and quality."

Protection in Action

After 1965, the theme "Protection in Action" became the company's operative watchword. Having learned from experience, EMCC was prepared for a tornado in Topeka, Kansas, in 1966. At the first warning, its catastrophe program was activated. The resident adjuster's office immediately became an around-the-clock control center for the work of five local agencies, 14 extra adjusters, and help from the Wichita Branch. Home Office Disaster Specialist Vic Mickunas hurried to Topeka. Four radio stations broadcast agents' names and telephone numbers in 82 spot announcements that urged insureds to report claims immediately.

After the storm, automobile claims were paid at once, and cars were towed to repair shops. Cash advances were given to homeowners who were assisted in finding temporary shelter and contractors to make repairs. Damaged buildings were covered with plastic to prevent further loss. One claimant wrote, "I am highly pleased with

the expeditious claim adjustment ... I feel your adjuster extended himself beyond his responsibilities ... His analysis was complete, comprehensive, and entirely fair ... These 'extra bits' of service are the things that point out to me the fact that Employers Mutual Casualty is truly a noteworthy company."

In 1967, EMCC's largest single loss to date — $211,000 — occurred when the deadliest tornado of the year damaged Highland Hospital in Belvidere, Illinois. Despite great damage to the premises, injuries to patients were minor. The company presented a check that would rebuild a modern, 80-bed facility.

The next year, a string of deadly tornadoes and hailstorms passed through Charles City, Oelwein, Iowa City, and LeClaire, Iowa. The Iowa Branch immediately established emergency service centers in all four towns, and radio and newspaper announcements informed policyholders how to proceed. Agents used disaster guidelines prepared by EMCC. Additional help was brought in from the Davenport Claims Office; adjusters came from Des Moines, Traer, and Dysart; and a Minnesota claims man helped in Oelwein.

Then Hurricane Camille hit the Mississippi Coast in August 1969. It was the strongest tropical cyclone to strike land ever recorded worldwide. Camille sustained 190 miles per hour winds and 24-foot surge flattened nearly everything along the coast, breaking up many portions of U.S. Highway 90. The Mississippi River flowed backwards for 125 miles and was backed up for an additional 120. Camille caused nearly 300 deaths, devastating floods throughout Appalachia, and $1.42 billion in damages before exiting into the Atlantic Ocean at Virginia Beach, Virginia. Only Betsy, four years earlier, had ever caused as much damage.

Camille was the worst of numerous storms that caused the Jackson Branch to change its underwriting practices. Although most writing was being done in the middle two-thirds of the state, it was primarily for personal lines, which have more storm exposure than commercial lines. When Bill Sandstrum became branch manager in 1975, he successfully turned the emphasis to commercial underwriting. The coast continued to be avoided, and all area south of Highway I-10 was referred to a pool for wind coverage.

■ ■ ■

Left: Wreckage of automobiles and homes showed what happened the night of June 8, 1966, in Topeka, Kansas. Steel beams in the foreground had supported large signs in front of a shopping center.

Right: Victor Mickunas, sent to Topeka from the Home Office, inspected wreckage of a home where the roof and walls were ripped away.

A "Super Outbreak" of tornadoes in 1974
affected Hamilton Mutual Insurance Company
of Cincinnati, which became EMCC's Cincinnati
Branch in 1997. Damage from 148 tornadoes
occurred over 900 square miles encompassed
by Illinois, Alabama, North Carolina, New York,
and Ontario. The deadliest individual tornado,
with winds over 318 miles per hour, killed
34, injured 1,150, and destroyed 1,400 buildings
in Xenia, Ohio. A similar tornado struck about
50 miles southwest in the Cincinnati area.
Hamilton Mutual's losses of $7.5 million
required using its total limit of reinsurance,
and their reinsurer also suffered severe losses.

Five years later, two or three tornados
locked horns and ripped across Wichita Falls
in northern Texas. Within 15 minutes, the
homes of 20,000 of the city's 96,000 residents
were wiped out, and 44 people were killed.
The office and home of the Wichita Falls agent
was damaged before he could contact the
Dallas Branch. But as soon as branch personnel

heard the news through radio and television
reports, they leased a motor home and equipped
it with manual typewriters and calculators,
claim forms, and file boxes. It arrived in Wichita
Falls the next day and was staffed with adjusters
and claims administrators from Dallas, Houston,
and San Antonio, who immediately began
making $2,000 living expense advances.

The experience made vivid the need to
educate agents about the importance of insuring
for replacement costs. About 75 of EMCC's 165
claimants were underinsured because an agent,
thinking he was giving clients the favor of lower
premiums, had written their policies for stated
value rather than replacement cost. Therefore,
EMCC was unable to provide complete relief
to many even though their insured limits were
paid up. Thanks to reinsurance, its $3.5 million
share of the $211 million total insured damage
was reduced to $1.03 million, spread over
a period of years.

Topeka, Kansas, 1966

Belvidere, Illinois, 1967

■ ■ ■

Top center: For EMC insureds in Topeka, automobiles too badly damaged to be driven were towed to a central parking area adjacent to a body repair shop.

■ ■ ■

Middle right: Don Squire, Iowa Branch, wearing a hard hat, talked with an EMC policyholder amid wreckage left by the Oelwein tornado.

Topeka, Kansas, 1966

■ ■ ■

Top left: Resident Adjuster Dean Twidwell viewed debris in the backyard of wrecked two-story row houses on Topeka's Huntoon Street. On the roof, workmen covered the stripped rafters with polyethylene sheets to keep out wind and rain and prevent further damage.

■ ■ ■

Lower left: Checking claims near Iowa City are agent W. V. Dunton of Dunton Insurance Agency, Inc., Iowa City; and EMC Claim Adjusters Bill Bresee, Des Moines; Bob Bohnsack, Dysart; Roger Barge, Traer; and John Ruhlman, Des Moines.

■ ■ ■

Top right: Highland Hospital check presentation with Carl Rosequist, fire claims adjuster, Chicago Branch; Chicago Branch Manager Dale C. Fry; Esther Hawkey, Highland Hospital administrator; Harold Kingren, Highland Hospital Board of Trustees president; and Don Tripp and Boyd Miller of the Tripp Insurance Agency, Belvidere, Illinois. (left to right)

■ ■ ■

Lower right: In spite of the devastation, some Wichita Falls residents retained their sense of humor.

■ ■ ■

Bottom center: Remnants of a dwelling insured for $22,500.

Oelwein, Iowa, 1968

Oelwein, Iowa, 1968

Wichita Falls, Texas, 1979

Wichita Falls, Texas, 1979

A New Home Office

Robb Kelley was a big man in every way — from his 6'8" height to his enormous energy and his ambitious vision for the company — and the accomplishments of his 19-year administration reflected the man. Through the decentralization program, the number of branches doubled, expanding the geographical area covered. Seven functional subsidiaries, the holding company, and several real estate-related organizations were created. Business boomed with the introduction of multiline policies, and EMCC's offerings proliferated with an increasing emphasis on large commercial accounts. Risk improvement services attained new levels of sophistication, and office procedures were increasingly automated. During the years of Kelley's presidency, 1963 through 1981, premiums increased 440%, surplus grew 600%, and assets rose 620%.

Early in his administration, growth was already crowding the Home Office beyond capacity. More space was needed for employees and functions as well as parking and storage. A building committee appointed by the board in late 1966, recommended that the Home Office be expanded downtown rather than follow the relocation trend to the suburbs. On the practical side, the company was already located downtown and owned several properties in the office's block. As president of the Des Moines Chamber of Commerce, Kelley also envisioned a larger purpose.

The chamber was promoting downtown development, and a number of major companies were enlarging their facilities or building new ones in the central business district. EMCC decided to go a step farther. It would risk building twice the size of its current needs with faith that future expansion would fill the space. In the meantime, it would create offices for tenants who could further contribute to downtown advancement. Several other companies subsequently followed this lead.

In 1967, EMCC completed acquisition of the entire south half of the Home Office block when it purchased the Ryan Parking Lot parcel owned by the Hubbell Company. Next, design features became the focus as planning began for a new structure at 717 Mulberry Street, immediately west of the existing office. Costs and integration of the existing building were major considerations. Kelley was adamant that there should be no space for pigeon or starling roosts on the building's exterior. Board committee members John Stoddard and Richard Booth visited stone quarries and other buildings to assess materials and designs. Alleys had to be closed and earth borings done to determine load-bearing capacity. Interior layout and rental space were planned.

In December 1968, Paul Skiles presented a concept and plans for an 188,800-square-foot, ten-story building. The ensuing design process was fluid. Structure changed from reinforced concrete to steel. The choice of a black slate outer skin was discarded when the supply from a Minnesota quarry proved insufficient. A granite substitute was, in turn, superseded by less expensive precast concrete panels of white quartz aggregate. There would be a basement, and mechanical equipment would be housed on the top two floors. Cost was projected at $7–8 million.

After approval of plans in March 1969, financing was secured from Bankers Life. Because money borrowed by insurance companies was subtracted from surplus, a subsidiary, EEMSEE Corporation, was formed in August 1969 to channel the funds so that surplus would not be affected. EMCC made an initial $3 million stock investment in the new subsidiary. After the construction loan was paid off, EEMSEE Corporation was dissolved on January 1, 1981. Construction began in mid-1969, the cornerstone was laid September 9, 1970, and the building was enclosed in early November.

A view of the completed building looking northeast from the corner of Eighth and Mulberry Streets.

Images from the December 12, 1971, building opening.

On December 12, 1971, a ribbon-cutting ceremony opened the building to the public with U.S. Senator Jack Miller and Iowa Governor Robert Ray in attendance. It was a double celebration. A series of open houses, special programs, and luncheons attended by approximately 4,000 people observed not only the opening of 717 Mulberry Street, but EMCC's 60th anniversary. Two special features were on display. First, the board room in the center of the eighth floor executive suite was an oval shape, designed to accommodate a "boat-shaped" table that allowed everyone to be seen. Second, a 16.5' x 12.25' tapestry of Picasso's "Volutes" graced the two-story lobby. It was unveiled on December 9, 1971, by Winifred Kelley and Mary Wilkinson, wives of President Robb Kelley and retired Executive Vice President Maurice Wilkinson.

At first, about half of the building was reserved for tenants who would share the cafeteria and 525-space parking area with EMCC employees. The first and largest was publisher Meredith Corporation in 1972. Four hundred of their data processing employees occupied parts of the fourth and fifth floors and all of the sixth and seventh. Four years later, two more tenants arrived: a subsidiary of Brenton Banks, Inc., and an animal-breeding subsidiary of Monsanto. Other tenants over the years were the Iowa Manufacturers Association, from which EMCC had sprung; Wesley Day Advertising, which did work for EMCC; the Des Moines Symphony; and the Piper Jaffray investment firm. EMCC gradually took occupancy of the entire building as the company grew.

Left: Iowa Governor Robert Ray, with Mrs. Ray by his side, cut the ribbon at the open house ceremonies.

Center: Taking part in the unveiling of the Picasso "Volutes" tapestry during December's open house events were Fred Weitz, Paul Skiles, Mrs. Weitz, Mrs. Skiles, Mr. and Mrs. Robb Kelley, and Mr. and Mrs. M. J. Wilkinson. (left to right)

Top right: U.S. Senator Jack Miller, Iowa Governor Robert Ray, and EMC President Robb Kelley in the formal opening of EMC's new building. (left to right)

Bottom right: Part of the crowd in the lobby following the formal ribbon-cutting ceremony and public open house.

Left: The new employee cafeteria on the building's third floor of the new Home Office.

Right: President Robb Kelley stands alongside the custom-built table in the Board of Directors room on the eighth floor of the new building.

Other Real Estate Matters

During the planning and construction of the 717 Mulberry Street building, EMCC purchased properties south of the Home Office for parking, storage, and investment purposes. Robb Kelley had seen prices escalate when it became known that companies were interested in purchasing particular properties. Acquiring miscellaneous properties as they became available would preempt price inflation, and the properties could be utilized for investment purposes or held for expansion.

First to be acquired was some property with a number of dilapidated and abandoned old warehouses and other buildings. They were demolished and the site was used for parking. After that purchase, other owners were eager to sell, and Kelley became popular with real estate agents. From 1967 through 1970, properties were purchased from such owners as Keck Parking Company, the Chicago Burlington & Quincy Railroad, Des Moines Bale and Tie Company, Gentec Hospital Supply Company, and others. Most of this land would be developed for parking, and EMCC would eventually own several city blocks.

A decade after the west building opened, EMCC made its crowning purchases — an assemblage of all the remaining properties in the block occupied by the Home Office. Ownership of the entire block provided options for future expansion along with control over current use of the property. Included in the purchases were the old Foster Hotel and a number of retail stores facing Walnut Street — Norman Cassiday's, Wolf's Ladies' Wear,

Walker's Shoes, The Plus Shop, Arnolds Fashion Center, and Stearns Apparel. EMCC purchased most of the leases and added other lessees — Walgreens, Lane Bryant, The American Agency, French Way Cleaners, Drake's Salad Bar Corporation, and Norwest Financial subsidiaries.

For the purpose of purchasing, developing, and managing this property, EMCC formed two new companies. First was Sixth Avenue Associates, Ltd., in April 1981, which purchased land and improvements and arranged long-term land leases with purchase options in the northwest quarter of the block. Then One Hundred LaSalle Corporation was formed in May to carry out the same functions in the northeastern quarter. After all the properties were purchased, Sixth Avenue Associates was merged into One Hundred LaSalle, effective November 15, 1981. One Hundred LaSalle Corporation would serve as EMCC's real estate arm until its dissolution in 1995.

...

The Foster Hotel on the southeast corner of Eighth and Walnut (top) and the Wolf's Ladies Wear building at 712 Walnut were both purchased by EMC.

Inside the Buildings

Personnel

After 1960, more and more employees were needed for administrative processing and reporting due to expanding operations and increasing government regulations and requirements. Many processes, from printing to handling investments, which had been done by outside contractors, became more economical to perform in-house. Technology created new types of jobs. Expanded employee benefits required new expertise. All of these factors made a larger and more diverse personnel department essential.

To meet this challenge, Employment Manager Dean Price added to the clerical staff and assigned specific functions to both existing and new staff — interviewing, recruiting, testing, new employee processing, administering benefit programs, promotions, salary increases, transfers, leaves of absence, terminations, and moving arrangements and expenses. In 1963, Darrell Southern was named vice president for administration, and personnel duties became a separate function under Price as personnel manager. Payroll was moved to his jurisdiction from Accounting and, then, journeyed to Data Processing in 1968 and moved back to Accounting in 1971 before returning permanently to Personnel in 1978.

Price retired in 1972 and was succeeded by Donald Long, assistant personnel director since 1970, who was given the title personnel director. Long left in 1973 and was replaced by Milwaukee Branch Administrative Services Manager Maurice L. "Maury" Hines, who had come to EMCC as an office services assistant in 1969, following college, seminary education, and service in the U.S. Army. Under his leadership, the scope of the Personnel Department expanded to include orientation and training programs, promoting good human relations, and recruitment and hiring for the Des Moines Branch.

Payroll grew to 1,200 by 1975. When it returned to Personnel in 1978, Katie Juliano,

who had supervised the operation since 1947, moved with the section and stayed until retiring in 1988. In 1959, she had been joined by Sally Drake who remained in the department into the next millennium. Nellie, the Cardatype machine, was replaced in 1964 by an IBM 1410 with magnetic tape drives as well as punched cards.

One significant change under Hines was creation of a new communications supervisor

* * *

Top: The new IBM 1410 series, which was installed at EMC in 1964, with John Atherton at the printer, John Isenhart seated at the console, and Dick White at the magnetic tape wall.

Right: Francis Young, a key punch machine operator in 1968.

...

Philip T. Van Ekeren held several positions at EMC, including administrative services manager, vice president of administration, and corporate secretary.

...

John D. Isenhart became manager of Data Processing and Methods in 1967.

position in 1974. It was filled in by Doug Zmolek, who transferred from Data Processing and immediately became editor of the *Circuit*. Dean Price had replaced Elizabeth Berens as editor in 1964, making the newsletter a Personnel responsibility, handled briefly by Don Long and Hines. Although Zmolek became employee relations director in 1975, he continued as editor until 1985.

Zmolek enlarged the format and made it more colorful, but his main contribution was promoting two-way communications with employee readers through such means as question & answer and letters-to-the-editor columns. More pictures and news from the branches were added. In 1983, a "Keeping Informed" series initiated discussion of company policies, procedures, and operations.

Robb Kelley supported this approach. In the April-May 1977 issue, he wrote, "Much of this paper is devoted to people. We believe people are our most important asset and knowing more about them is really meaningful. We are all working toward a common corporate end — serving the policyholder. How we do it and who is working at it should prove interesting. Finally, we have friends in our respective offices and around the circuit and like to keep up with their hobbies, activities and achievements."

When Hines left EMCC in 1985, Zmolek became Director of Human Resources and passed on the editorship to Bobby Holmes. Zmolek's new title reflected the broadening scope of responsibilities and also recognized that employees were one of the company's most valuable resources.

General Administration

As the Personnel Department was coming into its own, substantial changes were also taking place within broader administrative functions. When Robb Kelley became president in 1963, Darrell Southern succeeded him as corporate secretary and was promoted to vice president for Administration, where he served until his retirement in 1978. Following retirement, he compiled a body of documents related to the company's history, working at the task until several months before his death in 1988.

Just before Southern became vice president for Administration, an Office Services subunit, composed of Personnel, Purchasing, Reception, PBX, Supply, Mail, and Printing, was created. Interdepartmental Trainee Philip T. Van Ekeren, a Korean Conflict Army veteran who held a degree in business and economics from Central College in Pella, Iowa, and had prior experience with seed corn and railroad companies, was named supervisor. In 1968, he was promoted to administrative services manager (ASM), a new position that had emerged in several branches around 1965. When Southern retired, Van Ekeren succeeded him as vice president of administration and corporate secretary.

As ASM, Van Ekeren worked closely with branch operations, as well as Home Office functions. For example, in 1970, he directed a four-day workshop for administrative services managers from 11 branches and the Home Office. EMCC's fleet operations provided another connecting link. When John D. Hargett, who managed both fleet operations and premium audit in the Risk Improvement Department, retired in 1977, it was a logical time to transfer his fleet responsibilities to Administrative Services. Operations Supervisor Dennis M. Gooch was promoted to operations manager, and fleet operations were placed under his wing. Originally an interdepartmental trainee, who transferred to Administration from Data Processing, he would play an important role in company real estate matters until his retirement in early 2001.

Data Processing, Methods and Procedures

The Methods and Procedures Department, created in 1960, helped manage dramatic change after the Data Processing Department was created in 1963. Designed to facilitate both daily operations and long-range planning, it coordinated changing functions as business grew, organization became more complex, and data processing technology advanced. By the late 1960s, computer programming was added to the development of manual systems. Darrell Southern said, "Efficient utilization of our resources means better service to our agents, better working conditions for our employees, and more satisfied policyholders. Our Methods and Procedures Department

is constantly working in this direction." Staff was trained intensively for eight months by working in all departments of the company, attending IBM school, reading technical manuals, and reviewing forms and procedures to keep up with current trends.

There were shifts in management when Data Processing Manager Jim Stansell was succeeded by Methods and Procedures Supervisor Don Andrew in 1967, and Systems Analyst John D. Isenhart became methods manager. Isenhart had earned a mathematics and business administration degree from Drake University and taught school before joining EMCC. He was named manager of both Data Processing and Methods in 1970 when Andrew left the company, and Methods Analyst Robert D. Rinehart became methods supervisor.

Most dramatic were developments in computer technology. In 1962, a few "innocent-appearing cabinets" had landed in the Home Office according to a plan hatched by Southern. They were an IBM 1401 computer processing unit that used the Symbolic Programming System (SPS), capable of assembling specific commands. Accompanied by a card punch, printer, and memory core, the 1401 replaced the original IBM 650 and was expected to save over $2,000 per month in the Tabulating Department alone. The May 1962 *Circuit* reported that the

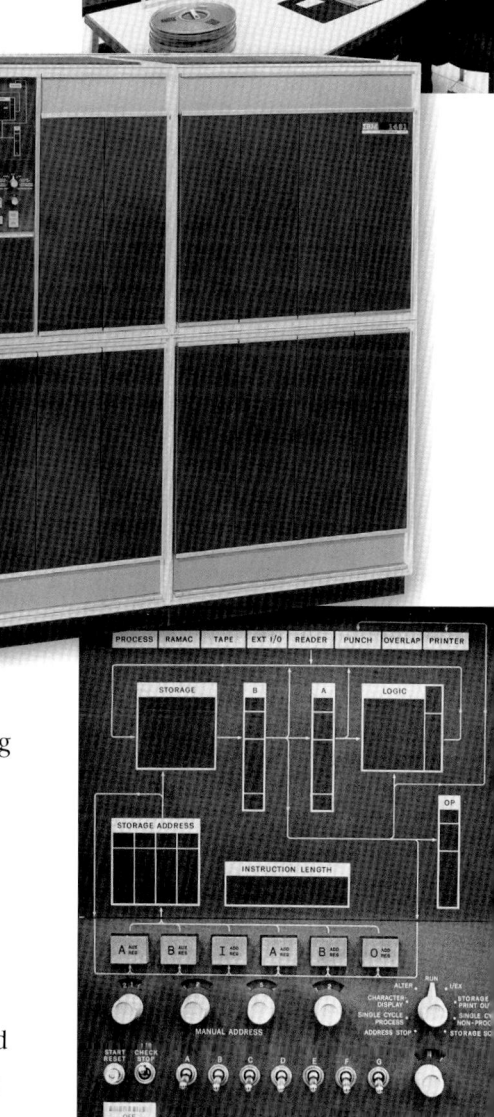

...

IBM 1400 series computer processing unit.

•••

Systems Analyst Gerri Lyon, who designed and implemented EMC's premium input system, stands behind one of the data terminal screens in 1973.

•••

Linda Fuson uses the optical character recognition scanner in 1970.

1401's "internal processing speeds ... stagger the imagination!" It could read 800 cards and print out 600 lines per minute, add two-digit numbers in 0.299 milliseconds, and multiply a six-digit number by a four-digit number in 15 milliseconds. A millisecond, it was noted, is one-thousandth of a second — a fraction of the blink of an eye. It also combined the work of collator, accounting machine, calculator, and summary punch for jobs completed.

Only two years later, after nearly 18,000 man-hours of planning, programming, and testing, an IBM 1410 system, with five magnetic tape drives, replaced the 1401. Housed in a specially constructed glass and aluminum space on the second floor of the Home Office, it was "one of the most modern electronic computer systems in the industry." Still operators had to feed punched cards, load and unload tapes,

store tapes, and perform tasks on auxiliary and noncomputer equipment. This required 38 keypunch employees, five tabulating operators, half a dozen computer room operators, and a dozen programmer analysts.

It was not until 1970 that EMCC began to replace punched cards with Control Data Corporation's Optical Character Recognition (OCR) system, the first company in Des Moines to do so. Material produced by a typewriter with the now familiar stylized font was scanned by an optical page reader from which data was transferred to the computer. While punched cards could accommodate only 80 characters and had to be totally redone if an error was made, the reader could scan 11" x 14" pages containing hundreds more characters, and mistakes could be corrected with strikeovers.

Then in 1973, a paper shortage hastened conversion of the OCR system to a visual data terminal system. Called the "premium input system," it had been developed over 20 months under the direction of Systems Analyst Gerri Lyon for use in the Statistical Input Department supervised by Flora Tallman (Wise). Just as the company was down to the last half-day's supply of the unavailable special paper required by OCR, a quick decision was made to switch to the new system, and the conversion was completed two months ahead of schedule. It enabled operators at 14 terminals to complete over 50,000 policy transactions each month and to produce statistical reports required by various bureaus, as well as internal documents such as the annual statement.

EMCC's first computer purchase was IBM's new 370/145 system in 1972. Acquisition

had become more cost effective than leasing, and this system was suited to long-range planning. Identified as the "foundation for future needs," the 370/145 had a technological capacity that extended out five years, and its capabilities could be expanded. According to John Isenhart, it could further put "the facilities and power of the centralized computer system in the hands of the people on the front line." One example was the automatic automobile and homeowners system in use at all but three branches by 1973. Policy information could be typed into a branch terminal and sent in batches over phone lines to the Home Office computer where it was processed overnight. The next morning, new policies were back at the branch ready for delivery to the agents.

Installation of a second IBM 370/145 in 1977, doubled capacity with 14 tape drives and six disc drives. It also increased heat generation. Cooling the computer area required 60 tons of air conditioning, which used about 100,000 kilowatt hours monthly — the equivalent of 100 homes — and equipment had to be arranged to distribute temperature evenly. Upgrading with advances in the IBM 370 series quickly followed in the next few years. These computers totally eliminated punched cards and instituted an "on line" system with terminals that had easy-to-read displays from which programs could be developed or edited. Processing steps were reduced, and an audit trail was created. Best of all, the system contained 5,000 programs and had a capacity for 8,000. Over 2,200 changes were made to these programs annually.

Data Processing had entered a new era, and it was made a separate major department with sole responsibility for management decisions about automation. The first major purchase under this authority was an IBM 303/358 in 1981. It increased processing capacity from 1.4 million to 2.6 million instructions per second.

As programming and system functions became more specialized and complex, a shortage of trained technicians developed across the country. To address this problem, EMCC tried using third-party software packages. But too often, the vendors were acquired by other companies, creating two problems, aside from the programs needing modification. Maintenance of the system became undependable, and other programs that did not fit were thrust upon EMCC. So the company turned to building its own programming staff with entry-level business

...

Computer Operator Linda Fuson sits at the central processing unit of a new IBM 370/145 computer system. In the background at one of the magnetic tape drives is Cecil Buckner, computer operator in 1972.

...

A computer operator sits at the console of the IBM 370 series.

analyst trainees. Although turnover was high, a stable core of technicians began to build up. After that, staff increased over the years until Data Processing and Methods became EMCC's largest Home Office department.

Professional Training

From the time he received his CPCU in 1952, Robb Kelley's advocacy for continuing insurance education encouraged EMCC employees to pursue professional development. Before he became president, EMCC had begun paying tuition for those who passed Insurance Institute of America, Inc. (IIA) and CPCU examinations. In 1970, an entire issue of the *Circuit* was devoted to training. The list of employees who had earned professional designations

and completed courses filled two and a half pages under the headings of CPCU (Chartered Property and Casualty Underwriter), CLU (Chartered Life Underwriter), LOMA (Life Office Management Association), LUTC (Life Underwriters Training Course), and IIA (Insurance Institute of America) and AMIA (American Mutual Insurance Alliance) courses. By 1981, EMCC ranked eighth of all U.S. fire and casualty companies in its ratio of employees taking educational exams to the total number of employees.

New courses and designations continued to be added. One was the Certified Safety Professional (CSP) designation created by the Board of Certified Safety Professionals. At EMCC, six employees had earned this

...

1968 Philadelphia American
Mutual Insurance Alliance
graduates/EMC employees:
(front row) Patricia Heil,
Linda Scafidi, Shannon
Raleigh, Anna Pagano and
(back row) Evelyn Herzstein,
April Lee, Mary Windisch,
Bob Mazur. (left to right)

designation by 1980: Bill Duncan, Roger Kilborn, Joe Lamb, Dennis Lamport, and Norman Anderson from the Home Office, and Jack R. Robertson from the Wichita Branch.

Of particular note is that seven of the 15 women who earned membership in the Iowa Chapter of CPCU, between its formation in 1956 and 1981, were from EMCC — Margaret A. Ball, Carole S. Hallenbeck, Avis Adams James, Donna M. Jones, LaRae N. Penny, Sherri A. Stanley, and Donna M. Brees. Ardith King in the Wichita Branch also held the designation. Ball and Penny both served as president of the Iowa Chapter, and Ball was inducted into the Iowa Insurance Hall of Fame in 2002.

Particularly popular in the branches was the General Principles of Insurance continuing education course sponsored by the American Mutual Insurance Alliance (AMIA), renamed the Alliance of American Insurers (AAI) in 1977. This was a flexible course, often taught in-house by EMCC personnel. It was first offered in 1968 at the Philadelphia Branch, which had 100% participation in 1973. While Providence claimed the largest class ever, with 50 in 1971, particularly large numbers from Dallas, Lansing, Wichita, and Milwaukee received certificates over time.

The dedication and perseverance of the many employees who earned designations, as well as a number of EMCC senior staff who frequently taught various courses, made a major contribution to the company's reputation for high standards of professionalism and service.

• • •

Roy H. Chatfield was director of the Accounting Department for more than 20 years.

• • •

Donald D. Klemme, named manager of internal audit in 1979, retired as senior vice president/administration in 2007.

Accounting and Internal Audit

Underpinning all EMCC operations, internal and external, was financial management. Accountability to policyholders, shareholders, and regulators was paramount. In the beginning, recording and reporting requirements were met simply with in-house bookkeeping and accounting, and the treasurer functioned as the chief financial officer.

By 1940, the Accounting Department had grown from one person, Helen Mulligan, to 11 women under her supervision. Their task was "first of all moulded to the requirements of the elaborate reports of the various state departments," and accuracy was their slogan. They viewed their department as a "keystone of all the activities of the company," and borrowed the line, "Check and Double Check," from radio comedians, Amos and Andy. Sixteen years later, the department had grown to 17 and was directed by Roy H. Chatfield, who had become EMCC's first controller following the retirement of Mulligan in 1944. The department was then described as having the answer to "most anything fiscal you want to know about Employers Mutual." Although the number of staff had been stable for a decade, the volume of work had doubled, a tribute to efficient methods conducted by three sections — Accounts Current, Payroll, and Investment Portfolio.

Chatfield left EMCC in 1966, and Raymond F. Vogel became controller and accounting department manager. A decorated World War II Army veteran and CPA with a B.S. in business administration from the Walton School of Commerce in Chicago, Vogel had held accounting positions with Froggatt & Company, EMCC's first outside auditor. He liked to joke that being the "watchdog function of the company's assets," did not win popularity contests. But with payroll under their wing, payday every other Friday improved the department's image "for a day or so." On Vogel's 15th anniversary at EMCC, President Robb Kelley compared him to the rudder of a ship — "He doesn't get much visibility as far as the public is concerned, but the ship would be in one heck of a fix if it had no rudder." Vogel retired in 1984 and was succeeded by Accountant John M. "Jack" Van Sloun, a Korean Conflict Army veteran with previous experience in data processing.

A new function was created in 1959 when outside auditor Peat Marwick Mitchell & Company discovered an act of embezzlement in the Accounting Department. They recommended a full-time internal position to audit both the Home Office and the branches. Jack Wagstaff was transferred from manager of the Statistical Department to be internal auditor and reported directly to the president and the board. Two staff positions were added before Wagstaff retired in 1973. Then a rapid series of personnel changes led to Des Moines Branch Premium Auditor Donald D. Klemme being named internal auditor in 1975 and manager of the Internal Audit Department in 1979.

To provide a direct link from Internal Audit to the board and to deal with new accounting regulations adopted by the New York Stock Exchange, an audit committee of the board was created in 1978. Initial members were

John M. Lockhart, John D. Stoddard, and Harlan T. Moses, with Robb Kelley, ex-officio. Meetings were also attended by the controller, internal auditor, and representatives from Peat Marwick Mitchell & Company.

Beyond Business: Good Citizenship

A gift of $4,800 in 1945 for the John A. Gunn Memorial Room at Methodist Hospital in Des Moines was EMCC's first charitable contribution noted in the minutes. That was followed during the mid-1950s by programs to orient teachers and students to the insurance business, donations to the U.S. Marine Corps' "Toys for Tots" drive, and dollar contributions to the YMCA and Mercy Hospital. In the

early 1960s, participation began in what would become three of EMCC's major citizenship thrusts in Des Moines — the United Campaign (United Way), Junior Achievement, and Des Moines downtown development.

Russ Wellman, Fred DuBois, and J. Earle Miller led EMCC's first participation in the United Giving Campaign in 1960 when 100.2% of the city's $1,725,000 goal was achieved. Robb Kelley, who had previously worked as a solicitor, team captain, and division commander, headed the citywide drive two years later, and the goal of $1,807,000 was exceeded. For years after that, EMCC "loaned" an executive for three months

...

Robb Kelley purchased a Junior Achievement product from students in his office in 1973.

to many annual campaigns, and different employees headed the Home Office drive every year. "Good Giver" plaques, trumping the previous year's giving, and topping goals became common. By 1981, EMCC raised nearly $50,000 — 108% of its goal with 83% of employees contributing.

Personnel Manager Dean Price was one of the original advisers for a Junior Achievement corporation program for high school students. EMCC began sponsoring student organized and managed companies in 1959. Over the next two and a half decades, many employees provided counsel about production, sales, and accounting as students learned the ups and downs of business. A wide range of products were produced and sold by the EMCC-sponsored student companies, and they were often applauded for profits earned and dividends paid to stockholders.

For several years in the mid-1980s, after a quarter century of advising student companies, participation turned to employees teaching business topics in classrooms through the Project Business program. Subsequently, fund-raising activities and corporate giving to Junior Achievement supplanted the participatory activities.

Records indicate that significant regular giving to community development began with annual contributions of $1,250 to the Des Moines Development Commission from 1961 through 1964. In 1967, $25,000 was given to the YWCA building fund, and the next year, Robb Kelley raised over $2.5 million as chair of the fund drive. EMCC set a new philanthropic standard for itself in 1975 with a $200,000 gift to the Downtown Redevelopment Project for building the Civic Center. Seen more as an investment in the future of business in Des Moines was the contribution of $270,000 to City Center Development for construction of the downtown Marriott Hotel at the end of the decade. When Living History Farms founder and brother of Winifred Kelley, William G. Murray, was organizing the 600-acre open-air museum in Des Moines in the early 1970s, EMCC provided office space. Since that time, EMCC has been the fourth largest corporate sponsor of the expanding attraction.

Spiderman Visit a Big Hit

Sometimes a contribution was unplanned, such as during a fund-raising auction for the Des Moines Science Center in 1978. EMC President Robb Kelley placed the high bid of $142.50 for what he thought was 500 gallons of Pester gasoline. What he actually won was a day with Spiderman.

So he invited Spidey to the lobby one December day to give 125 employees' and tenants' children autographs and pins before visiting the pediatric wards in Des Moines' three hospitals. The superhero was a bigger hit than Santa. ▪

Education also had high priority. In 1970, the company contributed $7,500 to the Dowling/St. Joseph Education Center Building Fund in memory of John F. Hynes. From 1972 to 1974, a $10,000 grant was paid to Simpson College in Indianola, just south of Des Moines. But Drake University would become EMCC's largest educational beneficiary. When Robb Kelley was chairman of the trustees in 1980, the company made its first major contribution — $750,000 to the capitol fund drive, to be paid over eight years.

Community service was not limited to corporate donations. It permeated the company at both the Home Office and branches where employees volunteered in local organizations and activities. Some of the contributions were company projects, and others were from individual employees who were recognized in company publications. The activities were wide-ranging — leadership in civic and religious organizations, support of health organizations, school functions, tutoring, vocational guidance and job training, fund-raising, blood donor drives, town councils and school boards, Friendship Force, Scouts, Campfire Girls, YWCA, YMCA, United Way campaigns, and more. ▪

A graphic of Halley's Comet used for EMC's
75th anniversary celebration materials in 1986.

Consolidation: 1980 – 1990
Base for the Future

Entry Into a New Business Era

The exuberant expansion of the 1960s and 1970s had reached its culmination. Robb Kelley and George Kochheiser had worked together as a team to oversee the remarkable growth. When the presidency was transferred from Kelley to Kochheiser on March 10, 1982, the team remained intact. Kelley stayed on as chairman of the board, treasurer, and chief executive officer, and Kochheiser became president and chief operating officer.

Under their ongoing leadership, the coming decade would be a period of consolidation, laying the groundwork for a new era of changed business patterns. A number of other companies foundered in the highly competitive market at mid-decade, but EMC ended up thriving, attesting to the soundness of its philosophy and practices and its ability to move ahead with changing conditions.

The Challenging 1980s

The underwriting cycle in the first half of the 1980s was what Robb Kelley called "the worst in modern times."

Many companies were not prepared for the consequences of falling interest rates in the early 1980s. Historically, with low single-digit interest rates for investment income, underwriting revenues give the most accurate picture of a company's financial status. But too many companies had focused on total net income, which left them unprepared for reduced investment returns. Raising premium rates to counter diminished investment income was not an adequate solution. The problem of lower interest rates was compounded by the failure of many companies to maintain adequate reserves for anticipated losses. Furthermore, reinsurance protection had been weakened because too many reinsurers did not create enough reserves for "long-tail" claims not contemplated when policies were written.

At the same time, the number of claims and lawsuits increased as public sentiment and legislation demanded more protection and higher compensation, particularly in areas such as bodily injury, pollution, and product liability. In 1984 and 1985, surpluses dropped precipitously and more reserves had to be put up. Fifty-five property and casualty companies entered insolvency from 1984 through 1986.

Legislation designed to alleviate the situation and prevent similar experiences in the future became "onerous and mindless" to the insurance industry. In 1985, the Iowa Department of Insurance required all companies to increase their reserves by a set percentage in an attempt to strengthen under-reserved insurers. President George Kochheiser reacted: "An across-the-board mandate isn't really fair. Why use a shotgun approach when a rifle will do?" Companies like EMC that maintained adequate reserves were penalized, not strengthened, by this action.

Another issue, "prior approval," required rate changes proposed by companies to be approved by the state insurance departments as a protective measure for the public. Insurance companies, however, generally preferred deregulated "open competition." They believed prior approval created inadequate rates and that they could better adjust based on their own experience. But, when a majority of states did deregulate through open competition laws, there was no protection against cutthroat rates. It would take several years of unprofitable underwriting before companies adjusted and brought their rates to a realistic level.

Within the industry, reinsurers took restrictive measures to get their own houses in order, which resulted in limiting the underwriting capacity of primary companies. For example, reinsurers required primary companies to retain more of their exposure, and they set limits on the types and amounts of coverage they would reinsure. This, in turn, limited coverage available to the public.

Chairman Robb Kelley took a middle ground, stating that fairness to everyone concerned was the key to reform. He saw the need for intelligent regulation as well as expert management. Ill-conceived rules and restrictions

· · ·
Employees in every branch
office took part in EMC's
75-year anniversary, including
Jackson (top), Lansing
(bottom left), and Phoenix
(bottom right).

Milestone Celebration

EMC chose Halley's Comet as its anniversary symbol in 1986. Posters sporting a pixelated image of the comet read, "Celebrating Our 75th Year in a Dramatic Way." They further explained, "The comet last appeared in 1911 when we began our operation. It will appear during our 75th anniversary, and will return to celebrate our 150th anniversary."

EMC's earliest days were commemorated by employees in period costumes riding tandem bicycles and 1911 automobiles to an office furnished in turn-of-the-century style. Magic shows and ragtime music abounded alongside antique displays, trivia games, baby picture contests, and costume judging. Wild West sheriff's deputies appeared in Phoenix where new rental space was also celebrated with an open house. Milwaukee combined the occasion with their 30th anniversary as a branch. The Denver Branch picnicked old-fashioned style by a pond, and Omaha had portraits taken 1911-style. Dashing men and ladies in high fashion displayed their Southern charm in Jackson and, up in Valley Forge, "old-timers" just plain partied. Throughout the company employees appeared as fancied characters of the period, in bustles and bonnets, knickers and caps, and straw hats and striped jackets. ▪

on reserves and rates could create obstacles and hamper growth and service. On the other hand, unfettered competition under deregulation could force many companies into unrealistic decisions and ultimate bankruptcy.

EMC, like the industry, reached its nadir when surplus declined 19% in 1983–1984 and underwriting losses became the highest to date — $47.6 million in 1984 and $41.3 million in 1985. By 1986, however, the company was benefiting from the effects of rising prices and demand, as well as a $21.4 million net infusion from a secondary offering of EMC Insurance Group Inc. stock in 1985. Also aiding the turnaround were lower catastrophe losses than in 1985, tightened in-house expense controls, selective underwriting, and the historic maintenance of reserves that had allowed capacity for growth all along. Not insignificant was an increase in written premiums from $296 million to $343.7 million in 1985–1986. In 1987, Robb Kelley reported that EMC was the largest Iowa company in general liability, second in workers' compensation, and third in inland marine. Nationally, A. M. Best ranked EMC 83rd in premium volume for domestic property and casualty companies.

Investments: A Conservative Approach

Even though underwriting losses became more common during the 1970s and going forward, total investment income grew most years, allowing surplus to keep increasing. For the rest of its first century, EMC would strive to maintain a reasonable balance between underwriting experience and investment income. Its focus would remain on building capacity through steady earnings from the insurance business itself by focusing on profitable classes of business and stressing superior claims and risk improvement services. Rate adequacy was the actuarial goal. Still, investment income would become increasingly important to the total profitability of the company.

EMC had made its first investment in 1917 when it purchased U.S. Liberty Bonds, and its only investments were in bonds until 1935. Then the company entered the more volatile stock market slowly and carefully. Stocks would not become a significant portion of investments until the 1950s when they averaged around one-fifteenth of total investments. The board limited investment in stocks to no more than 5% of the company's assets in 1951 and raised the percentage to 10% in 1958. After 1960, when stocks were first allowed to be 15% of total assets, they seldom represented more than one-fifth of investments. Only in the mid-1960s and early 1970s did the board allow stocks to rise to as high as 18% of the company's assets.

Further stability had come from what turned out to be a prescient investment action in 1984. Stock investments were reduced from $116.6 million to $63 million, while bonds were increased from $255.4 million to $323.5 million. Then, two months before the October 19, 1987, stock market crash, EMC sold $20 million in stocks, while bonds were further increased to $474.2 million. Within the pension fund alone, stock holdings were reduced from 76% to 40%. The company was well served by these transactions. Overall, 1988 was the company's "best year in history," according to Robb Kelley in a report to policyholders. Investment income quickly rebounded to over $57 million in 1989 and kept climbing.

At a board of directors meeting several months prior to the crash of 1987, Vice President Raymond W. Davis summarized the investment philosophy underlying this success: "Take the risk on the insurance side and *not* in the bond portfolio, do not buy junk bonds, attempt to match the maturities of assets and liabilities, do not manage on total rate of return, do not invest more than one percent in any one issue, and be guided by the after-tax return."

Davis had joined EMC as bond portfolio manager in 1979 after receiving a bachelor's degree in business administration from the University of Iowa and working five years with a bank in Des Moines. The next year he was the fifth Iowan to be awarded the Chartered Financial Analyst (CFA) designation by the Institute of Chartered Financial Analysts. He quickly advanced through officer ranks in EMC and its subsidiaries before becoming vice president in 1985. In 1989, he was named the company's first chief investment officer and wisely guided investments through the next two decades.

Setting Rates and Satisfying Regulators

EMC's early rate analysis activities focused on personal auto and homeowners lines. With development of the Actuarial Department by Ron Jean and Sam Colvin after 1979, regular rate reviews were instituted. Attention turned

•••

Raymond W. Davis, senior vice president/investments and treasurer, began at EMC in 1979 and retired in 2010.

increasingly toward commercial lines, first to commercial auto and workers' compensation and then to the expanding number of other commercial lines being written. The National Council on Compensation Insurance (NCCI) provided the basis for workers' compensation rates, while the rates for most other commercial lines came from the Insurance Services Office (ISO). From these bases, deviations could be filed. As EMC accumulated credible data over time, deviations were increasingly based on the company's own data, which also enabled filing of independent rates for specific programs or lines, as well as exceptions to the ISO rate structure to meet marketing needs.

Above: Kelvin Sederburg of the Actuarial Deparment.

Right: The Actuarial Department staff standing behind Ron Jean. Front row: Diane Thurston, Rhonda Simmons, Tony DiDonato, Chuck Ryherd, Kris Yerkey. Back row: Sam Colvin, Steve Peck, Lowell Nelson, Kelvin Sederburg. (left to right)

Other actuarial activities included the development and review of dividend plans for safety groups and creation of a loss reserve database for direct business. Quarterly reviews of direct loss reserve adequacy were started in 1981. Analysis of assumed reinsurance reserves was initiated in 1986 and became established as quarterly reviews over the next several years.

To carry out their daily work, actuaries were no longer making penciled entries on huge 16-column, 40-row spreadsheets. Nor were calculators, typewriters, and carbon paper used. In 1983, the demonstrated benefits of the Lotus 1-2-3 electronic spreadsheet program were quickly understood, and EMC's first purchase of IBM 8086 personal computers on which to run it was eagerly received. Two years later, the Actuarial Department took another technological leap when it acquired the company's first local area network (LAN), which allowed efficient sharing of information. A high-speed shared laser printer installed with the LAN system superseded the noisy dot-matrix machines at each workstation.

As commercial work increased, actuaries were assigned to either commercial lines under Jean's supervision or personal lines under Colvin's. In 1987, an executive underwriting rates committee was established to review proposed commercial lines revisions. Personal lines review was eventually added to its agenda. Developments at the end of the decade would make necessary new concepts in ratemaking and greater interaction with the branches.

The Rates and Filings Department was affected as regulations tightened and compliance requirements became more stringent, with regulators demanding more information.

In the early 1980s, filings increased to 150 annually. Because the insurance industry is regulated by the states, reports have to be filed in every state where EMC does business. In addition to filing reports state by state, the Rates and Filings workload was further increased in the 1980s by EMC adding more lines, deviated rates, branches, and subsidiaries. In accord with these changing conditions, Rates and Filings began reporting to Actuarial rather than Underwriting in 1985.

■ ■ ■

An IBM 8086 personal computer, the type purchased by EMC in 1983 to make actuarial activities easier and more efficient.

The States Rule

In 1869 the U.S. Supreme Court defeated efforts to institute uniform national standards, once preferred by John A. Gunn. The court ruled that issuing insurance policies was not commerce and was, therefore, not subject to federal regulation under the Commerce Clause of the U.S. Constitution. Thus, jurisdiction for insurance regulation resided with the states.

That ruling was reinforced in 1945 by the McCarran-Ferguson Act, which effectively left insurance regulation under state jurisdiction. McCarran-Ferguson has remained in place despite subsequent challenges and continuing debate. To address the need for nationwide standards, the National Association of Insurance Commissioners (NAIC) has established basic regulatory principles that can be adopted by state insurance departments as appropriate for their individual states.

Facilitating management of the increased workload was the introduction of personal computers in the mid-1980s. They multiplied access to information, made processing more efficient, and allowed rates to be entered directly without manual coding or keypunching. Analysts began typing their own filing letters instead of using transcriptionists, and clerical staff was reduced.

When Manager Jack Holtzbauer retired in 1985, he had established a good foundation for the department, as it centralized filing processes for forms, rates, and other information. Coughennower was well prepared to succeed him, having served as assistant manager since 1976. ■

Left: Bill Davis and
Melinda Krieg work on
the data processing end
of the Team for Automated
Commercial Systems Unit.

Center: Carl Evans explains
how the commercial lines
system will improve service
to agents and policyholders.

Right: Avis James
demonstrates the new
system to fellow EMC
employees.

Underwriting Reoriented

With the decentralization process complete
by the 1980s, most underwriting was processed
in the branches. Still, the Home Office had
responsibility for monitoring branch operations,
conducting specialized research, developing
products, handling special lines, and guiding
overall planning. As EMC looked to the future
from the bottom of the underwriting cycle
in 1985, it developed a five-year strategic plan
for the combined companies and a two-year
production plan. These plans tied underwriting
capacity to available surplus so that written
premiums would not exceed three times surplus.
Since 1980, EMC had generally adhered to this
standard and often maintained an even larger
proportionate surplus. The annual growth
rate goal for writings was set at about 10% and
was usually achieved over the five-year period.
Although the business mix was geared to
regional conditions, it generally shifted toward
more commercial products.

The mission stated in the strategic plan
was: "to provide insurance and related services
to the public in an efficient and responsible
manner. Service, savings, and strength are key
words embodying our purpose." To accomplish
its objectives, the company would stay within
the areas of its expertise for the five-year
projected period. There would be no further
acquisitions, no new investment programs,
no new territories opened, and no new lines
of business introduced. Attention would
be given to product development that would
provide defensive underwriting tools or
fit new niches. Advantage would be taken
of management by objectives, risk improvement
services, the wide range of coverages available,
and EMC's agility made possible by
decentralization. Variety in regional planning
and close contact with agencies and insureds

would be emphasized through the branch offices. These objectives were largely achieved.

The production plan provided detailed marketing, underwriting, and expense goals with specific targets for each branch. It began with upgrading underwriting standards and limiting capacity. Traditional middle-of-the-road business was to be re-evaluated, and less desirable categories were to be supplanted by increasing penetration into more desirable classes. Agents and renewal business that did not meet the new standards were to be identified and eliminated. It was anticipated that at least two years would be required to fully implement the program due to the advance notice required to terminate agencies and mandated policy continuations. Rate adequacy and a substantial volume of new business would also be required to increase capacity for significant growth. Implementation of these plans played a major role in setting EMC on course out of the mid-1980s slump.

Supporting these endeavors were new automated systems, primarily for commercial lines. In 1981, Underwriting and Data Processing joined forces to launch a commercial lines system to improve service to agents and policyholders. To coordinate the effort, a unit called Team for Automated Commercial Systems, composed of personnel from both departments, was formed. They sequenced the installation of rating and quoting ability, policy issuance, and statistical reporting for the various lines over the course of several years.

The Insurance Services Office (ISO) adopted a new statistical reporting program for commercial lines in 1979, and the company

developed a stellar record for accuracy. Errors could now be detected on a daily basis so that systems could be constantly upgraded to reduce future errors. Bureau Statistics Manager Mike Freel, who joined EMC as a statistical analyst at the time the ISO program was implemented, was instrumental in building the data quality program from the ground up. According to Freel, EMC has been at the top of the A range and ranked in the top 1% of all reporting companies since report card ratings began to be issued in the mid-1980s. Because of its reputation for accuracy, the company had become a test site for new industry programs and was active in enhancing data packages.

Senior Vice President for Underwriting M. O. Cooper oversaw a number of shifts in management personnel during the 1980s. Margaret Ball, who had served in various underwriting capacities at the Des Moines Branch and Home Office since 1971, became commercial property manager after Bob Ruby turned his full attention to EMC Underwriters, Inc., in 1980. Ball would be named EMC's first female vice president in 1983. That same year, Ron Hallenbeck became underwriting supervisor for commercial special lines, which included umbrella, directors and officers, and the linebacker policies. When EMC Reinsurance Company was formed in 1981, Wayne Goettsch, manager of commercial special lines since 1972, transferred to the new company as vice president, and Hallenbeck became EMC special lines manager.

Fred Schiek, casualty manager since 1972, was transferred to Omaha as branch manager in 1984. He was succeeded by Casualty and

Top: M.O. Cooper, senior vice president for underwriting, retired in 1990.

Bottom: Margaret A. Ball, vice president/underwriting, retired in 2000.

Multiple Lines Underwriter Jeffrey T. Dahms, an underwriter at the Minneapolis Branch and Home Office since 1972.

In 1984, 45% of EMC's premium volume came from personal lines, and a new personal lines unit was set up to provide stronger staff support to the branch offices. A year later, the first manager, Roger Stordahl, left to work for another company, and William A. Murray was hired as personal lines manager. A graduate of Upper Iowa University and a U.S. Army First Infantry Division veteran with service in Vietnam, Murray had 14 years' previous underwriting and management experience with Iowa National Mutual Insurance Company. In 1991, he transferred to Charlotte as assistant branch manager in preparation for becoming branch manager the next year. He was succeeded as personal lines manager by Ronald D. Iverson, who had worked in personal, farm fire, and special lines underwriting positions in the Des Moines Branch and Home Office since 1980.

M. O. Cooper's retirement in 1990 brought other shifts. Fred Schiek was named vice president for underwriting and returned from Omaha to succeed Cooper. Then in 1991, the board of directors created a new position, senior vice president of marketing, underwriting, and field operations. Schiek was named to fill it, and Margaret Ball replaced him as Vice President for Underwriting. Kevin J. Hovick, who had progressed through positions as Des Moines Branch underwriter and underwriting manager at the Phoenix and Birmingham Branches since 1979, succeeded her as commercial property manager. Schiek's

responsibilities would again broaden in 1992, when he was named executive vice president and chief operating officer.

Safety Dividend Groups Added

Perhaps the most significant underwriting development was building on the safety dividend group concept and program. Success of the Iowa school program begun in 1974 led, in 1980, to a similar program for the Iowa Association of Municipal Utilities, which eventually covered the majority of Iowa's towns and cities. Again, the Des Moines Branch, its special risk underwriting section, and managing general agent Jester Agency were the moving forces behind the new group program's initiation and development. In 1983, EMC initiated safety dividend group property and casualty coverage to members of the Petroleum Marketers of Iowa Association. This time, the program was marketed directly to independent agents by EMC, and there was no managing general agent.

In 1982, the Independent Insurance Agents of Kansas endorsed the Wichita Branch's safety dividend group plan for the Kansas Municipal Utilities Association and its members. Created the previous year, it was an auspicious beginning for Wichita's entry into the safety group program. Field supervisory employees Bob Brown and Donna Ensey worked closely with the Municipal Utilities Association's executive office. Agents spread details of the program across the state and arranged informational meetings for agents and city officials. Speakers included Home Office staff such as Dennis Lamport and Roger Kilborn

from Risk Improvement. Bob Brown and Bob Gusé from the branch detailed insurance coverages. When the program was implemented, Jim Harms handled day-to-day risk improvement duties and Bob Gusé had oversight of underwriting at the branch.

Two safety dividend groups were formed by the Minneapolis Branch: the Minnesota Manufactured Housing Association in 1981 and the Northwest Petroleum Marketers Association, later renamed the Minnesota Petroleum Marketers (MPM) Association, in 1983. Branch Commercial Underwriter Barbara Barr became, and remains, a big hit at MPM Association conventions, where she hands out the dividend checks. More importantly, she has built strong relationships with agents and customers through personal contact. She helps agents to sell accounts and customers to improve their safety records by working closely with Risk Improvement.

Safety dividend groups continued to be added throughout the decade. In December 1989,

the *Circuit* reported that 14 were operating in ten states. As the number of safety groups grew, interaction among the groups also increased. In 1991, the Risk Improvement Department formalized a partnership services program in which safety and job enhancement ideas from individual members were shared with the entire group. Thus, for example, suggestions for improvements in 15 to 20 school districts could be shared in published form with 350 other district members. EMC personnel also participated in seminars and brainstorming sessions for various job categories within the groups, such as groundskeepers or administrators.

New Ventures in Risk Improvement

Risk Improvement's continuing involvement with underwriting and safety dividend groups resulted in "win-win" situations for everyone. Eliminating risks and improving safety measures resulted in better working conditions for employees, cost savings and dividends for the insureds, and additional business for EMC. To achieve these results, the Risk Improvement Department took a two-pronged approach: (1) consulting with clients to improve their safety practices and records and (2) cost estimating for loss control.

On the safety side, Risk Improvement Manager Bill Duncan stated in 1983, "Our methods are derived from those used by NASA when planning space flights. We try to determine everything that could possibly

· · ·

Left: Wichita Branch Underwriting Manager Don Marhenke and Field Supervisors Donna Ensey and Bob Brown assist conventioneers at the Kansas Safety Group booth. (behind counter, from left)

Top: Fred A. Schiek, executive vice president and COO, retired in 2001.

Bottom: Kevin J. Hovick, executive vice president and COO, started with EMC in 1979.

go wrong, then suggest fail-safe features to minimize the risk." To accomplish this analysis, staff was assigned to specialized subunits to dig beneath the surface. Among the subunits were environmental health and ergonomics, building and sprinkler system analysis, fire consultation, accident investigation, and companywide training.

The first prong of EMC's approach, client consultations, often began with inspections. Because only 10–15% of workplace injuries were now caused by unsafe machines, EMC identified and evaluated other risks in the overall work environment — hazardous chemicals, asbestos, radon, air quality, injuries caused by repetitive motion, and noise. Computers were used to analyze work sites and identify injury-causing conditions. For example, an unusual number of wrist injuries at one plant were thought to have been caused by cumulative trauma from lifting heavy wood onto a cutting machine. But computer analysis, based on a videotape of the process, revealed that the true cause was holding the wood against stops to prevent misalignment. The stops were quickly retrofitted to increase shock absorption, and the potential for repetitive motion injury was reduced substantially.

Of particular interest to EMC were back injuries, the costliest of workers' compensation claims. In 1984, back injuries were 32% of the 1.9 million disabling claims filed nationally, but they accounted for a whopping 42% of benefits paid. To counter this problem, EMC developed a computer program called Static Strength, in which data from photographs, observations, and interviews were used to calculate stress factors associated with back injuries. Once stress factors were identified, administrative and engineering controls could be implemented to reduce or eliminate them.

In 1986, the Environmental Health Lab purchased Motion Analysis Corporation's 2-D LiftTrac ergonomics program. Workers, with reflectors on their major joints, were videotaped performing lifting, pushing, pulling, and reaching motions required to carry out work tasks. Exact body measurements, along with the tape and other data, were then fed into a dedicated computer that could analyze the amount of stress placed on different joints by the motions.

During the 1980s, Environmental Protection Agency (EPA) regulations regarding spray-on asbestos, used in an estimated 8,500 school buildings, opened a new area of service for Risk Improvement. Since 1973, schools had been given the responsibility for voluntary control of the banned substance, which became friable and flaked off in a fine dust of cancer-causing asbestos fibers that could be inhaled. Then, legislation in 1982 and 1986 introduced requirements to develop specific management plans that ranged from complete removal to regular inspection and maintenance. As soon as the 1982 bill passed, the Environmental Health Lab, under Dennis Lamport's direction, became involved with asbestos inspection and management.

At mid-decade, a particular concern was the potential for fire at Hy-Vee's 450,000-square-foot warehouse in Chariton because of its extreme size and the value of its contents. EMC became deeply involved with fire protection analysis

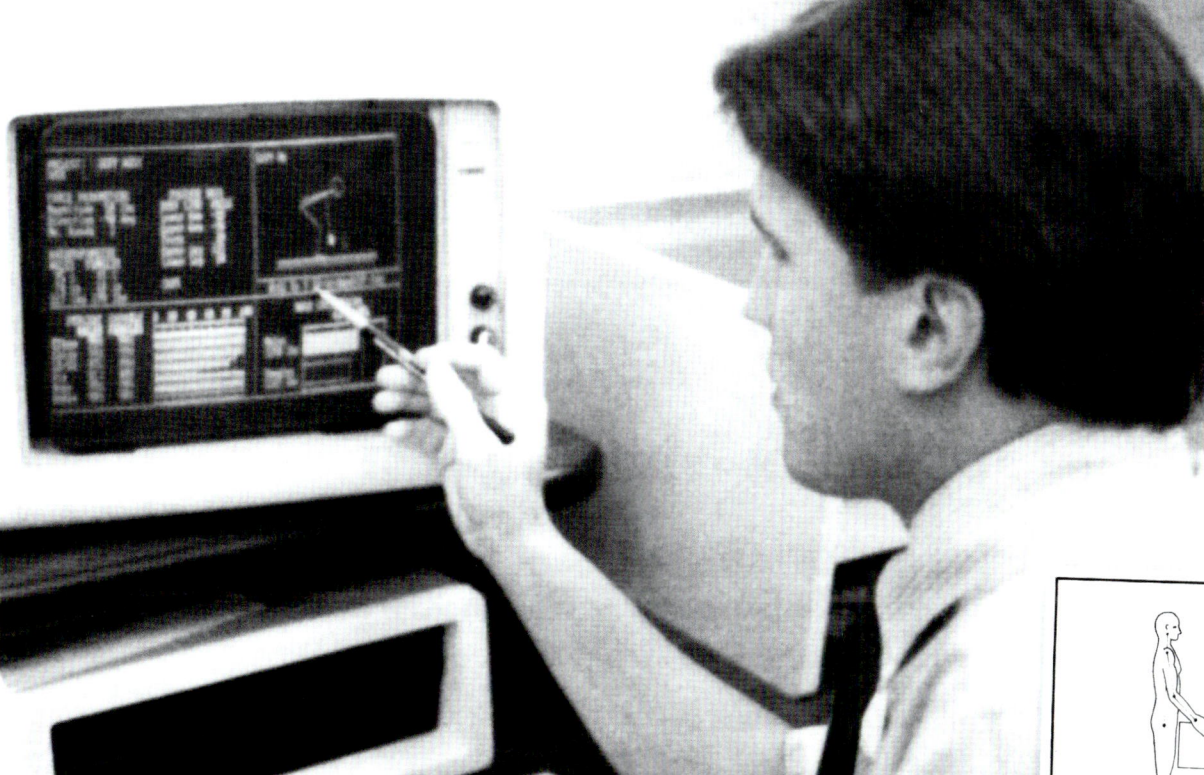

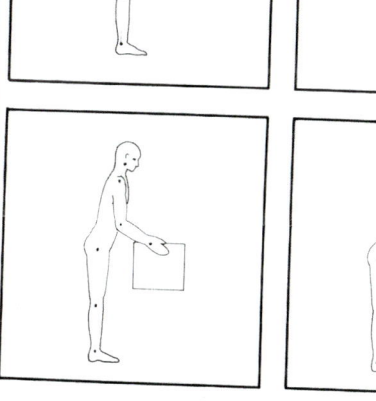

Bill Rankin coordinated the ergonomic programs at the Home Office.

there, and David Young was hired in late 1986 to work on fire protection with Hy-Vee and other accounts. At the end of the decade, Hy-Vee was also aided with OSHA compliance by EMC's standards assistance program, renamed compliance benchmarking in 2003.

By 1990, a new engineering services unit, managed by Systems Engineering Manager Norm Anderson, was reviewing all Risk Improvement reports on properties with sprinkler systems. They evaluated building configuration, flammability of contents, and current operations, as well as the pressure and capacity of public water supplies and fire pumps, to determine sprinkler protection adequacy. Sprinkler specifications were written and blueprints were reviewed for policyholders' new systems.

Along with prevention services, EMC offered training for response to injuries. Bill Duncan said, "If we can provide training and knowledge to those people first on the scene, we can reduce the pain and suffering of the victim. This means less hospital and rehabilitation time, as well as having a productive worker back on the job." Responder education programs leading to certification were created for industrial clients, and classes were given for small contractors

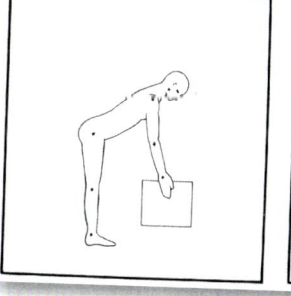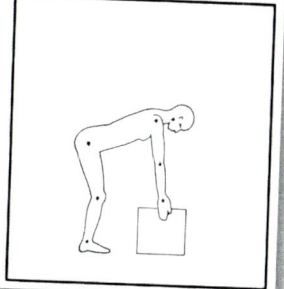

Static Strength, specially developed computer software, helped identify the probability of back injuries from specific work processes.

and EMC's own employees. First aid and CPR training were conducted in conjunction with the American Red Cross and the American Heart Association.

Helping clients develop their own safety programs continued to be an important thrust of Risk Improvement. The audio-visual division, managed by Roger Kilborn, played an important role. VHS was rapidly replacing 16mm film in safety communications, and EMC converted all of the films in its free loan library to VHS and, later, to DVD. These tapes presented information about both causes and prevention of injuries, ranging from workplace and driving safety to fire prevention and first aid. By 1991, the library had grown to 250 titles and would continue to grow in years to come.

Risk Improvement's second prong — cost estimating for loss control — remained a major emphasis of Bill Duncan, and many of the department's employees got their start in this area. Duncan believed that under-insurance was one of the greatest risk factors, and calculating replacement costs continued to be a major service. During inspections, Risk Improvement representatives recorded building dimensions, construction materials, location, use, layout, and occupancy as if the structure were being constructed from the ground up. The data was used to calculate total values and then forwarded to branch underwriting departments, which, in turn, passed it on to agents and their clients. Data received from the field could be processed in one day, and appraisals were ready for mailing the next morning. In 1983, about 15,000 such calculations were done for policyholders.

EMC moved to a total in-house computerized cost-estimating system in early 1982. H. Kenneth Barber and Arlo L. Weeks, who both had experience with property appraisal, construction, and development, were brought on board to review the previously used McGraw-Hill System and the feasibility of developing an in-house system. At year's end, they had an accurate homeowners system up and running. By 1985, they had developed, with Data Processing, a cost-estimating system for commercial properties that replaced McGraw-Hill's, for an annual savings of $1 million in processing fees.

In 1989, Weeks moved to a new management consulting services area designed to quantify hidden costs of employee injuries and to develop proactive methods to identify their

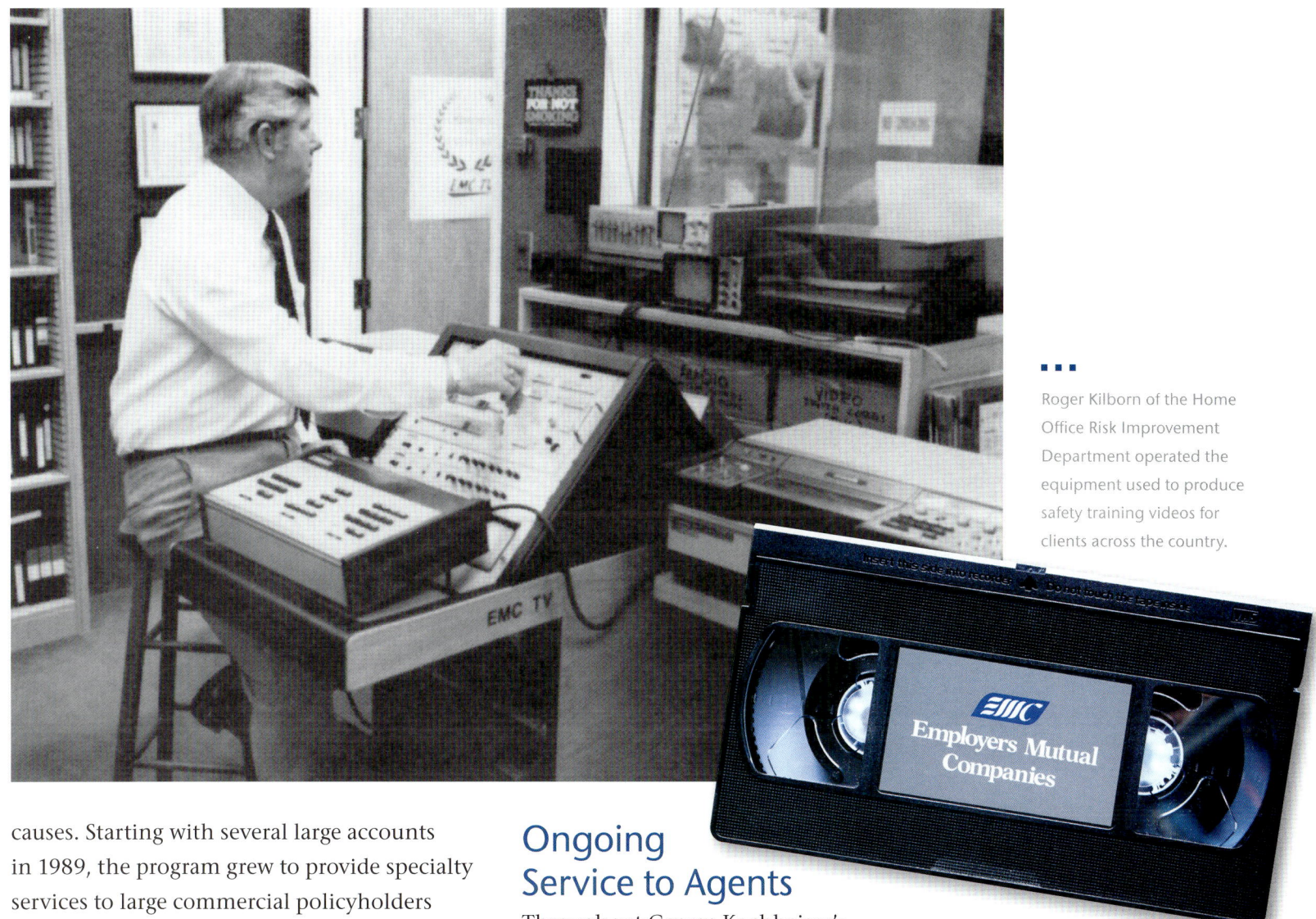

Roger Kilborn of the Home Office Risk Improvement Department operated the equipment used to produce safety training videos for clients across the country.

causes. Starting with several large accounts in 1989, the program grew to provide specialty services to large commercial policyholders and safety groups, particularly through the partnership services program initiated in 1991.

Also dealing with loss exposure was a loss information services program managed by Norm Anderson. Every commercial claim was reviewed and coded to build a loss database. By 1990, it contained information, including causal factors, from over 350,000 claims. New and small accounts that lacked sufficient data on their own losses could tap into this source. Eventually an online system, known as the risk management system (RMS), was developed for agents and large policyholders to monitor their claims.

Ongoing Service to Agents

Throughout George Kochheiser's administration, four important agents' benefit programs continued. First were the ever-popular annual production award trips, which began in 1960 and now spanned the globe from Munich to Hawaii and London to Alaska.

Second, EMC continued its scholarship program, begun in 1964, for the National Association of Mutual Insurance Agents (NAMIA) insurance school in Oberlin, Ohio. (The school was now called the Basic Insurance School, and NAMIA had changed its name to the National Association of Professional Insurance Agents in 1976.) Its 30th anniversary

■ ■ ■

Participants in the
1985 Commercial Lines
Underwriting School
held at the Home Office
in Des Moines, Iowa.

in 1986 was marked by a major change, when it was held at Drake University in Des Moines, and EMC's Risk Improvement Department provided an entire afternoon program. That year there were 127 attendees, ranging in age from 17 to 57 from 43 states, Puerto Rico, and the Virgin Islands. This program would continue into the 1990s.

Third was the annual Commercial Lines School, first held at Drake University in 1965. After two decades, a number of the students were sons and daughters of earlier attendees. Several agents from each branch generally attended. The school eventually moved from Drake University to the downtown Home Office. The focus would also shift from coverage to sales, and an Agents Sales Conference replaced the Commercial Lines School in 2005 and 2007.

The fourth program emphasized in the 1980s was the unique and popular agency profit sharing plan instituted by Kochheiser in the early 1970s. Payments were based on agencies' improvements in loss ratios

during three-year periods. EMC prided itself on making payments for the prior year as early as possible in January.

One of EMC's responses to competition was assisting agencies with business expansion loans. During the 1970s, banks became leery of business expansion loans, interest rates skyrocketed, and agencies needed an alternate financing source. President George Kochheiser learned that other insurance companies were making lower interest loans to selected agencies to help expand their businesses or buy out competing agencies. The incentive was to make the lender the number one carrier for the agency. Kochheiser adopted the idea and delegated to Surety Bond Manager Dick Haskins the development of an EMC loan program. Between 1983 and 1991, nine of 13 applications received were approved, and no loan was ever in default. As interest rates fell and bank loans once again became available, some agencies used cheaper bank loans to pay off their EMC loans, and all nine were retired according to contract terms.

New Steps in Claims Management

While there was turbulence within the insurance industry during the 1980s, the weather remained relatively calm, and catastrophe-related claims were relatively small. T. X. Wright, who had been claims manager since 1963, was elected senior vice president in 1978 and continued his able oversight of claims operations until he retired in 1989, after 41 years with EMC.

Vice President of Claims David O. Narigon, who succeeded Wright in 1988, ushered in a new administrative era. As he assumed his new position, Narigon noted that Wright was a navigator who had charted a good course, which he intended to follow. Any changes would not be philosophical, he said. EMC's reason for being would continue to be "the service afforded in paying claims and losses to alleviate human suffering and replace damaged resources."

The last decade and a half of Wright's tenure had witnessed the retirement or resignations of most of the "old guard." Now Narigon began filling vacant positions and making structural changes. While branch claims staff across the country could provide quick responses to policyholders and reduce costs in claims administration, he thought efficiencies could be achieved by returning some of the branch functions to new units and positions created in the Home Office.

The first step was hiring litigation attorney and former county prosecutor Mark Cullen in March 1990. His job at EMC was to establish a Home Office subrogation operation. He also provided support to local attorneys on EMC subrogation cases in jurisdictions where he was not admitted to the bar. By 1999, there was a staff of 18: lawyers, paralegals, legal assistants, adjusters, and support personnel in the subrogation unit.

The next step was creating what became known as medical claims review (MCR) in 1990. It brought on board a number of nurses to answer questions regarding medical diagnosis and prognosis for both casualty and workers' compensation claims. A workers' compensation bill review service was soon added, and all workers' compensation medical bills are now paid by MCR. Mary Jane Neswold started the unit as medical benefits manager and moved into other positions as they developed before her retirement in 2006. Kathleen Knutsen, who had 26 years of experience in group health and nursing, joined EMC as medical claims consultant supervisor in 1995 and became medical claims services manager in 2000.

■■■

David O. Narigon headed the Claims Department from 1988 to 2005.

The Branches Work Together

By the 1980s, EMC's branches were solidly established as profit centers. At the annual branch managers fall conference in 1989, George Kochheiser stated, "We've got a group of highly experienced branch managers. They have a good network. They have worked together for so many years they really know each other and know about each other's differences in operating areas." Indeed, the average tenure of the 18 branch managers

at that time was 25 years, and the branches were generally operating smoothly, receiving many accolades from their agency forces.

The branch managers conferences were now seen as multipurpose. The main objective was to analyze the insurance environment and develop a plan of action for the next year. This was accomplished by discussing individual branch concerns, ways to improve communications between the branches and Home Office, new products and services, the latest technology used to automate processes, and reports by Home Office specialists. Of no small import was the accompanying opportunity to build on the exchange of ideas that occurred throughout the year: how to strengthen agency relationships and further premium growth, ways to increase the proportion of commercial lines, office expansions and changes in location, personnel changes, and the promotion of cordial relationships among staff.

Subsidiaries Extend EMC's Scope

The EMC Family Tree

In 1983, 13 companies operated under the trade name Employers Mutual Companies. Besides EMC, there were 11 affiliates and subsidiaries, four of which functioned as branches, and the holding company, EMC Insurance Group Inc. Within EMC itself were 14 additional branches and three claims service offices.

EMC Insurance Group Inc.

Upon its formation, EMC Insurance Group Inc. (EMCI) became part of EMC's intercompany underwriting pool, which enabled more uniform underwriting by placing the capacity of all participants at the disposal of each company in the pool. The pool had originated with formation of EMC's first subsidiary, EMCASCO Insurance Company, in 1958 when the premiums and risks of both companies were pooled. EMC subsequently reinsured 100% of both Union Mutual Insurance Company of Providence and Dakota Fire Insurance Company, after affiliating with them in 1968 and 1973, respectively. That set the precedent for future subsidiaries and affiliates to cede all of their underwriting business to EMC and receive back their proportional share of the pool. EMCI's share was 17% in 1982.

To further ensure fairness and prevent conflict of interest issues, an intercompany committee of the board was formed in 1984. Three "outside" directors were chosen by EMC and EMCI to review and approve all transactions between the two corporations. Arms' length transactions were to prevent advantage or disadvantage to EMC's policy-holders and EMCI's shareholders. Initial EMC committee members were John M. Lockhart, Harlan T. Moses, and John D. Stoddard. George C. Carpenter, III, Crawford C. Hubbell, and Raymond A. Michel represented EMCI. Hubbell retired in 1985 and was replaced by David J. Fisher.

In 1988, EMCI's stock dividend was 13¢ per share, and the company was gaining respect. At the end of 1989, *Forbes* ranked EMCI in the top 5% of America's small publicly traded companies.

Farm and City Insurance of West Des Moines

Aside from American Liberty Insurance Company, which became the Birmingham Branch, EMC's only acquisition during the decade was specialty auto insurance carrier Farm and City Insurance Company of West Des Moines in 1984. Originally chartered in 1899 as Farm and City Mutual Insurance Association of Iowa, a fire company, its charter was purchased in 1960 by Farmers Casualty Company Mutual. Two years later, it was incorporated as a stock company, Farm and City Insurance Company, and began doing business as a writer of nonstandard auto insurance in Iowa, South Dakota, Kansas, and Nebraska.

Over time, other companies, in addition to Farmers Casualty Company Mutual, acquired ownership interest in Farm and City, and EMC Chairman Robb Kelley took stock of the possibilities. He viewed Farm and City as a good underwriter with "a proven facility to handle high-risk business profitably" and believed it would be a positive addition to EMC. Its nonstandard business could provide additional diversification to EMC's business, and there was less competition in the nonstandard field.

By early 1983, negotiations were underway to purchase the company, and agreement was reached at the end of December. For $8.6 million, EMC Insurance Group Inc. purchased all 30,000 shares of issued and outstanding stock, which were then held by three mutual companies and two of their subsidiaries. At that point, Farm and City's assets were over $10 million, surplus was over $6 million, underwriting profits were about $600,000, and it had an A+ rating from A.M. Best. About 80% of its business was in Iowa, with the remaining 20% in Missouri, Kansas, Nebraska, and the Dakotas. It was providing a market for nonstandard business to 1,500 independent agents.

The transaction was completed January 3, 1984. All Farm and City officers and directors resigned, but several were retained. General Manager Gene Mattise became president and general manager; Claims Manager Ralph Summa, a former EMC claims supervisor,

Individual branch office developments are presented in the "At the Branches" section of this book.

was named vice president; and Assistant
Claims Manager Robert Lineback was named
secretary. Farm and City's operations continued
with existing staff at their West Des Moines
location. Because its business was different,
it was not included in EMC's intercompany
pooling arrangement.

In 1987, EMC's five-year strategic plan
called for Farm and City's marketing emphasis
to be in rural and small town areas in
Midwestern states. There was little likelihood
that business could be profitable in
"tough metropolitan markets." Restraint
in underwriting was needed, but expansion,
in conjunction with EMC Underwriters, Ltd.,
was projected for motorcycle, residual dwelling,
and excess auto liability lines. The updating
of data processing, then underway, would
"further reduce their already enviable expense
ratio," while enhancing service and making
new products readily available. By 1988,
the company had moved to a new office
suite, and 14 employees handled $12.5
million of premiums.

Employers Modern Life Company

Employers Modern Life Company (EML)
observed its 20th anniversary in 1983 with
a reception for Home Office EML personnel.
Featured was a cake decorated to resemble
Robb Kelley's 1961 memo to himself,
reminding him to start the company.

John Button, president and COO, introduced
many changes as he led the company through
the decade. One of the first was offering
interest-sensitive universal life products made
possible by a Life/70 mainframe computer
system installed in 1983. By 1985, life managers
and agents were using hand-held computers
to illustrate the policies.

In 1986, EML Marketing Services, Inc.
(EMS), a brokerage subsidiary wholly owned
by EML, was formed to add the sales capabilities
of a brokerage to the existing direct sales
approach. EML Assistant Vice President Ralph
Varisco was named president. Its first personal
policy was issued in July, and contracts with
four companies soon initiated commercial
writings. After two years, EMS moved to
a separate office in the Des Moines skywalk,
and group insurance, long-term care,
cancer/dread disease insurance, and Medicare
supplemental insurance were added to
its offerings. Administrative and accounting
procedures were developed by Alan D. Huisinga,
an EML accountant since 1972, who would be
named EML vice president of operations and
treasurer in 1988 and president of EMS in 1989.

In 1987, J. Michael Dollar was hired to fill
a new position, special life marketing director.
His duty at EML was to phase out the life
manager system, used since its inauguration

by Ed Bird in 1964, and to introduce a new approach called managing general agent (MGA). MGA replaced salaried branch life managers with independent agents who specialized in life products. The agents worked with P&C agencies in their immediate geographical areas and were paid only when they sold business. Agent services were moved from the branches to EML's home office to create efficiency. Working in conjunction with EMS, new products were added to the life portfolio, and faster underwriting services and reduced expenses were developed for the MGA system.

The life manager system was fully converted to MGA in 1988. By year's end, $4,456,000 in new premium had been written and the seniors' market was being deeply penetrated. Results for amount purchased, amount in force, premium, and annuity business were all above national averages, while death payments were below.

To make room for expanding EMC departments in 1985, the life company relocated to the Robertson Building, which was part of the 1981 home block purchases. The 25th anniversary was observed in 1988 with the introduction of a special "EML designer" universal life policy for employees and their immediate families. John Button retired in 1990, and Alan Huisinga became president and treasurer in September.

EMC Premium Services Company

The number of accounts handled by EMC Premium Services Company grew during the first half of the 1980s from 2,255 in 1983, an increase of 27% over the previous

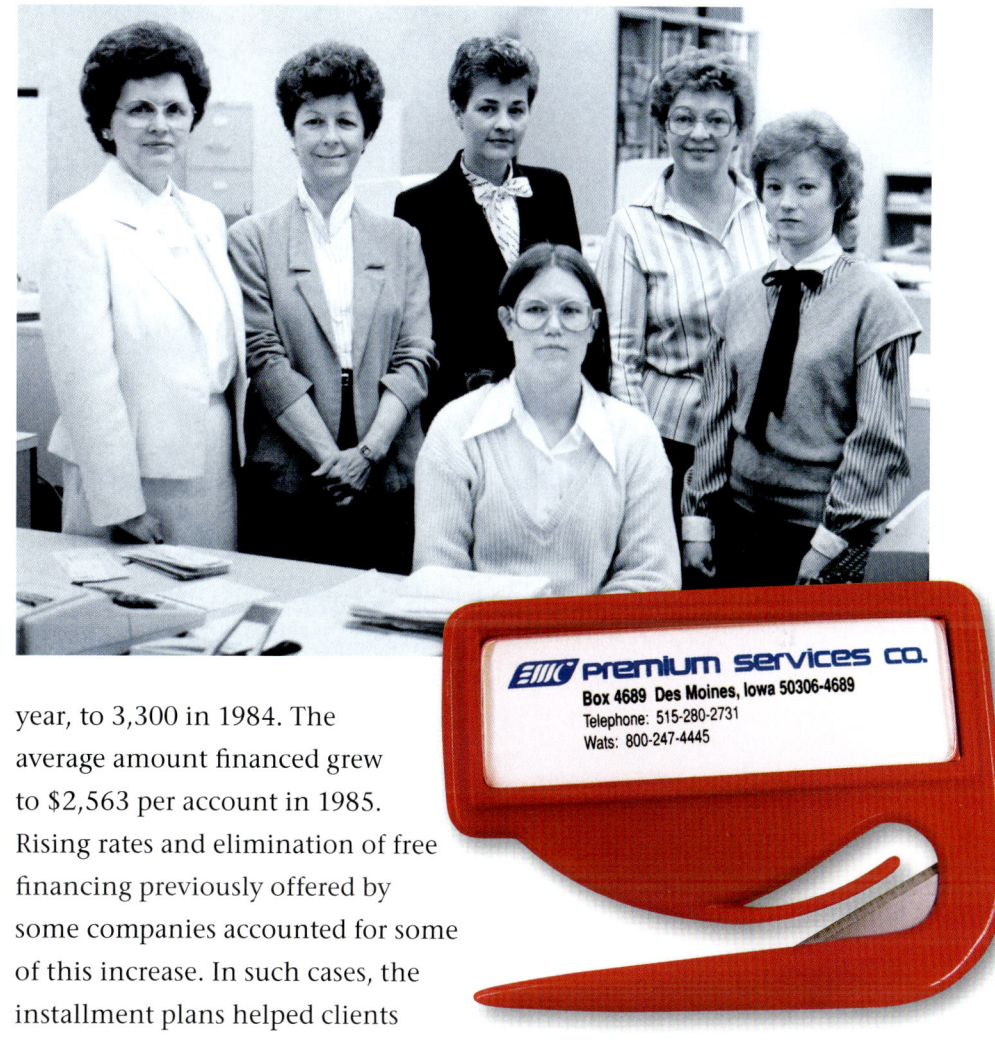

The staff of EMC Premium Services Company: Patricia Meyer, Lola Jackman, Sharon Townsend, Kay Morey, Rita Allsup, Kathy Babinat. (left to right)

year, to 3,300 in 1984. The average amount financed grew to $2,563 per account in 1985. Rising rates and elimination of free financing previously offered by some companies accounted for some of this increase. In such cases, the installment plans helped clients manage the higher costs.

Manager Pat Spowart Meyer was promoted to vice president in 1984 and to president in 1986, the year she also chaired EMC's 75th anniversary celebration. As the decade wound down, so did EMC Premium Services Company. The interest rates of commercial lenders were going down, reducing the need for other financing services, and Premium Service's volume became too small to offset its overhead. In 1989, Elizabeth Anne Heartney retired as home office services supervisor, and Meyer undertook those duties while phasing out Premium Services. The phase-out was completed in 1994, and Meyer retired four years later.

EMC Reinsurance Company

Perhaps most memorable for EMC Reinsurance Company (EMC Re) during the 1980s was the relationship with reinsurance underwriter Russell Reinsurance Services, Inc. (Russell Re), of Southfield, Michigan. Russell Re was looking for a company that could expand capacity for issuing reinsurance treaties, and EMC Re was a new and respected company wishing to build premium volume. In 1982, Russell Re contracted with EMC Re to issue policies that it underwrote, and volume was steadily built for EMC Re. All business was written in the name of EMC and ceded internally to EMC Re.

All seemed to be going well until early 1987, when EMC Re discovered that the nature of business being underwritten was leading to an unprofitable situation. The relationship with Russell Re was terminated in December. Because some of the reinsurers involved in protecting EMC on the Russell Re business became insolvent, EMC was left to handle not only its own obligations but also those of the insolvent companies. From then on, all underwriting for EMC Re's business was tightly controlled in-house, and results improved.

While EMC Re handled only assumed reinsurance, its principals, President Dick Haskins and Vice President Wayne Goettsch, continued to handle ceded reinsurance for the EMC companies. Goettsch retired in 1988 and was succeeded by Dean P. McClaflin, who had joined EMC Reinsurance Company as vice president in January, following a 29-year insurance career. When Haskins retired in 1992, McClaflin became president of EMC Re.

EMC Underwriters, Ltd.

"The key to success for EMC Underwriters, Ltd., has been its ability to find market niches, develop them, and leave that niche when it becomes unprofitable," wrote President Bob Ruby in early 1991 of this brokerage for uncommon coverages. Indeed, opportunity to sell these coverages were legion — the company received about 2,500 to 3,000 phone inquiries and requests for coverage each month — but EMC Underwriters chose carefully. It agreed to do business with only 15–20%, moving in and out of various types of risks as the marketplace changed. For example, coverage of medical malpractice and long-haul trucking, which had been vigorous during the 1970s, was greatly reduced in the 1980s, while that of snowmobile associations, apartment rehabilitation programs, and motor cargo increased.

The brokerage continued to focus on Iowa and contiguous states, where marketing was less expensive and demand for ultra-large or hazardous risks was lower. Staff was kept small at around a dozen, and automated processing was utilized to the maximum. The formula worked. In 1990, over $10 million of business was generated. At that point, EMC Underwriters moved from the Home Office to separate quarters in West Des Moines. Ruby explained, "Not only did we need more room, but we needed the autonomy that's associated with separate facilities." General supervision was placed under Fred Schiek when he was promoted to senior vice president for marketing, underwriting, and branch operations of EMC in 1991.

...

An increase in employees and new emerging issues created a need for a larger human resources staff in 1990. Back row: Betty Woodburn, Colette Wortman, Lynda Twine, Teresa Phillips, Mike Foggia, Sally Drake, Kathy Miller. Front row: Diana Cornish, Doug Zmolek, Cathy Ziebell, Tamara Bernard. (left to right)

Behind the Scenes

Human Resources

Doug Zmolek became human resources director in 1985, at a time when the vision of personnel functions was broadening. Not only were additional staff needed to service the number of employees, which increased to over 1,500 during the 1980s, but they also had to become more specialized to administer expanded and changing benefit plans.

New regulations demanded greater accountability. Emerging issues required response. For example, sexual harassment was defined, and a policy for dealing with it was added to the Employee Handbook. A policy for fair employment and advancement opportunities at both the Home Office and branches was established, and tools for enforcing it were spelled out. Interviews, tests, reference checking, and maintaining good relationships with labor sources were emphasized. Upgrading automation was an ongoing challenge.

Keeping Compensation and Benefits Competitive

Over the years, wages and salaries grew, and benefits were modified to meet employees' needs, while remaining competitive with benefits offered by other employers. Escalating medical costs were countered by a choice of insurance plans for employees. The company paid 100% of premiums as well as 65% of dependents' coverage and 80% of dental expenses. Employees were encouraged to become better "healthcare consumers."

A fitness facility was set up for Home Office and Des Moines Branch personnel where they could exercise, get basic medical tests, and take health education classes.

An opportunity for all employees to participate in the company's financial performance was made available with EMC Insurance Group's public offering in 1982. This was expanded in 1988, when an employee stock purchase plan was established. The plan gave greater incentive to contribute to the company's well being and also created potential for employees to accumulate some personal wealth as the company grew.

When 1988 turned out to be EMC's "best year to date," the company decided to share its success. A 3%-of-salary bonus totaling $780,000 was paid to approximately 1,250 employees not already in a bonus plan.

By the late 1980s, retirement benefits had not kept up with inflation and several actions were taken to ameliorate the growing deficiency.

...

Douglas J. Zmolek was named director of human resources in 1985 and retired as vice president/human resources in 2006.

Top: John D. Isenhart, senior vice president/data processing and methods, retired in 2003.

Bottom: Richard L. "Rick" Gass, senior vice president/ productivity and technology.

In 1988, payments to retirees under the defined benefits plan were upgraded, and supplemental plans were added later. EMC also participated in the 401(k) pension plan, established by Congress in 1978 and approved for implementation by EMC in 1988. EMC consistently matched 50% of each employee's investment, up to a maximum of 6% of salary. A wide variety of investment choices were offered to satisfy employees' range of high to low risk appetites. In 1991, a trust was established for pension fund assets.

From the 1980s, the company also sought to keep in line with industry standards related to officers, key employees, and nonemployee directors. Of particular concern was offering compensation packages that would attract and retain top-level executives. Over the years, officers and top-tier employees were given bonuses and stock options that allowed optimum tax consequences, in addition to commensurate salaries. Bonuses were tied to the company's performance, and stock options had to be held for specified periods before they could be exercised.

Growth of the company required expanded governance responsibilities for directors. To carry out this work, committees were formed that covered a wide range of functions: administration and audit, employee benefits, financial and investment matters, corporate governance, and intercompany relationships within the EMC family. As with key employees, nonemployee directors' pay for their growing active role in the company's governance increased over the years, and retirement plans and life insurance benefits were added to their compensation packages.

Technology

Technological changes had a great effect on general office operations throughout the company. Sometimes it was low-tech, such as using color-coding, terminal digits, microfiche, and linear shelving instead of file cabinets for records management. Higher tech was an Audix voice mail system installed in the Home Office. When installed, it was so new that the local telephone representative had to be taken to Minneapolis to become familiar with it. By late in the decade, use of FAX machines was an accepted method of communication. More dramatic were advances in computer technology.

Although lauded by individual users and departments, introduction of the personal computer in the early 1980s proved to be a headache as well as a benefit. Every department and line of business had a different type of machine, which created complexity, incompatibility, and duplication that was expensive and difficult to support. At the same time, there were problems with IBM mainframe operations. The solution came with use of MAPPER programs. MAPPER (**MA**intain, **P**rocess and **P**repare **E**xecutive **R**eport) could connect different platforms, terminals, and personal computers and combine various hardware and software combinations.

The first step was taken in 1980 when John Isenhart, vice president for data processing and methods, and Richard L. "Rick" Gass, director of information development, and a half-dozen staff members consulted with Sperry and developed several MAPPER programs on a Sperry Model 1100-60 computer purchased

Computer Operator
Judith Halbur mounts
a round reel tape
on an IBM 3420
tape drive in 1980.

•••

EMC moved to using
all UNISYS systems
in the early '80s.

by EMC in 1981. They used a fourth generation language that could build real-time systems and was easier to use, less expensive, and ten times faster. It reduced training time. The systems were demonstrated at the fall 1981 branch managers meeting, and terminals were installed in the branches in 1982. The programs replaced IBM's batch updating process for transferring data to the Home Office.

A commercial lines real-time system was developed and installed in the branches in late 1984, with Commercial Systems Manager Ann M. Erb in charge of the project. The new system was functional in 11 months at a cost of $360,000, giving EMC bragging rights and a tremendous competitive advantage. Five years after EMC's installation, no other company had successfully developed such a system, and a trade magazine reported that such an achievement was still on the horizon. In 1985, John Isenhart announced that all new EMC online systems would be built in MAPPER.

The result was significantly improved efficiency, as evidenced by the elimination of 154 clerical positions through attrition.

Rick Gass was promoted to manager of data processing in 1986 and charged with the responsibility for combining the IBM and Sperry systems. As he began this task, Sperry merged with Burroughs to become UNISYS, and EMC gradually moved toward using all UNISYS systems.

Using MAPPER, efficient new online systems were created in many areas. One striking example was a risk management program that the Des Moines Branch had spent six weeks trying to develop on a personal computer. With MAPPER, it was completed in three hours. When a third-party vendor to Farm and City Insurance Company threatened to raise its price, John Isenhart demonstrated how quickly EMC could build a new system with MAPPER. Suddenly, the vendor was happy to decrease the price. Within several years, a 40% annual savings was realized, and an in-house MAPPER system replaced the vendor's system.

In late 1985, the board's audit committee drew attention to the need for data processing security to protect the financial integrity of the company as well as for backup to service branches, agents, insureds, and claimants in the event of catastrophe. Discussions continued for several years before a business continuation plan was prepared by a working committee of department managers and key personnel. Data Processing Vice President John Isenhart coordinated committee activities and served as liaison to the policy committee, composed of key officers, which had oversight of the project.

Review of the plan and input from the branches and various departments took place from mid-1988 through 1990. Upon implementation, Assistant Vice President Robert D. Rinehart was named plan coordinator, with responsibility for keeping the system updated, daily if necessary.

Key to the plan was creating a remote secondary computer site, which was approved by the board in 1989. For about two decades, EMC had been among several companies that had an agreement to use disaster backup space provided by Drake University. This site, however, contained no equipment, and EMC needed a facility outside the Des Moines phone system and electric grid so that communication lines with the branches could be kept open in case of catastrophe. In late 1990, Ames, Iowa, located 30 miles north, was selected, and construction began on a 15,000-square-foot, $1.7 million data processing facility.

Completed in late 1991, the center housed approximately 50% of EMC's computer power with a staff of nine data processing professionals. Backup computer tapes were transported to the facility daily, and half of the company's daily computing processes — claims processing, rating, and issuance of commercial insurance policies — were handled there. The facility had dual power sources and communications lines as well as a motor generator. Air conditioning handlers were located in two different parts of the building. The center was on standby to assume 100% of vital data-processing functions if the Home Office computers became unusable.

· · ·

The Foster Building on the northwest corner of Eighth and Walnut Streets in downtown Des Moines circa 1930.

Real Estate: Acquisition, Renovation

After acquisition of the entire "EMC block" was completed in 1981, there was little new activity on the Home Office real estate front until plans began for a new East Tower Annex in 1991. One Hundred LaSalle Corporation handled most of the work related to maintaining, upgrading, and leasing the acquired properties. One renovation of particular interest was the Foster Building on the northwest corner of the EMC block. Built in the late 1800s, this three-story structure was originally the Foster Opera House and Academy of Music. In 1911, it was converted into hotel rooms over retail shops. Fifty years later, the hotel closed, and the last of the shops followed suit in 1983. After the shops closed, EMC remodeled the space into modern offices while preserving its historic outward appearance. Completed in 1986, the new space was used by EMC subsidiaries, and part was leased to Norwest Financial for a time.

Through One Hundred LaSalle Corporation, two additional properties were purchased south of the "EMC block." First were the Ladin Industries properties in 1983. Both the $275,000 purchase price and a five-year lease-back arrangement, which produced annual income of $31,000, were attractive. EMC was then spending $15,000 annually for off-site storage and expected storage needs to double in the near future. The ten-year-old, fully-sprinklered Lortex Building on site was in excellent condition, and when the tenant moved out, it was converted into a records storage facility. Two remaining structures were demolished, and the land became a parking lot. Second to be purchased, in 1987, was the Carpenter Building for $380,000. An older building located east of the Ladin properties, it was converted into records storage for less sensitive materials.

Service to the Community

Planned giving became desirable as the evolution of EMC's donations called for a stable giving pattern in the face of the cyclical nature of the insurance business. The losses of the early 1980s diminished EMC's ability to carry out its developing pattern of sizeable charitable contributions, which benefited recipients and also afforded tax advantages. To ensure annual contributions of at least $150,000, even in down times, and to retain tax benefits, the Charitable Clifford Trust was formed in 1984 to exist for ten years. Five years later, the nonprofit Employers Mutual Charitable Foundation was created to provide "a relatively stable level of giving ... while taking full advantage of the favorable tax treatment given to charitable contributions." The foundation complemented the trust until the trust's expiration in 1994. Since then the foundation has served as EMC's charitable arm.

Drake University, a major recipient of EMC's giving, had cut costs in the early 1970s by eliminating two insurance professorships. To prevent a recurrence, EMC endowed a Chair of Insurance in 1988 to honor former EMC Presidents John A. Gunn, John W. Gunn, and John F. Hynes. Robert W. Cooper was the first Distinguished Professor of Insurance in the chair. In 1990, EMC established an insurance scholarship for Drake undergraduates. For the first decade, it was $10,000 and then doubled after 2000.

Participation in a wide range of charitable activities continued to be sponsored by the Home Office and branches. From 1960 on, EMC's contributions of employee time and money to annual United Way campaigns was outstanding. Employees further initiated a wide range of United Way and other activities — for example, interaction with nursing home residents, food and clothing drives, Big Brother-Big Sisters, special needs programs, and raising funds for the Special Olympics.

Preparing for
New Leadership

As President George Kochheiser approached retirement age, plans began to take shape for transition to a new administration. Bruce G. Kelley, Robb Kelley's son, had earned a degree in history and government from Dartmouth College in 1976 and a J.D. from the University of Iowa Law School in 1979. While completing his education, he clerked three summers at the Des Moines law firm of Bradshaw, Fowler, Proctor, and Fairgrave where EMC General Counsel William Z. Proctor practiced. Upon graduation, Kelley joined the firm and rose from associate lawyer to partner. While at Bradshaw, he handled a number of EMC legal matters.

Then in 1981, when Proctor was completing his 40th year as general counsel, Kelley moved to a new position at EMC — assistant general counsel for EMC, EMCASCO Insurance Company, and Employers Modern Life. A year later, he was promoted to associate general counsel, and, in 1984, he was named to the boards of all three companies as well as Union Mutual Insurance Company (Providence Branch) and Dakota Fire Insurance Company (Bismarck Branch).

At the 1985 annual meeting, Proctor retired and was named general counsel emeritus, and EMC ended its practice of retaining outside

general counsel. Kelley was then named EMC's first in-house general counsel. At that time, he also became vice president of EMC, EMCASCO Insurance Company, Employers Modern Life, and EMC Reinsurance Company. While rising through these ranks, he gained an overview of the company's operations.

Kelley's next promotion — to executive vice president in 1989 — was part of what Kochheiser called a "broadening of the responsibilities shared by our executive staff." He defined it as "a logical recognition and extension of responsibilities for Bruce [that] is intended to involve him more deeply in operations and the planning process." Kelley was placed in charge of developing and managing annual marketing and expense projection plans, planning and coordinating the annual branch managers conference, branch staffing, and agency marketing matters. Branch managers now reported directly to him. He also began making the general executive reports to the

board of directors, while Chairman Robb Kelley, who had been handling that responsibility, presented written reports on the subsidiaries and miscellaneous financial matters.

Bruce Kelley continued in this capacity until he succeeded Kochheiser as president and COO at the annual meeting in 1991, several days before his 37th birthday. The next year, Robb Kelley retired as chief executive officer, and Bruce Kelley assumed that position in addition to the presidency.

When Bruce Kelley became executive vice president in 1989, Richard W. Hoffmann succeeded him as general counsel. Hoffmann studied law at Drake University and received a J.D. from the University of Colorado in 1979. Prior to joining EMC, he was in private law practice for several years before becoming an attorney for Northwestern Bell/U.S. West Communications in 1984. He was named a vice president in 2001.

Kochheiser Retires

George W. Kochheiser retired in 1991 with more than 41 years of employment at EMC. During his career, he never wavered from his modesty about his outstanding contributions, his own personal advancement within the company and industry, and his extensive service to the broader community. When he retired, he said, "The easiest job I've had with the company has been the job of president. After all, it was really the staff and agencies of EMC that did much of the hard work. To be perfectly honest, all I had to do was sound wise. I was lucky to have stumbled into an industry populated by decent, friendly, and bright people. EMC has some of the best. For 41 years, I've been fortunate enough to work with the finest staff and agents any insurance professional could ask for." His only regret was that EMC did not top $1 billion in assets during his presidency. At the end of 1990, assets stood at $901,331,422, but within months after his retirement, they reached the ten-digit goal. He would not be in error to claim major credit for that.

Kochheiser would remain on the EMC Board of Directors and other affiliated boards for 17 more years. During that time he was generous as a source of information and guidance and has played a supportive role in preparation of this book. He was honored in 2002 when his portrait was hung in the executive offices library, which was dedicated in his name.

When Kochheiser retired from the EMC Board on March 12, 2008, a resolution was passed commending his "distinguished career."

...

George Kochheiser, former EMC president and CEO, was inducted into the Iowa Insurance Hall of Fame in 2009.

The resolution noted, in part, his service as an officer of the company and a member of the EMC Board, his service on boards of affiliated companies, his chairmanship of EMC Insurance Group Inc., and his wide experience in the insurance industry. His innumerable contributions were cited as significant to the company's growth and prosperity as he "continually displayed a keen understanding of insurance underwriting and marketing, devotion, sound business judgment, valuable counsel and leadership skills." Capping Kochheiser's honors was induction into the Iowa Insurance Hall of Fame on May 21, 2009. ▪

•••

The EMC Board of Directors in 1989. Standing: L. Robert Bolton, John D. Stoddard, Robert M. Gunn, Lanning Macfarland Jr., Blaine A. Briggs, Richard W. Booth, John M. Lockhart, Dr. John H. Kelley, William H. Brenton, Phillip T. Van Ekeren, Albert C. Rawson, Harlan T. Moses. Seated: William Z. Proctor, George W. Kochheiser, Robb B. Kelley, Bruce G. Kelley, Webster M. Lehmann. (left to right)

•••

Left: EMC Insurance Group Inc. celebrated its 25-year anniversary on the NASDAQ in 2007.

A Company You Can Count On: 1990 – 2010

Passing the Torch

"My father's vision was instrumental in helping build the Company to be one of Iowa's largest Property and Casualty companies. His strong sense of midwestern values continues to set the tone for our company," said President Bruce Kelley when Robb Kelley died on September 1, 1997.

President John A. Gunn had laid a foundation, and his successors had added their vision and expertise to build on that foundation. The retirement and death of Robb B. Kelley was, in a sense, the end of an era, but it also opened the way for the next stage of the company's history.

Bruce Kelley would lead EMC into future challenges from a rock-solid base.

The guard began to change when George Kochheiser was named President in 1982. Then Robb Kelley's other responsibilities — treasurer, CEO, chairman, and director — were gradually transferred to his successors. In 1985, Elwin H. "Al" Creese was named treasurer. Bruce Kelley became CEO in 1992, a year after becoming president. Albert C. Rawson was the successor chairman in 1994. Finally, Kelley retired from the board of directors in 1996 and was named honorary chairman.

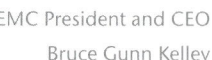

Staying the Course

As Bruce Kelley assumed leadership during EMC's 80th year, he articulated the traditions of EMC: financial stability; high ethical business standards; commitment to employees, agents, and insureds; and pride in its communities. "There will be no big changes at EMC," he promised. "We will keep a steady course. We will not make changes for change's sake. Changes will only be implemented when and where they are necessary for our continued growth and prosperity."

Nearly two decades into his presidency, he was recognized as having stayed the course with his own style of management. In May 2009, an article in the *Des Moines Business Record* called him "steady as he goes." It termed Kelley's executive style "low-key" with a gift for understatement, like that of his predecessor, George Kochheiser. Charlie Edwards, dean of the College of Business and Public Administration, Drake University, said, "[Kelley] doesn't have a big ego; he's just quietly effective." Seen by others as deflecting attention from himself whenever possible, Kelley described his own modus operandi

as one of assembling an "excellent staff" of "good, competent people in their areas, and then constantly trying to help those people work together to build the company." Kochheiser viewed him as both student and educator who understood the business well.

One event signaled a major change for EMC as Bruce Kelley began his presidency. In late 1992, the trade name "EMC Insurance Companies" replaced "Employers Mutual Companies," used since the 1960s, to avoid confusion with other "Employers Mutuals" and to reflect that both mutual and stock companies were now under parent company EMCC's wing.

The mix of mutual, stock, and publicly traded entities under the EMC umbrella, coupled with the growing importance of investments, demanded very sophisticated financial management and accounting. The increasing complexity and scope of operations required greater specialization. Internal structural reorganization to adapt to changing circumstances was ongoing. As technology leaped forward, vast amounts of information became easily accessible, requiring new analytical and management systems; communications accelerated and became less face-to-face; and ways of doing business changed dramatically.

The company adopted a new trade name, EMC Insurance Companies, and a new logo in 1992.

Addressing the position of EMC within this environment, President Kelley said, "What has taken nearly a century to build could be lost quickly if we do not follow a clearly understood code of ethical conduct." At the functional level, he spelled out, "It's a major accomplishment to stay in the insurance business through good times and bad times, to not get overly optimistic in the good times, and to prepare for those tough times that inevitably come because of the cycles."

A decade into his presidency, Kelley initiated a functional and organizational restructuring at the top executive level. As Fred Schiek, who had been promoted to executive vice president and COO in 1992, approached retirement in March 2001, a three-person executive management committee was created to have oversight of all functional areas. It was fully in place when Schiek retired.

Kelley retained his CEO functions and had oversight of Claims. Bill Murray was brought back from the Charlotte Branch as executive vice president and COO. In addition to assuming Schiek's former responsibilities related to branch operations — Underwriting, Marketing, Risk Improvement, and Premium Audit — he was given oversight of surety bonds, ceded reinsurance, and, later, corporate risk management. In 2004, the Claims Department was transferred to his area of responsibility. The third slot was filled by Ron Jean, who was promoted to a new position, executive vice president for corporate development. He was responsible for Actuarial, Data Processing, Human Resources, Budget and Planning, and EMC Reinsurance Company.

As these functions developed, Jean focused on their consistency and coordination.

The structural changes and operating principles put forth by Kelley paid off. From the beginning of his presidency in 1991 through 2009, premiums climbed from $504.6 million to $1.123 billion, surplus increased from $275.8 million to $1.001 billion, and assets rose from $1.002 billion to $3.094 billion. While the dollar amounts were doubling and tripling, the number of employees also increased — by roughly 38% from almost 1,600 to about 2,200.

EMC's strong financial performance has virtually always been recognized with consistently high ratings by A. M. Best Company, which rates the financial strength of insurance companies. From 1917, when Best first published ratings, through 1930, EMC ranked in the top of five tiers of A ratings with "A1" or "A2." Ratings during this period were based on a company's reputation for adjusting and paying losses. When other items such as surplus and ratios were factored in after 1930, the lettering system changed, and EMC was rated "A+" (superior) for 29 years and "A" (excellent) for 35 years. Only during a brief period from 1936 through 1941 was a less stellar performance reflected by a "B+" for five years and a "B" one year.

Stable Financial Management

Crucial to staying the course were several executives who played prominent roles in financial management. Among them was Ray Davis, who was named chief investment officer (CIO) in 1989, senior vice president

Executive Management
Committee members
Bill Murray, executive
vice president and COO;
Bruce Kelley, president
and CEO; and Ron Jean,
executive vice president
for corporate development,
2006. (left to right)

in 1998, and treasurer in 2000, when the title of CIO was discontinued. In anticipation of Davis's retirement in 2010, Lisa A. Stange was hired as assistant director of investments. A former senior portfolio manager and strategist for Principal Global Investors in Des Moines, she had two decades of experience with portfolio management, marketing, and financial strategy for institutional and retail clients. Upon Davis's retirement, she was named vice president and treasurer.

When Davis's CIO position was created in 1989, a chief financial officer (CFO) position was also created and filled by Elwin H. "Al" Creese. After joining EMC as vice president in 1984, he advanced to senior vice president and was a senior officer and/or director of most organizations under the EMC umbrella, including chief financial officer of EMC Insurance Group Inc., before retiring in 1997.

Creese was followed by Mark E. Reese, who had prepared EMC Insurance Group's Securities and Exchange Commission (SEC) filings for four years. Reese continued the SEC filings work in-house, and his responsibilities gradually broadened into the other EMC companies. He became controller in 1995, after Jack Van Sloun retired, and succeeded Creese as CFO. Soon after Reese arrived with his Apple computer and its Lotus 1-2-3 spreadsheet, the Accounting Department converted from the "longer than your arms" papers, prepared with pencils and adding machines, to personal computers.

Preparation of quarterly and annual financial statements to meet regulatory requirements is the primary function of the Accounting Department. In the early 1990s, EMC was one of the first companies to file GAAP statements electronically. Later, a system developed by the SEC called EDGAR (Electronic Data Gathering and Retrieval) was used and is now required for all public companies.

Great change came in 2002 with passage of the Sarbanes-Oxley Act (SOX), also known as the Public Company Accounting Reform and Investor Protection Act, in response to corporate scandals. Compliance with SOX increased interactions among the Accounting, Internal Audit, and Investment Departments. Accounting also worked closely with Data Processing to devise systems and with Human Resources to design executive compensation plans and file them with the SEC.

Changes in the Internal Audit Department coincided with the transfer of CFO responsibilities from Creese to Reese. Ronald A. Paine was hired as internal audit director in 1996, when Don Klemme left the position after 17 years to become vice president of administration.

Paine inherited a staff of three, and they audited all departments and organizations within the EMC structure. After passage of SOX, staff grew to nine to handle the increased volume of work. Iowa's Model Audit Rule brought another layer of regulation in 2010. The department viewed its role as assisting with compliance, rather than being a watchdog. Remaining independent of functional responsibilities within the corporate structure, it reported directly to the CEO and the Audit Committees of the EMC and EMC Insurance Group Boards.

The accounting and internal audit efforts were rewarded in May 2010 when EMC Insurance Group Inc. was included in the "100 Most Trustworthy Companies" list published by *Forbes* in April 2010. EMCI was one of 39 small-cap companies identified as "the most transparent and trustworthy businesses that trade on American exchanges." Inclusion on the list validated the company's core values of honesty and integrity, which have helped build its strong financial foundation and success.

Rate Making and Filing

Besides accounting and auditing functions, another key to strong financial management was rate making and filing. As more premium rates were "customized" for specialized projects, larger accounts, and self-insured entities, the Actuarial Department created three pricing units — one personal and two commercial — in 1990 to work with the branches. In 1996, the units were restructured, and a loss reserve analysis unit was added. Additional work was also created in 1991 when ISO began publishing standard, or manual, rates based on the amount of claims only. The final rates used, which had to cover all claims and underwriting expenses, then had to be calculated using a loss cost multiplier.

By the early 2000s, the actuarial role had expanded beyond pricing and reserving functions to investment and risk analysis, providing management information, and developing statistical models. After the turn of the millennium, spreadsheets were developed on computers that ran 8,000 times faster than the personal computers that used Lotus 1-2-3. Number crunching with spreadsheets was enhanced by modeling with computerized software programs for catastrophe modeling, dynamic financial analysis, and loss reserving. These programs incorporated variables of information, events, and contexts to project scenarios with different potential outcomes that could be evaluated. The internet multiplied the amount and kind of data available and offered a new generation of electronic premium comparisons.

The number of actuarial employees grew from about ten in 1990 to about 30 in 2010. There was also change at the top. When Ron Jean was promoted to executive vice president for corporate development in 2000, Vice President of Actuary Steven C. Peck was promoted to head the department. Peck retired in 2009 and was followed by Vice President Scott R. Jean, who reports directly to President Kelley. Both men had worked through the actuarial ranks after joining EMC in 1984 and 1993, respectively, and both earned the FCAS (Fellow, Casualty Actuarial Society) designation — Peck in 1989 and Scott Jean in 2007.

Paralleling growth in actuarial activities was a dramatic increase in the work of the Rates and Filings Department. The 150 annual filings with state insurance departments and regulatory agencies in the early 1980s increased to 1,800 at the turn of the millennium and to over 3,000 a decade later.

The department also had to update rates for agents in two ways. First, they worked with Data Processing to provide EMC's rates

...

Mark E. Reese,
senior vice president/accounting
and chief financial officer.

...

Ronald A. Paine,
vice president/internal audit.

Steven C. Peck,
vice president/actuary,
retired in 2009.

Scott R. Jean, vice president
and chief actuary.

to organizations that published many companies' rates, making comparisons more accessible to independent agents. Secondly, they updated the two agents' manuals — personal lines and commercial lines — for each state and converted them from paper to electronic versions on EMC's website.

Rates and Filings also used electronic technology to develop procedures for market conduct exams by state insurance departments. These exams make sure regulatory procedures and rules are being followed. They may be routine, as determined by each state, or triggered by a large number of complaints. To its credit, EMC has had few of the latter.

EMC was at the forefront in Iowa, and Iowa was at the forefront of the nation, in implementing electronic rate and form filings. Guided by the National Association of Insurance Commissioners as it developed the web-based System for Electronic Rate and Form Filing (SERFF), the Rates and Filings Department began electronic filings in Iowa in 2002. SERFF is now utilized by 49 states and the District of Columbia. The unique role of Rates and Filings in meeting regulatory requirements has kept it somewhat independent of EMC's internal systems, although it works closely with Data Processing in such areas as producing rates for manual pages and imaging for electronic storage.

Profitable Underwriting

EMC's goal of profitability has always taken precedence over total amount of insurance sold. To achieve sustainable growth in the soft market of the past two decades, major objectives have been selective underwriting and keeping the ratio of losses and loss expense low for written premiums. Strategies include targeting market areas where business can be adequately priced, developing competitive products responsive to market conditions, providing loss control assistance to policyholders, maintaining good relationships with independent agents, and developing effective employees who provide superior service.

Since 2006, commercial accounts have accounted for more than 85% of the company's business, most of which comes from property, liability, auto, and workers' compensation lines. Workers' compensation, EMC's oldest line, currently comprises close to 20% of total business. Personal policies have been targeted in highly competitive, smaller and mid-level markets. The bulk of business comes from non-metropolitan agents in the interior of the country, and property insurance writings on the coasts are limited.

In the early 1990s, Home Office Underwriting turned its attention to product development for select groups of businesses, internally called "focus groups." A market development unit, staffed by Underwriters Carole Hallenbeck and Alison M. Cate, was formed to develop a product offering that could be used by all branches. The result was the Medallion Series, designed to increase property production and to diversify the branches' business. Initiated in 1993, offerings during its first several years included a revised business owners policy (BOP), a financial institutions policy, and coverage for printers, religious institutions, hospitals, metal goods

manufacturers, wholesalers and distributors, boat dealers, laundries and dry cleaners, auto repair shops, and small artisan contractors. By 1998, Medallion premiums were over $15 million and rose to over $23 million the next year.

Beginning in 2005, many Medallion Series products were updated and re-marketed as EMC Choice® products, accompanied by clear guidelines for marketing. One example was a new BOP plan with 80 classes of business. Other EMC Choice products, such as coverage for motels and equipment dealers, were added over the next few years.

Complementing safety dividend groups were target market groups that began to be formed in the early 1990s. Both targeted risks of similar characteristics and classes of business and had

similar benefits, but their sales incentives differed: dividends to policyholders for safety groups and eligibility for agency profit sharing for target market groups. Over the years, group names changed, and some switched between safety dividend and target market structures, but group programs continued to be a mainstay. In 1996, there were 35 active safety dividend groups, generating about one-fourth of EMC's commercial premium with a loss ratio of 51.7%.

As it did with the Michigan Manufactured Housing Safety Dividend Group, the Lansing Branch spearheaded formation of EMC's first target market group. In 1991, Commercial Underwriter Pierce Kent worked with the General Agency Company, Mount Pleasant, Michigan, to form the Michigan Wholesale and Retail Petroleum Marketers Target Market Group.

...

Carole Hallenbeck and Alison Cate developed the Medallion Series products for a select group of businesses in the 1990s. (left to right)

EMC Choice™
METAL GOODS MANUFACTURERS

The EMC Choice™ Metal Goods Manufacturers program is designed

EMC Choice™
BUSINESSOWNE[RS]

SALES GUI[DE]

**EMC Choice™
Businessowne[rs]**

Offering your small businessown[er]
and protection they need – and [...]

EMC Choice™
WHOLESALERS

The EMC Choice™ Wholesalers program is designed for wholesale

...

The EMC Choice® product line, designed for small and midsize businesses, was introduced in 2005; several were updated Medallion Series products.

EMC Choice™
PRINTERS

The EMC Choice™ Printers program is designed for third party commercial

EMC Choice®
EQUIPMENT DEALERS

The EMC Choice® Equipment Dealers program is designed for a variety of retail dealers.

EMC Choice™
SMALL ARTISAN CONTRACTORS

The EMC Choice™ Small Artisan

EMC Choice™
BOAT DEALERS

The EMC Choice™ Boat Dealers program is designed

EMC Choice™
LAUNDRY AND DRY CLEANERS

The EMC Choice™ Laundry and Dry Cleaners program is designed for family or commercial laundry operations.

These operations generally provide dry cleaning services, laundering services and specialty cleaning services for specific types of garments and other textile items.

To be eligible for the EMC Choice Businessowners Laundry and Dry Cleaners program, risks must meet the following criteria (these apply on a per location basis):
- $4 million or less in gross annual receipts
- 25,000 square feet or less
- Do not exceed $3 million combined insurable value for buildings and business personal property

To be eligible for Laundry and Dry Cleaners Bailees coverage, the entire operation's gross annual receipts must be less than $5 million, regardless of the number of locations.

The EMC Choice Laundry and Dry Cleaners program is generally available for businesses with the following operations:
- Laundry and dry cleaning [...]ing stations
- Laundry and dry cleaning plants
- Laundry and dry cleaning stores

The following operations are generally not acceptable for the EMC Choice Laundry Dry Cleaners program:
- Self-service coin-operated laundries unless incidental to the overall operation (attended only)
- Dyeing plants
- Hand laundries
- Pickup and delivery to customers' homes unless an incidental part of the operation
- Routine handling of furs and high-valued textiles

- Converted structures or those not originally built for laundry and dry cleaning operations
- Operations serving food or alcoholic beverages
- Laundromats with sun tanning beds available for customer use
- Diaper service

The most preferred risks for the EMC Choice Laundry and Dry Cleaners program will:
- Show at least three years of profitable business experience
- Have verifiable prior premium and loss information
- Perform satisfactory handling and storage procedures for cleaning solvents and supplies
- Properly inspect and maintain duct work and ventilation components
- Have procedures for receipt, identification and return of stored items
- Maintain buildings and business personal property in an above-average condition
- Continually train employees on safe handling of materials and utilization of equipment
- Make clothing repairs or alterations only as an incidental part of the overall operations
- Place receiving area separate from working area

EMC offers a wide array of coverages to meet the needs of laundries and dry cleaners.

Property, liability, workers' compensation (selected territories), commercial auto, inland marine and others are available to customize for the protection needed.

- Require a signed agreement that includes a hold harmless clause when loaning equipment without an operator
- Deal with equipment manufactured in the United States; if not, a foreign liability policy or United States location is required

The following operations are generally not acceptable for the EMC Choice Equipment Dealers program:
- Dealers selling primarily used equipment
- Sales of mining, quarry, logging, road construction, maintenance equipment or conveyor-type equipment
- Manufacturing, modification, re-[...]gn or alteration of equipment
- [...]ations storing large [...]ts of tires
- [...]e sales of equipment [...] operations

[...] manufactured overseas [...] have a foreign [...] place or a United [...] location
[...] nt to [...]tor

[...] coverages to [...]ent dealers.

[...] compensation [...]al auto, [...]available [...]eded.

EMC Insurance Companies.

Then the branch again worked with General Agency to form the Michigan Charter School Group in 1996, a year after charter schools were authorized.

Before the Indiana and Ohio territory was transferred to the Cincinnati Branch in 1998, the Lansing Branch developed a Cities and Towns Group with the Downey Agency in Kokomo, Indiana. The Milwaukee Branch established a Schools Target Market Program in Wisconsin, marketed jointly by the TRICOR, Inc. and M3 Insurance agencies. After the Charlotte and Valley Forge offices merged in 2001, they continued to separately manage two important petroleum marketer groups they had previously initiated. One of EMC's longest-running petroleum groups, which covers the Carolinas and Virginia, is managed by Charlotte, while Valley Forge manages one that covers Pennsylvania. The Omaha Branch organized and managed the Nebraska Municipal Utilities Safety Group, which covers 230 of the state's 510 cities and over 100 rural fire districts.

Currently, EMC is recognized as an industry leader in underwriting group programs, with well over 100 active target market and safety dividend groups. Public entity programs have continued to be a major part of EMC's group business. In 2010, the company insured 1,345 educational institutions in 13 states from Ohio to Idaho and from North Dakota to Oklahoma. Also covered were 5,273 municipalities, townships, counties, fire departments, and rural water associations in 20 states from Montana to the Gulf Coast and from Colorado to Pennsylvania.

A New Marketing and Underwriting Synergy

Marketing Administrator Dick Fraser, who began working with George Kochheiser in 1962, retired at the end of 1995. For three decades, he had served as Kochheiser's right-hand man and became, essentially, a one-person marketing "department" in which the focus was on agency and branch sales support. In later years, he worked closely with COO Fred Schiek. Beyond his formal duties, Fraser helped new President Bruce Kelley establish his senior management team. Kelley later wrote to him, "Your support and encouragement was very special to me as it eased the transition during those difficult months."

Around the time of Fraser's retirement, personnel shifts were made in the Underwriting Department, and a Marketing Department emerged. After Ron Hallenbeck moved to EMC Reinsurance Company in 1993, Underwriting Specialist Jay L. Oster, who began as an underwriter in the Bismarck Branch, became special lines underwriting manager with responsibility for commercial umbrella, linebacker, employment practices, ceded on direct reinsurance, and the corporate insurance program. In 1996, Kevin Hovick was named marketing director to develop a separate Marketing Department, and Underwriter Shari Petersen Preston, who had transferred from Irvine two years before, succeeded him as commercial property underwriting manager. Casualty Underwriting Manager Jeff Dahms became vice president of commercial casualty lines in 2000.

...

Shari L. Preston, assistant vice president/commercial property underwriting.

...

Jeffrey T. Dahms, vice president/commercial underwriting.

Hovick was named vice president for marketing in 1997, and the market development unit was transferred from Underwriting to the new Marketing Department. They were given responsibility for maintaining close ties to underwriting while serving as primary contacts for the branch offices regarding safety dividend and target market groups and Medallion Series products. In 1999, Daniel C. Crew, an underwriting specialist since 1995 with previous experience at three other insurance companies, was brought in as marketing consultant. Cate moved to a new position as director of employee development in 2002.

Further restructuring occurred after Senior Vice President for Underwriting Margaret Ball retired at the end of 2000. Oversight for both Underwriting and Marketing was placed under a new vice president for business development position, filled by Kevin Hovick. He worked closely with Bruce Kelley, Fred Schiek, and Bill Murray to develop a new forum that formally recognized the intertwined nature of underwriting and marketing and facilitated their complementary work. Succeeding Hovick as director of marketing was Beech Turner, a Des Moines Branch underwriter and special risk supervisor since 1978, who became special risk manager after Wes Sticken's retirement in 1992.

With these changes, the company's marketing effort broadened beyond the traditional focus toward agents. More advertising was directed toward the general public to create consumer awareness, and consistency of image took on greater importance. The website,

created in 1998, provided new opportunities to present information about EMC's management, history, products, and services.

EMC's long-time ad agency, Thomas C. Porter & Associates, was instrumental in developing print ads for a larger audience in national and state independent agency association publications. New in the late 1990s, radio advertising became part of sports marketing programs in select branch territories. In 1999, a series of commercials for the Nebraska market took top honors at the Des Moines and Midwest region ADDY Awards sponsored by the American Advertising Federation.

The *Count on EMC®* brand was introduced in October 2001 to 1,000 employees at the Polk County Convention Complex in Des Moines. The kickoff culminated a two-year process after EMC labeled itself the "Company of Choice" in 1999. *Count on EMC* captured the company's core values of stability and superior service — and it has been the company's brand promise ever since.

As the marketing scope broadened, the Home Office worked with the branches to more effectively engage agents through product development and sales effectiveness endeavors. A consulting firm was hired to facilitate the "Fusion" initiative. Through this project, the sales orientation of branch staffs and agents was enhanced, and products they requested were brought to market more quickly.

To focus more resources on developing products and programs, a product management unit (PMU) was created in the Marketing Department in 2003. Michael A. "Mick" Lovell, who had more than 13 years of previous commercial underwriting and marketing management experience, was hired to organize and manage it. Under his direction, EMC Choice® products replaced the Medallion Series. His other priorities were developing safety dividend and target market groups with the branches, supporting programs already in place, adding new classes of business, and bringing new business acquisition abilities to agents via the internet.

For sales effectiveness, EMC staff and outside consultants trained branch personnel in sales, agency relations, and "marketing best practices." An agency performance value (APV) program was introduced at mid-decade to measure each agency's success in writing and retaining profitable business. Calculated annually, it uses several performance criteria to score all agencies and place them in performance bands. Based on this information, the top performing agencies are rewarded with an additional profit share payment and special benefits.

A series of planned promotions after Bill Murray retired in January 2011 ensured marketing and underwriting continuity.

In early 2010, Lansing Branch Manager Jason R. Bogart was brought to the Home Office to fill a new position, vice president for branch operations, reporting to the COO. He works with the branches on their plans for marketing, underwriting, growth, and agency development.

∎∎∎

Melissa Appenzeller, actuary, and Mick Lovell discuss the product development process as part of the Fusion initiative.

Kevin Hovick was promoted to executive vice president and COO, Mick Lovell replaced Hovick as director of business development, Dan Crew followed Lovell as director of product management, and Beech Turner remained at the helm of Marketing.

A Niche: Surety Bonds

From the first bonds that were written on war contractors in 1942, through the formation of a separate Surety Bond Department in 1959, to the present, surety bonds have always been written countrywide, directed by the Home Office. Contract bonds have produced the major volume.

When David Hixenbaugh left his Home Office underwriter trainee position to go to the Chicago Branch as a bond underwriter in 1975, he thought of himself as the "prototype bond field person." His assignment was to knock on doors to expand the business. Until that time, the Surety Department had been essentially an adjunct to property and casualty lines when a client needed a performance guaranty bond for a contractor.

Hixenbaugh's experience in the field initiated rethinking the role of the Surety Department. When he returned to the Home Office in 1978, the options were to retain the adjunct role or to pursue bond business itself. EMC opted for the latter, which had greater potential for growth and profit. EMC gradually expanded the number of bond-only agents to about a dozen in select territories and, over the years, added bond managers to branch staffs in those areas. Bond premiums grew from about $3–4 million to roughly $33–34 million

by the time Hixenbaugh retired in 2011. He was replaced by Jim Clough.

EMC's Surety Bond Department is unique within EMC in several ways. First, contract bond underwriting is done somewhat like bank lines of credit, based on contract amounts, rather than traditional insurance underwriting, which is based on actuarial determinations. Second, bond claims are serviced differently from property and casualty claims, using a countrywide network of specialist consultants and attorneys developed by Linda Hoffmann, bond claims manager since 1994. Finally, the Surety Department has its own reinsurance treaty using a different broker and reinsurers than does the property and casualty operation. This can be attributed to Dick Haskins, who, through the Independent Reinsurance Underwriters (IRU), helped spearhead what is believed to be the first excess of loss bond coverage in the industry. The treaty executed in 1983 stands today with just a few minor changes.

A nearly paperless automated bond underwriting system (BUS) facilitates the various levels of approval required for issuing bonds. Used by branch and Home Office personnel, it contains all contractors' financial statements, all submissions for approval, and other information. Approvals flow successively through as many as five levels from the bottom up. Entries can be made at any level, while messaging capabilities allow interchange up and down the line with all involved looking at the same thing at the same time. The entire approval process can take as little as a half hour.

Risk Improvement:
Service As a Product

Risk Improvement remained a specially emphasized EMC "product" as new safety and cost control measures for clients were introduced and the range and sophistication of services became more complex and comprehensive in the 1990s. For example, the company began using nurses to test for carpal tunnel syndrome and occupational therapists to assist with return-to-work issues. It provided funding to the State of Iowa's Fire Marshall for training a golden retriever to detect use of accelerants at suspected arson sites. Several years before OSHA's statement that violence, not terrorism, was the biggest threat to business, Risk Improvement created a 45-minute computer presentation, *Violence in the Workplace*, to assist clients with violence prevention strategies. New cost estimating practices and tools were developed in-house for buildings and equipment in 2003 and for wastewater treatment facilities in 2004.

Risk Improvement's work with safety dividend and target market groups and other large accounts continued to be a high priority, especially with schools, municipalities, contractors, and petroleum groups. The ability of its management consulting services program to bring together owners, managers, and employees to analyze business processes and share ideas for improvement was recognized by a Certificate of Excellence award from the National Professional Insurance Agents in 1997. Since 1999, this service has been managed by Senior Engineer Monte Ball, who had worked in cost estimating and fire protection engineering for EMC since 1990. In 2010, management consulting services was merged into engineering services under Ball.

New communications tools created by Risk Improvement included *Loss Control Insights*, a newsletter initiated in 1996 by then Charlotte Branch Manager Bill Murray. It won the Insurance Marketing and Communications Association's "Best in Show" award in 2003. Published in five editions geared to specific client groups, its circulation grew to 38,000 by 2010, in addition to appearing on EMC's website. More recently produced by the department were safety education CDs for agents to use with groups and other policyholders.

Environmental Health Services, which originated as the Environmental Health Lab in 1973, started working with the Des Moines Metro Waste Authority's Rehab the Lab program in 2001 to identify and control hazardous chemicals in Iowa schools. The program identified material for disposal and provided waste disposal training to schools via the Iowa Communications Network (ICN). The first year, 1,028 pounds of material for disposal were identified in eight school districts. Nine years later, the program had reached out to all Iowa school districts, identifying 159 having high hazard materials, 77 with controlled substances, and 164 with radioactive materials. More than 167 tons of materials had been identified for disposal. Rehab the Lab received two Iowa Governor's awards in 2004 — Overall Environmental Excellence and Special Recognition in Waste Management. The next year, the Environmental

David L Hixenbaugh, vice president/bonds, retired in 2011.

James D. Clough was named head of the Bond Department in 2011.

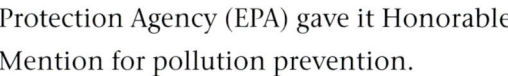

Protection Agency (EPA) gave it Honorable
Mention for pollution prevention.

The program has since grown to include
54 school buildings in 48 school districts
in Nebraska and has expanded into Wisconsin,
Kansas, Minnesota, and South Dakota. In 2007,
EMC became a partner in the EPA's similar
School Chemical Cleanout Campaign (SC3)
initiative, which in 2009 recognized the
company for continued "commitment to create
safer environments in which students can learn
and develop into the leaders of tomorrow."

In 2003, Risk Improvement established a
partnership with Benchmark Roof Consultants,
Inc., of Cedar Rapids, Iowa, to inspect school
building roofs and recommend maintenance
to prevent losses, leaks, and mold. The initial
program — completed in Wisconsin at the
end of 2005 and in Iowa, Nebraska, and

Kansas the next year — inspected more
than 166-million-square-feet of roof in 3,535
buildings in 942 school districts. South Dakota
and Montana were added to the program
in 2006 and Minnesota in 2007. Surveys have
continued in hundreds of school districts.

By 2010, half of the Risk Improvement
staff of 80 was located in the branches.
Significant shifts in management began when
Systems Engineering Manager Norm Anderson
succeeded retiring Manager Bill Duncan in 1994.
When Anderson retired in 2009, Engineering
Services Manager Bryon Snethen was named
vice president for risk improvement. Dennis
Lamport retired as environmental health
services manager in 2006 and was succeeded
by the department's third industrial hygienist,
Kent A. Candee, a former Air Force
bio-environmental engineering technician.

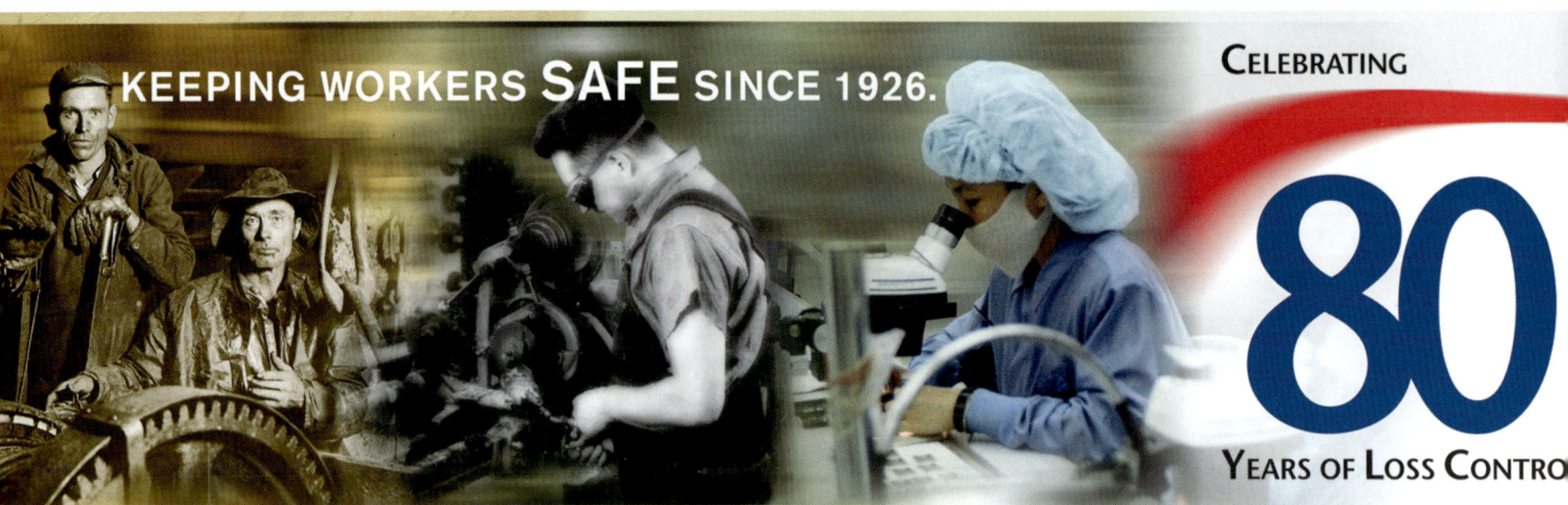

KEEPING WORKERS SAFE SINCE 1926.

CELEBRATING

80

YEARS OF LOSS CONTRO

EMC Insurance Companies.
Risk Improvement

Count on **EMC**

In 2010, Snethen structured the department into five functional areas and an administrative unit headed by Nancy Renda. Continuing in their roles are Monte Ball (engineering services), Kent Candee (environmental health), and Jerry Loghrey (loss prevention information). Former Material Handling Specialist Doug Brinkman has headed field services since 1994, and former Supervisor of Building Cost Estimating and Technical Services Charles Smith was named manager of building valuation.

Risk Improvement's 80th anniversary open house celebration in 2007 exhibited a history of fidelity to the objectives expressed in its present-day vision statement: "Be the best in loss control by providing exceptional services that make a difference."

Inner Workings

Staff Changes, New Functions

The retirements of two giants — Phil Van Ekeren (1996) and Fred Schiek (2001) — were followed by staff and structural changes in leadership. As they closed out their service, both men were elected to the EMC Board and both served as chairman, Van Ekeren from 2002 to 2005 and Schiek from 2005 to 2009. At the administrative level, Don Klemme, who succeeded Van Ekeren as senior vice president of administration, retired at the end of 2007, and Robert L. Link, who had served as administrative services manager in the Chicago Branch and the Home Office, became vice president for administration. The most significant structural change was formation of the Executive Management Committee and the Planning Team, which gave new attention to corporate strategic planning and risk management.

The *Corporate Strategic Plan*, revised every three to five years as needed, projects multiyear goals and strategies. Under the strategic plan, a Corporate Operating Plan is updated annually and reviewed at least quarterly by the planning team, under the direction of Executive Vice President Ron Jean. The team represents all functional areas in the Home Office and receives input from the branch managers. The team sets goals and objectives for growth, service, the combined trade ratio, and improved employee effectiveness and outlines specific action steps for the departments and branches.

Changes in the business climate necessitated new approaches to corporate risk management. In 2001, a Risk Management Committee composed of senior management was formed with five subcommittees. They deal with the risk areas of corporate insurance for property, casualty, and executive liability; business recovery in the face of catastrophe; employee practices; security and fraud; and workplace safety. In 2006, a Corporate Risk Management Department was formed, and Special Lines Underwriting Manager Jay Oster was promoted to manager.

By 2008, a centralized, enterprise-wide approach that recognized the interdependence of risks was put in place. An Enterprise Risk Management (ERM) Committee of the board, headed by Director and COO Bill Murray, began to work out an integrated, holistic

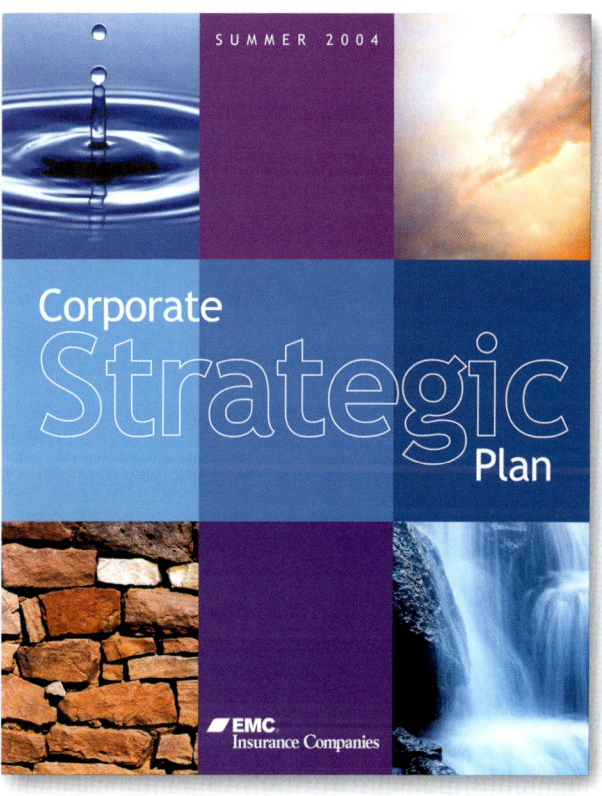

The *Corporate Strategic Plan* projects multiyear goals and strategies.

Robert L. Link, vice president/ administration and secretary of the EMC Board of Directors.

Jay L. Oster, vice president/ corporate risk management.

method with Oster and the planning team. They identified and prioritized risks, defined parameters, and projected means to incorporate risk management into business processes, and continue to develop policies and procedures to fully implement ERM. Top risks are recognized in three categories: 1) liability risks, which include risk selection, pricing, reserves, and catastrophes; 2) asset risks, which include investments and reinsurance recoverables; and 3) operational risks, which include computer systems, security, disaster recovery, legislative changes, and regulatory compliance.

At the operational level, three new departments were created: Corporate Communications, Employee Development, and Program Management. Corporate

Communications was instituted in 2002 when Lisa L. Hamilton was hired to coordinate the company's various internal and external communications. The department was charged with improving communications with employees, agents, policyholders, and the general public.

To clearly communicate the EMC business strategy and company information to employees, the department produces various internal communications, including *Circuit*, the employee newsletter, and the employee intranet site. For external audiences, Corporate Communications is in charge of the annual *Corporate Review*, and oversees the website content and media relations.

In 2004, to reinforce the corporate image and *Count on EMC*® brand, a new corporate graphic identity was established with consistent colors, fonts, and design, including the EMC flag shape as a window for images unique to each company publication. In 2009, Hamilton and her department were selected to head up the company's 100-year celebration in 2011.

Alison Cate's move from the Marketing Department to director of employee development in 2002 was the beginning of the second new department, Employee Development. Initially, Cate conducted surveys to determine employee expectations and training needs. The focus was on core skills and compliance training. Employee Development offers course work in business writing, dealing with confrontational issues, understanding personalities and behavior, and customer service. Leadership training was added later, including locating leadership libraries at the Home Office and each branch office. Initially, technical training was left to the specific department, but now Employee Development is creating an intensive underwriting training course for new underwriters.

The third function was an outgrowth of the Fusion project — creation of the Program Management Office (PMO) in late 2006. Headed by Kenneth J. Fitzgerald, its purpose is to bring central oversight and consistency to the way various projects are developed within the company. The PMO provides project management training resources and coordinates project teams of managers and subject matter experts for all major projects. An oversight committee of top executives and Fitzgerald determines the priority of each project.

Claims Department Expansion Completed
The Home Office Claims Department continued its expansion under David Narigon after 1990. Once the subrogation and medical claims review units were established, surety bond claims were

next to receive attention. Jewell Crouch, who had been responsible for surety losses since 1975, had retired in 1988. Narigon then assumed oversight until the function was moved to the Surety Bond Department in 1994.

An estimatics review unit (ERU), which uses electronic estimating systems, was formed in 1993 after an audit of the branches revealed duplication of processes in assessing auto physical damage claims. Since 1994, it has been headed by Wendell A. Adamson, who had extensive collision repair, body shop management, and casualty insurance experience. Marshall Hildreth, an expert in heavy equipment losses, has served as assistant administrator since 1995. By 2010, there were nine functional units, staffed by 49 employees. They handle all auto property damage estimates over $500 from the majority of branches, and assist them with response to catastrophic storms, including setting up drive-up claim centers. An express pay unit can pay physical damage

claims within a day, if liability is clear. Total loss specialists handle a settlement with vehicle owners, and salvage is sold to pools where a large number of closed bids give the greatest return possible.

A special investigation unit (SIU) was added in 1994 to detect, investigate, and prosecute insurance fraud as part of EMC's antifraud strategy and to ensure compliance with each state's antifraud reporting requirements. Since 1996, it has been managed by Laurie Salz, who joined the company as an adjuster in 1994 and then served as an SIU claims examiner.

Finally, a property review unit was formed in 2003 to assist branches with catastrophes and storms. Oversight is by Home Office Claims Superintendent Charles H. "Chuck" Herrold, who has worked with claims at the Des Moines Branch and Home Office since 1988. He is assisted by Gary Friess, who draws on his fieldwork, litigation, and loss adjustment experience to handle daily supervision.

Left: Lisa A. Simonetta, vice president/claims legal.

Center: Gregory P. Bird, vice president/claims technical.

Right: Richard K. Schulz, senior vice president/claims.

Claims Processing Restructured

Mediation, which complements EMC's arbitration committee work, began in the late 1950s. While arbitration forums are used for cases under $100,000, mediation resolves 90% of major litigated files, such as certain types of product liability cases and construction defect cases. Every effort is made to settle out of court, and, since the early 1990s, litigation specialists have served on staff to negotiate settlements in large cases.

One litigation specialist was Lisa Simonetta, a former California defense attorney who joined EMC in 1992. In an organizational restructuring ten years later, claims functions were divided into Claims/Legal under Simonetta and Claims/Technical under Gregory P. Bird, and the special investigation unit was retained. Simonetta is responsible for coverage counsel, litigation management, and subrogation. Bird, who had worked in claims supervisory and management positions in the Des Moines Branch and Home Office since 1977, has oversight of the estimatics review unit, medical claims review, the property review unit, and six claims superintendents.

Another change came after the company became concerned that funds set aside for payment of individual claims were inadequate and added significantly to reserves, resulting in an elevated combined ratio in 2004. Subsequent settlement of those claims confirmed that the strengthening efforts overshot the mark. At that point, David Narigon, having completed his reorganization work, left the company, and Chicago Claims Manager Richard K. Schulz was named senior vice president, home office claims. Before joining EMC in 1999, he had 25 years of field adjusting, litigation management, and claims supervisory experience.

Schultz immediately tackled the reserve problem, using an online claims management system (CLMS) that was developed by many people with strong input from Michael Boggs in Data Processing. Completed in 2002, it allows close tracking of reserve amounts, the development of reserving guidelines for probable outcomes of different kinds of claims, and a verification process to monitor changing reserves. These measures have improved consistency and allow accurate adjustments to be made to the company's overall reserves.

Shultz has also taken steps to ensure balance between centralized consistency and decentralized flexibility to respond to local and regional needs, including governance of the huge amounts of data generated. A division of labor allows the branches to handle the claims in which they have the most expertise, while the Home Office takes care of very large and complicated exposures as well as routine smaller claims, such as automobile glass, that can be handled en masse by specialists.

In 2008, the subrogation unit was reorganized to eliminate in-house attorneys and increase reliance on adjusters, who handle subrogation in about 75% of cases. Subrogation and salvage recoveries grew from $9.1 million in 1990 to $23.7 million in 2000 and totaled $17.2 million in 2009.

Behind the scenes, Claims Administrator Christine Brandenburg, a former Des Moines Branch Office adjuster and claims specialist, manages day-to-day departmental administration, including oversight of reporting to the National Council on Compensation Insurance, support of coding at the branches, and coordinating various project efforts.

Automation has created major changes in claims processing. In 1999, a new property estimating program allowed adjusters to write and pay estimates on the spot, using laptop computers. Installation of CLMS in the branch offices in 2002 placed all claims information online, eliminating paper flow and allowing instantaneous assignments to adjusters. With many small claims it takes only one day from receipt of the claim to sending a check to the insured. In 2008, online claim reporting was made available to policyholders through EMC's website.

Schulz anticipates that the next priorities will be improving customer service through work with adjusters, getting better settlements through accurate pricing of claims, and reducing expenses by using automation efficiencies.

EMC: A Good Place to Work

The company's tradition of ensuring employee satisfaction — in the belief that challenged, well-compensated and healthy employees are productive employees — remains strong as it moves into its 100th year. This is illustrated by enhanced employee benefits, increasing salaries and bonuses, and a variety of events and programs. During the war in Iraq, EMC made up the difference in pay for six months for employees who served in the military or were reservists called into active duty. The Contingent Salary Plan was adopted in 2002. Precursors to the plan were the bonus given

...

EMC has made employee satisfaction a No. 1 priority since day one.

for exceptional profitability in 1988 and given to all employees in 1994 and 1995. Since 2002, a substantial bonus, triggered by superior company profitability, has been paid to every employee almost every year.

EMC has received several awards from the Wellness Council of America and Iowa's Annual Worksite Wellness Conference for being one of America's healthiest companies. At the Home Office, there are company walks, health screenings, smoking cessation and weight loss assistance and annual flu shots. The branches conduct similar activities and receive support from the Home Office for such benefits as gym memberships for employees.

Since 1999, over 2,000 employees have been on EMC's payroll. Human Resources Director Doug Zmolek retired in 2005 and was succeeded by Assistant Director Kristi K. Johnson, former EMC associate general counsel, who was named senior vice president in 2009. The next year, she took a position with another company and was succeeded by Elizabeth A. Nigut, formerly an attorney with the Bradshaw Law Firm and general counsel for the Des Moines Public School District.

From Data Processing to Productivity and Technology

Technology and data processing functions have continued to mature. During the 1990s, subdepartments developed within the Data Processing Department, and system manager positions were created for all of EMC's functional areas. Branch, subsidiary, and Home Office systems were unified. Both internal and external communications were enhanced using internet and intranet capabilities.

At the turn of the millennium, EMC had little difficulty with potential Y2K problems. Many companies had to undertake massive programs to convert the dating systems on the computers vital to their businesses. They had used two-digit year numbers such as 1/1/00 so that, without conversion, when the century number changed, it would be impossible to distinguish between dates for the years beginning with 19 and those in the 2000s. EMC, however, had been using four-digit year numbers in the MAPPER system since the mid-1980s, and all other Y2K adjustments, including those for Hamilton Mutual, were completed by 1998.

That year, EMC was recognized by the State of Iowa for being one of the first companies to use electronic data interchange (EDI) to transfer workers' compensation data. In fact, Iowa was one of the first states to use this technology, and EMC had drawn on its large involvement with workers' compensation and advanced technology to assist with the initial setup. Today, EDI is used in most states and is overseen internally by Steve Tetzloff, external business systems manager.

Records retention, required by law, is managed through an up-to-date records management program. By transferring electronic records to the latest media every ten years, it ensures that they are preserved and remain accessible. The STORE (Standards to Organize Records Effectively) project was implemented in 2009 to review and set standards for companywide record retention. To keep procedures and policies in sync, Methods and Procedures keeps current with claim file retention rates, IRS regulations, and what will be needed for market conduct exams. Assistant Secretary Sean Pelletier of the Legal Department serves as compliance officer.

Director of Office Systems and Productivity Larry McCool directed computer-driven procedures for retention and disposal of documents after 2000. Upon McCool's retirement in 2005, Ken Fitzgerald assumed these duties as the manager of methods and procedures. When Fitzgerald became director of the newly created Program Management Office in 2006, he was succeeded by Max LaBlanc, a methods analyst since 1981.

John Isenhart, senior vice president for data processing and methods, retired in mid-2003 after 40 years of service. With his retirement, came a new department name — Productivity and Technology (P&T). For years, Isenhart had used the name informally to better describe the department's focus, functions, and responsibilities. It seemed only fitting for Rick Gass to make it an official name when he succeeded Isenhart as senior vice president for productivity and technology.

. . .

Elizabeth A. Nigut, vice president/human resources.

. . .

Richard L. "Rick" Gass, senior vice president/ productivity and technology.

Fred Schiek, Bruce Kelley, and Jeff Felts (left to right) with a picture of German Mutual Insurance Company founder H. A. Rattermann to the left.

Branch Office Changes

A New Branch: Hamilton/Cincinnati

The most significant branch development after 1990 was affiliation with Hamilton Mutual Insurance Company, which became the Cincinnati Branch on January 1, 1997. Its proud history dates back to 1858 when German immigrant Heinrich "Henry" Armin Rattermann founded Die Deutsche Gegenseitige Versicherungs Gesellschaft von Cincinnati, or German Mutual Insurance Company, in Hamilton County, Ohio. In 1957, Hamilton merged with the Druggists Mutual Insurance Company of Mansfield, Ohio, and was renamed Hamilton Mutual Insurance Company of

Cincinnati. Richard E. Felts, son of Druggist Mutual's President Charles C. Felts, became general manager of the merged company.

Hamilton Mutual entered the casualty business in 1962, and new lines were added through the mid-1970s. Challenges came from natural disasters, including the Xenia tornado in 1974 and stock market fluctuations, but the company continued to prosper into the 1990s. In 1992, Hamilton was named "The Number One Company in the State" by the Michigan Professional Insurance Agents Association. Then a series of losses, a huge computer installation overrun, and other factors led Hamilton to investigate partnering possibilities. Following negotiations, Hamilton and EMC agreed to affiliate through a pooling agreement.

1878.

Deutsche Gegenseitige

Versicherungs-Gesellschaft

von Cincinnati, Ohio.

Incorporirt 1858.

Office: Im Gebäude der Gesellschaft, Südwest-Ecke Walnut und 12ter Straße, eine Treppe hoch.

Baar Ueberschuß-Fond am 1 Januar 1879	$209,188 50
Gesammt-Aktiva am 1. Januar 1879	770,259 75
Passiva	Keine !
Gesammtsumme versichert am 1. Januar 1879	$14,878,731 00
Gesammtsumme Verluste bezahlt in 21 Jahren	136,123 52
Gesammtsumme Prämien-Noten unbenutzt-zurückerstattet an die Versicherten bis 1. Januar 1879	1,747,931 83

F. H. Roewekamp,   Präsident.

H. A. Rattermann,   Sekretär.

• • •

The Die Deutsche Gegenseitige Versicherungs Gesellschaft von Cincinnati (German Mutual Insurance Company) building in Cincinnati and the 1878 financial statement.

The need for sophisticated computer expertise for year 2000 computer compliance was a significant reason for Hamilton's choice in partnering with EMC.

Hamilton remained an Ohio corporation and effectively became EMC's Cincinnati Branch. Jeffrey E. Felts succeeded his father, Richard, in 1983, and was named branch manager. Most of Hamilton's staff of about 85 became EMC employees, but five of the nine directors were from EMC. Hamilton's force of 310 agencies provided strong personal lines business, new opportunities for commercial business in Ohio and Kentucky, and increased volume in Indiana and Michigan. To streamline operations, Hamilton's Michigan business was transferred to the Lansing Branch and Lansing's Indiana business was transferred to Cincinnati during the first few years of affiliation. A major task, completed in 1999, was transitioning Hamilton's existing 60,000 policies to the EMC operating system. Gradually, staff was trimmed to 70 and the number of agencies was reduced to 160. In 2003, Jeff Felts's retirement coincided with conversion of the Irvine Branch into a service office under the Phoenix Branch, and Irvine Branch Manager Kent Kochheiser's transfer to Cincinnati to succeed Felts. In 2005, Hamilton was redomesticated to Iowa for efficiency, accounting, and filing purposes.

EMC's Other Branches

While the Cincinnati Branch was added during this period, three other branches were converted into service offices that report to existing branches — Dallas to Wichita (1996), Valley Forge to Charlotte (2001), and Irvine to Phoenix (2003) — following analysis of impact on marketing, changes in management, and new opportunities for cost savings.

To recognize the leading branches for their ability to produce profitable business through joint underwriting and claims operations, the Hynes-Gunn Challenge Cup was instituted in 2001. Winners to date are: Denver (2002, 2003, 2005, 2009, 2010), Bismarck (2004), and Omaha (2006, 2007, 2008, 2011).

Changes in the EMC Family

EMC Insurance Group Inc.

In honor of the 25th anniversary of EMC Insurance Group Inc.'s (EMCI) initial stock offering, former President George Kochheiser rang the NASDAQ opening bell on February 9, 2007, as EMC employees across the country watched via live satellite feed. A dozen board and staff members joined NASDAQ officials to ring in the day. At that point, EMCI's stock had reached a high of over $34 per share, and quarterly dividends were 17¢, up from 12¢ at the first offering. The economic downturn of 2008 brought a low of about $16 per share, and prices would range in the mid- to lower $20s in the two years after that. But quarterly dividends rose to 18¢.

By 2010, company personnel held 3% of the stock; institutions held 28% in their investment portfolios; other shareholders, among them additional EMC personnel, held 8%; and EMC

∎∎∎

Maria Perez, NASDAQ;
David Fisher, EMCI board
member; Raymond A.
Michel, EMCI board member;
Donald D. Klemme, senior
vice president; George
C. Carpenter III, EMCI
board member; Mark Reese,
senior vice president and
CFO; George W. Kochheiser,
EMCI chairman of the board;
Anita Lake Novak, director
of investor relations; William
A. Murray, executive vice
president and COO; Bruce
G. Kelley, president and
CEO; Bruce Aust, executive
vice president, NASDAQ;
Fred Schiek, EMCI board
member; Margaret Ball,
EMCI board member;
and Joanne Stockdale,
EMCI board member.
(left to right)

∎∎∎

EMC Insurance Group
Inc. Chairman of the Board
George W. Kochheiser signs
the screen after opening
the NASDAQ market
on February 9, 2007.

retained 61%. Besides income to shareholders, EMCI had provided needed capital to EMC Insurance Companies to help stabilize marketplace cycles. In addition to a total net of over $23.9 million from the first two stock offerings in 1982 and 1985, a third offering of two million shares in 2004 had netted $34.89 million.

EMC Risk Services, Inc./LLC

In 1996, EMC purchased the stock of EMC Risk Services, Inc. (ERS) for $497,500 to capitalize the subsidiary that had been incorporated in 1981 but never activated. By that time, there was a growing trend of large businesses toward "alternative insurance mechanisms" such as self-insurance, and it made sense to activate ERS as a third-party administrator, reporting to the Claims Department. Tailored, fee-based risk management, loss control, and claims management services could be provided to businesses that did not want traditional coverage. ERS could also handle EMC's employee claims to avoid conflicts of interest.

The doors opened when Jean Bloomburg, who had experience with a number of insurance agencies and companies, was hired as general manager in 1996. Two months after opening, Casey's General Stores, with about 1,000 convenience stores in seven states, became the first account. Others followed quickly in response to cold calls and working with the branches and independent agents.

ERS became profitable after the Hy-Vee account was rewritten in 2003. Handled by the Des Moines Branch's Special Risk Underwriting Department since 1973, the account had been lost in 1995, when Hy-Vee moved its corporate headquarters to West Des Moines and changed insurance agencies. EMC, however, had continued to handle its open and pending claims. When Hy-Vee returned to EMC, it became ERS's largest account, covering 229 stores in eight states. The account was set up in two weeks, during which 19 additional people were hired to staff it.

Effective in 2005, EMC Risk Services changed its name from "Inc." to "LLC," which better reflected its limited liability form of corporate governance and allowed significant state tax savings. It began reporting to Business Development, rather than Claims, but continued to work closely with EMC's other departments and subsidiaries to provide a full range of services to clients: claims management, risk analysis, medical cost review and case management, vocational rehab, ergonomics, auto estimatics, and fraud investigations. "Service is paramount," Bloomburg said. She attributes ERS's success to the staff, whom she described as "people who recognize our focus is on clients, rather than growth," and concluded, "Growth occurs naturally as a result."

In its first ten years, ERS grew from one to nearly 30 employees and revenues increased 1000%. By 2010, staff was nearly 40 strong, some having come from EMC's intern program which originated in 1997. New accounts continue to be sought and existing ones further developed with an eye toward diversity and adapting to each customer. Even during the economic downturn of 2008, revenues and service fee income increased.

Employers Modern Life/
EMC National Life

The managing general agent program,
inaugurated in 1988, did not solve the sales
management problems of Employers Modern
Life Company despite the best efforts of both
President John Button, who retired in 1990,
and Alan Huisinga, who followed him. By the
mid-1990s, production was flat or decreasing,
and surplus was not increasing enough
to support growth. Following an evaluation
by the Life Insurance Marketing Research
Association (LIMRA) in 1998, many territories
returned to Ed Bird's vision of the formative
years — using employee marketing
representatives instead of life agents.

In 1999, Ralph Varisco, who had experience
with the life manager program of the 1970s,
was named vice president. He had responsibility
for developing a simplified portfolio and

providing more marketing assistance to
property and casualty agents who sold life
products. For the first time since the 1980s,
production goals were achieved in 1998 and
1999. In 2000, insurance in force hit $3 billion,
premiums rose to $44.4 million, and production
reached 105% of the goal, EML's best ever
results. That year, Varisco was promoted
to senior vice president, where he remained
until his death in 2004.

In 2001, a "Teledex" system that speeded
up policy issuance was initiated by Insurance
Services Manager Jeff Varisco, who had joined
EML in 1997 and soon moved into Insurance
Services. A website for agents reduced the
expense of mailings and proposal duplications.

Eric J. Faust, executive vice president and COO, EMCNL.

John R. Kelley, executive vice president and chief marketing officer, EMCNL.

By 2002, insurance in force topped $4 billion, premiums were $73.7 million, surplus stood at $32.9 million, and the A.M. Best rating was A-.

At this time, a cooperative arrangement with the Des Moines-based National Travelers Life Company (NTL) was explored. Unlike the 1971 attempt, this one resulted in a merger. The companies were similar in size, and both used the same computer program for policy administration, contributing to familiarity with operations. EML's focus on individual life production was complemented by NTL's specialization in worksite marketing, and EMC's commercial accounts were a ready source of prospects for worksite marketing.

A merger agreement between the parties was executed in March 2003, and EMC National Life Company (EMCNL) became a stock company affiliate of EMC, which owned 49% of the voting stock. Because NTL was a mutual company, their policyholders' interests were placed in a new EMC National Life Mutual Holding Company, which owned 51% of EMCNL's voting stock. The merged company's operations began on July 1, when a board of directors and officers were elected, the organizational structure was approved, and Alan Huisinga was named president and COO.

The new company had 115 employees, $8.5 billion in force, $120 million in annual premiums, $70 million surplus, $500 million assets, and an A. M. Best rating of B++. Employees of the merged companies had already moved to a shared office in Urbandale. By the end of September, agents' contracts were renegotiated, and the new company was reauthorized in 46 states.

Spring 2009 brought major changes in EMCNL's leadership. Alan Huisinga retired, and Bruce Kelley became president. Eric J. Faust, a former underwriter and administrator with National Travelers Life, was named executive vice president and COO. He had become vice president of insurance services for EMCNL, upon merger, and then senior vice president, insurance operations in late 2008. To oversee marketing, former Birmingham Branch Manager John R. Kelley was promoted to executive vice president and chief marketing officer. He had relocated to Iowa in spring 2008 as senior vice president, with responsibility for long-term strategic initiatives in marketing life products to property and casualty companies.

Two significant events occurred in October 2009 under the new leadership. Since 2001, National Travelers had a 10% interest, through reinsurance, with a block of Equi-Trust business, which it carried to EMCNL. Now, EMCNL recaptured 100% of the Equi-Trust block in a new agreement. In another transaction, EMCNL's cancer coverage was transferred to Central United Life Insurance Company, a sister company in the Manhattan Insurance Group based in Houston, Texas. Central United took responsibility for the cancer coverage by reinsuring it 100% as well as handling all management responsibilities.

The second quarter of 2010 witnessed a major milestone as EMCNL's assets topped one billion dollars. At that point, there were 81 employees, 116,000 policies with $12.2 billion in force, $129 million in annual premiums, $70.7 million adjusted capital and surplus, and an A.M. Best rating of B++.

EMC Underwriters, Ltd./LLC

EMC Underwriters, Ltd., converted to a limited liability company (LLC) at the end of 1998. When President Bob Ruby retired in 2007 after 44 years of service, the subsidiary was blended with Home Office Special Lines to form a new Emerging Markets Department within the Business Development section. Dan Crew was named manager of emerging markets and president and COO of EMC Underwriters. Since that time, Marcel D. "Marcy" Boggs, who began as a secretary/policy typist in 1980 and worked up to vice president of operations in 1990, has been handling most of the underwriting.

Efforts have been refocused on writing business in support of the branch offices. For example, EMC Underwriters has been working to provide additional opportunities to branches by converting some forms and coverages that begin as nonadmitted lines into filed, admitted lines through a process of evaluation, development, and incubation. The tradition of insuring special events has continued with coverage for the annual Des Moines Arts Festival, Iowa's largest arts festival.

EMC Reinsurance Company

When Dean McClaflin retired as president of EMC Reinsurance Company (EMC Re) in 1994, Ron Hallenbeck was ready to fill the position. He had worked with purchasing facultative reinsurance (for individual risks) his entire career. As special lines underwriting manager for EMC, he became involved with treaty reinsurance (for classes of risks) around 1987. His move to assistant manager

of EMC Re in 1993 gave him a year of "invaluable lessons" from McClaflin about assumed reinsurance.

The centralized reinsurance underwriting, accounting, and claims staff that McClaflin developed and fostered during his tenure was an enduring legacy. He drew on his wealth of reinsurance and computer system experience to teach Hallenbeck and others how the reinsurance system works and how premium and loss data is booked into the system. Because each contract is unique and accounting reports are not standardized among brokers, reinsurance systems require manual entries. Assisting McClaflin was Vicki Freese, who worked with reinsurance in administrative, accounting, and underwriting capacities since 1983, and began working with assumed reinsurance in 1987. After McClaflin's retirement, she advanced to the position of vice president and secretary of EMC Re and also handles broader reinsurance functions.

McClaflin opened employees' eyes to the value of establishing personal relationships with reinsurance intermediaries through whom business is brought in the door. Currently, a brokers' school, initiated and coordinated by Assistant Vice President Howard Garnett, advances these relationships. The two-day event utilizes volunteer subject matter experts from EMC's direct operations and the West Des Moines Fire Department to educate reinsurance brokers, who may have limited experience with primary insurance company operations. Many of the school's past attendees have gone on to be influential in their respective brokerage offices and have

...

Marcel D. "Marcy" Boggs, vice president of operations for EMC Underwriters, LLC.

Ronnie D. Hallenbeck, president, EMC Reinsurance Company.

aided EMC Re's marketing long after their attendance at the school.

While the bulk of EMC Re business continues to be done through brokers, consolidation has reduced the number from 30 brokers in 1994 to approximately ten in 2010. Most direct reinsurance contracts are written through the Mutual Reinsurance Bureau (MRB) or pools such as the Mutual Atomic Energy Pool and the American Nuclear Pool. EMC Re is now one of four assuming companies in MRB, which does business with about 45 ceding companies. Although EMC Re has been challenged by major industry loss events, its surplus has grown from $21 million in 1990 to $36 million in 1999 and to $121 million in 2010.

Currently, EMC Re has two main priorities. One is improving its pricing models and proficiency of use in order to gain experience as a reinsurer that has more influence over pricing and, in some cases, to be the reinsurer that determines the "lead terms." The other is continuing the venture into international business. In 2005, EMC Re joined the International Cooperative and Mutual Insurance Federation (ICMIF) to network with mutual companies eager to do business with other mutuals around the world. This has opened up a number of opportunities to reinsure mutual companies in Europe, Japan, and elsewhere. Care is taken to keep abreast of cultural differences through study and travel as EMC Re seeks a diverse book of property business. International business has grown from 1% of EMC Re's $35.9 million total written premiums in 1995 to 12% of more than $85 million in 2010.

•••

Vicki L. Freese, vice president, assistant manager of EMC Re.

•••

Howard L. Garnett, assistant vice president and marketing manager, EMC Re.

Farm and City Insurance Company of West Des Moines

Since acquisition by EMC Insurance Group Inc. in 1984, Farm and City had marketed nonstandard auto products from its own office, essentially as a separate company. As premiums fell from $12.5 million to $10 million between 1988 and 1997 and the ratio of surplus to premiums became inadequate, it became clear that the business was not succeeding. In response, Robert Morlan, who became manager in 1990 and president and COO in 1998, changed course to bring the subsidiary more in line with EMC's regular business by moving the office downtown to the skywalk area, changing business strategy to integrate the nonstandard market into the branches, enhancing service levels, and bringing Farm and City into EMC's intercompany pool to improve its financial position.

In the meantime, competition became stiffer as more traditional carriers began to offer nonstandard business. Further costs for upgrading and transition would be greater than the benefits, and management decided to phase out the business. At the end of 2007, Farm and City was merged into EMCASCO Insurance Company and ceased to exist. Morlan then moved into three new, concurrent positions: community relations specialist, government affairs manager, and executive director of Employers Mutual Charitable Foundation.

The Impact of Outside Forces

The greatest impact on EMC's financial position has come from outside forces, including disasters caused by Mother Nature and those caused by corporate scandals, market fluctuations, and terrorist attacks.

Disasters Caused by Humans

Many people with whom EMC Reinsurance Company did business on a daily basis were deeply affected by the terrorist attack on the World Trade Center in New York City on September 11, 2001. Two of EMC's reinsurance brokers were particularly hard hit: The Guy Carpenter/Marsh McLennan (MMC) and AON. The MMC offices in the north tower of the World Trade Center were located on the floors struck by the first plane; all 295 employees and 60 consultants who were in the office at the time died. One hundred seventy-six of AON's 1,100 employees in the south tower were not able to evacuate before the second plane hit that building about 20 floors below their offices.

EMC entities and personnel responded to the losses with total pledges of $68,000 to the MMC Victim's Relief Fund and the AON Memorial Education Fund. On April 9, 2002, President Bruce Kelley presented the pledges in New York City, and $34,290 was distributed to each organization. In addition to reinsurance coverage and charitable contributions, EMC also helped restore some of the Guy Carpenter company records.

EMC's only primary claim from the terrorist attack was from RLI Insurance Company of Peoria, Illinois, which the Chicago Branch had insured for business interruption and property damage. RLI's New York branch office was in the south tower of the World Trade Center, 12 stories below the second plane's impact. Fortunately, only three employees were in the office when the plane struck, and all escaped via the stairs before the building collapsed. Within an hour, RLI's New York business was being routed through their Peoria home office where all documents were backed up. By the next day, all operations were up and running from alternate locations. The cost to EMC was $250,000 for damage to office furniture and equipment.

EMC was less directly affected by the corporate scandals that began breaking in the following years. Charges against companies had to do with manipulation of markets, improper booking, accounting fraud, overstated earnings, bribery, tax evasion, and improper use of funds. First to fall were Enron and its accounting firm, Arthur Andersen. Nineteen more errant companies were listed by *Forbes* magazine in 2002 alone. Among them was WorldCom, where EMC experienced its first loss on a bond purchased by the company. A victim of WorldCom's estimated $11 billion overstatement of total earnings, EMC eventually recovered 80 cents on the dollar when WorldCom emerged from bankruptcy and merged with MCI a couple of years later.

That loss was rare. And it could have been worse, with a recovery of only 30-35 cents on the dollar, had EMC's investment been in a lower class portion, or traunch, of the bond offering. Here again, EMC benefited from its conservative investment philosophy — to invest

...

Top: Howard Garnett at the podium for the 2004 Broker School.

Middle and bottom: Broker School participants suit up for demonstrations at the West Des Moines Fire Department.

in high-quality, rather than high-risk, securities. Although EMC seldom trades bonds, its strategy has been to sell occasional investments that appear to be headed toward default, even if the price is below par. A known smaller loss is considered better than riding out a potential bankruptcy with an uncertain outcome.

The company's cautious planning and conservative investment strategy, however, could not spare it serious losses — along with most business and personal investors in the United States — in the economic downturn and financial turmoil of 2008. The value of EMC's stock portfolio fell from $663 million in 2007 to $427 million in 2008. By the second quarter of 2009, however, stocks were on the rebound. Including new investing activities, the value of the company's stock investments rose to $514 million by the end of 2009.

Hurricanes

EMC's storm experience during the 1960s and 1970s prepared it well for a new era of activity that began with Hurricane Hugo in 1989.

Chief among the company's responses on direct business were its catastrophe or "cat" teams, which were ready to go before storms arrived. Hugo, the most damaging hurricane yet recorded, caused widespread destruction in the Caribbean. It struck Isle of Palms, South Carolina, and played havoc in the Charleston area before traveling 200 miles inland to Charlotte. Within hours, the Charlotte "cat" team began taking loss reports and assessing damages on 1,500 claims that averaged about $2,500 per claim and closed with a total loss of over $3.5 million. Reinforced by 17 adjusters

from United Storm Adjusters and claims personnel from the Home Office and Birmingham and Jackson Branches, they operated out of a makeshift office equipped with fax machines and telephones. Nightly planning sessions were held at a motel.

When it was over, Chairman and CEO Robb Kelley commended those involved, saying, "Hurricane Hugo was a challenge for our agents and claims department ... Our experience ... is an excellent example of insurance in action. *It's why we are in business!"*

Hurricane Andrew came next in 1992, Charley and Ivan in 2004, Katrina and Rita in 2005, and Ike in 2008. Andrew was one of the most destructive hurricanes in U.S. history with total insured losses estimated at $15.5 billion. It first struck the southern tip of Florida, devastating the town of Homestead before moving across the Gulf Coast to strike the Louisiana coast south of Baton Rouge. Even though EMC had chosen to have only minimal direct exposure on the coasts, this 1992 event brought a gross loss of $20.6 million to EMC Re.

Hugo and Andrew caused EMC Re to make changes. Retrocessional protection reduced Hugo's impact from $13.1 million to $6.8 million and Andrew's to $12.6 million, but protection did not come without a price. After catastrophe claims are made, reinstatement premiums must be paid before coverage can be obtained for subsequent events, adding expense on top of paying losses. This caused EMC Re to restrict its writings and to take additional protective measures. An intercompany quota share arrangement,

∎∎∎

Gulf Shores, Alabama,
September 16, 2004 –
Hurricane Ivan makes
landfall in the United States
with sustained winds of
near 120 mph.

∎∎∎

Brewton, Alabama,
September 23, 2004 –
Downed trees remain in
areas hit by Hurricane Ivan.

FEMA Photo/Jocelyn Augustino

which capped occurrences losses to a manageable level at a consistent and fair price, was created in 1993.

Six hurricanes affected EMC Re in 2004, although none were large enough to trigger retrocessional coverage or industry loss warranty payments. The strongest of these was Ivan, which caused 124 fatalities after striking the coast near the Alabama-Florida state line and traveling north. EMC Re, with help from the intercompany quota share capping arrangement, paid $5.8 million for Charley, $6.1 million for Ivan, and lesser amounts for the others.

EMC's direct losses for Ivan were much greater — $19.7 million — with the Birmingham Branch alone processing 1,400 claims. While providing a great deal of protection to policyholders, EMC reduced its direct loss to $11.4 million through ceded reinsurance recoverable.

In 2005, Hurricane Katrina destroyed much of the Mississippi coast and caused devastating losses as far north as Pennsylvania. The total insurance industry property loss was $41.1 billion. EMC's direct loss of $22.3 million included $9.9 million in Mississippi and $2.7 million in Louisiana. Losses would have been greater if prior decisions had not been made in the 1970s to reduce Gulf Coast exposure, to increase the proportion of commercial accounts, to refer wind coverage to the pool, and to obtain reinsurance coverage that mitigated the loss to $11.8 million. For EMC Re, Katrina produced its greatest loss ever — $27.5 million, most in Louisiana and Mississippi. Here, like never before, the value of

retrocessional protections and industry loss warranty coverage came into play, reducing the reinsurance assumed net loss to $11.6 million.

Through Employers Mutual Charitable Foundation, EMC responded immediately with a $100,000 contribution, which the Jackson Branch directed to the Central Mississippi Chapter of the American Red Cross. President Bruce Kelley said, "Our hearts go out to those who have suffered from Katrina in our Gulf Coast locations. All of our customers who were affected by the hurricane should know that not only are we here to support them through swift claims service, but that we also support the efforts of relief workers." Branch Manager Frankie Box responded, "The people of Mississippi, Alabama, and Louisiana are deeply appreciative."

...

Top left: Mauriceville, Texas, October 2, 2005 – Many homes in southeast Texas were crushed by trees felled by Hurricane Rita's high winds.
FEMA Photo/Bob McMillan

Top right: Bruce Kelley presented a $100,000 check from the EMC Insurance Foundation to Jackson Branch Manager Frankie Box to donate to the Central Mississippi Chapter of the American Red Cross.

Bottom: A hurricane-damaged house in Cameron, Louisiana, is checked by FEMA inspectors in preparation for demolition.
FEMA Photo/Marvin Nauman

Although a record breaking number of storms occurred in 2005, EMC's only other major exposure was Hurricane Rita, which struck Texas and Louisiana. Here, the company experienced its second largest direct loss ever — $38.3 million. Through reinsurance, $25.9 million was recovered, reducing the net direct loss to $12.4 million. EMC Re sustained a $6.6 million loss that was only slightly reduced by ceded retrocessional recoveries. The company did not experience another large hurricane loss until Ike hit Texas in 2008, leaving EMC Re with a $13.6 million gross loss, reduced to $11.4 million by retrocessional recovery. EMC's direct loss from Ike was $13.2 million, and $2.5 million was recovered from reinsurance.

- - -

Sand bags were piled
around the EMC Home
Office at 717 Mulberry Street
in an effort to keep rising
flood waters at bay.

- - -

Waters flooded the parking
lots on Eighth Street south
of the Home Office.

Deluge in Des Moines

Des Moines began flooding on Friday, July 9,
1993. In the early hours of Sunday, July 11,
the Des Moines Water Works, about a mile
from the confluence of the Raccoon and
Des Moines Rivers, was overwhelmed, along
with several electric utility substations near
downtown. The city lost its running water
for 12 days, and another week lapsed before
it could be certified potable.

EMC's Home Office and Des Moines Branch,
which employees had banked with sandbags,
were not spared. Although floodwater never
reached the offices, the parking lots and
Carpenter storage building were inundated.
All buildings were without water, power,
or telephone service. Immediately, Senior
Vice President John Isenhart implemented
the business continuation plan completed
in 1990. Dennis Gooch, head of the Building
and Operations Department, and department
heads worked 12-hour shifts around the clock
to carry out recovery efforts. A recently installed
emergency diesel generator was quickly put

to work, and EMC had lighting and a phone
system before city electricity was restored
at 4:00 a.m. on Monday, July 12.

Water was a different matter. How could
employees and computers operate without
the water-cooled air conditioning system?
And what about restrooms? The computer
overheating problem was tackled by EMC's
building engineers, among them Navy veteran
Bruce Alan Cram, who would be with the
company 41 years. Using his previous disaster
experience, he rigged a pump to a hose that
could spray water on the cooling coils of the
air-conditioning unit. Employees hauled water
from surrounding farms and communities
and carried it up the freight elevator to a
holding tank on the ninth floor. By Tuesday
noon, all systems were up and running. Four
college interns had their duties changed from
auditing data quality to carrying trashcans
and buckets of flushing water to six restrooms.
A portable toilet near the front entrance
supplemented their efforts.

The next challenge was air conditioning
throughout the facility. Four hundred gallons
an hour were needed just to cool the three-story
east building. Water pumps and two 800-gallon
plastic tanks were easily purchased for that
task, and water was available from surrounding
areas. Risk Improvement Manager Bill Duncan
assumed a new job description — trucking water
from Altoona, 20 minutes away. His conveyance
was the 1,600-gallon tank he used to fill his
swimming pool, mounted on a truck and
trailer. Cooling the larger west building simply
required expanding the process. Additional
water "pumps, piping, and water tanks with

Top left: Des Moines River, Iowa, July 1993 — An aerial view of floodwaters showing the extent of the damage.
FEMA Photo/Andrea Booher

Above: Water was trucked in from farms and surrounding areas for use at the EMC Home Office.

Top Right: Fleur Drive looking toward the Des Moines Water Works and Gray's Lake Park just south of downtown Des Moines.

Above: College interns switched from their normal duties of auditing data quality to carrying trashcans and buckets of flushing water to restrooms.

Left: EMC building engineer and Navy veteran Bruce Alan Cram used his previous disaster experience to devise a way to cool the computer system.

· · ·

During the flood of 1993, heavy rains throughout June and early July left Des Moines without running water for 12 days and without drinking water for 20 days. Companies like Anheuser-Busch donated drinking water to help during this critical time.

· · ·

Northridge, California, January 17, 1994 – Buildings, cars, and personal property were destroyed when a 6.6 magnitude earthquake struck the Los Angeles suburb.

FEMA News Photo

a capacity of 6,600 gallons were purchased, and a local trucking firm was hired to haul water from other communities.

By Thursday morning all was ready for employees, but there was still a problem. Due to fire and safety concerns, the mayor had limited the occupancy of downtown offices. Although 23% of the Home Office and 70% of the Des Moines Branch staffs were allowed to operate half days, the remaining employees could not be brought in as planned. Some worked from other offices or their homes. Many who came had to navigate around water-covered and damaged roads and bridges. They received free cafeteria food for their effort. All were kept on the normal payday cycle. To eliminate downtown congestion, two shopping mall parking lots became paycheck pick-up sites.

Because the company itself was a victim of the flooding, it was inevitable that claims became backlogged; however, EMC made every effort to maintain its expected level of service. As soon as security guards could be hired to serve as fire guards, an additional 20 employees were brought into the office. Still, there was

a significant backlog on July 22 when city water was restored and all employees were allowed to return. The Workers' Compensation and Employers Modern Life Company staff members joined the Claims Department until the backlog was caught up.

In recognition of the entire event, President Bruce Kelley commented, "Employees handled the situation masterfully. Their energy, creativity, and patience helped us start up faster than other businesses in the area. We appreciate all the employees who came in under trying circumstances and the understanding of branch employees and agents. Thanks to you, we brought EMC to the end of July in good fashion."

EMC's business continuation plan had proved its worth. In fact, the ingenuity, quick action, and hard work of everyone involved had made one element of the plan unnecessary. The off-site data processing backup facility in Ames remained on standby, but was not needed.

The Earth Shakes

Early on January 17, 1994, the 6.6 magnitude Northridge Earthquake struck the San Fernando Valley of California, some 70 miles from the Irvine Branch office. It had the highest ground acceleration ever recorded in a North American urban area. Freeways and buildings collapsed. Severed gas and water mains caused fires to burn through floods. Landslides abounded, their dust causing an outbreak of Valley Fever respiratory disease. Hospitals became unusable. Seventy-two people were killed and over 12,000 were injured.

EMC Re's hit was $9.1 million, but EMC had little direct exposure to earthquakes, and protection brought EMC Re's net loss down to $5.1 million. EMC's direct side underwriting decision to minimize exposures to earthquake had been prudent.

Tornadoes

When about 70 tornadoes touched down in Oklahoma and Kansas in less than 21 hours on May 3, 1999, the Wichita Branch location was in the storm's path, and the homes of several employees were among the 10,000 hit. There could have been no more personal reminder that responding to accidents and disasters is at the heart of insurance work. Branch action was quick and effective. Nearly 300 claims were handled the first two days without the help of additional outside adjusters. EMC's direct loss for this storm approached $5.7 million, with the Haysville school system producing a single loss of over $500,000.

It was the beginning of a big storm year. Of EMC's total direct losses of $49.5 million

...

Greensburg, Kansas,
May 16, 2007 –
The center of town
12 days after it was
hit by an EF5 tornado
with 200 mph winds.
FEMA Photo/Greg Henshall

in 1999, three of four other storms that produced losses of $5.6 million to $9.4 million also hit Kansas. About $1.9 million total was recovered through reinsurance. EMC was heavily exposed in Kansas as the insurer of 75% of its school districts and 49% of the incorporated municipalities.

Kansas was again hit on May 4, 2007, when an outbreak of 123 tornadoes ripped across the state. The town of Greensburg was wiped out, and 14 people were killed by one EF5 tornado packing winds of over 200 miles per hour. As soon as claims adjusters and property specialists were allowed access to the damaged area, EMC was working with policyholders. Between May 8 and 10, they inspected all covered properties, which included homes, businesses, the town's school district, and the county government. Of the $30.3 million

direct claims paid by EMC, $10.5 million was recovered through reinsurance.

The next year, nearly half of Parkersburg, Iowa, was flattened, and over a dozen people were killed on May 25 by another EF5 tornado. Its path of destruction was half a mile to a mile wide for over 40 miles across Butler and Black Hawk Counties. That event produced EMC's largest-ever direct loss — $45.3 million. This time, $12.7 million was recovered through reinsurance. EMC Re's gross loss for tornadoes, wind, and hail across seven states that season was small by contrast — under $2 million.

Since 2000, EMC's direct property value exposures have increased over 60%, and direct storm loss activity has increased as well. EMC Re has also experienced increased storm loss activity during this period, although their larger losses tend to be non-Midwestern events.

∎∎∎

Left: Parkersburg, Iowa,
May 28, 2008 – A couple
stands among the debris
of their home, of which
only a kitchen wall
remains standing, after
an EF5 tornado razed nearly
the entire town.

Right: Parkersburg High
School was reduced
to a pile of rubble, with
a collapsed roof, twisted
structure beams, and
fallen brick walls.
FEMA Photos/Barry Bahler

A Good Citizen

EMC's service philosophy extends beyond policyholders to the larger community. In a March-April 2006 *Circuit* article, President Bruce Kelley could easily have been talking about either. He said, "Service performed out of duty or obligation alone yields a less positive result than service performed with the heartfelt intention to do what is good or right." He also emphasized caring and empathy, attentiveness to the other, and cooperation among individuals.

The EMC Insurance Foundation is EMC's primary channel for charitable corporate giving to nonprofit organizations. Ten years after its formation in 1989, funding was granted to 300 of 1,700 requests received, with 10% going to civic organizations, 25% to community funds, 30% to cultural organizations and facilities, and 35% to education and scholarships. Today, 0.1% of surplus is the guideline for total annual giving, and about $1 million is granted each year.

From the foundation's beginning, its management and funding decisions have been made at the executive and board level. Staff assistance was added in 1995 when Joseph A. Smith, former vice president of fundraising for the United Way of Central Iowa, was hired to handle administration and to serve as community relations officer. After the executive director position was created and filled by Bob Morlan in 2008, the name was changed from Employers Mutual Charitable Foundation to EMC Insurance Foundation. Morlan retired in 2011 and was replaced by Sean Pelletier.

United Way and Drake University continue to be major recipients. Employee-conducted

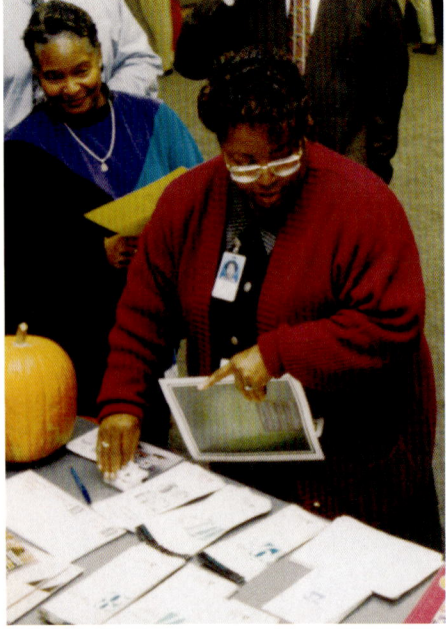

annual United Way campaigns in the Home Office and branches are a tradition. With the company's match, the total passed $500,000 in 2006 and grows each year. Impetus to support Drake University's insurance program stems from EMC's experience of hiring innovative leaders, such as George Kochheiser, John Isenhart, Fred Schiek, and others who are Drake graduates. Funding professorships and scholarships for insurance students assures continuation of the program, which has supplied a number of EMC employees. Complementary support, such as a special $90,000 award in 1999 for a two-year study on workers' compensation insurance, rounds out EMC's contributions to Drake.

...

Top left: Cedar Rapids, Iowa,
native Steven Lauterwasser
paints Iowa's rural landscapes;
two were purchased by
EMC in the 2005 Art EMC
competition, and another
one in the 2007 competition.

Top right: EMC presented
a $500 check to Lynnville-Sully
Elementary School Principal
Teri Bowlin, in partnership
with KCCI TV-8, to use toward
the purchase of new books
for the school library. Also
pictured: Marcus Macintosh,
KCCI TV-8.

Bottom left: Roger Elliott
(center), husband of
EMC employee Deb Elliott,
presented a certificate
and a flag flown in Iraq
to Bill Murray (left)
and Ron Jean (right)
in appreciation for EMC's
support of troops and in
thanks for the Iowa Troops
Care Packages the company
sent while he was
stationed abroad.

Bottom right: EMC received
the Impact Award from
United Way and
was recognized
as a leader
in giving.

Among other EMC-sponsored projects over the years has been Art EMC, a biannual online art show for Iowa artists initiated in 2005. Judges select pieces of art from those submitted, then employees vote online for their favorites. The winners are purchased by the company and hung in various workspaces.

Beyond corporate philanthropy, the company has sponsored many employee-staffed programs. "Meals on Heels," begun by employees in 1994, delivers daily meals to residents at a downtown Des Moines retirement home. Emergency food pantry drives are frequent. Literacy and educational programs have proliferated. Examples include "Reading Is Fundamental," "Communities for Literate Iowa Kids" to improve early childhood literacy, Omaha's "Cash-in for Schools" project, "Read With Me!" in several states, and the "EMC Teacher Scholarships in Poetry" given to 20 inner-city public school teachers across the country for a seven-day workshop. Many shipments of Iowa Troops Care Packages have been sent to Iraq and Afghanistan.

Employees participate in Paint-A-Thons, races against cancer, and numerous other charitable activities.

EMC's charitable activities have been recognized by many awards. Among them are a number from the United Way, each received several times: the Bill McReynolds Memorial Award, the Leadership Award,

and the "Leader in Giving." EMC was named for "Outstanding Corporate Philanthropy" by the National Society of Fund Raising Executives in 1999. Participation in the Dollars for Scholars program won the Advance America Award of Excellence from the American Society of Association Executives in 2003 and the National Trustees Award from Scholarship America, a national network of over 1,200 grassroots scholarship foundations, in 2004. The Economic Impact Award from the Des Moines Chamber of Commerce in 1994 and the Mayor's Spirit of Des Moines Award in 2001 were received for community improvement in Des Moines.

Beacon to the Future

In the early 1990s, a report by Senior Vice President of Administration Phil Van Ekeren and Director John Stoddard indicated that more space was needed for the company's operations. Plans began to take shape under two slogans: "Shape of the Future" and "Reaching for the Sky."

The commitment to downtown development made while planning the west building in the late 1960s remained solid. In March 1993, architects Brooks Borg & Skiles, who had designed the west building, presented to the EMC Board of Directors a conceptual plan for a tower building in the northeast quadrant of the "EMC block." Oversight for the project came from the board's ad hoc building committee — L. Robert Bolton, John H. Kelley, Webster M. Lehmann, and John D. Stoddard — with additional consultative help from Director Richard W. Booth.

In September 1993, expansion plans were announced for a $50 million, uniquely shaped, 20-story office tower, containing over 425,000 square feet and underground parking for use by EMC and lessees. By spring 1994, plans were completed, and demolition of existing structures and skywalks took place during the summer.

Energy efficiency was a key factor in the new design. Insulation would be on the outside of the building, covered by a recycled aluminum skin to protect the exterior from moisture and extreme temperatures. This was expected to reduce the load on mechanical heating and cooling systems by 20%. Specially stored ice would further reduce electric consumption. Layering of glass and plastic in the windows would make them four times more efficient than traditional windows — equivalent to solid walls — and would block all ultraviolet rays. A $250,000 rebate and a $30,000 per year

energy curtailment agreement was given by MidAmerican Energy for installing energy-efficient motors, chillers, boilers, and lighting.

The partnership of Neumann Brothers, Inc. of Des Moines and Kiewit Construction Company of Omaha was selected as general contractor in July 1994. Neumann Brothers had been building Des Moines landmarks for 82 years and had established relationships with city officials. Kiewit, one of the three largest contractors in the United States, had high-rise construction experience particularly useful for the tight building site.

Although a number of structural elements were already in place, construction began officially with a groundbreaking on September 13, following a combined board meeting of EMCC and Dakota Fire Insurance Company. It was a festive occasion attended by both boards, Iowa Lt. Governor Joy Corning, Des Moines Mayor Pat Dorian, City Council members

Chris Hensley and Preston Daniels, and Des Moines Development Corporation President Robert N. Houser. Businessman John Ruan paid a call on President Bruce Kelley to express his thanks for the decision to build downtown, and the *Des Moines Business Record* commended the decision.

By December 1994, a 10-story crawler crane was in place, and a tower crane was being erected. A topping off ceremony was held November 17, 1995, when the final steel girder — painted white, signed by employees, and decked out with flags and a Christmas tree — was put in place. By mid-1996, the building was enclosed, and work proceeded on schedule.

Mechanical systems were installed and offices began to take shape. The airflow system was capable of filling a Goodyear blimp in less than two minutes. A 90,000-gallon secondary water source, powered by an emergency generator, gave added fire protection. A security system and communications systems were

...

Left: EMC Board members at the groundbreaking ceremony for the new building at 700 Walnut Street in downtown Des Moines on September 13, 1994. EMCC Board Members: Dr. John Kelley, Lanning Macfarland, John M. Lockhart, Richard Booth, L. Robert Bolton, Robb Kelley, Bill Brenton, Blaine Briggs, George Kochheiser, Robert Gunn, David Proctor, John Stoddard, Bruce Kelley, Harlan Moses, Albert Rawson, and Webster Lehmann. (left to right)

Right: Des Moines Mayor John Pat Dorian addressed the crowd at the groundbreaking ceremony.

700 WALNUT

EMC INSURANCE COMPANIES
BROOKS BORG SKILES ARCHITECTURE ENGINEERING
NEUMANN–KIEWIT CONSTRUCTORS

• • •

Left: Cornerstone inside
the first floor lobby.

Right: Construction of the
700 Walnut building begins
with the elevator towers.

Inset: The south façade
during construction.

Bottom: Ribbon cutting
ceremony with Iowa
Governor Terry Branstad;
EMC Board Chair L. Robert
Bolton; Rod Nelson, architect;
Bill Anderson, architect;
Larry Hopp, Neuman/Kiewit;
Art Whitmack, Neuman
Brothers; to celebrate the
opening of the new building.

installed. The new skywalk opened with
a ribbon-cutting ceremony just before winter
1997 set in.

Gradually, the new building became
habitable as interior portions were completed
in late 1996, and a Thanksgiving feast was
held in the newly opened cafeteria. The final
departmental move took place August 1, 1997,
and tenants followed — AmerUs Bank, Piper
Jaffrey Brokerage Firm, and the Nyemaster
Goode McLaughlin Voigts West Hansell
& O'Brien law firm.

The east tower officially opened for business
before occupancy was complete. On Sunday,
April 20, 1997, a ribbon-cutting ceremony
was led by President Bruce Kelley. Dedication
of the building to Robb B. Kelley was conducted
by Executive Vice President Fred Schiek.
Kelley's portrait was unveiled by his wife,
Winifred, and recently retired Senior Vice
President Phil Van Ekeren, who had been
instrumental in the building process.
Van Ekeren and Schiek placed a time capsule
in long-term storage to be retrieved in 2097.
In the lobby, a large welded steel sculpture,
"Prairie Wind," by Mac Hornecker, an artist
teaching at Buena Vista University, Storm
Lake, Iowa, was presented. Two representatives
from the German company that supplied the
aluminum siding were present. Iowa Governor
Terry Branstad, Board Chairman L. Robert
Bolton, and representatives from the
architecture and construction firms cut
the ribbon to open the building.

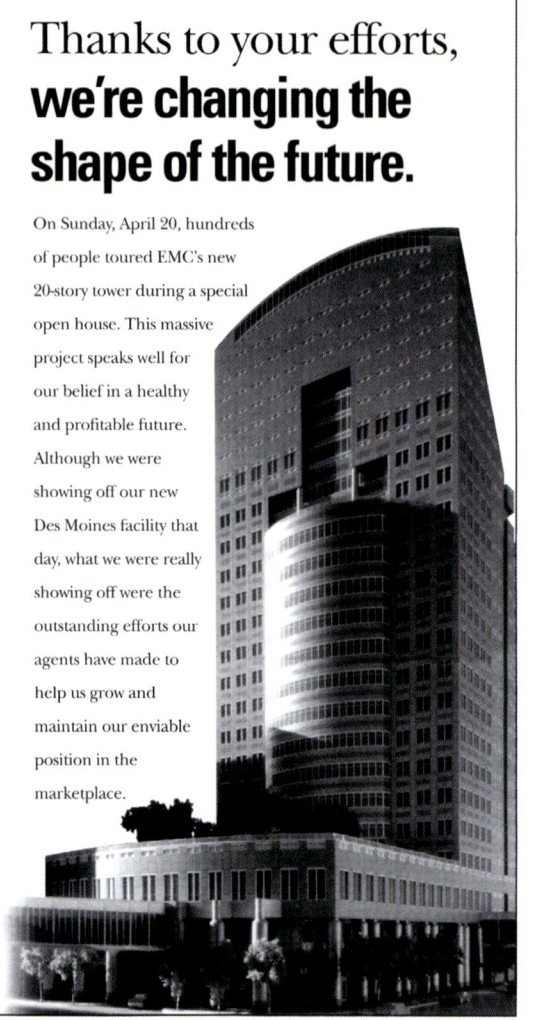

Thanks to your efforts, we're changing the shape of the future.

On Sunday, April 20, hundreds of people toured EMC's new 20-story tower during a special open house. This massive project speaks well for our belief in a healthy and profitable future. Although we were showing off our new Des Moines facility that day, what we were really showing off were the outstanding efforts our agents have made to help us grow and maintain our enviable position in the marketplace.

"Insurance is our business and we intend to stay in it."

The new east tower commanded local and national attention. It was voted the best addition to Des Moines by the *Des Moines Business Record*, and a *Wall Street Journal* article included it as one of the progressive elements that dispelled Des Moines' "cow town" reputation. On a lighter note, newspapers across the country picked up on a separate *Wall Street Journal* article about the 20-story Absolut vodka bottle image on the south side of the building, which came to light near the end of construction. An Absolut advertising agency representative suggested the architect had "some mental relationship with Absolut," but architects Brooks Borg & Skiles representatives offered different opinions. One said, "It would be great publicity for our city. It's great vodka and a great building." Another countered with, "I'm sure EMC, being a casualty insurer, probably would just as soon not have the publicity."

When the east tower was being built in 1995, EMC was either utilizing or had demolished all properties that had been leased out after purchase, and the need for One Hundred LaSalle Corporation was greatly diminished. On June 30, 1995, the corporation was dissolved and all of its assets were assigned to EMC. Parking lot adjustments followed and, in 2004, a parking facility was built in the block immediately south of the Home Office complex. Designed by Brooks Borg & Skiles and constructed by Neumann Brothers, Inc., half was for EMC parking, and a lease-purchase arrangement was made with the City of Des Moines for the other half.

During its 100th year, EMC enlarged its footprint even further in downtown Des Moines. In December 2010, the 20-story, 280,000-square-foot Hub Tower, then in foreclosure and located immediately northeast of the EMC block, was purchased for $7 million and insured for $77 million. Initially, the facility will house EMC National Life Company and tenants. The availability of expansion space for the Home Office and Des Moines Branch is an investment in the future.

The Hub Tower on the northeast corner of Seventh and Walnut, purchased by EMC in 2010.

The EMC Executive Management Team, 2011: Kevin J. Hovick, executive vice president and COO; Bruce G. Kelley, president and CEO; Ronald W. Jean, executive vice president for corporate development. (left to right)

A Salute

EMC's success over the past century has been shaped by those who have led the company — their vision and actions, their principles and practices. That has been recognized in recent years by inductions of EMC personnel into the Iowa Insurance Hall of Fame, created in 1997 to honor outstanding contributions to the Iowa insurance industry. Candidates are evaluated according to their impact on the industry, their ethical standards, their role model qualities and their Iowa connection.

The EMC personnel honored in the Iowa Insurance Hall of Fame are:

- 1997: **Robb B. Kelley**
  President, CEO, Chairman

- 2002: **Margaret A. Ball**
  Senior Vice President, Underwriting

- 2007: **John A. Gunn**
  Founder, President, Chairman

- 2009: **George W. Kochheiser**
  President, COO

EMC's recognized leaders could not accomplish their plans without the people who carry out the tasks. This narrative ends with a tribute to the many people whose names could not be included in these pages. They are the company's mainstay — its heart and soul. For 100 hundred years, they have worked diligently from day to day to make EMC a success. They are the people at the desks, out on the roads, and at disaster scenes. They live our company's guiding beliefs of honesty and integrity, service, teamwork, and continuous improvement. Most of all, they demonstrate the *Count on EMC*® promise to policyholders, agents, shareholders, and fellow employees each day. Thanks to all EMC employees, past and present, for what you have done and where you will take EMC in the future! ▪

OUR GUIDING BELIEFS

Guiding beliefs are the fundamental principles and values that shape and direct the way we work at EMC. Keeping our guiding beliefs in mind while we work with fellow employees, agents, and policyholders will enable us to fulfill our company mission.

CELEBRATING
100 YEARS

COUNT ON EMC.

HONESTY AND INTEGRITY

Honesty is the bedrock of all our relationships. We say what needs to be said, when it needs to be said, despite how difficult or unpopular this may be. If we make a mistake, we own up to it and expect others to do likewise. In this way, we can quickly move toward solving problems. Integrity means we do the right thing — always. Our agents, policyholders, and fellow employees expect nothing less. We are counting on all EMC employees to exercise the principles of honesty and integrity in their daily work.

SERVICE

Service is every employee's job at EMC. We must all take personal responsibility for addressing fellow employee, agent, and policyholder concerns and questions and for solving their problems. We must prove ourselves every day. As we demonstrate these values through our individual actions and behaviors, customers, agents, and fellow employees know that they can *Count on EMC*. We are counting on all EMC employees to provide excellent service in their daily work.

TEAMWORK

Collaboration is the key to our team-oriented workplace. By sharing ideas and seeking input from coworkers, agents, policyholders and others, EMC employees seek win-win solutions. This collaboration must extend beyond our individual work areas to integrate unit, department, and branch operations. We are counting on all EMC employees to exercise teamwork principles in their daily work.

CONTINUOUS IMPROVEMENT

Continuous improvement is the relentless pursuit of excellence. All of us at EMC must continually look for ways to improve what we do and how we do it. By evaluating past performance, setting challenging goals and searching for new opportunities, we will always be making improvements at EMC. We are counting on all EMC employees to exercise continuous improvement principles in their daily work.

MISSION STATEMENT

Our mission is to grow profitably through partnership with independent insurance agents and to enhance the ability of our partners to deliver quality financial protection to help the people and businesses we mutually serve.

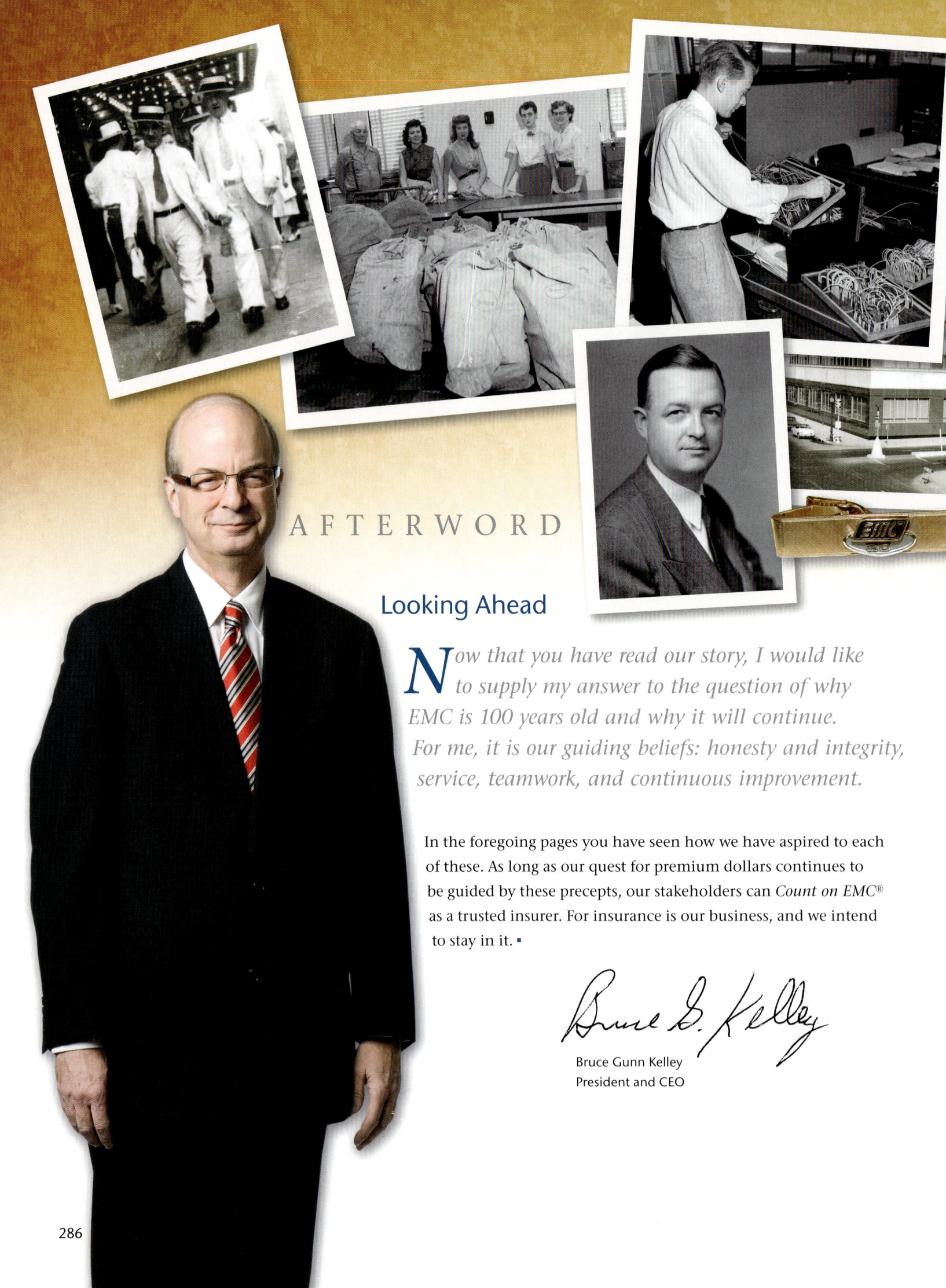

AFTERWORD

Looking Ahead

*N*ow that you have read our story, I would like
to supply my answer to the question of why
EMC is 100 years old and why it will continue.
For me, it is our guiding beliefs: honesty and integrity,
service, teamwork, and continuous improvement.

In the foregoing pages you have seen how we have aspired to each
of these. As long as our quest for premium dollars continues to
be guided by these precepts, our stakeholders can *Count on EMC*®
as a trusted insurer. For insurance is our business, and we intend
to stay in it. ▪

Bruce G. Kelley

Bruce Gunn Kelley
President and CEO

• • •

The EMC Board of Directors at their annual meeting on March 13, 1953, at the Home Office in Des Moines. Seated: M. J. Wilkinson, vice president and superintendent of agents; John F. Hynes, president; J. W. Gunn, chairman of the board and treasurer; Dr. L. E. Kelley, physician and surgeon in Des Moines. Standing: W. Z. Proctor, attorney in Des Moines; Carl Muelhaupt, secretary of Center Service Company, Des Moines; Dr. D. E. Baughman of Fort Dodge; H. L. Hjermstad, president of Citizens Fund Mutual Fire Insurance Company, Red Wing, Minnesota; R. W. Weitz, contractor in Des Moines; W. J. Hynes, secretary; and Frank Kohrs, president of Kohrs Cold Storage Company, Davenport. Not shown: Dr. R. W. Wood of Newton, W. H. Brenton of Brenton Brothers in Des Moines, and Amos C. Pearsall, general manager of Pittsburgh-Des Moines Steel in Des Moines. (left to right)

• • •

The EMC Board of Directors in 2009. Seated: Gale L. Griffin, retired executive, Bestfoods, Williamstown, Massachusetts; Chairman of the Board David J. W. Proctor, J.D., practicing attorney and shareholder, Bradshaw, Fowler, Proctor & Fairgrave, Des Moines, Iowa; Mary O'Gorman Murray, retired executive, Towers Perrin Reinsurance, Media, Pennsylvania. Standing: William A. Murray, retired executive vice president and COO, EMC; Thomas W. Booth, vice president, operations services, Service Experts, Inc., Richardson, Texas; John C. Burgeson, chairman and CEO, Iowa State Bank, Des Moines, Iowa; H. Terrill Watts Jr., CPA, Proprietor/CPA Firm, Atlanta, Georgia; John H. Kelley, M.D., retired orthopaedic surgeon, Boca Raton, Florida; Bruce G. Kelley, J.D., president and CEO, EMC; Richard Koch Jr., president/owner, Koch Brothers, Des Moines, Iowa; J. Thomas Lockhart, vice president of finance and administration, United Theological Seminary, Minneapolis, Minnesota; Ronald W. Jean, executive vice president for corporate development, EMC; Robert L. Link, secretary and vice president of administration, EMC. (left to right)

AT THE BRANCHES

Territory

Alabama
Florida
Georgia
Tennessee

...

Thomas C. O'Connell
CPCU, CIC, ARM, AU,
AMIM, AIM
Resident Vice President

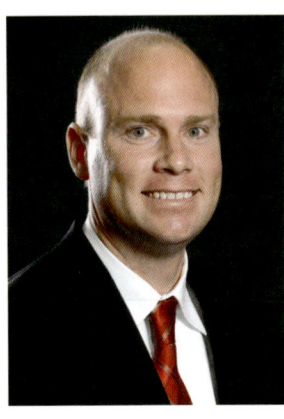

Birmingham Branch

(EMC Property and Casualty Company)

Highlights

1953 American Liberty Insurance Company incorporated in Birmingham

1968 American Liberty acquired by the Statesman Group, Inc. of Des Moines; Statesman officer Robert L. "Bob" Stewart transferred to Birmingham as president and CEO

1982 EMC purchased American Liberty Insurance Company; many American Liberty personnel retained, including the bond manager, a position that was continued

1983 All policies converted to EMC systems

1994 Birmingham Branch took over servicing Tennessee, and Jackson Branch took over servicing Louisiana in a territory swap

1996 Redomesticated to Iowa

1998 Large storm losses with Hurricanes Bonnie and George and ten other catastrophic storms; record number of other large losses; increase in lawsuits

1999 Name changed to EMC Property and Casualty Company

Key Personnel

Branch Managers

Thomas C. O'Connell	2008 –
John R. Kelley	1995 –2008
M. Eugene "Gene" Harris	1988 –1995
Robert L. "Bob" Stewart	1983 –1988

Underwriting Managers

Mary Webb	2008 –
Thomas O'Connell	2004 – 2008
R. Jean Beadles	1992 – 2003
Kevin J. Hovick	1987 – 1992
M. Eugene "Gene" Harris	1972 – 1987

Claims Managers

Terry Hardesty	2002 –
Russ Musgrove	1998 – 2002
Marc Schudel	1996 – 1998
Lee Froedge	1976 – 1996

Administrative Services Managers

Anna Price	2008 –
Suzanne McClellan	2003 – 2006
Joan Long	1988 – 2002
David Petway	1984 – 1988

Total staff 2010

53 employees, 152 agencies

Office Locations

1984 Riverchase, suburb of Birmingham, AL
1997 800 Concourse Parkway, Birmingham, AL

Written Premiums 2010

78% commercial, 22% personal;
7 target market groups

1983: 17,817,609	2002: 47,391,574
1984: 19,218,551	2003: 47,157,157
1985: 14,694,985	2004: 45,700,978
1986: 15,503,851	2005: 45,528,600
1987: 13,587,721	2006: 46,054,074
1988: 13,196,400	2007: 45,789,016
1989: 13,395,234	2008: 41,259,785
1990: 15,537,493	2009: 37,823,017
1991: 17,761,632	2010: 38,692,217
1992: 18,743,904	
1993: 18,930,952	
1994: 19,727,798	
1995: 24,573,930	
1996: 29,840,560	
1997: 34,002,881	
1998: 36,666,502	
1999: 38,329,630	
2000: 38,399,475	
2001: 41,473,511	

Bismarck Branch

(Dakota Fire Insurance Company)

Highlights

1957 Dakota Fire Insurance Company incorporated on August 23

1973 EMC acquired majority stock in Dakota Fire Insurance Company of Bismarck in a $1.7 million share transfer

1979 Remaining shares of Dakota Fire stock
– 80 acquired through additional tender offer; Dakota Fire a wholly owned subsidiary of EMCASCO, Inc.

1990 First annual Agent Advisory Committee held with branch management, field supervisors, and agents

1994 Idaho added to territory; marketing manager position added to staff

1995 Eleven catastrophic storms but ended year with a loss ratio below 60%; focus on increasing volume by adding agencies and larger accounts for which the branch could not previously compete

1997 $9 million in weather-related claims ("winter of the decade" in Dakotas, 500 year flood in Red River Valley, hail in North Dakota and Montana)

1998 Organized Montana Building Industries Association safety group; developed Y2K plan of action

1999 Organized South Dakota School and Idaho Building Contractors Association safety dividend groups

2001 South Dakota territory transferred from Bismarck to Omaha Branch

2004 Branch received third Hynes-Gunn Challenge Cup

2006 Oregon added to territory

2008 50th Anniversary of Dakota Fire celebrated

Key Personnel

Branch Managers

Marilyn R. Ternes	2008 –
Dennis J. Prindiville	2001 – 2008
Merle L. Croy	1983 – 2001
Bob J. Jones	1972 – 1982
Richard J. Smith	1961 – 1972
Donald A. Taylor	1958 – 1961

Underwriting Managers

Tammy S. Olson	2011 –
Brad Johnson	2008 – 2011
Marilyn R. Ternes	2002 – 2008
Rick Siewert	1992 – 2002
Jerry K. Harlow	1985 – 1992
Ross Warner	1983 – 1985
Merle L. Croy	1974 – 1982

Claims Managers

Tony Burbach	2003 –
Vern Jurgens	1978 – 2003
Dick Senger	1973 – 1978

Administrative Services Managers

Jeff Lawler	1994 –
Dennis J. Prindiville	1984 – 1994
Sheila Cleveland	1983 – 1984
Rick Bock	1982 – 1983
John Liston	1982 – 1982
Grace Henson	1978 – 1982

Total staff 2010

77 employees; 268 agencies

Office Locations (All in Bismarck, ND)

1958 Provident Life Building, 316 N. 5th Street
1961 904 East Divide Avenue
1980 1838 East Interstate Avenue

Written Premiums 2010

70% commercial, 30% personal; 3 safety groups, 8 target market groups

1975: 3,290,625
1976: 3,744,289
1977: 3,755,117

Territory

Idaho
Montana
North Dakota
Oregon

...

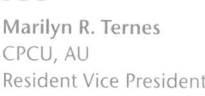

Marilyn R. Ternes
CPCU, AU
Resident Vice President

1978: 4,501,046	1989: 16,262,350	2000: 55,127,668
1979: 4,899,484	1990: 16,802,114	2001: 57,508,120
1980: 6,076,900	1991: 18,519,485	2002: 62,283,992
1981: 7,380,688	1992: 20,724,906	2003: 63,973,084
1982: 9,073,770	1993: 21,337,803	2004: 67,160,862
1983: 11,090,682	1994: 23,658,341	2005: 66,955,471
1984: 12,907,817	1995: 24,538,684	2006: 67,447,764
1985: 12,912,771	1996: 28,160,935	2007: 66,951,600
1986: 12,959,685	1997: 32,982,114	2008: 64,255,696
1987: 13,877,281	1998: 42,048,892	2009: 66,906,972
1988: 14,685,783	1999: 47,558,249	2010: 67,514,784

Territory

Vancouver

British Columbia Branch

Highlights

1953 EMC entered British Columbia through the British Columbia Automobile Association (BCAA, formed in 1905) at the suggestion of D. K. MacDonald & Company (formerly Carter, MacDonald & Company); BCAA incorporated A.A.A. Insurance Agency, Ltd., headed by David W. Bird

1954 Exclusive contract between EMC and A.A.A. Insurance Agency Limited executed; John F. Hynes Jr. set up and headed the EMC office as chief agent; Ross E. MacKinnon was in charge of accounting; first four Canadian auto policies were issued in April

1959 John F. Hynes Jr. transferred to Minneapolis; Ross E. MacKinnon became chief agent; Walter Waskel became claims supervisor

1963 Total of 14,830 policyholders

1964 BCAA obtained legislative approval to form its own insurance company

1966 Robb Kelley, John Isenhart, Thomas X. Wright,
– 68 and George Kochheiser made investigative trips to analyze operational problems

1967 EMC was the second largest writer of auto business in British Columbia; David W. Bird promoted to BCAA general manager; Thomas E. Holmes became A.A.A. agency manager

1968 Total of 44,229 policyholders

1968 Large increase in premium volume caused
– 69 capacity problem; B.C. Parliament passed a no-fault auto plan, and Canadian agitation to form a Crown corporation with exclusive auto insurance rights was underway

1969 A.A.A. Insurance Agency Limited changed name to BCAA Insurance Agency Limited; EMC terminated contract with BCAA; BCAA activated its own insurance company, British Columbia Motorist Insurance Company

1970 EMC transferred its business to B.C. Motorist Insurance Company

1971 MacKinnon and Waskel returned to Home Office and their responsibilities were transferred to Canadian firms; EMC office closed

1974 EMC's last B.C. license for auto and personal accident expired

1981 Joint release between EMC and BCAA ended further obligations and potential legal actions

Key Personnel

Chief Agent
Ross E. MacKinnon	1959 – 1971
John F. Hynes Jr.	1954 – 1959

Chief Accountant
Ross E. MacKinnon	1954 – 1959

Claims Manager
Walter Waskel	1959 – 1971

Total staff 1968

29 employees

Office Locations (All in Vancouver, BC)

1961   B.C. Automobile Association Building
          845 Burrard Street
1972   999 West Broadway

Written Premiums

1954: 68,094	1964: 1,399,590
1955: 257,835	1965: 2,321,597
1956: 370,190	1966: 3,441,668
1959: 784,112	1967: 4,172,051
1960: 758,705	1968: 4,906,428
1961: 833,825	1970: 6,296,822
1962: 926,885	
1963: 1,091,900	

Charlotte Branch

Highlights

1943   Kelleher & Associates, Inc., owned by Don J. Kelleher, began operations as a general agency

1945   Charlotte Claims Office opened with Clarence Johnson as claims supervisor; succeeded by Max A. Wilson in 1947 and Albert W. Green about 1966

1946   Accident prevention added to services (Lawrence "Larry" Pye, first safety engineer)

1960s Telephone claims adjusting implemented; high praise was received for settlement of an accident and theft claim from an event in San Francisco (handled by Irene Whalen, one of the few EMC women adjusters)

1972   EMC purchased Kelleher & Associates, Inc. and continued operating under their name

1973   Juanita DeArmound became one of first EMC women to hold a technical position when she was promoted to claims service representative

1975   Converted into the Charlotte Branch when Don Kelleher retired and Kelleher & Associates was dissolved

1975   Twenty Year Club formed

1992   Judy Funderburk was the first EMC woman to become a branch claims manager

1994   New accounts were added to the North Carolina Rural Water Association Safety Dividend Group; petroleum marketers loss control and risk improvement research project completed

1996   Losses from Hurricanes Bertha and Fran, but production increased 6.6% with a 59.3% loss ratio; Agency Advisory Council established to facilitate joint planning

1999   80% of claims from Hurricane Floyd settled within 30 days and 95% were closed at year's end; loss ratio was 57.7%; marketing administrator position added

2001   Merger completed with Valley Forge Branch, which became Valley Forge Service Office

2002   Marketing manager position added to staff

2005   Expansion in South Carolina business

Key Personnel

Branch Managers

Lonnie D. Schwab	2010 –
R. David Orr	2001 – 2010
William A. Murray	1992 – 2001
Robert N. "Bob" Holden	1975 – 1992
Don J. Kelleher	1972 – 1975

Underwriting Managers

D. Stephen "Steve" Long	2006 –
Oliver S. Moore	2001 – 2006
James R. Sides	1995 – 2001
Oliver S. Moore	1990 – 1995
Ralph M. Jones	1975 – 1989

Territory

Delaware
Maryland
New Jersey
North Carolina
Pennsylvania
South Carolina
Virginia
Washington, D.C.

...

Lonnie D. Schwab
AU
Resident Vice President

Claims Managers

Judy B. Funderburk	1992 –
John P. Strother	1973 – 1992
Albert W. Greenbout	1966 – 1973
Max A. Wilson	1947 – 1966
Clarence D. Johnson	1945 – 1947

Administrative Services Managers

Jane R. Whitley	1985 –
Ed Thomas	1983 – 1985
Wayburn H. Birmingham	1976 – 1983

Total staff 2010

85 employees, 245 agencies

Office Locations (All in Charlotte, NC)

1947	Kelleher/Charlotte Claims Offices Johnston Building, 212 South Tryon Street
1955	Cole Building, 207 Hawthorne Lane
1957 – 58	Keldon Building; 515 Insurance Lane
1987	8303 University Executive Park Drive
2006	11020 David Taylor Drive

Written Premiums 2010

100% commercial; 10 safety groups, 8 target market groups

1964: 1,487,037[1]	1992: 17,177,333
1965: 1,629,764[1]	1993: 16,894,174
1966: 1,731,059[1]	1994: 20,348,070
1967: 1,910,678[1]	1995: 22,076,654
1968: 2,014,364[1]	1996: 23,427,957
1969: 2,320,352	1997: 22,317,245
1970: 2,274,330	1998: 22,910,732
1971: 2,453,879	1999: 22,639,589
1972: 2,665,999	2000: 24,929,241
1973: 3,200,915	2001: 59,430,625[2]
1974: 4,031,690	2002: 66,428,528
1975: 4,159,895	2003: 73,705,252
1976: 4,807,540	2004: 78,701,956
1977: 5,660,218	2005: 85,131,324
1978: 5,529,155	2006: 85,508,622
1979: 6,430,399	2007: 90,835,291
1980: 7,557,954	2008: 93,442,518
1981: 8,028,439	2009: 90,468,460
1982: 9,529,697	2010: 87,278,444
1983: 10,960,994	
1984: 11,291,055	[1] Kelleher and Associates, Inc.
1985: 11,955,402	
1986: 12,632,408	[2] Merged with Valley Forge (Philadelphia) Branch
1987: 13,498,017	
1988: 15,544,424	
1989: 17,256,250	
1990: 18,827,947	
1991: 18,481,021	

Territory

Illinois

Chicago Branch

Highlights

1934 Office established with Gordon Nelson supervising underwriting and one stenographer; reported directly to the Home Office because there was no branch manager

1936 Safety engineer position added (Lawrence "Larry" Pye)

1937 Chicago Service Office formed to handle underwriting, claims, and inspections, with William J. Hynes, acting manager; basic conditions were illustrated by Adjuster Abe Shapiro's workstation being a card table

1950 Office reorganized as a full Chicago Branch

1954 Agency force had grown to 170 as agencies were appointed outside the Chicago area

1967 Major personnel shift when the office moved from Chicago to Oak Brook, where the new office building served as the prototype for EMC's uniform plan buildings; marketing manager position added to staff and discontinued in 1978; in-house study group formed for IIA (Insurance Institute of America) courses

1976 Illinois EMCASCO Insurance Company formed; branch's 90 employees served as staff; bond manager position added to staff

1978 Indiana business transferred to Lansing Branch when it reached $1 million

1989 One-third of the branch's business had moved to central and southern Illinois; Chicago business tended to be commercial, and the rest of the state leaned toward personal; approximately 60 employees

1994 "Hall of Fame" award received from Professional Independent Insurance Agents of DuPage County; "Recognition of Excellence" award received from Chicago Board of Underwriters

1997 Transition period — new service standards, – 00 products, and pricing; formal agency review and new agency selection program

2001 Ilinois EMCASCO redomesticated as an Iowa firm to improve efficiency; personal property and time loss when policyholder RLI Corporation lost World Trade Center offices during terrorist attack (80% reinsured)

2007 "CPCU Champion of the Year" award received from Chicago-West Suburban CPCU Society

Key Personnel

Branch Managers

Gary A. Kohnke	1996 –
Robert E. "Bob" Smith	1983 – 1996
John C. Pollock	1978 – 1983
Dale C. Fry	1958 – 1978
John S. Kerper	1951 – 1958
A. N. "Abe" Shapiro	1946 – 1951
W. J. Hynes	1937 – 1946

Underwriting Managers

Linda Borgstrom	1997 –
Susan Zieche	1996 – 1997
Edward M. Mayer	1983 – 1996
Robert E. "Bob" Smith	1982 – 1983
Frank Kish	1978 – 1982
Robert E. "Bob" Smith	1966 – 1978
George K. Lindmeier	1953 – 1957
Byron H. Sistler	1950s
E. C. Finn	1940s
Gordon Nelson	1934 – 1952

Claims Managers

Mike Genender	2005 –
Richard K. Schulz	1999 – 2005
Janet Leifel	1996 – 1999

Mitchell O. "Mick" Riley	1977 – 1996
Charles Burnett	1967 – 1977
Thomas M. Boland	1946 – unknown
A. N. "Abe" Shapiro	1938 – 1946
J. J. Faith	1937 – 1938

Administrative Services Managers

Jeanne Hammer	2006 –
Joseph Fougerousse	1997 – 2006
Tony Mendola	1989 – 1997
Robert L. Link	1978 – 1989

Total staff 2010

53 employees, 141 agencies

Office Locations

1930s Insurance Center Building, 330 South Wells Street, Chicago, IL

1958 Franklin-Adams Building, 222 West Adams Street, Chicago, IL

1967 715 Enterprise Drive, Oak Brook, IL (prototype for uniform plan buildings)

1992 815 Commerce Drive, Oak Brook, IL

2001 1815 S. Meyers Road, Oak Brook Terrace, Oak Brook, IL

Written Premiums 2010

89% commercial, 11% personal; 1 safety group, 2 target market groups

1936: 897,870		
1937: 1,101,447	1952: 2,134,020	1967: 5,166,255
1938: 823,223	1953: 2,233,445	1968: 5,794,931
1939: 644,840	1954: 2,511,168	1969: 7,597,116
1940: 637,101	1955: 2,436,476	1970: 8,378,930
1941: 613,815	1956: 2,617,088	1971: 8,713,830
1942: 556,921	1957: 3,152,384	1972: 9,169,409
1943: 512,862	1958: 4,233,711	1973: 10,475,656
1944: 524,867	1959: 4,340,721	1974: 13,339,005
1945: 574,824	1960: 4,598,898	1975: 16,532,871
1946: 760,687	1961: 4,040,227	1976: 18,389,346
1947: 1,078,413	1962: 3,834,210	1977: 19,725,876
1948: 1,404,045	1963: 3,945,120	1978: 16,381,696
1949: 1,678,754	1964: 3,492,622	1979: 17,582,184
1950: 1,562,085	1965: 4,251,545	1980: 19,358,014
1951: 1,744,550	1966: 4,763,120	1981: 16,945,767

...

Gary A. Kohnke
CPCU
Resident Vice President

1982: 13,718,446	1990: 22,921,353	1998: 32,198,684	2006: 42,166,430
1983: 16,454,973	1991: 25,297,553	1999: 32,631,900	2007: 41,467,246
1984: 19,683,014	1992: 28,306,490	2000: 37,371,508	2008: 37,988,235
1985: 19,286,105	1993: 28,369,420	2001: 40,151,853	2009: 36,182,108
1986: 18,176,080	1994: 29,767,468	2002: 41,678,395	2010: 37,412,036
1987: 17,721,742	1995: 33,315,950	2003: 41,428,097	
1988: 18,376,907	1996: 31,821,957	2004: 41,114,156	
1989: 19,123,394	1997: 31,846,632	2005: 41,019,219	

Territory

Indiana
Kentucky
Ohio

...

Kent A. Kochheiser
CPCU
Resident Vice President

Cincinnati Branch

(Hamilton Mutual Insurance Company)

Highlights

1858 The German Mutual Insurance Company (Die Deutsche Gegenseitige Versicherungs Gesellschaft von Cincinnati, Ohio) founded by German immigrant Heinrich (Henry) Armin Rattermann on May 10

1918 Name changed to Hamilton County Mutual Fire Insurance Company due to World War I bitterness against Germans; "Germania" sculpture on their office building changed to "Columbia," and "E Pluribus Unum" and an American eagle were added

1957 Hamilton Mutual merged with Druggist Mutual Insurance Company of Mansfield, Ohio, to become Hamilton Mutual Insurance Company of Cincinnati, Ohio

1997 EMC purchased Hamilton Mutual's surplus notes and it became an EMC affiliate; about 85 Hamilton staff, including bond manager, retained; business was about 30% commercial

1998 60,000 Hamilton policies and billing
–99 operation were converted to EMC's systems

1999 Hamilton's Michigan business was transferred to Lansing and Lansing's Indiana business to Cincinnati

2005 Hamilton redomesticated to Iowa; personal lines growth targeted; home policies increased 63% and auto policies 117%

Key Personnel

Branch Managers
Kent A. Kochheiser   2003 –
Jeffrey E. Felts   1997 – 2003

Underwriting Managers
Phil Goedde   1997 –

Claims Managers
Mike Loftus   2004 –
William Rhoads   1995 – 2004

Administrative Services Managers
Don Harmeyer   2000 –
Brent Rouse   1997 – 2000

Total staff 2010

70 employees, 175 agencies

Office Locations

1957 1520 Madison Road and Chapel Street, Cincinnati, OH

2005 Cornell Center, 11311 Cornell Park Drive, Blue Ash, OH

Written Premiums 2010

56% commercial, 44% personal;
10 target market groups

1998: 30,669,674	2005: 63,407,659
1999: 34,732,364	2006: 63,397,298
2000: 39,375,310	2007: 65,435,492
2001: 43,011,746	2008: 63,416,382
2002: 52,455,977	2009: 69,566,072
2003: 57,829,314	2010: 74,653,872
2004: 62,297,142	

Dallas Branch/Service Office

Highlights

1939 Williamson & Nelson General Agency opened by George Eric Williamson and Richard R. "Dick" Nelson Sr. to write business for EMC; became Williamson, Nelson & Kent when joined by William J. Kent in 1941; became Nelson & Kent in 1945

1946 Texas Claims Office opened; housed with Nelson and Kent; John J. Dunn and Carl Wildenstein were first claims representatives

1952 Russell A. Engelmann took new southwestern divisional claims superintendent position; subsequently, Texas Office became Dallas Claims Office (headed by Charles C. O'Dell) and service offices were established in Houston (headed by Roy H. Schaller), San Antonio, and Austin; John P. Strother and Franklyn Y. Wright were each key staff in several of these offices

1954 Nelson & Kent produced $2.2 million premium for EMC

1959 New Mexico Claims Service Office established in Albuquerque, NM, by Harry E. Wishard to service the New Mexico Motor Club

1964 New Mexico business expanded when EMCASCO Insurance Company qualified to do business, thereafter being issued a $75,000 surety bond by Employers Reinsurance Corporation

1967 EMC purchased Nelson & Kent General Agency and combined it with the Claims Services operations to form the Dallas Branch; most Nelson and Kent employees became EMC staff

1976 Eight Twenty Year Club members; 95 agencies served by 44 staff

ca. 1984 Bond manager position added to staff

1980s First branch outside of Iowa to establish an underwriting unit for large special risks

1989 Added town & country unit geared toward agencies outside metropolitan areas

1996 Became a service office in merger with Wichita Branch; provides underwriting, claims, risk improvement, audit, marketing, and rating services to Texas agents and policyholders

Key Personnel

Branch Managers

William "Bil" Anderson	1992 – 1996
Ronald Cheshire	1982 – 1992
Franklyn Y. Wright	1969 – 1982
Francis E. Baker	1967 – 1969

Claims Managers

Don Wiese	2002 –
Howard Dugger	1984 – 2002
Charles C. O'Dell	1978 – 1984
Paul C. Smith	1974 – 1978
Russell A. Engelmann	1967 – 1973

Total staff 2010

38 employees (Service Office)

Office Locations

1967	3631 Cedar Springs Road, Dallas, TX
1973	1341 West Mocking Bird Lane, Dallas, TX
1977	1200 Frito-Lay Tower, Richardson, TX
1990	1702 North Collins Road, Richardson, TX
2002	2505 North Plano Road, Richardson, TX

Written Premiums

1995, 91% commercial, 9% personal

1967: 2,031,925		
1968: 3,131,878		
1969: 3,775,117	1980: 6,231,856	1991: 9,959,022
1970: 4,040,778	1981: 6,868,385	1992: 8,208,584
1971: 4,142,973	1982: 8,707,283	1993: 11,551,260
1972: 4,296,338	1983: 10,618,526	1994: 11,375,569
1973: 4,881,536	1984: 13,408,883	1995: 14,243,293
1974: 5,725,413	1985: 11,056,613	1996: 19,598,462
1975: 5,079,604	1986: 11,641,786	1997: merged with
1976: 5,667,725	1987: 10,753,394	Wichita
1977: 5,467,177	1988: 13,607,119	
1978: 5,804,726	1989: 21,576,903	
1979: 6,350,744	1990: 24,962,235	

Territory

New Mexico
Texas

Territory

Colorado
Utah
Wyoming

Dennis J. Prindiville
CPCU, AU
Regional Vice President

Denver Branch

Highlights

1935   O. B. "Mac" McKinney, who brought EMC into his Cedar Rapids agency in the early 1920s, started McKinney Fire Insurance General Agency in Denver

1940   EMC established Denver Claims Office managed by Clarence E. Johnson; succeeded by Walter J. Ellwood (1943) and Louis J. Campbell (1946)

ca.   McKinney died and S. John Johns and
1949   Henry Walz assumed management of McKinney Agency

1981   EMC purchased McKinney Fire Insurance Agency when Mrs. McKinney died; the agency and claims office were combined to form the Denver Branch, with five employees; 80% personal lines being written

1984,   Large losses from major hail storms
1990   in Colorado

1988   Total of 24 staff

1991   Bond manager position added to staff

mid-   80% commercial lines being written
1990s

1993   Wyoming added to territory

1994   Utah added to territory

1998   Christmas Eve fire in Boulder medical building caused $5 million property damage

2001   Risk improvement representative added to staff

2002   Received first Hynes-Gunn Challenge Cup for successful branch performance; won cup again in 2003, 2005, 2009, 2010

2005   Established oil and gas target market program

2006   25th anniversary celebrated with an open house for over 100 agents; received "BIG HITTER" bat award from Van Gilder Insurance Corporation for long years of service; marketing manager added to staff

Key Personnel

Branch Managers

Dennis J. Prindiville	2008 –
Roger L. Ford	1981 – 2008

Underwriting Managers

Mark K. Schonebaum	2008 –
Vernon L. Limbrecht	1981 – 2008

Claims Managers

Dan Hare	2001 –
Douglas A. Cossette	1991 – 2001
James W. Robinson	1965 – 1991
Walter Waskel	1958 – 1959
Louis J. Campbell	1946 – 1958

Administrative Services Manager

Carol Eaton	2005 –
Lois Wilson	1999 – 2005
Nancy Allan	1989 – 1999

Total staff 2010

54 employees, 127 agencies

Office Locations

1935   McKinney/Denver Claims Offices: Security Exchange Building;

early   Converted house at 1640 Logan Street;
1940s   both in Denver, CO

1947   1107 Security Building, Denver, CO

1981   2260 South Xanadu Way, Aurora, CO

1983   3150 South Vaughn Way, Aurora, CO

early   Aurora Corporate Center, South
1990s   Peoria Street, Aurora, CO

1996   12100 East Iliff, Aurora, CO

2003   Denver Tech Center, 8181 E. Tufts Avenue, Denver, CO

Written Premiums 2010

85% commercial, 15% personal;
4 target market groups

1964: 772,396	1969: 1,128,175
1965: 889,127	1970: 1,379,283
1966: 913,022	1971: 1,536,538
1967: 907,064	1972: 1,620,276
1968: 903,533	1973: 1,775,683

1974: 1,835,249	1982: 2,989,685	1990: 9,167,666	1998: 21,683,613	2006: 55,738,709
1975: 1,921,372	1983: 4,308,577	1991: 11,006,690	1999: 24,014,417	2007: 57,781,546
1976: 2,141,369	1984: 4,851,058	1992: 11,950,299	2000: 28,527,352	2008: 51,475,574
1977: 2,350,469	1985: 5,579,733	1993: 12,754,826	2001: 33,913,084	2009: 43,867,017
1978: 2,449,810	1986: 5,621,004	1994: 15,903,614	2002: 39,922,655	2010: 40,283,360
1979: 2,592,811	1987: 5,967,283	1995: 18,245,664	2003: 44,073,496	
1980: 2,688,081	1988: 6,866,186	1996: 18,565,328	2004: 48,714,299	*McKinney Agency
1981: 2,729,883*	1989: 7,381,995	1997: 19,431,057	2005: 52,405,660	purchased by EMC and became branch office

Des Moines Branch

Highlights

Iowa business initially handled by Home Office

1947 Polk County Office established to provide underwriting and claims assistance to agents and policyholders in Polk County

1952 Polk County Office had premium volume of $1.2 million and claim load of 6,500

1958 High volume (about $5 million) necessitated opening Iowa Branch with jurisdiction over the entire state of Iowa; LeRoy E. Bruce was branch manager with 21 employees; high school students were brought in to photocopy all Iowa policies to make them readily available to both the branch and Home Office

1960 Third annual Workmen's Compensation Clinic held by Branch Claims Department at Hotel Kirkwood in Des Moines; premium audit manager added to staff

1968 Wes Sticken organized the special risk underwriting unit; marketing manager position added to staff

1969 Premium audit-risk Improvement representatives added to staff

1971 Name changed to Des Moines Branch in keeping with the company policy of naming branches after metro areas

1972 Branch Underwriting Department, managed by Wayne Goettsch, restructured to achieve benefits of specialization; Risk improvement manager added to staff

1973 Davenport Claims Service Office opened with an adjuster and a secretary; by 1999, there were nine employees, a risk improvement representative, and three field adjusters

1974 Iowa Association of School Boards safety dividend group established

1975 More than 40 employees processed over 8,000 new workers' compensation claims and 22,500 claims from other lines. To handle this load, Claims Manager Gene H. Bailey divided Iowa into four supervisory territories comprising 15 outside adjuster territories and formed a special workers' compensation unit managed by Mitchell O. "Mick" Riley, who was succeeded by Gregory P. Bird (1977)

1977 Underwriting Department divided into subunits to manage 420 agencies writing almost $30 million property and casualty premiums (Ed O'Hair, Marketing Department) and $605,000 life premiums (Life Manager John R. Smith). Fifty employees in five units: town and country (Robert C. Pearson), special risk (Wes Sticken and Lorrel E. "Pete" Peterson), personal lines (Jo Etheridge), and two general commercial lines (James E. Wright Jr. and Donna Jones); ten Records Department employees processed 200,000 dailies (Ruthan Young); cashier unit; administrative support (mail and control, terminal-issue, transcription)

1980s Branch consistently wrote approximately 25% of EMC's total premiums

Territory

Iowa

1980 Iowa Association of Municipal Utilities (IAMU) safety dividend group established; managed by Jester Agency; 465 cities participating in 1999

1983 Petroleum Marketers of Iowa (PMI) safety dividend group program established; marketed to Iowa independent agents by EMC

1993 Disaster Recovery Plan used to combat the flood of 1993

1997 Recognized as "Company of the Year" by Professional Insurance Agents of Iowa

1998 6,000 additional claims handled due to severe weather; Iowa Telecommunications Insurance Program developed in partnership with Jester Agency; Iowa Association of Business and Industry group program established; both groups marketed through EMC independent agents

2004 Personal lines underwriting manager position created to increase personal lines business

Key Personnel

Branch Managers

James C. Fontanini	1998 –
Ed O'Hair	1990 – 1998
Miles R. "Dick" Barnhart	1966 – 1990
LeRoy E. Bruce	1947 – 1966
(Supervisor, Polk County Office; Manager, Iowa Branch)	

Underwriting Managers

Jerry McClelland	1998 –
James C. Fontanini	1990 – 1998
Bernie Zalaznik	1986 – 1990
Ed O'Hair	1978 – 1986
James C. Aldridge	1972 – 1978
Wayne W. Goettsch	1970 – 1972

Claims Managers

Bruce Boock	2000 –
Charlie Wells	1996 – 2000
Gene H. Bailey	1975 – 1996
Jewell C. Crouch	1967 – 1975
Addison Hayne	1963 – 1967
Morris R. McCleary	1959 – 1963
Thomas X. Wright	1959
Clarence D. Johnson	1948 – 1958

Administrative Service Managers

Linda Heintz	2010 –
Allan Whitaker	1982 – 2010
Pat Addison	1978 – 1982
Don Johnson	1972 – 1978
Wes Hirsch	1970 – 1972

Special Risk Managers

John Schumacher	2000 –
Beech Turner	1992 – 2000
John Wesley "Wes" Sticken	1968 – 1992

Total staff 2010

187 employees, 375 agencies

Office Locations (All in Des Moines, IA)

1958 First Floor, Home Office, 210 7th Street

1971 Expansion to Second Floor, 210 7th Street

1994 Moved temporarily to 222 5th Avenue (formerly J.C. Penney's) when 210 7th Street building was demolished

1996 700 Walnut Street

Written Premiums 2010

80% commercial, 20% personal; 4 safety groups, 10 target market groups

1959: 6,833,097	1979: 46,212,510
1960: 6,980,637	1980: 45,925,006
1961: 7,118,420	1981: 48,720,487
1962 6,906,921	1982: 47,377,118
1963: 7,400,542	1983: 47,402,102
1964: 8,141,898	1984: 52,496,454
1965: 9,420,856	1985: 63,872,398
1966: 10,723,169	1986: 85,718,772
1967: 11,518,898	1987: 96,404,316
1968: 12,593,689	1988: 103,262,448
1969: 13,811,985	1989: 111,814,121
1970: 15,391,131	1990: 121,215,504
1971: 16,939,157	1991: 141,547,392
1972: 17,843,357	1992: 144,995,979
1973: 18,632,500	1993: 140,910,290
1974: 22,396,202	1994: 126,592,594
1975: 25,418,645	1995: 120,507,509
1976: 29,813,366	1996: 114,534,864
1977: 37,996,942	1997: 118,794,706
1978: 41,714,457	1998: 128,041,080

1999: 129,645,091	2002: 163,506,590	2005: 178,856,111	2008: 174,792,109
2000: 140,659,123	2003: 172,714,513	2006: 172,259,239	2009: 181,657,903
2001: 159,258,466	2004: 182,624,083	2007: 171,360,428	2010: 179,597,180

Jackson Branch

Highlights

1929 Southern Underwriters founded by George Eric Williamson

1935 Southern Underwriters became statewide agency for EMC

1946 Jackson was listed as one of twelve "Branch Claim Offices" and John L. Beach was listed as attorney in 1947 in the *Co-Operator*

1956 Jackson Claims Office opens

1966 EMC purchased Southern Underwriters, Inc. general agency to establish the Jackson Branch, staffed by Southern Underwriters and Claims Office personnel; most of the business was personal lines

1968 Purchase of Union Mutual Insurance Company in Providence, RI, brought transfer of its Tennessee business to the Jackson Branch

1975 Tornado in McComb, MS, caused large claims; began to change business from 90% personal to more commercial

1980 Marketing manager position added to staff

1981 Risk improvement representative added to staff

1988 Business was 70% commercial, 30% personal

1994 Jackson Branch took over servicing Louisiana, and Birmingham Branch took over servicing Tennessee in a territory swap; this added hurricane exposure to Jackson's territory

1995 30th anniversary observed

1999 Several agencies canceled in storm-prone areas

2005 Hurricane season devastation, especially Katrina, was abated by anticipatory preparations

2006 Five agencies recognized for 25 years of service with the branch

Key Personnel

Branch Managers

Frankie Box	1993 –
William S. Sandstrum	1975 – 1993
James Frazier Scott	1966 – 1974

Underwriting Managers

Coleman Cummins	2006 –
Ron Hicks	2001 – 2006
Tom Luscomb	1996 – 2001
Robert "Rusty" Nevels	1983 – 1996
Wayne Durham	1980 – 1983
Frankie Box	1978 – 1980

Claims Managers

Charles Brock	2003 –
Richard Farlee	2001 – 2002
Bill Lumpkin	1985 – 2000
Louis S. Bills Jr.	1966 – 1985

Administrative Services Managers

| Pat Green | 1994 – |
| Melanie Booth | 1983 – 1994 |

Total staff 2010

35 employees; 108 agencies

Office Locations

1966 233 East Hamilton Street, Jackson, MS

1977 5330 Executive Place, Jackson, MS

1990 460 Briarwood Drive, Jackson, MS

2003 877 Northpark Drive, Ridgeland, MS

Territory

Louisiana
Mississippi

...

Frankie Box
CPCU, CLU, ChFC, AIM
Resident Vice President

Written Premiums 2010				
100% commercial; 2 target market groups	1970: 1,852,895	1982: 7,361,868	1994: 16,257,058	2006: 36,319,338
	1971: 1,972,271	1983: 7,399,937	1995: 17,753,948	2007: 37,901,273
	1972: 2,219,210	1984: 6,988,681	1996: 18,759,274	2008: 36,918,434
	1973: 2,436,654	1985: 8,372,905	1997: 19,671,470	2009: 35,386,696
	1974: 2,558,830	1986: 8,617,915	1998: 22,024,857	2010: 33,718,277
	1975: 2,891,904	1987: 8,632,975	1999: 22,759,342	
1964: 773,777	1976: 3,083,239	1988: 10,869,339	2000: 24,428,945	
1965: 973,466	1977: 3,569,132	1989: 11,205,655	2001: 27,285,823	
1966: 1,107,010	1978: 4,006,974	1990: 12,401,596	2002: 30,349,722	
1967: 1,039,148	1979: 4,568,559	1991: 13,961,715	2003: 34,063,237	
1968: 1,212,074	1980: 5,175,912	1992: 13,098,105	2004: 35,931,751	
1969: 1,762,733	1981: 5,443,222	1993: 13,693,034	2005: 36,740,934	

Territory

Arkansas
Kansas (NE)
Missouri

Kansas City Branch

Highlights

1928 EMC entered Missouri through agencies in St. Louis and Kansas City

1946 Kansas City Claims Office opened by Harry Wishard to service the George Eric Williamson General Agency and others; Wishard was succeeded by Ronald R. Schwartz (1947), Hugh A. Randall (1949), and Joseph R. "Dick" Harbin (1951)

1948 St. Louis Claims Office opened; safety engineering position added to Kansas City staff (Lawrence "Larry" Pye)

1950 Francis E. Baker brought on staff as state agent to oversee production; succeeded by Charles A. Hartman (1951)

1954 Arkansas territory entered through Lewis & Norwood General Agency, Little Rock

1955 Miles R. "Dick" Barnhart added to staff as special field supervisor with responsibility for underwriting and agency production in western Missouri

1957 Springfield, MO, Service Office opened

1958 Jefferson City, MO, Service Office opened

1959 Little Rock Claims Office opened to handle claims from Lewis and Norwood General Agency

1962 Kansas City Branch was the first organized according to the O'Toole study decentralization recommendations

1966 EMC withdrew from Arkansas and closed the Little Rock Claims Office due to companywide capacity problems

1968 Underwriting for the St. Louis territory business moved from the Home Office to Kansas City

1969 New St. Louis Claims Office opened

1982 Arkansas re-entry was facilitated by Field Supervisor John Hanna, and the Little Rock Claims Office re-opened; succeeded by John Adams (1990) and Gary Morrison (2000)

1984 Bond manager position added to staff

1994 New Little Rock Claims Office opened by H. B. Moran Jr. who began by working out of his parents' living room; succeeded by S. Lee Valdez (2000)

1991 Twenty Year Club organized with 14 members who had a combined service of 351 years

1992 EMC selected from 350-400 companies as "Company of the Year" by the Professional Insurance Agents of Arkansas

1997 Arkadelphia, AR, tornado caused major losses; Little Rock Claims Office relocated to enhance service

Key Personnel

Branch Managers

Benjamin K. DeHart	2006 –
Dennis Johannsen	1998 – 2006
Thomas J. "Tom" Wilkinson	1968 – 1998
Ken Munn, Acting Manager	1967 – 1968
Miles R. "Dick" Barnhart	1962 – 1966

Underwriting Managers

David Vavak	2006 –
Benjamin K. DeHart	1998 – 2006
Dennis Johannsen	1975 – 1998
Dennis Williams	1968 – 1975

Underwriting initially handled by Jim Williams, Gary Reed, Sam Kidd, Ed Burr

Claims Managers

H. B. Moran Jr.	2000 –
Larry Valentine	1994 – 2000
Fred Viar	1964 – 1994
Joseph R. "Dick" Harbin	1962 – 1964

Administrative Services Managers

Amy M. Brush	2009 –
Jeff Siler	2007 – 2009
James M. Moore	1981 – 2007
Barry Fisher	1973 – 1981
Dick Sheldon	1969 – 1973

Total staff 2010

60 employees, 150 agencies

Office Locations (All in Kansas City, MO)

1946 918 Dwight Building

1952 3509 Broadway

1955 Pickwick Building, 903 McGee

1962 Graphic Arts Building, 934 Wyandotte

1971 Professional Park Plaza, 11225 Colorado Avenue

1996 Executive Hills Office Complex, 1300 East 104th Street

Written Premiums 2010

87% commercial, 13% personal; 1 safety group, 2 target market groups

1962: 2,643,976	1976: 5,998,589	1990: 12,992,593	2004: 40,552,112
1963: 2,782,709	1977: 6,351,903	1991: 15,222,641	2005: 38,255,879
1964: 2,190,871	1978: 6,528,540	1992: 15,668,648	2006: 36,212,312
1965: 2,467,031	1979: 6,870,694	1993: 14,891,623	2007: 38,939,814
1966: 2,764,744	1980: 5,175,912	1994: 15,848,094	2008: 40,868,583
1967: 2,791,139	1981: 7,012,492	1995: 17,165,912	2009: 45,017,536
1968: 2,992,773	1982: 7,860,038	1996: 16,929,284	2010: 50,079,166
1969: 3,365,815	1983: 9,908,676	1997: 18,500,786	
1970: 3,283,234	1984: 13,181,646	1998: 20,152,244	
1971: 3,525,650	1985: 11,096,003	1999: 22,787,839	
1972: 3,881,463	1986: 10,374,274	2000: 26,697,213	
1973: 4,927,434	1987: 10,454,863	2001: 32,291,222	
1974: 5,904,659	1988: 9,937,192	2002: 36,456,747	
1975: 5,531,493	1989: 10,748,464	2003: 39,551,326	

...

Benjamin K. DeHart
CPCU, ARM, ARe
Resident Vice President

Lansing Branch

Highlights

1940 EMC Marketing Representative John S. Kerper opened Michigan by appointing agents in midstate; due to World War II rationing, he traveled with a marketing representative from another company and his home served as the office

1946 Full Lansing Branch opened with five employees

1955 Staff of 24 employees; engineering services provided by Chicago Branch

1957 Began to write property lines when Michigan law allowed companies to write both property and casualty; in a prior reciprocal arrangement, Michigan Miller agents had written property for EMC, and EMC agents had written casualty for Michigan

Early 1960s Upper Peninsula business discontinued due to capacity problems

1960 Claims Service Office opened in Detroit; little effect from five days of civil disturbance in 1967 because little underwriting was done in the inner city; office closed at the end of the decade because it was more efficient to handle claims in Lansing

Territory

Michigan

Gary E. Pingel
CPCU, AU
Resident Vice President

1973 EMC's first safety dividend group organized by the Hempstead-Barrett Agency, Pontiac, MI, for the Michigan Manufactured Housing, RV, and Campground Association; new Michigan no-fault law caused drastic changes in auto insurance

1978 Indiana business transferred to Lansing from Chicago; manufactured housing business extended into Indiana; Indiana business managed by Marketing Manager E. Anthony "Tony" McNair

ca. 1990 Ownership of office building transferred from EML to EMC

1992 Michigan Wholesale and Retail Petroleum Marketers target market group formed

1995 Indiana Petroleum Marketers group formed

1996 Began target market groups for Michigan Charter Schools, Ohio Municipal Utilities, and Ohio Manufactured Housing Industry

1997 – 99 Hamilton/Cincinnati's Michigan business and agents transferred to Lansing and writing in the Upper Peninsula resumed; Lansing's Indiana and Ohio business transferred to Cincinnati

2000 Michigan Essential Insurance Act and Michigan No Fault Auto made it difficult to follow countrywide rate and underwriting adjustments

Key Personnel

Branch Managers

Gary E. Pingel	2010 –
Jason R. Bogart	2003 – 2010
Joseph M. Carr	1993 – 2003
Robert E. Kelley	1957 – 1993
Francis E. Baker	1951 – 1957
John S. Kerper	1940 – 1951

Underwriting Managers

Floyd Baker	2010 –
Gary E. Pingel	2004 – 2010
Kathleen Fowler	1999 – 2004
Robert Bailey	1978 – 1999
Herbert D. Shartle	1971 – 1978
Norman Brazil	unknown – 1971

Glen Dutcher	1957 – unknown
Robert E. Kelley	ca. 1950 – 1957

Claims Managers

Rick Whiters	2000 –
Robert K. "Tim" Rainey	1994 – 2000
Leland D. Spitzbergen	1970 – 1994
John Hynes Jr.	1964 – 1970
Edward J. Pilon	1960 – 1964
John J. Dunn	1947 – unknown
H. P. Van Patten	ca. 1946 – 1947

Administrative Services Managers

Ron Durga	1994 –
Carol Lovelady	1987 – 1994
Garry Underwood	1979 – 1984
Mike Rust	1976 – 1979
Jim Bowman	unknown – 1976
Gary Clark	unknown

Total staff 2010

58 employees, 95 agencies

Office Locations (All in Lansing, MI)

1940	John Kerper's home, Jenison Street
1946	Converted dwelling, 300 South Pine Street
1947	1113½-1115 North Washington Avenue
1957	2401 East Grand River Avenue
1974	5826 Executive Drive

Written Premiums 2010

100% commercial; 8 target market groups

1939: 6,484	1952: 1,037,392
1940: 75,098	1953: 1,069,761
1941: 129,648	1954: 1,243,378
1942: 153,514	1955: 1,328,521
1943: 197,317	1956: 1,582,879
1944: 320,048	1957: 1,837,210
1945: 580,903	1958: 2,245,490
1946: 792,149	1959: 2,482,258
1947: 740,049	1960: 2,510,234
1948: 668,464	1961: 2,561,761
1949: 708,146	1962: 2,673,743
1950: 807,030	1963: 2,643,773
1951: 892,298	1964: 2,862,463

1965: 3,202,642	1975: 5,313,973	1985: 9,350,606	1995: 21,275,724	2005: 45,048,726
1966: 3,597,621	1976: 4,848,966	1986: 10,483,246	1996: 21,035,736	2006: 45,197,384
1967: 3,152,299	1977: 5,537,161	1987: 11,412,514	1997: 21,121,246	2007: 44,953,170
1968: 3,064,806	1978: 5,919,740	1988: 12,752,878	1998: 24,145,200	2008: 40,592,821
1969: 3,230,708	1979: 6,251,858	1989: 13,459,974	1999: 27,020,208	2009: 38,160,948
1970: 3,289,290	1980: 6,283,174	1990: 14,861,573	2000: 32,353,767	2010: 37,115,110
1971: 3,426,198	1981: 6,787,819	1991: 13,453,648	2001: 39,204,866	
1972: 4,118,345	1982: 6,744,234	1992: 16,182,687	2002: 52,241,167	
1973: 4,631,220	1983: 8,035,564	1993: 18,484,337	2003: 54,235,841	
1974: 5,059,199	1984: 9,565,890	1994: 21,715,188	2004: 47,262,604	

Milwaukee Branch

Highlights

1945 Entered Wisconsin in contract with Wylie C. Sampson General Agency

1947 Milwaukee Claims Office opened, headed by Roy Schaller and John Bliss

1951 Office was at the forefront of the post-war trend of moving to the suburbs when it relocated to the new Southgate Shopping Center, which provided "ample breathing and parking space" and was a "terrific" traffic draw

1956 Milwaukee Branch (also called Wisconsin Branch) opened after EMC purchased the Wylie C. Sampson Agency in 1955 and converted it into a branch office with seven employees

1958 Auditing and marketing manager positions added to staff; 23 employees and 160 agents producing business

1963 Started direct bill automobile under EMCASCO

1967 Risk improvement manager added to staff

1968 Began writing life products through Employers Modern Life Company (EML)

1972 Special risk supervisor added to staff; discontinued in 1985

1977 Organized service club for employees with 15 or more years of service

1980 Employee's station wagon blew up in the parking lot when the sun's heat caused pressure to build up on a carbon dioxide cartridge for a beer keg in the rear of the car; the car's roof landed on top of the office building causing minor damage; no one was hurt, but the car was totaled

1988 Branch was one of the state's eight servicing carriers for the Wisconsin Compensation Insurance Pool with over $10 million premium written; also participated in the Wisconsin Compensation Assigned Risk Pool

1989 Branch was one of EMC's largest linebacker policy writers through the Wisconsin Town Association

1994 Open house for a new office addition was attended by Bill Young, Fred Schiek, and Dick Fraser, the last time "Pete Lemley's boys" got together

1998 Branch-sponsored essay contest scholarship program for Wisconsin's sesquicentennial resulted in 17 new school districts being added to Wisconsin's School Safety Group program

2006 50th anniversary celebrated with a 1950s theme party

Key Personnel

Branch Managers

Philip R. Lucca	2010 –
Lonnie D. Schwab	2005 – 2010

Territory

Wisconsin

···

Philip R. Lucca
CPCU
Resident Vice President

Robert G. Cascioli	1996 – 2005
William L. "Bill" Young	1974 – 1996
John E. Schmidt	1969 – 1974
Eugene W. Reese	1962 – 1969
George Kochheiser	1956 – 1962

Underwriting Managers

James A. Pousha	1995 –
Robert G. Cascioli	1974 – 1995
William L. Young	1972 – 1974
Elmer G. Possin	1969 – 1972
George Walters	1965 – 1969
Maurice O. Cooper	1960 – 1964
Robert L. Young	1956 – 1959

Claims Managers

Mark McClusky	2002 –
Clyde R. Schweitzer	1969 – 2002
John E. Schmidt	1964 – 1969
George Higbee	1957 – 1964
John Bliss	1950 – 1957
Roy Schaller	1947 – 1950

Administrative Services Managers

Marie Biernacki	1973 –
Maurice L. Hines	1971 – 1973
Almer Perkins	1969 – 1971
James A. Pousha	1968 – 1969
Donna Sclender	1967 – 1968

Total staff 2010

73 employees, 69 agencies

Office Locations

1947   Marine National Bank Building,
633 North Water Street, Milwaukee, WI

1951   Southgate Shopping Center,
3333 South 27th Street, Milwaukee, WI

1958   2629 West Greenfield Avenue,
Milwaukee, WI

1963   6525 West Bluemound Road,
Brookfield, WI

1970   16455 West Bluemound,
Brookfield, WI

Written Premiums 2010

91% commercial, 9% personal; 1 safety group,
7 target market groups

1956: 628,670	1998: 29,095,753
1957: 870,963	1999: 30,692,009
1958: 1,034,149	2000: 36,183,119
1959: 1,274,642	2001: 43,486,893
1960: 1,444,803	2002: 49,839,589
1961: 1,377,427	2003: 57,918,351
1962: 1,358,462	2004: 60,494,509
1963: 1,314,855	2005: 60,464,374
1964: 1,220,030	2006: 62,027,242
1965: 1,593,223	2007: 60,742,612
1966: 1,940,599	2008: 59,722,911
1967: 2,399,040	2009: 62,569,654
1968: 2,806,467	2010: 64,327,291
1969: 3,740,050	
1970: 4,395,971	
1971: 4,678,238	
1972: 4,953,482	
1973: 5,488,624	
1974: 6,216,537	
1975: 6,479,717	
1976: 7,153,292	
1977: 8,961,720	
1978: 11,191,286	
1979: 12,161,579	
1980: 11,855,592	
1981: 10,431,907	
1982: 10,388,092	
1983: 9,763,073	
1984: 11,061,121	
1985: 15,151,125	
1986: 20,041,186	
1987: 22,734,754	
1988: 23,835,389	
1989: 28,239,769	
1990: 32,325,850	
1991: 34,337,992	
1992: 34,652,818	
1993: 33,787,398	
1994: 29,222,546	
1995: 28,866,714	
1996: 25,575,971	
1997: 26,892,951	

Minneapolis Branch

Highlights

1934 EMC appointed Citizens Fund Mutual Fire Insurance Company in Red Wing as general agent for Minnesota; Claims Office established in Red Wing under the management of William J. Hynes

1942 Minneapolis Branch formed to fully serve Minnesota, the Dakotas, and western Wisconsin

1954 Staff of about 30 employees

1961 Home Office assisted with resolving problems caused by the unexpected death of Branch Manager James T. Larson

1968 Branch Manager John C. Pollack trained young and inexperienced staff and boosted business processing and morale after a troubled period, and the office was stable and productive by 1972; Administrative Services Manager Melvin "Tommy" Thompson aided the process using his ability to handle "people problems" with a poker face

ca. 1970 Employee safety became a concern when a protester set off an explosive a block and a half away from the office

1972 Open House and Agency Conference hosted at new Bloomington office; branch had lowest loss ratio of all branches

Early 1970s Thief unlocked the back door with a credit card and stole some claim drafts; easily caught because he made out the drafts in his own name

1974 Dakota Fire Insurance Company/Bismarck's Minnesota business transferred to Minneapolis

1981 Minnesota Manufactured Housing Association safety dividend group formed

1983 Minnesota Petroleum Marketers Association safety dividend group formed and grew rapidly to 400 participants by 2000

1998 Large number of storm losses (one tornado, three major wind and hail) reinforced EMC's reputation as a valued and trusted insurer

2005 Minnesota Schools target market group increased premiums from $747,416 in 2004 to $2,106,117 (193.6%)

Key Personnel

Branch Managers

Jerry K. Harlow	1992 –
William L. "Bil" Anderson	1978 – 1992
John C. Pollock	1968 – 1978
John Skurdalsvold (Acting Branch Manager)	1968
J. George Huglin	1961 – 1967
James T. Larson	1957 – 1961
M. H. "Jim" Jamar	1942 – 1956
Joe Elliot	1937 – 1941
William J. Hynes	1934 – 1937

Underwriting Managers

Jim Matthees	2004 –
John R. Koehler	1968 – 2004
John Skurdalsvold	1961 – 1967
J. George Huglin	1957 – 1961
James T. Larson	1953 – 1957
Ned Finn	1942 – unknown

Claims Managers

Mike Huttner	2006 –
Dennis Petrucelli	1994 – 2006
Robert Brinkworth	1989 – 1994
James W. Lanning	1978 – 1989
William L. "Bil" Anderson	1969 – 1978
William J. "Bill" Cree Jr.	1967 – 1969
E. I. "Barney" Barron	1944 – 1967
Joe Elliot	1942 – 1944

Administrative Services Managers

Denise Best	2006 –
Barbara Snow	1975 – 2006
Melvin "Tommy" Thompson	1967 – 1975

Total staff 2010

44 employees, 134 agencies

Office Locations

1942 1009-1014 Northwestern Bank Building, Minneapolis, MN

1954 Mutual Exchange Building, 1926 Nicollet Avenue, Minneapolis, MN

Territory

Minnesota

...

Jerry K. Harlow
CPCU, AU
Resident Vice President

1961 111 East Franklin Avenue,
– 67 Minneapolis, MN

1972 Metropolitan Stadium area,
Bloomington, MN

1976 6120 Blue Circle Drive,
Minnetonka, MN
(uniform plan building)

Written Premiums 2010

69% commercial, 31% personal; 2 safety groups,
3 target market groups

1942: 295,628	1951: 1,068,697	1960: 2,252,264
1943: 307,555	1952: 1,239,367	1961: 2,326,425
1944: 348,837	1953: 1,274,182	1962: 2,427,841
1945: 493,855	1954: 1,172,263	1963: 2,168,565
1946: 702,726	1955: 1,076,662	1964: 2,497,682
1947: 849,745	1956: 1,156,888	1965: 2,456,166
1948: 854,629	1957: 1,395,552	1966: 2,645,936
1949: 832,960	1958: 1,831,139	1967: 2,987,975
1950: 951,529	1959: 2,223,799	1968: 2,806,467

1969: 3,689,870	1991: 24,404,092
1970: 4,352,203	1992: 25,256,932
1971: 4,459,986	1993: 25,960,165
1972: 4,360,098	1994: 25,966,582
1973: 4,567,694	1995: 23,401,779
1974: 4,643,041	1996: 21,204,099
1975: 5,442,369	1997: 22,490,184
1976: 5,372,105	1998: 23,892,004
1977: 5,955,702	1999: 24,911,141
1978: 6,935,956	2000: 26,537,515
1979: 6,737,621	2001: 29,641,821
1980: 7,952,713	2002: 30,796,920
1981: 7,602,019	2003: 33,766,501
1982: 7,846,628	2004: 33,089,951
1983: 9,319,572	2005: 32,174,604
1984: 11,359,772	2006: 32,074,570
1985: 13,021,203	2007: 32,396,185
1986: 15,110,030	2008: 33,645,117
1987: 16,555,008	2009: 36,493,664
1988: 18,735,805	2010: 39,484,381
1989: 21,273,743	
1990: 23,939,299	

Territory

Nebraska
South Dakota

Omaha Branch

Highlights

1939 EMC purchased Turk-Somerville General
Agency and established the Nebraska Branch
Office with Robert S. Somerville, manager;
Thomas Turk retired to devote time
to livestock raising enterprises

1950s Great success in writing for schools (50%),
counties (one-third of Nebraska),
municipalities, townships

1960s Emphasis placed on education about
products and processes through seminars
and meetings for agents and claims personnel

1961 Branch was supervising Claims Service
Offices at Grand Island, Alliance, and Lincoln,
NE; 57 employees, 290 agents

1964 Seven counties in southwest Iowa added
and name changed to Omaha Branch Office

1967 70 employees, 262 agencies; branch was
second to occupy a new uniform plan office

1975 Three tornadoes hit Omaha, but branch
building was not heavily damaged

1984 Staff trimmed to 53 employees; 215 agencies

1987, Received "Company of the Year" award
1996 from Omaha Professional Insurance Agents
Chapter

1988, Received "Listening Ear Award" from
1989, Professional Insurance Agents of Nebraska
1998

1989 50th anniversary celebrated; 60 employees,
230 agencies

1999 60th anniversary celebrated; received
recognition from Nebraska Autobody
Association and Omaha Fire Department

2000s Partnered with local television station in
"Cash In For Schools" program that awards
funds to Nebraska and Iowa school projects

2006, Branch received Hynes-Gunn Challenge
2007, Cup three consecutive years
2008

2010   Branch began writing new business
for South Dakota

Key Personnel

Branch Managers

Jay Sillau	2011 –
John R. Smith	1990 – 2010
Fred A. Schiek	1984 – 1990
Howard D. Peterson	1970 – 1984
Lester Crow	1961 – 1969
Donald E. Hendrix	1956 – 1961
Robert S. Somerville	1939 – 1955

Underwriting Managers

Ralph Bluedorn	2011 –
Jay Sillau	1994 – 2010
Terrence M. "Terry" Connelly	1970 – 1994
Howard D. Peterson	1964 – 1969
Gerald Sohl	1939 – 1964

Claims Managers

Laura Vitek	2008 –
Bob Wetzel	1995 – 2007

Quentin P. Gerhard	1957 – 1995
Charles Absher	1949 – 1957
Lee Kious	1939 – unknown

Administrative Services Managers

Pam Cope	2007 –
Michael J. Gaughan	1970 – 2007
Jack West	1965 – 1970

Total staff 2010

82 employees, 301 agencies

Office Locations (All in Omaha, NE)

1939   Service Life Insurance Company
Building, 1904 Farnum Street

1954   3172 Dodge Street

1967   7315 Mercy Road

1992   11819 Miami Street

2002   2121 N. 117th Avenue

Written Premiums 2010

90% commercial, 10% personal; 7 safety groups,
10 target market groups

...

Jay Sillau
CPCU
Resident Vice President

1939: 410,329	1958: 1,821,122	1977: 11,084,569	1996: 52,969,727
1940: 413,185	1959: 2,012,150	1978: 11,623,358	1997: 53,005,415
1941: 470,945	1960: 2,228,400	1979: 13,003,613	1998: 56,391,414
1942: 439,831	1961: 2,479,320	1980: 14,808,677	1999: 59,210,217
1943: 499,940	1962: 2,468,567	1981: 15,708,842	2000: 67,655,332
1944: 567,432	1963: 2,472,980	1982: 15,372,563	2001: 73,278,957
1945: 691,596	1964: 3,040,292	1983: 15,846,737	2002: 79,050,472
1946: 900,510	1965: 3,560,345	1984: 17,357,343	2003: 84,927,107
1947: 1,042,607	1966: 3,676,177	1985: 18,793,149	2004: 81,303,156
1948: 1,158,590	1967: 3,889,118	1986: 19,798,979	2005: 72,743,593
1949: 1,254,226	1968: 4,004,303	1987: 23,726,622	2006: 70,159,152
1950: 1,259,573	1969: 4,593,205	1988: 26,574,476	2007: 68,463,091
1951: 1,354,089	1970: 5,183,355	1989: 29,405,661	2008: 67,916,755
1952: 1,474,852	1971: 5,653,726	1990: 34,832,215	2009: 68,130,248
1953: 1,578,094	1972: 6,324,401	1991: 41,332,421	2010: 68,273,817
1954: 1,650,856	1973: 7,178,449	1992: 45,307,737	
1955: 1,703,701	1974: 8,390,200	1993: 45,815,762	
1956: 1,439,082	1975: 9,309,423	1994: 50,128,650	
1957: 1,531,153	1976: 10,595,275	1995: 52,072,833	

Orange County/Irvine Branch and Service Office

Territory

California

Highlights

1981   Orange County Branch opened in Laguna Hills to do commercial business in Orange and San Diego Counties; Alpel Insurance Agency appointed first agency

1984   Ronald Foglesong became claim manager (claims previously handled by Phoenix Branch)

1980s Losses caused by litigation that resulted in condominium association members being granted large awards from a spurt of condominium construction, induced by favorable tax treatment, in which defective buildings were erected on unstable ground; corrective action from the courts and legislation did not come until 2000 and 2002

1988   Proposition 103, designed to provide consumer protection, required a 20% rate rollback from 1987 rates on most lines of insurance and cost the branch about $1 million

1990   Became Irvine Branch when the office moved to Irvine

1997   Serving Orange, San Diego, Riverside, and San Bernadine Counties; 24.1% loss ratio best in company for third year

1998   Loss ratio of 38.0% was EMC's best for fourth consecutive year; agents appointed in San Joaquin Valley

2003   Converted to Irvine Service Office reporting to the Phoenix Branch

2004   Phoenix Branch absorbed Irvine business, completing merger

Key Personnel

Branch Managers
Kent A. Kochheiser   1981 – 2003

Underwriting Managers
Sally Loiacono   1994 – 2004
Shari Peterson (Preston)   1983 – 1994

Claims Managers
Ronald Foglesong   1984 – 2003

Administrative Services Managers
Phyllis Rankin Foglesong   1987 – 2003
Debora Barnhart   1981 – 1987

Total staff 2002

24 employees, 40 agencies

Office Locations

1981   23441 South Pointe Drive, Laguna Hills, CA

1983   23461 South Point Drive, Laguna Hills, CA

1985   Mill Creek Drive, Laguna Hills, CA

1990   8001 Irvine Center Drive, Irvine, CA

1997   23382 Mill Creek Drive, Laguna Hills, CA

2007   25541 Commercentre Drive, Lake Forest, CA

Written Premiums 2002

99% commercial, 1% personal

1981: 26,226
1982: 1,317,671
1983: 2,401,922
1984: 5,068,678
1985: 4,610,591
1986: 4,697,201
1987: 4,527,878
1988: 5,423,929
1989: 6,964,996
1990: 10,272,284
1991: 10,584,282
1992: 10,524,538
1993: 10,005,747
1994: 9,626,024
1995: 7,259,170
1996: 10,198,403
1997: 10,232,628
1998: 10,448,231
1999: 10,564,044
2000: 12,049,618
2001: 14,781,449
2002: 17,477,339
2003: 18,138,960
2004: merged with Phoenix

Philadelphia Branch

Highlights

1939 R. A. Downes General Agency began representing EMC in Pennsylvania and Maryland

1946 Philadelphia Branch opened by Robb Kelley when EMC bought out the business relationships of R. A. Downes

1956 Branch served Pennsylvania, Maryland, New Jersey

1967 "Operation Eyeball" meetings at different locations promoted better staff-agency understanding; branch first to introduce improved risk mutuals (IRM)

1968 "One-Shot Speedie," a procedure for quick claims processing (developed by the branch and introduced to EMC by John Button), went into effect one day before a violent storm bombed Charlottesville, VA, with baseball-sized hail; "A Look at Life" tour introduced Employers Modern Life to Pennsylvania agents

1969 Office adjuster program used telephone and all-lines concept for efficient claims adjusting and salesmanship

1971 Staff of 54 employees; Virginia and District of Columbia had been added to the territory; an attempt to use EML as the lender for the new uniform plan office building failed when owner Eighth-Moore Corporation secured "a more favorable mortgage commitment from another lender"

1979 Dramatic shift from personal to commercial
– 94 lines made under Branch Manager Herbert D. Shartle

1980s Amish claimant donated his claim check to his church in honor of Claims Supervisor Robert A. Red

1984 Renamed Valley Forge Branch

1990s Safety group programs developed for Municipal Market, Manufactured Housing, Association of Auto Service Providers, Pennsylvania Moving and Storage

2001 Merged with Charlotte Branch and became Valley Forge Service Office to create economies of scale by combining strong features of both branches (municipalities and safety group programs in Valley Forge and underwriting and claims expertise and petroleum marketers groups in Charlotte); motels added after the merger

Key Personnel

Branch Managers

Lonnie D. Schwab	2010 –
(Charlotte Branch Manager)	
R. David Orr	1994 – 2010
Herbert D. Shartle	1978 – 1994
John Button	1971 – 1978
Rex L. Davis	1966 – 1971
R. Gordon Coulter	1956 – 1966
Robb Kelley	1946 – 1956

Underwriting Managers

Paul Eggert	1995 – 2000
Michael Derewitz	1989 – 1994
Dave Kendrick	1973 – 1983
John W. Button	1969 – 1971
John C. Pollock	mid-1960s – 1968

Claims Managers

James N. Zeigler	1994 –
Frank M. Mattucci	1963 – 1994
Giles K. Riley	1950s
George W. Buchanan	1946 – unknown

Administrative Services Managers

Joann DiPasquale	1995 – 2000
Shirley Pirone	1987 – 1995
Ronald Gundel	1980 – 1987
Paul Martucik	dates unknown
Robert J. Civera	1969 – 1979
Richard J. Lubicky	dates unknown

Total staff 2010

36 employees

Office Locations

1946 Western Savings Fund Society Building, 111 Broad, Philadelphia, PA

Territory

Pennsylvania

1956 1616 Walnut Street, Philadelphia, PA

1963 1339 Chestnut Street, Philadelphia, PA

1971 1010 8th Avenue, King of Prussia, PA

1996 1610 Medical Drive, Pottstown, PA

Written Premiums 2000

85% commercial, 15% personal

1946: 232,404	1958: 2,325,203	1970: 4,205,443	1982: 7,012,977	1994: 8,476,485
1947: 270,844	1959: 2,325,182	1971: 4,638,344	1983: 7,063,112	1995: 10,857,369
1948: 288,483	1960: 2,393,721	1972: 4,896,775	1984: 6,251,056	1996: 12,886,673
1949: 385,312	1961: 2,273,331	1973: 5,433,523	1985: 6,522,038	1997: 13,758,209
1950: 540,432	1962: 2,216,954	1974: 5,752,257	1986: 7,841,838	1998: 15,879,987
1951: 652,445	1963: 2,205,390	1975: 5,523,375	1987: 7,402,322	1999: 19,786,476
1952: 918,008	1964: 2,853,783	1976: 5,809,388	1988: 6,494,897	2000: 24,358,445
1953: 1,266,501	1965: 3,446,528	1977: 6,333,269	1989: 5,971,219	2001: merged
1954: 1,426,977	1966: 3,342,479	1978: 6,944,037	1990: 6,339,695	with
1955: 1,589,168	1967: 3,684,787	1979: 7,212,084	1991: 6,575,731	Charlotte
1956: 1,904,189	1968: 4,143,514	1980: 7,605,515	1992: 6,737,862	
1957: 2,189,853	1969: 4,152,867	1981: 6,814,261	1993: 7,220,984	

Territory

Arizona
California
Nevada
New Mexico

Phoenix Branch

Highlights

1958 John Kerper opened service office in Phoenix to write personal lines; Bob Camp from Prescott became first agent

1962 Claims manager and field supervisor positions added to staff

1963 Official recognition of Phoenix Branch

1978 Special risk supervisor added to staff (Kent Kochheiser)

1982 Full-time risk improvement representative (Paul Stein) added to staff

1987 EMC Board meeting held in Phoenix with recognition of branch reaching $10 million in premiums; branch had risen from 18th in 1973 to 12th in premiums produced

1997 Branch entered Nevada

2000 Branch entered New Mexico

2004 Branch absorbed Irvine business after Irvine Branch was converted into a service office

2008 New internal quarterly newsletter created; called CANN for states served (CA, AZ, NV, NM)

Key Personnel

Branch Managers

Carl L. Doot	1982 –
Ron Cheshire	1978 – 1982
R. Gordon Coulter	1966 – 1978
Rex L. Davis	1963 – 1966
John S. Kerper	1958 – 1962

Underwriting Managers

Doug Lincoln	1994 –
Sloan Amos Jr.	1987 – 1994
Kevin J. Hovick	1982 – 1987
Carl L. Doot	1977 – 1982
Stan Vernia	1965 – 1977

Claims Managers

Michael Boyce	2007 –
Sloan Amos Jr.	1994 – 2007
Darrell Vigil	1988 – 1994
Hubert G. Mote	1967 – 1988
Rex L. Davis	1962 – 1963

Administrative Services Manager

Terrie Reynoso   1987 –
Kathie Hovick   1982 – 1987

Total staff 2010

83 employees, 202 agencies

Office Locations

1958 John Kerper's home, 4634 N. 44th Street in Phoenix, AZ

1962 1429 North First Street, Phoenix, AZ

1963 1439 North First Street, Phoenix, AZ

1966 96 West Osborn Road, Phoenix, AZ

1973 333 West Indian School Road, Phoenix, AZ

1981 3424 North Central Avenue, Phoenix, AZ

1986   9630 North 25th Avenue, Phoenix, AZ

2000 16150 N. Arrowhead Fountain Center Drive, Peoria, AZ

Written Premiums 2010

95% commercial, 5% personal;
6 target market groups

...

Carl L. Doot
CPCU, CLU, AU
Resident Vice President

1958: 41,050	1969: 687,965	1980: 4,020,500	1991: 16,885,247	2002: 48,055,982
1959: 126,905	1970: 821,253	1981: 4,692,760	1992: 17,738,162	2003: 53,519,525
1960: 216,444	1971: 1,061,883	1982: 5,915,974	1993: 18,718,137	2004: 78,928,598
1961: 247,494	1972: 1,289,732	1983: 7,726,156	1994: 20,619,913	2005: 79,274,533
1962: 246,910	1973: 1,690,184	1984: 8,268,886	1995: 21,379,997	2006: 81,379,848
1963: 269,364	1974: 1,915,936	1985: 8,608,908	1996: 23,599,078	2007: 81,966,338
1964: 366,008	1975: 1,679,624	1986: 9,254,992	1997: 24,995,742	2008: 66,154,210
1965: 429,864	1976: 1,790,082	1987: 10,936,432	1998: 28,303,370	2009: 59,652,546
1966: 489,452	1977: 2,141,972	1988: 13,250,695	1999: 31,251,747	2010: 55,552,522
1967: 542,988	1978: 2,659,882	1989: 14,976,388	2000: 36,824,166	
1968: 560,772	1979: 3,385,650	1990: 16,261,867	2001: 42,828,633	

Providence Branch

(Union Insurance Company of Providence)

Highlights

1854 Firemen's Mutual Insurance Company incorporated as a member of the Factory Mutual group established in 1835 by textile manufacturer Zachariah Allen

1863 Union Mutual Fire Insurance Company organized as an affiliate of Firemen's Mutual

1953 Renamed Union Mutual Insurance Company of Providence; charter powers broadened to permit multiple line underwriting

1963   Governor John Chafee issued a citation for "distinguished service" on the 100th anniversary

1967 Union Mutual ended affiliation with Firemen's Mutual, which eliminated personal lines written by Union Mutual

1968 EMC acquired Union Mutual in April as an affiliate to service all of New England; recognized as the Providence Branch in December; Union Mutual personnel retained; Union's Tennessee business transferred to Jackson Branch; Maine, New Hampshire, and Vermont territories transferred from Philadelphia to Providence

1970 Staff of 88 employees, 300 agents

1971 Branch had the largest class ever (50) to complete the American Mutual Insurance Alliance study course, organized by Luther Cloxton

Territory

Connecticut
Maine
Massachusetts
New Hampshire
Rhode Island
Vermont

Raymond L. Geary
CPCU
Resident Vice President

1975 Twenty Year Club formed with seven members who had service records from 27 to 41years; 23 members in 2010

1977 Special risk supervisor position created

1979 New Hampshire Department of Labor recognized the branch with a Certificate of Merit for its workers' compensation claims procedures

1980s Rhode Island economy was good as business relocated from Boston to Providence; main street business dominated branch writings; unique service was "Exit Drills In The Home" (EDITH) conducted in area schools during Fire Prevention Week by Risk Improvement Representative Al McIntyre

1990 Total experience of 11 members of the Twenty Year Club was 336 years; efficiency had allowed staff reduction to about half that at acquisition in 1968

1994 Union Mutual demutualized (converted to stock ownership) and changed name to Union Insurance Company of Providence; EMC purchased 97% of the stock, making the company a subsidiary

1996 Redomesticated to Iowa

Key Personnel

Presidents/Branch Managers

Raymond L. Geary	1991 –
Ernest G. Ashton	1976 – 1991
Franklin N. Folsom	1968 – 1976

Underwriting Managers

Kenneth F. Provost Jr.	1993 –
Thomas G. Cormier	1993
LaRae Penny	1991 – 1992
Raymond L. Geary	1989 – 1991
George Yencho Jr.	1968 – 1988

Claims Managers

Michael D. Morris	2005 –
Robert A. Coon Jr.	2002 – 2005
Frank Robinson	1988 – 2002
Eugene T. Martin	1968 – 1988

Administrative Services Managers

Susan A. Newkirk	2003 –
William A. Arnold	2000 – 2003
Deborah Pontifice	1991 – 2000
John M. Barry	1982 – 1989
Luther E. "Luke" Cloxton Jr.	1968 – 1982

Total staff 2010

44 employees, 108 agencies

Office Locations

1968 Blue Cross Building, 444 Westminster Mall, Providence, RI

1970 60 Jefferson Park, Warwick, RI

2008 200 Crossings Boulevard, Warwick, RI

Written Premiums 2010

69% commercial, 31% personal

1969: 5,496,952	1980: 7,571,251	1991: 19,496,002	2002: 33,878,652
1970: 5,087,842	1981: 8,530,020	1992: 18,358,028	2003: 36,234,317
1971: 5,679,392	1982: 9,216,258	1993: 20,202,442	2004: 39,875,216
1972: 6,067,956	1983: 10,784,300	1994: 21,637,096	2005: 41,753,603
1973: 6,632,462	1984: 11,812,894	1995: 21,968,175	2006: 40,146,100
1974: 7,173,455	1985: 11,884,977	1996: 22,329,943	2007: 41,297,130
1975: 6,357,314	1986: 11,925,939	1997: 22,229,249	2008: 35,245,535
1976: 4,865,666	1987: 14,217,861	1998: 25,480,045	2009: 34,366,778
1977: 5,588,835	1988: 14,582,771	1999: 27,539,550	2010: 33,429,585
1978: 6,071,549	1989: 16,655,092	2000: 29,530,955	
1979: 6,660,837	1990: 17,617,233	2001: 30,755,022	

Wichita Branch

Highlights

1927 EMC entered Kansas through affiliation with State General Agency

1933 M. J. Wilkinson opened EMC's first branch office in McPherson, KS, when the State General Agency relationship proved unprofitable

1934 Wilkinson trimmed the business from $400,000 to $80,000 and organized a complete Wichita Branch in Wichita

1941 Production again reached $400,000; 14 employees

1948 Staff of 35 employees, over 300 agents; first branch to have a new office built to EMC specifications, a precursor of the uniform style adopted by EMC in the 1960s

1955 Oklahoma entered about this time

1959 Physical Damage School used wrecked 1953 Ford two-door hardtop to train adjusters; by 1962 it had become a three-day seminar with a Physical Damage Manual, visual aids, and participation of top company personnel

1965 Branch was first to handle its own fire claims under Fire Claims Supervisor James D. Hobson

1967 Oklahoma City Claims and Production Office opened under supervision of the Wichita Branch; resident claims adjusters were also stationed at Hays, Topeka, Independence, and Garden City, KS

1969 First "telephone adjuster" added to staff; increased to three employees by 1971

1970 More than 80 employees

1975 Club formed for employees and retirees with 15 or more years of service

1979 Began "Underwriters' Agent of the Month" award, and Stucky-Graber Insurance Agency of Moundridge, KS, was first recipient

1980s Efficient use of technology allowed reduction of staff to around 60

1982 Kansas Municipal Utilities Association safety group initiated, endorsed by Independent Insurance Agents of Kansas (Big I)

1996 Dallas Branch merged into Wichita Branch; bond manager for Kansas and Oklahoma added to staff

1999 Loss control manager and bond manager for Texas added to staff

2008 Risk improvement manager added to staff

Key Personnel

Branch Managers

Bernie Zalaznik	1990 –
Ed O'Hair	1986 – 1990
T. Gale Eales	1981 – 1986
Lester E. Crow	1970 – 1981
Harold C. Dabler	1941 – 1970
M. J. Wilkinson	1933 – 1941

Underwriting Managers

Robert Gusé	1999 –
Don Marhenke	1981 – 1999
T. Gale Eales	1961 – 1981
Lester Crow	1954 – 1961

Claims Managers

Ron Hoffman	1989 –
James D. Hobson	1978 – 1989
Hugh A. Randall	1955 – 1978
Richard D. Woodward	1952 – 1955
Russell A. Engelmann	1939 – 1952
H. W. Tharp	unknown – 1939

Administrative Services Managers

Beverly Martin	2000 –
Jane Sharp	1974 – 2000
Norman Whitcomb	early 1960s – 1974

Total staff 2010

174 employees, 356 agencies

Territory

Kansas
Oklahoma
Texas

Bernard E. Zalaznik
CPCU
Resident Vice President

Office Locations

1933 Main Street, McPherson, KS

1934 200 Ellis Singleton Building
(later Petroleum Building),
221 South Broadway, Wichita, KS

1948 2431 East Douglas, Wichita, KS

1968 6530 East 13th Street, Wichita, KS

1993 245 North Waco Street, Wichita, KS

Written Premiums 2010

92% commercial, 8% personal; 4 safety groups,
5 target market groups

1936: 150,317	1951: 1,911,141	1966: 4,184,420	1981: 15,882,840	1996: 55,627,791
1937: 179,721	1952: 2,350,989	1967: 4,079,854	1982: 16,602,799	1997: 83,627,357*
1938: 204,663	1953: 2,730,652	1968: 4,540,925	1983: 19,050,648	1998: 85,641,087
1939: 252,667	1954: 2,776,556	1969: 5,214,218	1984: 19,762,894	1999: 95,951,011
1940: 310,322	1955: 2,864,718	1970: 6,102,927	1985: 19,991,752	2000: 116,164,838
1941: 397,902	1956: 2,860,121	1971: 6,620,936	1986: 20,338,798	2001: 132,317,551
1942: 396,426	1957: 3,157,095	1972: 7,154,918	1987: 21,355,507	2002: 149,238,562
1943: 448,690	1958: 3,621,502	1973: 8,188,758	1988: 22,660,419	2003: 159,846,853
1944: 523,361	1959: 4,023,927	1974: 9,389,339	1989: 23,682,829	2004: 166,469,800
1945: 641,311	1960: 4,232,588	1975: 10,240,640	1990: 25,655,881	2005: 163,342,716
1946: 898,053	1961: 4,582,742	1976: 10,939,285	1991: 31,814,584	2006: 167,532,294
1947: 1,286,611	1962: 4,473,280	1977: 11,074,427	1992: 39,317,178	2007: 170,912,796
1948: 1,546,787	1963: 4,707,008	1978: 11,315,979	1993: 40,751,449	2008: 167,807,633
1949: 1,632,055	1964: 4,275,978	1979: 12,331,294	1994: 47,361,114	2009: 169,854,715
1950: 1,716,425	1965: 4,196,196	1980: 14,542,015	1995: 52,648,578	2010: 165,500,410

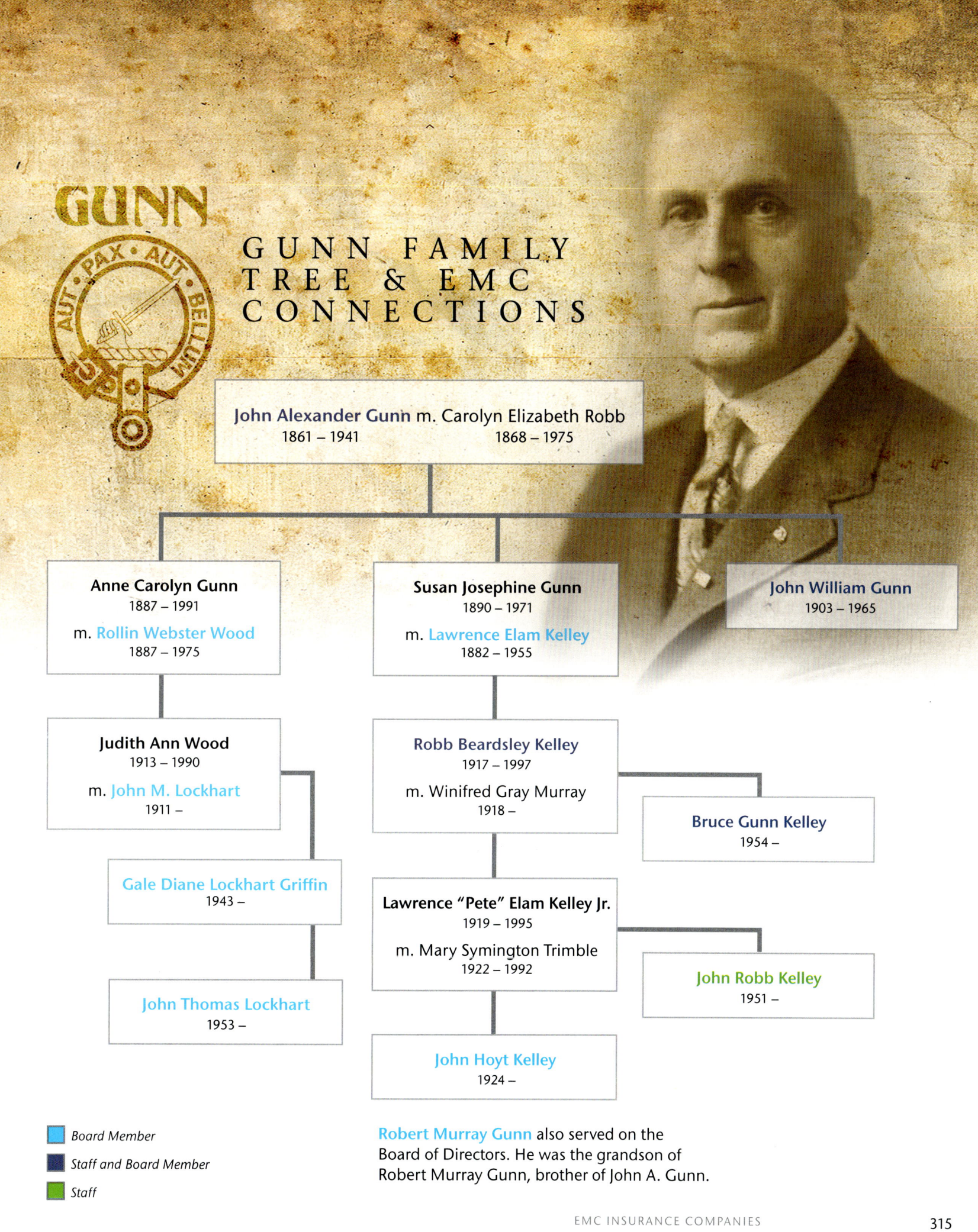

GUNN FAMILY TREE & EMC CONNECTIONS

John Alexander Gunn m. Carolyn Elizabeth Robb
1861 – 1941   1868 – 1975

Anne Carolyn Gunn
1887 – 1991

m. Rollin Webster Wood
1887 – 1975

Susan Josephine Gunn
1890 – 1971

m. Lawrence Elam Kelley
1882 – 1955

John William Gunn
1903 – 1965

Judith Ann Wood
1913 – 1990

m. John M. Lockhart
1911 –

Robb Beardsley Kelley
1917 – 1997

m. Winifred Gray Murray
1918 –

Bruce Gunn Kelley
1954 –

Gale Diane Lockhart Griffin
1943 –

Lawrence "Pete" Elam Kelley Jr.
1919 – 1995

m. Mary Symington Trimble
1922 – 1992

John Robb Kelley
1951 –

John Thomas Lockhart
1953 –

John Hoyt Kelley
1924 –

- Board Member
- Staff and Board Member
- Staff

Robert Murray Gunn also served on the
Board of Directors. He was the grandson of
Robert Murray Gunn, brother of John A. Gunn.

BOARD MEMBERS

Name	Dates of Service
Baughman, Dr. D. E. – Fort Dodge	1/23/39 – 3/10/54
Bellamy, Fred E. – Cedar Rapids	3/10/54 – 6/13/62
Berwanger, Jay – Chicago, IL	9/13/72 – 12/14/72
Black, Joseph Gaily – Des Moines	6/15/27 – 2/14/28
Black, M. F. – Creston	6/5/14 – 1/24/38
Bolton, L. Robert – Des Moines	3/9/88 – 3/11/98
Booth, Edward C. (Ted) – Marshalltown	6/10/59 – 4/13/74
Booth, Richard W. – Marshalltown	6/6/74 – 3/13/02
Booth, Thomas W. – Richardson, TX	3/13/02 –
Brenton, William Henry (Bill) – Des Moines	12/12/68 – 1/28/03
Brenton, Woodward Harold – Des Moines	1/24/44 – 9/30/68
Briggs, Blaine A. – Des Moines	12/14/72 – 3/9/05
Burgeson, John C. – Des Moines	3/13/02 –
Christopherson, Christopher C. – Des Moines	4/24/11 – 7/14/11
Cochrane, William – Red Oak	1/9/24 – 1/25/37
Deering, Charles Clift – Des Moines	6/13/14 – 1/25/37
Eddy, John A. – Des Moines	7/10/12 – 9/8/20
Fisher, J. H. – Marshalltown	3/9/21 – 1/24/38
Frankel, Anselm – Des Moines	1/25/37 – 1/28/46
Griffin, Gale L. – Williamstown, MA	3/13/96 –
Griffith, John L. – Evanston, IL	3/14/73 – 12/13/84
Gunn, John A. – Kellogg and Des Moines	7/14/11 – 11/23/41
Gunn, John W. – Des Moines	3/7/30 – 10/18/65
Gunn, Robert Murray – Glencoe, IL	3/13/85 – 3/13/02
Hanlon, Frank J. – Mason City	7/10/12 – 1/15/13
Harrison, Cephas – Keokuk	1/15/13 – 6/13/14
Hill, James W. – Des Moines	10/13/20 – 6/13/24
Hjermstad, Hjalmar L. – Red Wing, MN	1/25/37 – 9/4/71
Hunt, Fred L. - Fairfield	11/10/26 – 3/13/29
Hynes, John F. – Des Moines	1/14/25 – 5/17/68
Hynes, William J. – Des Moines	12/10/47 – 6/25/72
Jean, Ronald W. – Altoona	3/11/09 –
Kelley, Bruce G. – Des Moines	3/14/84 –
Kelley, Dr. John H. – Des Moines	3/10/65 –
Kelley, Dr. Lawrence E. – Des Moines	1/25/37 – 9/1/55
Kelley, Robb B. – Des Moines	12/14/55 – 6/5/96
Koch, Richard, Jr. – Des Moines	3/11/98 –
Kochheiser, George W. – Des Moines	6/6/74 – 3/12/08
Kohrs, Frank – Davenport	1/23/39 – 12/14/55
Leefers, J. F. – Cedar Rapids	6/13/14 – 1/11/28
Lehmann, Webster M. – Des Moines	3/9/66 – 11/18/97
Lockhart, John M. – Cincinnati, OH	3/11/70 – 3/14/01
Lockhart, John Thomas – Minneapolis, MN	3/12/08 –

Logan, Guy E. – Des Moines	4/11/28 – 1/24/38
Macfarland, Lanning, Jr. – Chicago, IL	3/10/71 – 3/31/05
Manhard, E. E. – Des Moines	1/15/13 – 6/5/14
Matless, A. E. – Keokuk	7/10/12 – 1/15/13
McCardell, H. C. – Newton	3/10/26 – 1/25/37
McKinney, O. B. – Denver, CO	1/25/37 – ca. 1944
Miller, Jesse A. – Des Moines	4/24/11 – 6/13/14
Miller, Oliver H. – Des Moines	4/24/11 – 7/10/12
Morrell, George A. – Ottumwa	6/12/57 – 3/10/71
Moses, Harlan T. – Johnston, RI	6/12/68 – 3/11/98
Muelhaupt, Carl – Des Moines	1/28/46 – 3/14/73
Mulroney, J. R. – Fort Dodge	1/9/24 – 9/15/26
Murray, Mary O'Gorman – Media, PA	3/14/07 –
Murray, William A. – Des Moines	3/12/08 –
Olson, Bruce F. – Rockford, IL	12/9/71 – 1977
Palmer, E. C. – Sioux City	11/4/29 – 10/18/38
Patterson, George E. – Des Moines	1/25/37 – 8/30/44
Pearsall, Amos C. – Des Moines	1/28/46 – 6/23/58
Phillips, Henry – Ottumwa	7/10/12 – 6/13/14
Power, Howard W. – Davenport	3/9/21 – 1/25/37
Proctor, David J. W. – Des Moines	3/11/92 –
Proctor, William Z. – Des Moines	1/25/37 – 3/11/92
Rawson, Albert C. – Venice, FL	12/1/78 – 3/13/96
Rawson, Charles A. – Des Moines	7/10/12 – 9/2/36
Read, H. W. – Oskaloosa	1/23/39 – 3/12/47
Ricker, B. J. – Grinnell	7/14/11 – 10/14/25
Sale, A. R. – Mason City	6/13/14 – 1/23/33
Schiek, Fred A. – Des Moines	3/11/98 – 3/11/09
Soller, John A. – Davenport	1/9/24 – 2/9/27
Southern, Darrell B. – Des Moines	3/14/73 – 1/24/88
Stoddard, John D. – Des Moines	12/14/55 – 6/29/98
Turk, Thomas H. – Omaha, NE	1/25/37 – 1/26/42
Van Ekeren, Janice Rae – Wilton, CT	5/26/05 – 3/8/06
Van Ekeren, Philip T. – Des Moines	6/12/96 – 3/9/05
Wallen, E. J. – Sioux City	3/9/21 – 1/11/22
Wallingford, J. D. – Des Moines	4/24/11 – 7/14/11
Watts, H. Terrill, Jr. – Atlanta, GA	11/18/97 –
Weitz, Frederick W. – Des Moines	3/8/78 – 9/20/78
Weitz, Rudolph W. – Des Moines	1/26/42 – 5/26/74
Wilkinson, Maurice J. – Des Moines	1/25/37 – 2/18/73
Wise, W. W. – Des Moines	1/10/17 – 1/25/37
Wood, R. L. – Des Moines	10/18/38 – 5/8/43
Wood, Dr. Rollin Webster – Newton	1/24/44 – 3/1/70
Wormhoudt, Henry E. – Des Moines	5/26/25 – 2/13/29
Wrightman, George A. – Des Moines	4/24/11 – 1/10/17

FACTS AND FIGURES

Employers Mutual Casualty Company numbers are listed through 1974; consolidated numbers are listed from 1975 on. The first consolidated/combined statement was produced in 1975 and included EMCC, EMCASCO Insurance Company, Union Mutual, and Dakota Fire. Illinois EMCASCO was added in 1976. EMC Reinsurance was added in 1981. American Liberty was added in 1983. Farm and City was added in 1984 and removed in 2007. Hamilton Mutual was added in 1997.

EMC Financials

Year	Assets ($)	Net Written Premium ($)	Surplus ($)	Net Underwriting Gain/Loss ($)	
1914	40,431	52,526	7,093	6,751	
1915	55,080	66,574	9,101	4,108	
1916	58,616	67,695	18,652	8,156	
1917	64,979	78,454	22,555	9,026	
1918	105,843	110,305	58,232	33,319	
1919	152,281	122,560	107,560	45,458	
1920	181,389	173,996	120,692	15,205	
1921	217,779	202,086	130,089	10,634	
1922	260,202	204,271	140,012	(6,611)	
1923	301,583	256,468	147,545	(1,917)	
1924	367,424	329,126	128,703	(29,636)	
1925	411,397	342,073	140,126	(1,104)	
1926	500,777	416,300	155,107	(2,308)	
1927	620,152	475,559	207,147	28,543	
1928	717,962	582,125	202,745	(23,685)	
1929	915,244	855,272	204,573	(20,512)	
1930	1,102,678	964,198	210,737	(40,320)	
1931	1,129,972	915,608	206,099	(47,649)	
1932	1,161,325	847,676	223,421	(5,269)	
1933	1,226,374	906,250	279,819	35,775	
1934	1,711,259	1,539,971	358,936	(8,275)	
1935	2,224,739	2,193,404	503,654	90,910	
1936	2,944,531	2,881,707	559,529	(107,458)	
1937	3,082,290	3,238,928	528,154	(28,652)	
1938	3,612,397	3,227,447	674,688	139,873	
1939	3,809,680	3,041,272	872,791	15,135	
1940	4,221,138	3,272,340	971,244	58,131	
1941	5,044,899	4,059,931	1,100,000	82,130	

Net Investment Gain/Loss ($)	Combined Trade Ratio (%)	A.M. Best Rating
211	64.8	–
1,119	91.2	–
1,395	91.0	–
1,651	97.1	A2
2,359	71.5	A2
3,871	62.5	A2
5,545	92.5	A2
6,762	90.7	A2
8,534	100.4	A2
9,438	97.1	A2
14,300	106.4	A2
9,021	97.0	A2
17,289	100.1	A1
23,496	90.8	A1
19,283	99.0	A1
22,341	96.1	A1
46,485	101.5	A1
43,011	103.3	A
22,591	100.3	A
32,416	93.8	A
87,392	95.0	A
53,808	91.5	A
104,843	99.2	B+
59,906	102.6	B
114,308	93.2	B+
104,100	99.1	B+
66,169	97.4	B+
94,163	97.0	B+

EMC Financials (*continued*)

Year	Assets ($)	Net Written Premium ($)	Surplus ($)	Net Underwriting Gain/Loss ($)	
1942	5,802,147	4,345,138	1,485,252	458,305	
1943	6,807,589	4,514,530	1,700,000	297,863	
1944	7,825,960	4,817,353	1,953,871	395,877	
1945	9,154,193	6,347,895	2,122,835	452,388	
1946	10,955,030	9,144,849	2,123,908	193,178	
1947	13,266,824	11,836,138	2,142,912	390,273	
1948	16,320,395	13,499,720	3,059,794	1,476,188	
1949	19,539,231	14,611,733	4,297,241	1,820,528	
1950	21,789,139	15,247,937	5,052,466	1,031,655	
1951	23,763,182	17,725,897	5,341,451	128,825	
1952	27,482,107	21,200,305	6,011,076	1,052,752	
1953	31,872,701	24,147,646	7,668,482	1,880,149	
1954	36,520,144	24,938,119	10,141,648	2,649,341	
1955	39,701,331	25,994,681	11,179,705	1,950,018	
1956	41,908,448	27,614,284	12,642,214	1,888,212	
1957	43,864,586	31,277,451	11,838,179	(592,370)	
1958	48,233,994	35,277,985	13,213,670	523,521	
1959	52,083,850	38,646,619	13,289,037	(863,061)	
1960	55,470,262	41,066,313	13,848,477	1,716,222	
1961	60,037,941	41,895,945	15,017,133	(212,976)	
1962	58,264,517	41,280,896	17,435,041	1,663,162	
1963	62,577,882	43,066,244	17,863,574	(1,846,830)	
1964	64,905,120	44,910,876	18,440,495	(755,125)	
1965	69,082,025	49,110,965	19,100,064	(207,402)	
1966	74,369,239	55,267,561	19,445,092	(478,136)	
1967	81,578,290	57,583,239	20,675,287	1,328,439	
1968	90,672,522	66,251,690	22,070,048	279,082	
1969	96,952,726	72,929,800	22,185,969	(2,147,402)	
1970	100,076,745	75,664,197	22,457,329	(509,185)	
1971	112,892,534	82,230,812	26,027,601	4,452,735	
1972	128,457,030	88,545,279	35,270,953	9,155,931	
1973	139,302,913	99,440,628	37,933,518	1,526,972	
1974	147,964,515	115,685,726	31,268,690	(4,856,399)	
1975	163,329,519	122,732,168	30,478,934	(11,914,062)	
1976	192,473,204	131,577,734	38,403,959	(214,145)	
1977	229,427,520	147,223,332	43,256,892	1,107,160	

Net Investment Gain/Loss ($)	Combined Trade Ratio (%)	A.M. Best Rating
71,434	91.4	A
59,226	94.4	A
115,552	92.1	A
148,623	93.0	A
218,943	97.9	A
175,228	97.2	A
246,316	90.1	A
326,686	89.1	A
311,078	95.3	A
416,633	101.4	A
466,969	95.4	A+
580,680	93.0	A+
805,077	92.5	A+
880,404	95.3	A+
901,994	96.0	A+
940,308	102.9	A+
1,058,272	99.2	A+
1,159,743	103.8	A+
1,405,808	96.7	A+
1,543,004	101.9	A+
1,805,375	99.0	A+
2,795,506	104.6	A+
2,548,849	103.4	A+
2,586,310	101.3	A+
2,411,862	101.9	A+
2,235,299	99.0	A+
3,358,183	99.5	A+
3,441,491	104.6	A+
3,597,846	101.9	A+
3,599,065	95.4	A+
3,681,319	90.7	A+
4,576,182	99.4	A+
4,993,423	105.2	A+
5,490,663	111.5	A+
7,291,947	101.1	A
9,950,218	99.7	A

EMC Financials (*continued*)

Year	Assets ($)	Net Written Premium ($)	Surplus ($)	Net Underwriting Gain/Loss ($)	
1978	272,714,177	156,631,642	54,196,905	1,845,330	
1979	316,309,455	170,171,915	71,820,479	6,912,578	
1980	358,896,634	187,426,824	99,807,651	4,822,394	
1981	387,024,225	191,458,623	107,147,870	(6,711,220)	
1982	440,842,083	201,334,949	122,124,518	(28,317,046)	
1983	501,178,124	241,792,781	118,821,684	(34,007,571)	
1984	504,455,577	282,800,078	98,826,322	(47,627,559)	
1985	534,665,201	295,940,466	120,709,380	(41,254,409)	
1986	606,196,765	343,705,727	126,012,945	(18,747,186)	
1987	696,932,102	354,994,045	155,187,054	(6,682,957)	
1988	771,391,823	366,987,095	202,187,584	13,549,428	
1989	849,018,344	401,206,018	228,212,474	(6,352,725)	
1990	901,331,422	457,708,630	240,492,142	(19,032,839)	
1991	1,001,721,223	504,606,206	275,797,328	(29,117,044)	
1992	1,079,064,760	538,410,428	288,065,289	(35,094,071)	
1993	1,228,334,292	562,816,504	304,501,964	(17,454,306)	
1994	1,289,722,903	583,288,995	316,783,613	5,247,590	
1995	1,416,051,098	586,502,641	391,929,460	16,151,875	
1996	1,451,019,234	594,018,148	447,454,048	(6,288,840)	
1997	1,578,904,744	667,816,063	561,040,212	(29,525,767)	
1998	1,711,927,532	716,820,636	591,459,018	(114,621,007)	
1999	1,795,916,904	771,615,762	590,072,289	(112,359,159)	
2000	1,847,557,298	856,924,003	556,431,814	(107,277,897)	
2001	2,147,141,332	960,095,683	489,358,194	(140,367,076)	
2002	2,067,497,320	1,089,297,388	463,584,085	(15,103,517)	
2003	2,329,732,085	1,152,805,411	586,968,483	(30,675,613)	
2004	2,649,512,476	1,181,925,786	665,683,022	(117,312,608)	
2005	2,792,795,021	1,157,368,302	769,825,768	47,949,377	
2006	2,973,253,222	1,136,813,086	923,484,695	104,211,939	
2007	3,132,428,167	1,156,314,423	1,055,113,700	48,096,184	
2008	2,956,756,093	1,121,769,668	848,574,936	(82,111,163)	
2009	3,094,064,079	1,122,857,566	1,000,807,027	(552,038)	
2010	3,258,467,656	1,125,278,642	1,079,590,060	(22,403,441)	

Net Investment Gain/Loss ($)	Combined Trade Ratio (%)	A.M. Best Rating
13,444,739	98.9	A
17,252,959	96.2	A+
19,967,880	97.8	A+
23,992,579	104.3	A+
26,196,814	114.6	A+
31,878,756	114.5	A+
47,393,476	117.7	A
47,623,853	115.2	A
42,360,970	105.6	A
48,007,102	102.1	A
46,139,509	97.1	A
57,425,142	103.6	A
60,832,409	105.8	A
69,606,118	107.7	A
78,811,552	108.5	A
82,590,272	105.2	A
82,128,688	101.2	A
83,889,251	99.4	A
100,407,072	103.7	A
83,098,331	106.0	A
80,096,985	117.2	A
100,134,202	115.4	A
105,764,628	112.9	A
102,210,464	115.1	A-
78,788,563	100.7	A-
79,818,835	102.8	A-
105,515,730	110.7	A-
113,214,113	97.6	A-
121,848,173	93.0	A-
134,468,024	97.4	A-
41,913,403	109.8	A-
153,152,626	101.9	A-
192,590,347	103.8	A-

Notes on Facts and Figures:

- Financial information is taken from the annual statements.
- A. M. Best ratings were obtained from A.M. Best resources.
- These numbers may not total due to rounding.

ACKNOWLEDGMENTS

The idea of creating a centennial commemorative book for EMC originated with a committee of employees and retirees who wanted to preserve the company's history as its 100th year approached. Headed by Dick Haskins (retiree) and Joe Smith (staff), they gathered information and stories from numerous sources, including essays written by the various branches and departments.

Freelance historian and writer Virginia Wadsley was then commissioned to complete the research and write the manuscript. Her work was guided by Bruce Kelley, Dick Haskins, George Kochheiser, Bill Murray, Fred Schiek, and Phil Van Ekeren. Further assistance was provided by EMC employee Dan Miller, who located and organized archival materials, created search aids, and assisted with visuals. Consultant Gale Griffin provided invaluable assistance in enlivening the text and paring down the manuscript.

A publication committee composed of Bob Link, Jim Moore, and Lisa Hamilton worked with WDG Communications Inc., Cedar Rapids, Iowa, on the design, printing, and final publication work for the book.

An effort has been made to obtain the names of all who have contributed to production of the manuscript. Apologies go to those whose names have disappeared from the record or were inadvertently lost in the process. The following people have provided information and advice, given interviews, reviewed parts of the manuscript, and provided backup support over the full course of the project: Wendell Adamson, Norm Anderson, Gene Bailey, Sherry Baker, Margaret Ball, Dick Barnhart, John Barry, Shari Becker, Denise Best, Marie Biernacki, Greg Bird, Jodi Bitterman, Jean Bloomburg, Lauri Bloss, Jason Bogart, Marcy Boggs, Frankie Box, Edwin Burr, Marie Burzette, Sarah Bush, John Button, Kent Candee, Harold Capps, Virginia Carpenter, Joe Carr, Luther Cloxton Jr., Terry Connelly, Tina Cornelius, Don Coughennower, Al Crease, Dan Crew, Merle Croy Jr., Jeff Dahms, Ray Davis, Ben DeHart, Carl Doot, Lori Drafahl, Mary Dropp, Lisa Eckstein, Donna Ell, Deb Elliott, Eric Faust, Brad Fels, Jeff Felts, Ken Fitzgerald, Jim Fontanini, Roger Ford, Mike Freel, Vicki Freese, Judy Funderburk, Rick Gass, Michael Gaughan, Ray Geary, Nancy Green, Barbara Hadley, Brenda Hadley, Carole Hallenbeck, Ron Hallenbeck, Lisa Hamilton, Jeanne Hammer, Dick Harbin, Jerry Harlow, Kevin Hennosy, Ron Herman,

Chuck Herrold, Dave Hixenbaugh, Dick Hoffmann, Bob Holden, Kevin Hovick, Bill Hynes Jr., Ron Jean, Scott Jean, Bob Jester, Dennis Johannsen, Tracy Johnson, Mary Jane Kamm, Jennifer Kebler, Bob Kelley, John R. Kelley, Winifred Kelley, Roger Kilborn, Margie Kling, Kent Kochheiser, Gary Kohnke, Mrs. Ralph G. Kral, Max LaBlanc, Joe Lamb, Jeff Lawler, Al Leiserowitz, Vern Limbrecht, Bob Link, Loren Littrell, Jerry Loghry, Brian Lohse, Joan Long, Fred Lorber, Mick Lovell, Phil Lucca, Ted Lussem, Gerri Lyon, Lawrence Matthews, Joyce McMickle, Jenifer Mercer-Klimowski, Sarah Miller, Jim Moore, H. B. Moran, Bob Morlan, Hubert Mote, Maureen Murphy, Eugene Myers, Eleanor Burgeson Newell, Melvin Nielsen, Anita Novak, Virgil Nutt, Tom O'Connell, Ed O'Hair, Gerri Ohde, David Orr, Jay Oster, Ron Paine, Rocky Palmer, Sarah Paoli, Lisa Pierce, Gary Pingel, James Pousha, Carla Prather, Anna Price, Dennis Prindiville, Ted Rasmusson, Mark Reese, Amy Reimers, Nancy Renda, Arden Reusink, Christina Riedel, Robert Riley, Robert Ruby, Ray Russell, Linda Samson, Bill Sandstrum, Sue Sapp, Rich Schulz, Lonnie Schwab, Barbara Scotti, Jay Sillau, Lisa Simonetta, John R. Smith, Robert E. Smith, Bryon Snethen, Nichole Starkman, Wes Sticken, John Strother, Marilyn Ternes, Beech Turner, Ralph Varisco, Joyce Waters, Vicki Waugh, Thomas X. Wright, Bill Young, Frances Young, Marshall Young, Bernie Zalaznik, and Doug Zmolek. ▪

SOURCES &
PHOTO CREDITS

Books and Periodicals

Annals of the American Academy of Political and Social Science. Vol. 38, No. 1, "Risks in Modern Industry." July 1911.

Bainbridge, John. *Biography of an Idea: The Story of Mutual Fire and Casualty Insurance.* Garden City, New York: Doubleday & Company, Inc., 1952.

Bernstein, Peter L. *Against the Gods: The Remarkable Story of Risk.* New York: John Wiley & Sons, Inc., 1996, 1998.

Carruth, Gorton. *What Happened When: A Chronology of Life and Events in America.* New York: Signet Book by Penguin, 1991.

Columbia Encyclopedia. New York: Columbia University Press, 1968. Third edition. Edited by William Bridgwater and Seymour Kurtz.

Downey, E. H. *History of Work Accident Indemnity in Iowa.* Iowa Economic History Series, edited by Benjamin F. Shambaugh. Iowa City: State Historical Society of Iowa, 1912.

Giese, Henry. *Of Mutuals and Men: The Story of the Rise of Mutual Insurance in Iowa.* Des Moines: Garner Publishing Company, 1955. Published by Iowa Association of Mutual Insurance Associations.

Journal of American Insurance. Alliance of American Insurers. Reprints of "History of American Insurance" published September 1923, September 1924, October 1924.

McCosker, M. J. *The Historical Collection of Insurance Company of North America.* Philadelphia: Beck Engraving Company, 1967.

Shankland, Frank S. "Liability Is Big Industrial Issue," *Des Moines Register and Leader,* 5/14/1911: 6.

Wadsley, Virginia. *Bear Ye One Another's Burdens: The First 100 Years of Farmers Mutual Hail Insurance Company of Iowa.* Des Moines: Farmers Mutual Hail Insurance Company of Iowa, 1993.

"We Gotcha Covered: The Iowa Insurance Story." *Prairie Voices.* http://www.uni.edu/iowaonline/ prairie voices/images/we_Gotcha-Covered.pdf.

Internal Publications and Archival Sources

Biographical profiles compiled by Virginia Wadsley in nine-volume notebook set; EMC personnel listing and *Circuit* photo index. EMC Archives.

Circuit. All extant issues. 10/1953 – present.

Company Digest. 1941 – 1958.

Corporate Review. 2003 – 2009.

Cooperator. All extant issues. 10/15/1928 – present.

DuBois, Frederic M. Historical Project. EMC Archives.

The Employer. All extant issues. 1921 – 1922.

Great Hurricane and Tidal Wave: Rhode Island. Providence Journal Company, 1938. Courtesy of Raymond L. Geary.

Gunn, John A. Insurance Hall of Fame nomination papers.

Haskins, Richard E. Historical Project. EMC Archives.

Hurricane Carol Lashes Rhode Island: August 31, 1954. Providence Journal Company, 1954. Courtesy of Raymond L. Geary.

Iowa Factories. Selected articles. 1912 – 1915.

Kelley Family History tape. 1972.

Kochheiser, George W. "EMC Insurance Companies: The Middle Years." Paper, ca. late 1980s – early 1990s.

Kochheiser, George W. Insurance Hall of Fame nomination papers.

Minutes of Employers Mutual Casualty Association/ Company. 4/24/1911 – present.

Minutes of Iowa Manufacturers Association. 1/27/1904 – 2/15/1922.

Miscellaneous papers by branch and department personnel.

Pawtucket Times, 9/30/1938. Hurricane Souvenir. Courtesy of Raymond L. Geary.

Policyholders Report. 1989 – 2002.

Southern, Darrell B. Historical Project. EMC Archives.

Turpin, Kathleen Gunn. *The Gunns of Kinlochlaggan...A Scottish Diaspora*, 1979.

Wadsley, Virginia. Historical Project. EMC Archives.

Wood, Anne Gunn. *Remembering Our Family*. Edited by Gale Lockhart Griffin, 2002.

Interviews

Haskins, Richard E. with Elizabeth Ann Heartney. undated

Haskins, Richard E. with Merle Kessler. undated

Haskins, Richard E. with George Kochheiser. undated

Haskins, Richard E. with George Kochheiser, Dick Barnhart. undated

Haskins, Richard E. with George Kochheiser, Marshall Young, Tracy Johnson. 11/2/05

Haskins, Richard E. with Eugene Meyers. 7/30/03

Haskins, Richard E. with Eleanor Burgeson Newell. 8/28/97

Kelley, Bruce G. with George Kochheiser. 1/31/00

Wadsley, Virginia with Norman H. Anderson. 12/11/09

Wadsley, Virginia with Margaret Ball. 10/17/08

Wadsley, Virginia with Jean S. Bloomburg. 4/16/10

Wadsley, Virginia with Virginia Carpenter. 4/15/10

Wadsley, Virginia with Don L. Coughennower, Linda S. Samson. 4/21/10

Wadsley, Virginia with Raymond W. Davis. 2/22/10

Wadsley, Virginia with Richard L. Gass. 4/14/10

Wadsley, Virginia with Ron D. Hallenbeck. 4/16/10

Wadsley, Virginia with Richard E. Haskins. 4/17/07, 5/17/07, 6/27/07

Wadsley, Virginia with David L Hixenbaugh. 7/22/10

Wadsley, Virginia with Kevin J. Hovick. 4/28/10

Wadsley, Virginia with William J. Hynes Jr. 5/1/08

Wadsley, Virginia with Ronald W. Jean. 4/15/10

Wadsley, Virginia with Winifred Kelley. 6/5/08

Wadsley, Virginia with Al Leiserowitz. 7/11/07

Wadsley, Virginia with Robert C. Morlan. 4/14/10

Wadsley, Virginia with Jay L. Oster. 7/22/10

Wadsley, Virginia with Mark E. Reese. 8/13/10

Wadsley, Virginia with Richard K. Schulz. 7/23/10

Wadsley, Virginia with Ronald A. Paine. 3/11/10

Wadsley, Virginia with P. Bryon Snethen. 7/21/10

Wadsley, Virginia with A Beech Turner. 7/21 – 22/10

Photo Credits

EMC Archives photo collection

Sarah D. Bush

Wichita-Sedgwick County Historical Museum

INDEX